DATE DUE			
MAY 0 1996			

The SARAH GRAHAM KENAN FOUNDATION, Inc. takes pride in assisting in the publication of this new edition of *County Government in North Carolina,* in further recognition of—

The great public service the Institute of Government has rendered the people of North Carolina and elsewhere;

The vision and wisdom of its founders, Albert and Gladys Coates; and

The enlightened and loyal public service to North Carolina of many other persons and families.

The Institute of Government is grateful for the
assistance of the Sarah Graham Kenan Foundation, Inc.
in the publication of this book.

University of North Carolina at Chapel Hill. Institute of Government.

COUNTY GOVERNMENT IN NORTH CAROLINA

Revised Edition

edited by
JOSEPH S. FERRELL

Andrew S. Thomas Memorial Library
MORRIS HARVEY COLLEGE, CHARLESTON, W.VA.

INSTITUTE OF GOVERNMENT
University of North Carolina
at Chapel Hill / 1975

97068

352.0073
Un3c
1975

Copyright 1975
Institute of Government
University of North Carolina at Chapel Hill
Printed in the United States of America

CONTRIBUTORS

With three exceptions, the authors of all the material in this book are members of the Institute of Government faculty. Their names appear in the table of contents and at the end of their respective chapters. Inquiries concerning a given subject should be addressed to the author who wrote on that subject at the Institute of Government, Post Office Box 990, Chapel Hill, North Carolina 27514.

Robert E. Stipe, who wrote the chapter on recreation, is a former Institute faculty member and is now Director of the State Division of Archives and History. Elaine von Oesen, who collaborated on the libraries chapter, is Assistant State Librarian. David G. Warren, who wrote the chapters on coroners and medical examiners and health services, is also a former Institute faculty member. He now teaches medical and hospital law in the School of Medicine at Duke University.

CONTENTS

Preface / ix

1 Counties and County Commissioners / 3
  Joseph S. Ferrell

2 Administering the County / 18
  Donald B. Hayman

3 Legal Aspects of County Finance and Fiscal Control / 43
  David M. Lawrence and Joseph S. Ferrell

4 The Property Tax / 88
  Henry W. Lewis

5 Elections / 160
  H. Rutherford Turnbull, III, and James C. Drennan

6 County Property: Acquisition, Sale, and Disposition / 172
  H. Rutherford Turnbull, III, James C. Drennan, and Warren J. Wicker

7 Purchasing and Contracting / 187
  Warren J. Wicker

8 Public Relations / 206
  Elmer R. Oettinger

9 Records Management / 218
  William A. Campbell

10 Legal Liabilities of Counties and County Commissioners / 224
  Joseph S. Ferrell

11 The Courts / 242
   C. E. Hinsdale

12 The Criminal Justice System / 260
   Douglas R. Gill

13 Coroners and Medical Examiners / 268
   David G. Warren

14 Alcoholic Beverage Control / 278
   Ben F. Loeb, Jr.

15 Health Organization and Services / 285
   David G. Warren

16 Public Education / 307
   Robert E. Phay

17 Social Services / 344
   Mason P. Thomas, Jr.

18 Public Library Services / 358
   Elaine von Oesen and Rebecca S. Ballentine

19 Recreation / 370
   Robert E. Stipe

20 Planning for Physical and Economic Development / 378
   Philip P. Green, Jr.

21 Interlocal Cooperation and City-County Consolidation / 392
   David M. Lawrence and Warren J. Wicker

22 Environmental Affairs / 400
   Milton S. Heath, Jr.

23 Public Enterprises / 416
   Warren J. Wicker

24 Fire Protection / 434
   Ben F. Loeb, Jr.

PREFACE

A few years ago, the National Aeronautics and Space Administration published a remarkable photograph taken by an astronaut from thousands of miles above earth. The picture shows a vast green expanse of land bordering a dark blue sea. There are no visible signs of life, yet a thin line of sand bars enclosing two large sounds identifies this apparently empty land as North Carolina. A Florida-bound New Englander looking down from seven miles up on a clear day through the window of a jet aircraft would see an enlarged view of the same land seen by the astronaut. To the New Englander, the green expanse becomes a crazy-quilt pattern of red clay fields delicately shaded in tints of green and pine woods, criss-crossed by the spidery lines of highways, threaded by meandering streams and broad rivers, and dotted with small farm ponds and an occasional large lake. Still, the New Englander would see few direct signs of life other than an occasional automobile moving at what seems a snail's pace along a rural road. He would see a few small towns, and perhaps a small city. But if our traveler were to return from his vacation on a clear night, what seemed deserted during the day would spring to life in thousands upon thousands of tiny points of light. The city that seemed small in the daytime would be transformed into a brilliant nebula of light covering many times its apparent daytime area, and the pine woods and green fields would be dotted with the lights of homes, stores, and factories. Below him would be the people of North Carolina. This book is about one aspect of their lives; their county governments.

If our astronaut were equipped with a road map and a good imagination, he might see in his mind's eye dotted lines running here and there across the face of the earth marking the boundaries between North Carolina and its neighboring states, and dividing the state itself into subdivisions called counties. Each acre of land within North Carolina is located in one of 100 counties. These counties vary tremendously in size, population, urbanization, economy, topography, and distance from one another. To a lesser degree, they vary in climate, fertility of the soil, natural resources, and access to transportation. Some of the extremes are illustrated by Chowan's area of 173 square miles as opposed to the nearly 1,000 square miles covered by Robeson or Sampson;[1] by Tyrrell's population of 3,860 and Mecklenburg's 354,656; by Hyde's population density of 9.1 persons per square mile and Mecklenburg's 669.2. Some are growing rapidly, while others are experiencing a decline in population. Between 1960 and 1970, Warren lost almost 20 per cent of its people, while Cumberland grew by nearly 43 per cent. Dare County lies hardly more than 10 feet above the surrounding water, while the highest mountain east of the Mississippi lies in McDowell County. The fields of Pasquotank grow potatoes, cabbage, corn, soy beans, and peanuts while tobacco is king in Pitt. Guilford is a hub of transportation with excellent access to rail, air, and highway transportation; Tyrrell has no railroads and lies nearly 100 miles from the nearest commercial airport or interstate highway. Manteo, the easternmost county-seat town, lies more than 500 miles from Murphy, the westernmost, and a northbound traveler beginning his journey at Elizabeth City would reach New York City several hours before a westbound traveler starting from the same point at the same time would get to Cherokee.

Not too long ago, many city residents thought of the county as the local government of people living "in the country," and country folk were content to manage the county's affairs without the interference or advice of their city cousins. These old attitudes persist—as is evidenced by a young newspaper reporter who came up after class and asked an Institute of Government faculty member whether city residents could vote for county commissioners—but they are passing rapidly. A visitor to the 1974 conventions of the North Carolina Association of County Commissioners and the North Carolina League of Municipalities would be hard put to separate the county commissioners from the city councilmen if they were all together in the same room, or to identify areas of concern not shared in common by county and city officials other than those dictated by the functional differences between counties and cities. County government is still the local government of country folk, but it is just as much the government of people who live in parts of the county that lie within the corporate limits of cities and towns, and county officials are becoming increasingly sensitive to this basic fact.

Many factors have contributed to the renaissance of the county in recent years. The most important of these have to do with the people themselves. Three-quarters of a century of universal education, fifty years of automobiles and good roads, thirty years of uninterrupted prosperity, and twenty years of television have erased most of the economic and social dividing lines between rural and urban people. The old stereotypes of the country bumpkin and the city slicker now seem as

1. Robeson and Sampson both claim to be the state's largest county. The United States Bureau of the Census gives the edge to Robeson by less than 10 square miles.

dated as the two-wheeled cart. While the percentage of North Carolinians who live in cities and towns has remained at around 50 per cent for more than twenty years, the number of people employed in agriculture, forestry, or fisheries continues to decline with each census.

A second factor grows directly out of the increase in the rural non-farm population and its attendant increase in the pressure on county government to provide services formerly thought of as appropriate only for cities. For at least twenty years, the state has pursued a policy that county government should be empowered to undertake virtually all of the services and functions of cities and to possess many of the regulatory powers of cities. Counties are now operating water and sewer systems and solid waste disposal systems. Since 1969, counties have had the authority—and are exercising it—to adopt ordinances regulating private conduct outside incorporated municipalities. Counties are extensively engaged in land-use regulation with planning boards, zoning ordinances, subdivision control ordinances, and enforcement of the State Building Code. A recent study done at the Institute of Government lists all of the services, functions, and regulatory powers authorized by law for cities and counties. It shows that counties now possess virtually the same legal authority to provide urban services as do cities, except for street construction and maintenance and traffic regulation. Counties have acquired the legal authority to provide urban services to rural residents in response to the needs and demands of the people as those needs and demands have been expressed to county commissioners and state legislators.

Another factor at work in changing county government is the increasing professionalization of county administration. The council-manager form of government was conceived and designed for city government, but counties have found it adaptable to and useful for their own purposes. More than half of the state's 100 counties now have a county manager vested with all of the powers prescribed by law for that position, or an officer entitled administrator, coordinator, or executive officer vested with a substantial portion of those powers. County commissioners are discovering that a professional administrator responsible to the board for planning, supervising, and coordinating all aspects of county government subject to the board's jurisdiction is becoming almost indispensable as the scope and complexity of county activities constantly grows.

Finally, in recent years the National Association of Counties on the national level and the North Carolina Association of County Commissioners on the state level have emerged as well-organized, well-staffed, and well-funded spokesmen for county interests in the formulation of national and state policy. No longer do the cities of the state and nation have a monopoly as the acknowledged representatives of the local governmental point of view.

The succeeding chapters of this book describe the functions and powers of North Carolina counties. With but one or two exceptions, the authors are faculty members of the Institute of Government of the University of North Carolina at Chapel Hill who specialize in the subject about which they write. We have tried to write in plain language without sacrificing accuracy, and we have emphasized the role of the board of commissioners in each county function or activity.

Joseph S. Ferrell
Professor of Public Law
and Government

Chapel Hill
Spring 1975

1 / Counties and County Commissioners

A Brief History / 3
From 1776 to 1868 / 3
From 1868 to 1876 / 4
Constitutional Changes of 1875 / 5
The County As a Body Politic and Corporate / 6
The Board of County Commissioners / 9
Selection / 10
Taking Office / 11
The Chairman / 12
Meetings / 12
Procedure / 13
Formal Actions of the Board / 14
Ordinance Procedure / 15
Public Hearings / 15
Organizing the Administration / 16
The County Manager / 16
The Clerk to the Board of Commissioners / 16
The County Attorney / 16

1 / COUNTIES AND COUNTY COMMISSIONERS

A BRIEF HISTORY

From 1776 to 1868

As did its neighboring colonies, pre-Revolutionary North Carolina relied heavily upon the county for local government purposes. Justices of the peace, as a body or court, administered the affairs of the county. They were men of standing, often men of substance, and generally leaders in their communities. Independence from England brought no wrenching changes in the system. In the early days of North Carolina's statehood the justices were appointed by the governor to serve for good behavior; but in making his appointments the governor relied on recommendations from the General Assembly. Thus, as a matter of practical politics, the members of the legislature from a given county had a powerful voice in the selection of that county's justices of the peace and, thus, in the government of the county.

Taken as a group, the justices in a county formed a court known as the Court of Pleas and Quarter Sessions. Any three justices, sitting together, constituted a quorum for the transaction of business. It was common practice for the justices to meet each January, select a chairman, then elect five of their number to hold the regular sessions of the court for the year. At first, the Court of Pleas and Quarter Sessions appointed the county sheriff, the coroner, and the constables. Later these offices were made elective—sheriff and coroner from the county at large and constables from captain's districts (a militia-mustering area). The justices were also responsible for appointing a clerk of court, a register of deeds, a county attorney, a county trustee (treasurer), a surveyor, and overseers or wardens of the poor.

The Court of Pleas and Quarter Sessions had a task that was dual in nature, Although called a court—and it did perform judicial functions—it also had administrative duties. Thus, the justices were responsible for assessing and levying taxes; they were charged with establishing and maintaining roads, bridges, and ferries; they granted licenses to taverns and controlled the prices charged for food; and they were responsible for the erection and control of mills. Through the powers of appointment already noted, they supervised the work of the law enforcement officers, the administrative officers of the court, the surveyor, and the wardens of the poor. Taxes were collected by the sheriff.

In its judicial capacity, the Court of Pleas and Quarter Sessions heard civil cases (except those assigned by law to a single justice or to a higher court); it was responsible for probate, dower, guardianships, and the administration of estates; and it had jurisdiction in criminal cases in which the punishment did not extend to life, limb, or member.

The county itself was a single political unit; there were no townships; and the Court of Pleas and Quarter Sessions, through its appointive and administrative powers, exerted strong control over county affairs. However, it should be emphasized that at the time, the voters had no direct control over the court and thus no direct control over county government. Such was the situation until the end of the Civil War.

From 1868 to 1876

When the North Carolina Constitution was rewritten in 1868 its draftsmen, many of whom were acquainted with local government systems in other parts of the country, devised a new and apparently more democratic plan of organization for the counties. It bore strong resemblance to the plans developed in Pennsylvania and Ohio.

Although the position of justice of the peace was retained, the old Court of Pleas and Quarter Sessions was eliminated. Its judicial responsibilities were distributed between the justices and the superior court. Its administrative work was assigned to a board of county commissioners composed of five members elected by the voters of the county at large.

The county commissioners were made responsible for public buildings, schools, roads and bridges, and the financial affairs of the county, including taxation. The wide appointive powers of the Court of Pleas and Quarter Sessions were not transferred to the board of county commissioners. Instead, the voters of the county elected the sheriff, coroner, clerk of court, register of deeds, surveyor, and treasurer. The sheriff continued to serve as tax collector.

Each county was divided into townships—a distinct innovation—and the voters of each township elected two justices of the peace and a clerk who served as the governing body of the township. Under the county commissioners' supervision, the township board was responsible for roads and bridges and for the assessment of property for taxation. Each township had a constable and each had a school committee.

This long ballot system was consciously constructed to favor the newly formed Republican Party, whose support was gathered from the newly enfranchised black people who had been slaves only three years before, from native whites of small means who had opposed secession and remained loyal to the Union throughout the Civil War, and from a relatively small number of prominent citizens who believed that the state's shattered fortunes could be recovered only through cooperation and understanding between the races and accommodation with the dominant national political party. It was intended to destroy forever the political power of the landowners, professional people, and merchants who had dominated state government, and thus local government under the old system, for nearly a century. Although most of these people were disenfranchised by the Fourteenth Amendment to the United States Constitution because they had "engaged in insurrection or rebellion against the United States, or given aid or comfort to the enemies thereof" by actively supporting the Confederacy, they formed a new political party called the Conservative Party devoted to restoring as much of 'the pre-war social and governmental system as was possible under the circumstances. The new system of county government contained in the Constitution of 1868 became one of their major targets.

Constitutional Changes of 1875

Seven years after the Constitution of 1868 established the county commissioners and township systems, political control shifted to the conservatives. By convention in 1875, the Constitution was amended to authorize the General Assembly to modify the plan of county government established in 1868. And the legislature was quick to exercise its power. The board of county commissioners was not abolished, but members were to be chosen by the justices of the peace of the county rather than by the people at large. While the commissioners retained their responsibilities, decisions on matters of substance could not be put into effect without the concurrence of a majority of the justices—all of whom were elected by the legislature. The justices were made responsible for conducting all elections. And this was only the general law—in more than a few counties, the board of commissioners was also made subject to legislative appointment.

This hobbling arrangement lasted for twenty years. In 1895, the right of the people to elect county commissioners was restored in most counties, and the necessity for approval of the board's decisions by the justices of the peace was repealed.

Townships were stripped of their powers, but they were retained as convenient administrative subdivisions, primarily for road building and maintenance purposes. Finally, in 1905 the people of all 100 counties regained direct control over the board of commissioners through the ballot box.

THE COUNTY AS A BODY POLITIC AND CORPORATE

A county, as a defined geographic subdivision of the state, serves many purposes. Churches, civic clubs, and other societal institutions use counties as convenient subdivisions for their own purposes. The business world may assign sales territories and franchises to areas composed of one or more counties. The county may play a role in the psychology of people born and raised "in the country"—it serves to establish where they are from and who they are, thus becoming a part of their personal identity. But the county was created in the first instance by the state as a political unit, and this remains its primary purpose.

Nearly forty years ago, the North Carolina Supreme Court was called upon to define what a county is from a legal point of view. (The case before the Court was one in which Wake County was a litigant; thus the court spoke in terms of that county, but what the Court had to say is equally true of the other ninety-nine counties).

> Wake County is a body politic and corporate, created by the General Assembly of North Carolina for certain public and political purposes. Its powers as such, both express and implied, are conferred by statutes, enacted from time to time by the General Assembly, and are exercised by its Board of Commissioners. . . . "In the exercise of ordinary governmental functions, [counties] are simply agencies of the State, constituted for the convenience of local administration in certain portions of the State's territory, and in the exercise of such functions they are subject to almost unlimited legislative control, except when the power is restricted by constitutional provisions." In *O'Berry, State Treasurer v. Mecklenburg County*, 198 N.C. 357, 151 S.E. 880 [1930], it is said, "The weight of authority is to the effect that all the powers and functions of a county bear reference to the general policy of the State, and are in fact an integral portion of the general administration of State policy."

It is instructive to examine some of the phrases used in this quotation: A county is a "body politic and corporate," according to the Court. A body politic is a civil division of the state for purposes of governmental administration. A body corporate is a legal entity. In private law, a corporation is a legal person. A county is a legal entity or corporation of a special sort and with a public function. As such, it can buy and hold property, sue and be sued, and enter into contracts—all functions necessary to make its work as a body politic effective.

Historically, the *primary* purpose for erecting a county was to serve state purposes and to perform state functions in a given area rather than to serve the purposes of a particular geographic community. (By way of contrast, a city was *primarily* formed at the request of the people within its jurisdiction to serve the needs of the inhabitants.)

For the Supreme Court to say that "all the powers and functions of a county bear reference to the general policy of the State and are in fact an integral portion of the general administration of State policy" is not as restrictive as might at first reading appear. "State policy" is a very broad frame of reference; it can touch any aspect of local government. Thus, the truly significant nugget in the Supreme Court's definition of the role of counties is its statement that in the exercise of their functions counties "are subject to almost unlimited legislative control, except when the power is restricted by constitutional provisions." In effect, if the General Assembly can be persuaded to assign counties any given power or responsibility, and if the Constitution does not prohibit it, that assignment becomes state policy for county administration.

The Court's phrases should not be drained of meaning, but they must be read in the light of the freedom the General Assembly has in withholding, assigning, withdrawing, and supervising the specific powers of any agency of government—state, county, municipality, or special district. The development of "state policy" with regard to the allocation of functions among governmental units and agencies is necessarily determined by successive legislatures' changing ideas of what is best calculated to achieve desired results.

Experience plays a major role in the determination of state policy. Not infrequently financial emergency and stress have produced a climate favorable to re-examination of the allocation of governmental responsibilities. Until Governor McLean's administration, the state allowed counties, cities, and other local units almost unlimited freedom in borrowing money and issuing bonds. With no one to advise them, no one to warn them, in marketing their securities, many counties overextended their obligations and saw their credit ratings drop to the point where they had to pay crippling rates of interest; eventually, some faced bankruptcy. In 1927, on the basis of this experience, and recognizing a statewide concern, the legislature established the County Government Advisory Commission and gave it the supervisory powers necessary to correct the situation. This commission effected a reversal in local government financing, and its successor, the Local Government Commission, remains one of the bulwarks of North Carolina government today.

Experience with various local arrangements for road building and maintenance had a comparable effect on state policy. It is not accidental that North Carolina counties are no longer responsible for this work.

Reflecting the concern of the people of the state, the legislature recognized a community of interest in roads wider than the single county and defined state policy on roads accordingly. Comparable redefinitions of the area of concern have affected governmental responsibility for operating schools, conducting elections, housing the state's system of lower courts and their records, maintaining property ownership and mortgage records, enforcing much of the state's criminal law, administering public health and public welfare programs, and carrying on state programs designed to promote the development of agriculture. Some of these functions are the responsibility of the boards of county commissioners, and some are assigned to other boards with varying relationships to the board of county commissioners. Thus, apart from the role played by the commissioners in any of these fields, it is the policy of the state to make extensive use of its counties in carrying out a large number of essential governmental operations.

From the beginning, the county has been used as the basic local unit in the judicial system and for law enforcement—there one finds the court, the courthouse, the sheriff, the jail, the clerk, and the court records. But the court is not a *county* court; it is a unit of the *state's* judicial system. The judge, the solicitor, the clerk, and the magistrates are state officials who administer state law, not county law.

Until 1966, the county was the accepted unit for popular representation in the General Assembly. Each county was guaranteed at least one member of the House of Representatives, and although legislative representation must now be allocated among districts designed to achieve equitable distribution of population, those districts do not cross county lines. In this way the county retains some significance as a unit in the state's legislative system.

The General Assembly expresses and codifies its state policy decisions by enacting statutes. In assigning duties and powers to counties, the legislature sometimes speaks in terms of mandate or command and sometimes in terms of permission and discretion. Thus, for example, counties are required to provide adequate housing for public schools, while they are given discretionary authority to exercise planning and zoning powers.

The General Assembly makes two kinds of laws. It enacts general statutes that apply statewide, but it also enacts local or special laws that apply exclusively within named counties or cities. The State Constitution contains limitations on legislative authority to enact local laws dealing with a substantial list of topics, but in the absence of constitutional restriction, the legislature is free to permit local variety and experiment, a freedom once denounced by students of government but now seen as a useful device for demonstrating new ideas and approaches to governmental problems. Given this legislative freedom, any discussion of county powers and responsibilities must always be prefaced with a caution that what is being said about counties in general may not be true for a particular county.

THE BOARD OF COUNTY COMMISSIONERS

We have seen that the county, as a body politic and corporate, is a legal person capable of holding and managing property and possessed of many powers conferred on it by law. The county exercises its powers and discharges its responsibilities through its board of commissioners. In the words of G.S. 153A-12,

> Except as otherwise directed by law, each power, right, duty, function, privilege and immunity of the corporation [i.e., the county] shall be exercised by the board of commissioners.

This statute goes on to say that the county's legal powers shall be carried into execution as provided by the laws of the state, but if a power is "conferred or imposed by law without direction or restriction as to how it is to be exercised or performed," the power or responsibility "shall be carried into execution as provided by ordinance or resolution of the board of commissioners."

Each county in the state has a board of commissioners, but no two boards are exactly alike. In many states, general laws prescribe a form of government for all counties, or for all counties in classes defined by population. In these states, one would expect to find essentially the same form of government in counties of comparable size. Not so in North Carolina. Our boards of county commissioners vary in size, term of office, method of election, method of selecting the chairman, and administrative structure. And these variations bear no correlation to the population of the county or any other objective criteria.

In number of members, the boards of commissioners vary from three to seven, with the great majority (76 out of 100 as of 1974) having five members. Only twelve of the boards serve two-year terms; nearly two-thirds (64 as of 1974) serve staggered four-year terms. The remainder serve either straight four-year terms (that is to say, the terms of all members expire at the same time), or a combination of two-year and staggered four-year terms. Fifty-eight boards, as of 1974, are elected at large; the remaining 42 counties are divided into districts for the purpose of nominating and electing the commissioners. However, in only eight of these 42 are the board members either nominated or both nominated and elected by district voters only. In the remaining 34 counties the districts are used only as representational devices; the members are required to reside in and represent districts, but all nominations and elections are conducted at large. In the great majority of the counties, the chairman of the board of commissioners is selected by and from the board itself, but in nine counties, all in the far west, he is elected separately. In mid-1974, more than half of the counties employ a manager, coordinator, or administrator to supervise all county departments as the board's chief administrative officer. In the remaining counties, the board appoints all department heads directly and supervises each separately.

Selection

All county commissioners are elected by the people in partisan elections held in November of even-numbered years—the same time as the elections for members of the General Assembly and other state officers. But not every county elects all members of its board every two years. Because of the interplay of staggered four-year terms, two-year terms, and straight four-year terms, about half of the state's county commissioners are elected at each general election. Newly elected commissioners take office on the first Monday in December following their election by taking the oath of office. There is no requirement that a person be nominated as the candidate of a political party in order to run for the office of county commissioner, but this is almost invariably the practice. After the 1974 elections, 396 of the 477 county commissioners were affiliated with the Democratic Party, 80 belonged to the Republican Party, and one was independent.

Vacancies in the board of commissioners are filled by appointment of the remaining members. A person appointed to fill a vacancy must be a member of the same political party as the person he replaced (if that person was elected as the nominee of a political party), and the executive committee of that political party has the right to be consulted before the appointment is made, although the board is not bound to follow any advice the committee may give. If the vacancy occurs in a two-year term or in the last two years of a four-year term, the appointment is for the remainder of the unexpired term. If the vacancy occurs in the first two years of a four-year term, the appointment runs only until the next general election, when an election is held to fill the office for the remainder of the unexpired term.

Occasionally, a board of commissioners finds itself deadlocked and unable to fill a vacancy. Since nearly all of the boards of commissioners have an odd number of members, one vacancy means that the remaining members can be equally divided between two candidates, so that neither candidate can receive a majority vote. Recognizing this problem, the law provides that when a board of commissioners fails to fill a vacancy in its membership for 60 days, the clerk to the board of commissioners must report the vacancy to the clerk of superior court, who must fill the vacancy within 10 days after the day the vacancy is reported to him.

The law also provides for another contingency that has not yet occurred. If the number of vacancies on the board is such that a quorum cannot be obtained, the chairman of the board must appoint enough members to make up a quorum and the board then proceeds to fill the vacancies. If this situation exists and the office of chairman is also vacant, the clerk of superior court may act in the chairman's stead on petition of any remaining member of the board or any five registered voters of the county. Whoever makes appointments to the board is bound by the rules that each appointee must be a member of the same political party as the person he is to replace and that the party executive committee must be consulted.

Taking Office

A newly elected or appointed county commissioner assumes the powers and duties of his office by taking the oath of office prescribed by the North Carolina Constitution in the following words:

> I, ... , do solemnly swear (or affirm) that I will support and maintain the Constitution and laws of the United States, and the Constitution and laws of North Carolina not inconsistent therewith, and that I will faithfully discharge the duties of my office as County Commissioner of . . . . . . County, so help me God.

The law gives to several public officials the authority to administer oaths, but in most counties it is customary to have the oath of office for members of the board of commissioners, the sheriff, and the register of deeds administered by the resident superior court judge, the chief district judge, or the clerk of superior court.

A person elected to public office may take the oath of office at any time on or after the date fixed by law for him to do so. For a newly elected county commissioner, that date is the first Monday in December following his election. This is also the regular meeting date for the board in most counties. If a newly elected commissioner is unable to take the oath then due to illness or for some other reason, he may take it at a later time. However, the Constitution provides that public officers continue to hold office until their successors are chosen and qualified. Thus, a member of the board of commissioners who was defeated in the election or chose not to seek re-election retains his office until his successor takes the oath of office.

The Chairman

In all but nine counties, the chairman of the board of commissioners is selected by the board itself. In eight counties the office of chairman of the board of commissioners is a separate office, and the chairman is elected as such by the people. In one county, the commissioner elected with the highest vote is automatically designated chairman of the board. In all counties, the board itself must choose a vice-chairman to act in the absence or disability of the chairman. Except in the nine counties mentioned, the board designates its chairman at its first regular meeting in December for a term of one year. Customs vary as to how the selection is made. In most counties, it is customary for the chairman to serve as long as he is re-elected and retains the confidence of his colleagues. In others, the member elected with the highest vote is usually designated the chairman. In still others, the chairmanship rotates among the members.

The chairman of the board presides at all meetings. By law, he has not only the right but also the duty to vote on all questions before the board unless he is excused by a standing rule of the board or by consent of the remaining members. However, he may not vote to break a tie vote in which he participated. He is generally recognized by law as the chief executive officer of the county and may acquire considerable prestige and influence by virtue of his position. Although as a general rule he has no more legal power than other members of the board, he does have special authority to declare states of emergency under the state laws governing riots and civil disorders. He also has authority to call special meetings of the board on his own initiative.

Meetings

The board is required by law to hold at least one meeting each month, although it may meet as frequently as necessary. Many counties have found in recent years that two regular meetings each month are needed. The board may select any day of the month and any public place within the county for its regular meetings, but in the absence of a formal resolution of the board selecting some other time or place, the law requires the board to meet on the first Monday of the month at the courthouse. Ten o'clock in the morning is the customary time of day for commissioners' meetings, although the law has never specified the time of day. In recent years, some boards have begun to hold some of their regular meetings in the evening to allow greater public attendance.

Special board meetings may be called by the chairman or by a majority of the other board members. The law lays down specific rules for calling special meetings. A special meeting must be called by written notice stating the time, place, and subjects to be considered. This notice must be posted on the courthouse bulletin board and delivered to each member of the board at least 48 hours before the meeting. Unless all members attend or sign a written waiver, only business related to the subjects stated in the notice may be transacted at a special meeting. The usual rules do not apply to special meetings called to deal with an "emergency," which is not defined by the law, but even then the persons who call the meeting must take "reasonable action to inform the other members and the public of the meeting."

The board of commissioners is subject to the Open Meetings Statute, enacted in 1971. This law forbids most public bodies, both state and local, to hold meetings that are not open to the public. The law is broadly worded and often difficult to interpret. In general, it prohibits a majority of the members of a board of commissioners from gathering together in closed or secret session for the purpose of "conducting hearings, participating in deliberations or voting upon or otherwise transacting public business," except when the subject of discussion falls within one of the exceptions set out in the statute. The exceptions are:

(1) Acquisition, lease, or sale of property;
(2) Negotiations with county employees or their representatives as to the terms or conditions of employment;
(3) Matters concerning hospital management, operation, and discipline;
(4) Any matter coming within the physician-patient or lawyer-client privilege;
(5) Conferences with legal counsel and other deliberations concerning court actions or proceedings.

(These descriptions of the exceptions are summarized from the statute and should not be taken as complete.)

Procedure

The law leaves most procedural matters to the discretion of the board, but it does set out a few rules that must be followed. The board may take no action unless a quorum is present, and the law defines a quorum as a majority of the full membership of the board without regard to vacancies. For example, a quorum of a five-member board is always three members even though there may be two vacancies. Once a quorum is present at a meeting, a member cannot destroy the quorum by leaving the room without the consent of the remaining members. The law provides that if a member withdraws from the meeting room without being excused by a majority of the members remaining, he is counted as present for quorum purposes. The board also has the legal power to command the sheriff to take absent members into custody and bring them to the meeting place. However, such action can be taken only when a quorum is already present.

The law places a duty on each member to vote on each question before the board unless he is excused by his colleagues, and excuses are permitted only when the matter before the board concerns the financial interest or official conduct of the member requesting the excuse. Although this duty is clearly present in the law, there are no enforcement provisions for it.

The board must see to it that the clerk to the board keeps full and accurate minutes of its proceedings. The minute book must be open to public inspection, and the results of each vote taken by the board must be recorded in it. Each member has the right to demand a roll-call vote on any question put to the board; and when such a demand is made, the names of those voting on each side of the question must be recorded.

The board has the power to adopt its own written rules of procedure. The only legal restraint on these rules is that they must be "in the spirit of generally accepted principles of parliamentary procedure."

Formal Actions of the Board

Except for the few special powers held by the chairman of the board, the legal powers and duties of county commissioners are vested in the board of commissioners acting as a body. An individual commissioner has no power of his own; but when he meets with his fellow commissioners in a validly called and held meeting, a majority of the board has and may exercise control of those functions of county government confided to the care of the board of commissioners. The board takes formal action in one of three forms; orders, resolutions, and ordinances. Although these terms are often used interchangeably, their definitions may be useful to illustrate how the board acts.

An *order* is usually a directive to a county administrative officer to take or refrain from taking a specified action. For example, a board of commissioners may enter an order directing the county manager to advertise for bids for a new office building. An order may also formally declare the existence of a given state of fact, such as an order declaring the results of a bond election. Finally, an order may sometimes be used to decide a question before the board, such as an order awarding a construction contract to the lowest responsible bidder.

A *resolution* usually expresses the sense of the board on a question before it. For example, the board may adopt a resolution requesting the county's legislative delegation to introduce a local bill, or it may resolve to petition the State Department of Transportation to pave a rural road.

An *ordinance* is an action of the board taken in its capacity as the county's legislative body. As such, an ordinance is analagous to an act of the General Assembly. The board of commissioners may adopt ordinances relating to such varied matters as zoning, subdivision control, dogs running at large, use of county parking lots, street numbers on rural roads, use of the county landfill, and so forth.

Ordinance Procedure

The law does not regulate the manner in which orders and resolutions are adopted by a board of commissioners, beyond the minimum requirements of a valid meeting at which a quorum is present, but there are several laws governing the adoption of ordinances. An ordinance may be adopted at the meeting at which it is introduced only if it receives a unanimous affirmative vote, all members of the board present and voting. If it passes but with less than this unanimous vote, it may be finally passed by a majority vote at any time within 100 days after its introduction. This rule does not apply to the budget ordinance (which may be passed at any meeting at which a quorum is present), or to a bond ordinance (which always requires a public hearing before passage and in most cases approval by the voters as well), or to any ordinance on which the law requires a public hearing before adoption (such as a zoning ordinance).

Once an ordinance is adopted, it must be filed in an ordinance book, separate from the minute book. The ordinance book must be indexed and made available for public inspection. The budget ordinance, bond ordinances, and ordinances of "limited interest or transitory nature" may be omitted from the ordinance book, but the book must contain a section showing the caption of each omitted ordinance and the page in the minute book at which it appears.

The board of commissioners has authority to adopt and issue a code of ordinances.

Public Hearings

In the course of a normal year, a board of commissioners will hold several public hearings. Some hearings will be required by law, such as the hearing on the budget ordinance, or on a bond ordinance, or on a zoning ordinance or amendment thereto. Some of them may be held on the board's own initiative to give interested citizens an opportunity to make their views known to the board on controversial issues such as a dog-control ordinance. Laws requiring public hearings do not set out how the hearing must be conducted; they only require that one be held. However, the law does allow the board itself to adopt reasonable rules governing the conduct of public hearings. These rules may regulate such matters as the time allotted to each speaker, designating spokesmen for groups, selecting delegates from groups when the hearing room is too small to hold everyone who wants to attend, and maintaining order and decorum.

Organizing the Administration

The law dictates many, if not most, features of how the county government will be organized. The sheriff and register of deeds are elected by the people. There is a board of education, a board of health, a board of social services, and a board of elections for each county and, in many counties, a board of alcoholic beverage control. The tax supervisor, tax collector, county attorney, county manager, and clerk to the board of commissioners are appointed directly by the commissioners. Yet in every county there are a number of county departments, agencies, or offices that are directly under the administrative jurisdiction of the board. With respect to these agencies, the board of commissioners has authority to organize the county government in any way it sees fit.

The County Manager

Except for a few counties in which the chairman of the board is a full-time administrative officer, each board of commissioners has discretionary authority to adopt the county manager form of government by appointing a manager. The basic features of the manager system are discussed in more detail in Chapter 2.

The Clerk to the Board of Commissioners

The board of commissioners must have a clerk, who is responsible for keeping the minute book and the ordinance book. The clerk also has a wide variety of miscellaneous duties, all directly related to official actions of the board of commissioners. In the past, the register of deeds usually acted as clerk to the board, but this custom is passing. A few boards now have a clerk who has no other duties, but most boards have designated some county official or employee such as the manager or finance officer to act as clerk to the board. The clerk is appointed directly by the board and serves as its pleasure.

The County Attorney

The board of commissioners must appoint a county attorney, who serves as the board's legal adviser. The exact nature of the county attorney's duties varies from county to county, as does the amount and method of his compensation. A few counties have established a full-time position of county attorney, and in those counties the county attorney may provide legal services to nearly all county agencies except the board of education (which always employs its own attorney.) The county attorney is not appointed to a definite term; he serves at the pleasure of the board.

— *Joseph S. Ferrell*

2 / Administering the County

Introduction / 18
Organization / 19
The County Manager Plan / 21
Appointment of a Manager / 21
Powers and Duties of the County Manager / 23
The Role of the Manager / 26
County Administrators and Coordinators / 27
Acting County Manager / 28
Information About the Manager Plan or
  Employing a Manager / 28
Commissioner Form of Government / 29
County Employment / 29
Commissioners' Powers As to County Officials
  and Employees / 30
Oath of Office / 30
Filling Vacancies / 30
Bonds / 30
Fixed Fees / 31
Number of Employees / 31
Compensation / 31
Adopt Rules and Regulations / 32
Restrictions on Political Activity / 33
Personnel Board / 33
Training / 34
Defense of Employees and Purchase of
  Liability Insurance / 34
Group Insurance / 35
Workmen's Compensation / 35
Social Security and Retirement / 36
Recruitment of County Employees / 36
County Employee Unions / 38
Power to Discharge or Remove County Employees / 38

2 / ADMINISTERING THE COUNTY

INTRODUCTION

Forty years ago Franklin D. Roosevelt described county government as the "dark continent of American politics." Why did the President find counties inadequate? During the depression of the 1930s, the central administration of county affairs in North Carolina and elsewhere was virtually impossible. Most of the major functions of county government were the responsibility of officers elected by the people. In North Carolina, these included the sheriff, the register of deeds, and the clerk of superior court in all counties and such other officers as the treasurer, the auditor, and the tax collector in some counties. In most states, the ballot was even longer. Many of the elected officers and their deputies were dependent for their compensation on the fees collected for performing their official duties. Although the governing boards of nearly all counties were elected by the people, the boards could not formulate and implement public policy because they lacked direct control over independently elected officers, lacked control over the fiscal affairs of these officers (because of the fee system), and lacked control over general administration of county affairs. As citizens who had to earn a living first, they lacked the time to do the county's business.

In Roosevelt's words, people were "ill-clad, ill-fed, and unemployed." The nation was paralyzed by the most severe economic depression in history, and people looked to county government for help. County government was the closest to the people because counties were responsible for public education, health, and welfare. But in the early '30s county government was completely unprepared to meet the challenges of the times. County governing boards had inadequate funds, limited time, and insufficient skill to develop and administer programs to solve the "people" problems. Earlier scandals in some midwestern states involving excessive fees collected by elected officers, and widespread financial irresponsibility of local governing boards had undermined public confidence in county government. The magnitude of the problems facing county government, the lack of administrative organization, and the low ebb of public confidence combined to prevent even the most concerned boards of county commissioners from developing meaningful programs.

In North Carolina several instances of misappropriation of county funds and fiscal mismanagement caused the North Carolina Association of County Commissioners in 1925 to ask Governor Angus W. McLean to appoint a commission to study and make recommendations for improving county government. The Governor did so, and the commission's report singled out the organization of county government and the lack of central financial administration as the two subjects most in need of attention. To improve the general administration of the county, the commission recommended the enactment of legislation to permit counties to adopt the county manager plan of government. To improve financial administration, it recommended passage of a county fiscal control act that centralized control of county fiscal affairs in a county accountant appointed by and directly responsible to the board of commissioners. Both of these recommendations were enacted by the General Assembly. The fiscal contol act was mandatory on all counties. The manager plan was optional.

The problems identified in 1925 were not solved by the legislation enacted in the '20s. They remain with county government to this day, but a beginning had been made. Perhaps if the depression had not intervened and counties had not been overwhelmed by the staggering problems of those times, counties might have emerged by a gradual evolution from the "dark continent" into the mainstream of American political life. But the twin crises of depression and world war arrested that evolution for twenty years after Governor McLean's beginning.

The thirty years since the end of World War II have seen county government in North Carolina pick up the threads dropped at the beginning of the depression. The fee system has all but died out; the General Assembly has adopted a policy of granting counties more and more control over local affairs and reduced the use of local legislation to control local affairs; the county manager plan of government has spread to more than half of the 100 counties and some of its features have been adopted in others; county fiscal affairs are well administered in most counties; and the authority of the board of commissioners to control the general administration of the county has greatly increased. The remainder of this chapter will trace the development of these themes and describe the present organization for the administration of county government.

ORGANIZATION

The reduction in local legislation and the enactment of more discretionary "home rule" statutes have increased the authority and responsibility of boards of county commissioners. These increases have enhanced the policy-making role of the commissioners and, with the wide adoption of the county manager plan, brought the North Carolina county government more in line with modern administrative theory.

G.S. 153A-76, enacted in 1973, has clarified the authority of the board of commissioners to organize county government:

> The board of commissioners may create, change, abolish, and consolidate offices, positions, departments, boards, commissions, and agencies of the county government, may impose ex officio the duties of more than one office on a single officer, may change the composition and manner of selection of boards, commissions, and agencies, and may generally organize and reorganize the county government in order to promote orderly and efficient administration of county affairs, subject to the following limitations:
>
> (1) The board may not abolish an office, position, department, board, commission, or agency established or required by law.
> (2) The board may not combine offices or confer certain duties on the same officer when this action is specifically forbidden by law.
> (3) The board may not discontinue or assign elsewhere a function or duty assigned by law to a particular office, position, department, board, commission, or agency.
> (4) The board may not change the composition or manner of selection of a local board of education, the board of health, the board of social services, the board of elections, or the board of alcoholic beverage control.

The statute has removed doubt and increased the ability of the board to act on organizational problems.

The 1970 revision of the North Carolina Constitution as to double officeholding and the enactment of G.S. 128-1.1 have eliminated another possible area of confusion by permitting a person who holds an appointive office to hold concurrently one other appointive or elective office. Also, Article III, section 6, of the State Constitution has been rewritten to delete eligibility to vote as a requirement for appointive office. These new provisions further clarify the position of county officials and foster professionalism.

G.S. 153A-77, which applies only to Mecklenburg County (because it is now the only county with a population over 325,000), authorizes the Mecklenburg board of commissioners, after a hearing, to assume all powers and duties of any county board or commission, including the boards of health, social services, and mental health.

THE COUNTY MANAGER PLAN

North Carolina has more county managers and administrators than any other state in the nation. As of July 1974, 64 counties had designated a county official as a manager, administrator, or coordinator (see page 28 for a discussion of the distinction implied by these different terms). Fifty-one of these counties have adopted the manager plan. In three counties the manager is the elected chairman of the board. In 47 counties, the appointed official is designated as county manager. In eight counties, this appointed officer is designated a county administrator; in six counties, he is designated as county coordinator (see Table 2-I). There are an estimated 325 appointed county managers or administrators in the nation.

Appointment of a Manager

The appointment of county managers was authorized by the General Statutes in 1927. Though three other counties adopted the plan briefly in 1927, Robeson County, which adopted the plan by local act in 1929, has operated under it longer than any other county in the nation. All other counties that now have managers adopted the plan under the general enabling statutes of 1927 or under legislation pertaining to counties that were revised in 1973 (G.S. Ch. 153A).

G.S. 153A-81 provides that the board of commissioners may by resolution adopt or discontinue the county manager plan. The board may choose among the following three alternatives in adopting the county manager plan.

(1) Appoint the manager on the basis of his executive and administrative qualifications to serve at the pleasure of the board. The manager need not be a resident of the county or state when he is appointed.
(2) Confer the duties of manager upon the chairman or some other member of the board of commissioners.
(3) Confer the duties of manager on any other county officer, employee, or agent.

This section, and G.S. 153A-76 described above, served as the pattern used by the Advisory Committee on Intergovernmental Relations established by Congress in preparing suggested "model" county organization legislation for adoption in all states.

Table 2-I

Form of County Manager Government in North Carolina (By Most Recent Date of Change), July 1974

County	Full-Time Chairman	Manager	Administrator	Coordinator
Alamance		1971		
Alexander			1971	
Anson		1962		
Ashe		1973		
Bertie		1973		
Brunswick		1970		
Buncombe	1917			
Burke		1968		
Caldwell		1967		
Catawba		1937		
Cherokee		1972		
Chowan				1973
Cleveland		1965		
Cumberland			1972	
Currituck		1973		
Dare		1973		
Davidson		1955		
Davie		1970		
Durham		1930		
Edgecombe		1971		
Forsyth		1956		
Franklin				1973
Gaston		1957		
Gates		1973		
Graham		1971		
Guilford		1942		
Haywood	1939			
Hertford		1959		
Hoke		1966		
Hyde				1973
Iredell		1964		
Jackson			1974	
Lincoln		1967		
Macon		1969		
Mecklenburg		1962		
McDowell		1968		
Moore			1974	
Nash		1969		
New Hanover		1966		
Northampton		1964		
Onslow		1970		
Orange			1963	
Pasquotank				1973
Person			1973	

ADMINISTRATION 23

County	Full-Time Chairman	Manager	Administrator	Coordinator
Pitt		1970		
Randolph		1972		
Richmond			1971	
Robeson		1929		
Rockingham		1957		
Rowan		1967		
Rutherford				1972
Sampson		1974		
Scotland		1964		
Stanly		1970		
Stokes		1972		
Surry		1971		
Transylvania	1972			
Tyrrell				1973
Union		1965		
Wake		1964		
Warren		1974		
Washington		1973		
Wayne			1965	
Wilson		1970		
Total	3	47	3	6

Powers and Duties of the County Manager

G.S. 153A-82 provides that the manager is the chief administrator of county government and is responsible to the board of commissioners for administering all departments of county government under the board's general control. The manager has the following powers and duties:

(1) He shall appoint with the approval of the board of commissioners and suspend or remove all county officers, employees, and agents except those who are elected by the people or whose appointment is otherwise provided for by law. The board may by resolution permit the manager to appoint officers, employees, and agents without first securing the board's approval. The manager shall make his appointments, suspensions, and removals in accordance with any general personnel rules, regulations, policies, or ordinances that the board may adopt. The board may require the manager to report each suspension or removal to the board at the board's first regular meeting following the suspension or removal; and, if the board has permitted the manager to make appointments without board approval, the board may require the manager to report each appointment to the board at the board's first regular meeting following the appointment.

(2) He shall direct and supervise the administration of all county offices, departments, boards, commissioners, and agencies under the general control of the board of commissioners, subject to the general direction and control of the board.
(3) He shall attend all meetings of the board of commissioners and recommend any measures that he considers expedient.
(4) He shall see that the orders, ordinances, resolutions, and regulations of the board of commissioners are faithfully executed within the county.
(5) He shall prepare and submit the annual budget and capital program to the board of commissioners.
(6) He shall annually submit to the board of commissioners and make available to the public a complete report on the finances and administrative activities of the county as of the end of the fiscal year.
(7) He shall make any other reports that the board of commissioners may require concerning the operations of county offices, departments, boards, commissions, and agencies.
(8) He shall perform any other duties that may be required or authorized by the board of commissioners.

G.S. 153A-92 makes the manager responsible for preparing position classification and pay plans for submission to the board and for administering the plans in accordance with general policies adopted by the board.

G. S. 153A-82 makes five additions or clarifications and one deletion to the 1927 enabling act: (1) Subsection (2) above specifically provides that the manager shall direct and supervise the administration of all county offices under the general control of the board of commissioners. (2) The manager is directed to prepare and submit the annual budget and capital program to the board. (3) He is to prepare classification and pay plans and administer the plans adopted by the board. (4) The board is authorized by resolution to permit the manager to appoint officers and employees without first securing the board's approval. (5) The manager's appointments and removals must be made in accordance with general rules and policies adopted by the board. The provisions of the 1927 act authorizing the adoption of the manager plan by popular vote was deleted on the theory that a manager could not function effectively with a board of commissioners who did not support the plan. With board support, an election is unnecessary.

The county manager's appointive powers were increased, but they are still less than the powers of county managers in some other states and less than the powers of most city managers.

The existence of two independently elected officials in all counties—the sheriff and the register of deeds—limits the appointive and supervisory

ADMINISTRATION

jurisdiction of the manager. The General Assembly could give a board of commissioners or manager the authority to appoint the register of deeds, but the manager's authority is now limited by G.S. 153A-103, which recognized the exclusive right of each sheriff and register of deeds to hire, discharge, and supervise the employees of his office.

The appointive powers of the county manager are also restricted by other statutory provisions. G.S. 153A-111 provides that the board shall designate a clerk to the board. The board also appoints the county attorney (G.S. 153A-114), tax supervisor (G.S. 105-294), tax collector (G.S. 105-349), and surveyor (G.S. 153A-441). The local board of health appoints the health director after consultation with the Secretary of Human Resources and the board or boards of county commissioners in the county or district (G.S. 130-18). The health director appoints all employees of the department in accordance with the provisions of the state personnel act found in G.S. Ch. 126. The board of social services appoints the social services director, who appoints the social services employees (G.S. 108-17, -19). The contract governing agricultural extension employees provides for them to be jointly appointed by the board of commissioners and the state extension service. Nor does the county manager appoint the employees of such independent boards as the board of elections (G.S. 163-35, -41, -67.1), the hospital board [G.S. 131-98(8)], and the board of education (G.S. 115-44, -57, -58, -72).

In some counties the county manager appoints or recommends the appointment of all appointive officials. The distinction between making an appointment subject to the approval of the board and recommending a person for appointment by the board is sometimes clouded in actual practice.

In other counties the manager from habit may recommend for appointment rather than appoint officers and employees whose appointment is not otherwise provided by law. In small counties the manager may appoint only a few clerical and maintenance employees. However, a variety of department heads are appointed by county managers.[1]

G.S. 153A-82, quoted on page 24, sets forth the legal powers and duties of a county manager. Most managers have a strong sense of responsibility and will work diligently to exercise these powers and carry out each duty. In their work, the Code of Ethics of their professional associations, the Inter-

---

1. Each of the following is appointed by a county manager subject to the approval of a board of commissioners or upon board resolution: animal shelter superintendent, budget director, building inspector, building maintenance superintendent, commodity distribution superintendent, county auditor, director of air pollution, director of bail program, director of center for human development, director of emergency services, director of general services, director of juvenile diagnostic center, director of youth center, fire administrator or marshal, garage superintendent, manager of the data-processing center, park director, personnel director, public service and information officer, purchasing agent, and veterans' service officer.

national City Management Association (ICMA) and the North Carolina City and County Management Association, requires them to follow seventeen principles: For example, the Code requires (1) a dedication to the concepts of effective and democratic local government; (2) a dedication to the highest ideals of honor and integrity in all public and personal relationships; (3) submission of policy proposals and facts and advice on matters of policy to elected officials; and (4) resistance to any encroachment on the manager's responsibilities, as "he should be free to carry out official policies without interference, and handle each problem without discrimination on the basis of principle and justice."

The Role of the Manager

Although the legal powers and duties of all county managers are the same, the manager's role may vary because of (1) the manager, (2) the elected and appointed officials in the county, and (3) the particular problems of the county at the time.

Because of individual differences in personality, ability, training, experience, skill, and interests, the manager's role may vary from county to county. It may also vary as the manager moves from one county to another because of differences in the personality, ability, training, experience, skill, and interests of board members and elected and appointed officials. No less important, the economic and social needs of the citizens of the county, the political atmosphere, citizen interest or antagonism, and many other factors may affect the manager's role.

The typical county manager in North Carolina has been described as "the eyes, ears, and legs of his board of commissioners." He gathers facts, does research, receives information, communicates the views of the commissioners, explains policies to employees and the public, and does the many other things required to help commissioners make policy and to carry out the policies made.

The anticipation of future needs of citizens for governmental services and the development of reasonable administrative programs and plans to meet those needs is a technical and involved job requiring long hours and a wide variety of skills. Commissioners find that small and relatively insignificant problems can take hours if the facts and circumstances are not known. Few commissioners can spare the time from their business or occupation to research a fraction of the questions brought for them to decide. Under these circumstances, the commissioners request the manager to gather information and make recommendations on policy issues. After the board adopts policies, administrative decisions are turned over to the manager to be made within those established policies.

Many boards require the manager to serve as a coordinator or liaison officer among groups within the county and between the county and state and federal agencies. Within the county, the manager may be directed to work on problems with the boards of education, elections, health, and social services, with chambers of commerce and industrial promotion groups, with airport, drainage, fire, planning, sanitation, water, and zoning boards and authorities, and with numerous other public and private groups.

The typical manager spends considerable time on intergovernmental relations. He may work with officials of cities within the county, neighboring counties, the Agricultural Extension Service, the district board of health, the Local Government Commission, and the state departments responsible for education, civil defense, forest fire protection, health, industrial development, anti-poverty, and social service programs.

Many managers are now spending an increasing percentage of their time in representing the county's interests before a host of federal departments administered through regional offices or from Washington.

Because of the position the county manager occupies, he is a community leader. Although managers diligently strive to avoid partisan political involvement, they will be asked and expected to explain and defend the policies adopted by the board whose members are elected in partisan elections. Citizens are demanding more services, higher levels of services, and more information as to county policies and problems. Because the manager has an office in the courthouse and is readily available, more and more citizens call on him for information and to register complaints, concerns, and requests. Commissioners find it administratively advantageous and politically desirable to refer citizens who have questions on administrative matters to the manager.

County Administrators and Coordinators

Eight counties have county administrators and six have county coordinators. A question frequently asked is, "Are county administrators and county coordinators county managers?" To answer this question, one must study the resolution appointing the official and subsequent practice.

Some county administrators are an "other officer" upon whom the duties of county manager have been conferred as authorized by G.S. 153A-81(3). They are "administrators" because the resolution adopting the county manager form uses that title; it provides for the duties of manager to be exercised by the "county administrator." Administrators are called by a different name simply because the board of commissioners preferred the term administrator. Orange is one county where the manager's duties are exercised by an administrator.

However, most administrators and all county coordinators are not legally county managers. The resolutions appointing them have not given them the appointive powers delegated to county managers. Some administrators and some coordinators do everything else that managers do. At the other extreme, some county coordinators serve in only a research and clerical capacity to the board of commissioners.

Acting County Manager

G.S. 153A-83 provides that the county manager may designate a qualified person to exercise the powers and perform the duties of manager during the manager's temporary absence or disability. The designation is to be made by letter filed with the clerk and is subject to the approval of the board of commissioners. During the absence or disability, the board may revoke the designation at any time and appoint another person to serve until the manager returns or his disability ceases.

G.S. 153A-84 provides that if the position of county manager is vacant, the board shall designate a qualified person as interim manager. The person designated may be the chairman or a member of the board.

Information About the Manager Plan or Employing a Manager

Commissioners who are considering the adoption of the county manager plan or the hiring of a manager have a number of agencies to help them. Richard S. Childs, the "father" of the manager form of government and a proponent of the county manager plan since 1914, is still active in supplying information regarding the plan. A number of his publications can be secured from the National Municipal League, 47 East 68th Street, New York, N.Y.

The International City Management Association has a handbook for councilmen and publications on the role of the manager and how to select a manager that is as helpful to county commissioners as to councilmen. The National Association of Counties in 1973 published a National Survey of the Appointed Administrator in County Government which contains helpful information about county managers and administrators. The International City Management Association publishes a bi-weekly newsletter that lists all governmental units that have adopted the manager plan and all governmental units that wish to employ a manager. By writing to the International City Management Association, 1140 Connecticut Avenue, N.W., Washington, D.C. 20036 (telephone 202-293-2200), a board of commissioners can have its manager vacancy given immediate national publicity. The typical notice of vacancy contains the following information: name of county, population, number of employees, annual budget, the date when the manager plan was adopted, number of managers since the plan was adopted, education and experience preferred or required, approximate salary, name and address of the person to whom applications should be sent, and last date for filing application.

The staff of the North Carolina Association of County Commissioners and the Institute of Government have for years provided information to counties about the county manager form of government and helped counties in securing the services of qualified professional managers.

Several North Carolina counties, when they have first gone to the manager plan, have adopted a supplementary resolution setting forth the duties of the manager in detail. Such a document alerts both the manager and the members of the board to their obligations. It may increase the likelihood that both will follow their new role. At least two North Carolina counties have signed a contract with a first manager that outlines his duties. One contract guarantees the new manager three months' severance pay if he should be dismissed during the first year of the contract.

COMMISSIONER FORM OF GOVERNMENT

The general powers of the board of county commissioners have been described in Chapter 1. In counties that have not adopted the county manager plan, certain appointive powers are exercised by the board of commissioners. G.S. 153A-87 provides that in counties that do not have a manager, the board shall appoint, suspend, and remove all county officers, employees, and agents except those who are elected by the people or whose appointment is otherwise provided for by law.

G.S. 153A-88 authorizes any department head, subject to the approval of the board of commissioners, to designate an acting department head to serve during his absence or disability. During this interval the board may revoke the designation at any time and appoint another person. When a position as department head is vacant, the board may designate a qualified person to exercise the powers of that position until the vacancy is filled.

In counties without a county manager, the commissioners shall appoint or designate a personnel officer, who shall then be responsible for administering the pay plan and any position classification plan in accordance with general policies and directives adopted by the board.

COUNTY EMPLOYMENT

Employment in county government in North Carolina has increased an estimated 66 per cent in the last ten years. This is twice as fast as the increase in municipal employment and only slightly less than the 75 per cent increase in North Carolina state employment during the same period. An estimated 21,395 full-time equivalent employees were working for the 100 counties in October 1973.

As Chapter 1 indicates, this increase reflects an effort by local officials to (1) provide service for the growing population, (2) provide a higher standard of service in keeping with citizen demand, (3) provide additional services demanded by citizens, and (4) extend county-wide the services that have been provided heretofore to residents of cities by municipal governments.

Commissioners' Powers As to County Officials and Employees

Although boards of county commissioners are limited by the State Constitution, state and local statutes, and federal standards, they have major responsibility for determining policy relating to county personnel administration. County commissioners exercise their power over personnel by (1) appropriating or refusing to appropriate funds; (2) fixing qualifications for appointive office (G.S. 153A-35); (3) fixing the pay and expense allowances of officials and employees (G.S. 153A-92); (4) appointing, supervising, and dismissing some groups of employees;[2] (5) approving or refusing to approve the appointments of the manager or administrator; and (6) adopting rules and regulations governing hours and days of work, holidays, leave, pay, expense allowances, working conditions, and any other measures that promote the hiring and retention of capable, diligent, and honest career employees (G.S. 153A-92, -94).

Oath of Office

Each elected county official is required to be at the regular meeting place of the board of commissioners on the first Monday in December following each general election and take an oath of office. Each appointive officer must also take an oath of office before entering on duty [G.S. 153A-26; G.S. 105-349(g)].

Filling Vacancies

The board of commissioners is authorized to fill vacancies in the elective offices of sheriff, coroner, and register of deeds (G.S. 162-5; G.S. 152-1; G.S. 161-5). If an elected official abandons his office, a quo warranto proceeding may be brought in the name of the Attorney General. After a finding of fact that the official has abandoned his office, the board of commissioners may fill the vacancy.[3]

Bonds

The commissioners are required to determine the amount of, and to approve, the bonds of the coroner, register of deeds, sheriff, and tax collector

---

2. The commissioners are authorized to fill vacancies in the office of register of deeds [G.S. 161-5(a)] and sheriff (G.S. 162-3) and to appoint and remove the tax collector and deputy tax collector [G.S. 105-349 (a) and (f)].

3. Letter of the Attorney General to Robert W. Proctor, August 1, 1957.

before these officials are inducted into office. In addition, each employee who handles or has custody of more than $100 at any time is required to give a faithful performance and true accounting bond [G.S. 153A-19 (a)].

The county may adopt a system of blanket faithful performance or true accounting bonding as an alternative to individual bonds for all county officials except elected officers, finance officers, and tax collectors. The county may pay the premium on any bond [G.S. 153A-29 (b)].

Fixed Fees

The board of commissioners may fix the fees and commissions charged by county officers and employees for performing services or duties permitted or required by law, but it may not modify the statutory fees set for the General Court of Justice or register of deeds or the filing fees imposed by statute on candidates for election. In a recent survey of all counties, only 20 officials were reported to be paid entirely or in part from the fees they collected. Officials compensated entirely by fees included one register of deeds, three tax collectors, one building inspector, and eight electrical inspectors. The officials who received fees as part of their compensation were three register of deeds, three sheriffs, and two deputy sheriffs. The use of fees to compensate county employees declined sharply after the passage of the Uniform Civil Process Fee Act. G.S. 7A-311 requires all civil process fees to be remitted to the county.

Number of Employees

The board of commissioners determine the number of county employees, in effect, when it approves a budget for each department and establishes a pay plan that sets salary ranges for each class of position. A technical limitation on this authority is G.S. 153A-103, which guarantees each sheriff and register of deeds at least one deputy.

Compensation

The board of commissioners may fix the compensation and allowances of the chairman and other members of the board and of all county officers and employees, whether elected or appointed (G.S. 153A-28, -92), subject to six restrictions: (1) The compensation of the register of deeds or sheriff may not be reduced during his term of office without his approval. (2) Commissioners must give notice of intent to reduce the compensation of the register of deeds or sheriff no later than 14 days before the last day for filing for the office. (3) If disagreement results from a reduction in the salary of either elected official, the dispute must be taken to the senior resident superior court judge for arbitration if it cannot otherwise be reconciled. (4) The salaries paid to employees of the health, mental health, and social services departments must conform to the pay plan adopted for those departments by the State Personnel Board in accordance with G.S. 126-9. (5) All employees must be paid the minimum wages and overtime wages required by the federal Fair Labor Standards Amendments of 1974. (6) The Law Enforcement Officers Minimum Salary Act establishes minimum salaries to be paid five levels of law enforcement officers and provides for the Criminal Justice Training and Standards Council to pay the difference between the minimum salaries set out in the act and the salaries paid officers as of January 1, 1973.

An estimated 46 counties have adopted position classification plans and pay plans governing county employees. In counties with managers, the manager is responsible for preparing the classification and pay plan. In the other counties, G.S. 153A-92(c) requires the commissioners to designate a personnel officer to prepare the classification and pay plan.

Local pay plans may or may not incorporate the salary ranges established by the State Personnel Board for local jurisdictions. With approval of the State Personnel Board, the commissioners may modify the state salary plan applicable to health, mental health, social services, and civil defense employees to conform to local financial ability and fiscal policy. If the county's pay plan is modified, the same pay relationships must be maintained among all professional, administrative, and technical positions other than the administrator and among all clerical and sub-professional positions in the county "merit system" departments.

In spite of specific legislation authorizing the board of social services to set the salary of the director of social services, the Attorney General has ruled that the commissioners may, in accordance with G.S. 126-9(a), determine the salary to be paid the director.

Failure of a county to adhere to the State Personnel Act governing the compensation of county employees not only makes it ineligible for state and federal funds, but also results in an illegal expenditure of public funds.

The Memorandum of Understanding—a contract entered into by the board of commissioners and the North Carolina Agricultural Extension Service—provides that the salaries of all extension personnel will be determined jointly by the Agricultural Extension Service and the commissioners.

G.S. 153A-92(d) authorizes a county to provide other fringe benefits to county employees as a part of their compensation.

Adopt Rules and Regulations

The commissioners may adopt rules and regulations concerning, but not limited to, annual leave, sick leave, special leave with full or partial pay supplementing workmen's compensation payments, hours, workdays, holidays, service award and incentive award programs, and any other measures that promote the hiring and retention of capable, diligent, and honest career employees (G.S. 153A-94).

When a board of commissioners adopts rules governing the above items and the administration of the pay plan for county employees and files the rules with the State Personnel Director, the county rules will supersede the State Personnel Board rules for local employees subject to the act (G.S. 126-9). County rules as to leave, hours of work, and holidays also apply to county extension employees. In the absence of local rules, the personnel rules of the State Personnel Department and the Agricultural Extension Service govern their respective employees (G.S. 153A-439).

Restrictions on Political Activity

Rules adopted by several boards of county commissioners provide that no county appointive employees shall (1) engage in any political activity while on duty; (2) be required as a duty of his office or employment, or as a condition of employment or promotion or tenure of office, to contribute to, solicit for, or act as custodian of funds for political or partisan purposes; or (3) coerce or compel contributions by any other county employee of funds for political or partisan purposes.

Civil defense, health, mental health, and social services employees are subject to the federal Hatch Act. These employees may not use their official authority or influence to interfere with an election or affect the results thereof. They may not stand for election to a partisan political office or coerce campaign contributions. However, the federal Elections Campaign Act of 1974 rewrote the Hatch Act to provide that state and local employees after January 1, 1975, may engage in certain activities previously prohibited by the Hatch Act. For example, unless prohibited by state or local acts, employees subject to the Hatch Act may serve as an officer in a political party or campaign, may organize political campaigns, may solicit votes, may endorse or oppose candidates for political office, and may serve as a delegate to a political convention.

Personnel Board

G.S. 153A-95 authorizes the board of commissioners to establish a personnel board with authority to administer tests; to conduct appeal hearings for employees who have been suspended, demoted, or discharged; to hear grievances; and to undertake any other duties relating to personnel administration that the commissioners may direct. The board's authority extends only to the employees under the board's general control.

No county is known to have used this authority. Mecklenburg and Gaston counties have civil service boards that administer tests and conduct appeal hearings for employees of their rural police departments. A 1973 act created a Buncombe County Personnel Advisory Board to have advisory and investigative duties respecting personnel administration in the sheriff's department. The board is empowered to hear appeals, receive evidence, determine facts, and make recommendations to the sheriff in cases of employee suspension, demotion, or dismissal. The act also provides for all appointments and promotions to be solely on the basis of merit and fitness and restricts political activity of employees of the sheriff.

Training

The State Supreme Court has held that the expenditure of funds by a governing unit to train an employee is for a public purpose and a necessary expense. The Attorney General has cited the case in which this opinion was given as authority for a board of county commissioners to grant a leave of absence with pay to an acting director of social service to do graduate work and qualify for the position of director. Such leave with pay must be approved by both the board of social service and the commissioners.

The personnel resolutions of several counties provide (1) for employees to be reimbursed for the cost of tuition and books after they have satisfactorily completed an approved course of study that will contribute to the professional advancement of the employee, (2) for employees to be granted educational leave at full pay for a limited period of time or on a part-time basis with the approval of the department head and the county manager, and (3) for a leave of absence at full or part pay for up to nine months with the approval of the board of county commissioners. Employees granted educational leave with pay are usually required to agree to return to the service of the county when they have finished training and remain for a period equal to twice the length of the leave or reimburse the county for all compensation received while on leave.

Defense of Employees and Purchase of Liability Insurance

G.S. 153A-97 authorizes the county upon request to provide for the defense of any civil or criminal action or proceedings brought against an employee in either his official or individual capacity on account of an act or alleged act made or omission or alleged omission made in the scope and course of his employment. The defense may be provided by the county by employing counsel or by purchasing insurance. G.S. 153A-435 also authorizes a county to insure itself and any officer or employee against liability for wrongful death or negligent or intentional damage to person or property caused by the officer or employee when acting within the scope of his authority and in the course of his employment.

Group Insurance

G.S. 153A-92(d) authorizes a county to purchase life or health insurance or both for all or for any class of county employees as a part of their compensation. Group life insurance policies may be issued covering a minimum of 10 county employees. The premium may be paid by the county, by the employee, or jointly and severally. If the county pays the entire premium, all eligible employees, or all except any whose individual insurability is not satisfactory to the insurer, must be insured. If part of the premium is to be derived from funds contributed by the insured employees, at least 75 per cent of the then eligible employees, excluding any whose individual insurability is not satisfactory to the insurer, must elect to make the required contributions [G.S. 58-210 (1)a,b,c and (6)]. A policy or policies may not insure a single employee for more than $100,000. As of January 1974, 77 counties were paying part or all of the cost of some life insurance for their employees.

Group hospital, medical, and dental insurance may be purchased by a county for county employees. The premium may be paid by the county, by employees, or jointly and severally (G.S. 57-1.2). As of January 1974, 66 counties were paying part or all of the cost of a hospital insurance policy for their employees.

Group accident and health insurance may be issued covering county employees. The premium may be paid by the county or by the employee, or jointly and severally. If part of the premium is to be derived from funds contributed by the insured employee, at least 75 per cent of all eligible employees of any class or classes must be included in the group (G.S. 58-254.4).

Workmen's Compensation

A county cannot reject workmen's compensation coverage for county employees. Under the workmen's compensation law, a county is liable only for accidents arising out of and in the course of employment. All county employees except deputy sheriffs in twelve counties are automatically covered. A county's liability for compensation payments under the Workmen's Compensation Act may be met by the purchase of insurance or by the county's being self-insured.

Volunteer firemen who belong to rural fire departments are covered by the workmen's compensation law. Most counties that provide financial assistance to rural fire departments require the departments to carry workmen's compensation insurance. Compensation payable to a volunteer fireman disabled under compensable circumstances is calculated upon his earnings in his principal employment [G.S. 97-2 (5)].

G.S. 153A-94 provides for the board of commissioners to adopt rules including "special leave with full pay or with partial pay supplementing workmen's compensation payments for employees injured in accidents arising out of and in the course of employment."

Social Security and Retirement

The boards of commissioners of all 100 counties have brought their county employees under Social Security. The boards in ninety-one counties have brought their employees under the Local Governmental Employees' Retirement System. Some employees in the remaining counties have become members of the retirement system as health, social service, library, and ABC employees have been covered. Forsyth County is the only county now operating a local retirement system. One county provides some retirement benefits to its employees by purchasing annuities from a private insurance company.

Law enforcement officers primarily engaged in enforcing the criminal laws of the state are eligible for membership in the Law Enforcement Officers' Benefit and Retirement Fund. Newly appointed county law enforcement officers who do not join the Law Enforcement Officers' Benefit and Retirement Fund must join the Local Governmental Employees' Retirement System if their county is a member.

G.S. 153A-93 provides that no county may make payments into a retirement plan or into a retirement system established by a local act unless the plan is certified to be actuarially sound by a qualified actuary.

The Attorney General has ruled that a board of commissioners may adopt a resolution providing for the compulsory retirement of all county employees under its jurisdiction, including employees appointed or employed under the merit system.

Recruitment of County Employees

In a majority of counties, recruitment is handled informally. Turnover is low, and friends and neighbors of present employees frequently learn of vacancies first and have an advantage in obtaining county employment. Little publicity is given vacancies, and replacements may be hired before vacancies are generally known. More formal recruitment procedures tend to be followed in counties that designated personnel officers as required by G.S. 153A-92(c).

Ten counties—Alamance, Buncombe, Catawba, Cumberland, Edgecombe, Forsyth, Gaston, Guilford, Mecklenburg, and Union—have appointed personnel officers. Some are full-time personnel officers, and some perform other duties as assistant to the manager. The personnel officer is the finance director in nine counties, the purchasing agent in two counties, the register of deeds in one county, and probably the county manager in the remaining counties with managers.

G.S. 126-16 provides as follows:

> All State departments and agencies and all local political subdivisions of North Carolina shall give equal opportunities for employment, without regard to race, religion, color, creed, national origin or sex, to all persons otherwise qualified.

Federal standards governing merit system employees provide:

> Equal employment opportunity will be assured in the . . . system and affirmative action provided in its administration. Discrimination against any person in recruitment, examination, appointment, training, promotion, retention, discipline or any other aspect of personnel administration because of political or religious opinions or affiliation or because of race, national origin, or other nonmerit factors will be prohibited. Discrimination on the basis of age or sex or physical disability will be prohibited except where specific age, sex, or physical requirements constitute a bonafide occupational qualification necessary to proper and efficient administration.

Under the federal Age Discrimination in Employment Act, most people who are at least 40 but less than 65 years of age are protected from age discrimination by counties in matters of hiring, discharge, compensation, or other terms, conditions, or privileges of employment. This act is administered by the United States Department of Labor.

The Equal Employment Opportunity Act of 1972 extended the Civil Rights Act of 1964 to county governments. The 1964 act prohibited discrimination because of race, color, religion, sex, or national origin and charged a federal agency, the Equal Employment Opportunity Commission, with responsibility for investigating charges of discrimination. A county employee or applicant who believes he has been discriminated against may ask the EEOC to investigate the alleged unlawful employment practice. If the Commission finds that discrimination has occurred, it is authorized to use informal methods of conference, conciliation, and persuasion to seek an agreement that discriminatory practices will cease. If the EEOC is unable to achieve a successful conciliation of the discriminatory practice, the EEOC may file a civil action in federal court against the county.

If the court finds that a county has engaged in an unlawful employment practice, the court may order the employee reinstated with or without back pay. Back pay is limited to that which accrues from a date not more than two years before the charge is filed with the Commission.

Under the Civil Rights Act, court costs and attorneys' fees may be levied against the discriminating employer.

Counties that receive Law Enforcement Assistance Administration (LEAA) grants are required to prepare affirmative-action plans to increase the employment of groups that may be underrepresented in county employment.

Some boards of county commissioners have adopted rules prohibiting the employment or promotion or transfer of employees if such employment will result in an employee's supervising a member of his immediate family. G.S. 153A-103(1) provides that to be effective, the appointment by the register of deeds or sheriff of a relative by blood or marriage of nearer kinship than first cousin or of a person who has been convicted of a crime involving moral turpitude must be approved by the board of commissioners.

County Employee Unions

In several North Carolina counties groups of county employees have joined unions and have threatened to strike, walked out, or threatened to resign if their wage or other demands were not met. In 1969 a federal district court [*Atkins v. City of Charlotte,* 296 F. Supp. 1068 (W.D.N.C. 1969)] held that local government employees may join labor unions and that G.S. 95-97 was unconstitutional. That statute had prohibited membership of fire and police employees in any national or international labor union. But the court found nothing unconstitutional in G.S. 95-98, which voids contracts between North Carolina units of government and labor unions.

The result of this case is that county employees may join unions, but any agreement or contract between the county and any labor organization, as bargaining agent for county employees, is illegal, void, and of no effect. Boards of county commissioners and managers have followed varying courses of action. When rural policemen in one county joined a union, local legislation was secured authorizing the board of commissioners to abolish the rural police department. In another county, unionized employees were permitted to petition the board and to discuss grievances as any other employee would with his employer or as any citizen would with the board, but the union members were told that the county could not enter into any agreement or contract with the employees.

Power to Discharge or Remove County Employees

In the absence of specific statutory provisions to the contrary, the power to appoint for an indefinite term of office includes the power to remove or replace. G.S. 153A-82(1) authorizes the county manager to suspend or remove all county officers and employees in accordance with policies adopted by the board except those who are elected or whose appointment is otherwise provided for by law.

County commissioners have no authority to discharge health, mental health, or social services directors; nor have they authority to discharge health, mental health, or social service employees. Health, mental health, and social service directors may be discharged only by their respective boards. Employees of each department may be discharged only by the director of that department.

A number of counties have adopted appeal and grievance procedures to permit employees with a grievance or an employee who has been suspended, demoted, or discharged to receive a hearing. Such a procedure does not deprive a merit system employee of his opportunity to appeal to the State Personnel Board.

A county employee subject to the State Personnel Act may be dismissed if negligent or inefficient in his duties, if unfit to perform his duties, if found to be guilty of gross misconduct, or if convicted of any crime involving moral turpitude.

If a county employee subject to the State Personnel Act is discharged or suspended and appeals to the State Personnel Board, the Board will hold a hearing and make a recommendation to the appointing authority. The action of the appointing authority is final, but the appointing authority must consider the recommendations of the State Personnel Board before taking final action.

G.S. 163-271 provides that it is unlawful for any county employee to discharge or intimidate any other county employee because of the way he or his family votes, or for a county employee to say that the position or salary of his subordinates depends on the way they or their families vote. Violation of G.S. 163-271 is a misdemeanor punishable by a fine or imprisonment, or both, at the discretion of the court.

— *Donald B. Hayman*

3 / Legal Aspects of County Finance and Fiscal Control

PART I. CONSTITUTIONAL LIMITATIONS / 43
Public Purpose / 43
Source of the Public Purpose Limitation / 43
Judicial Interpretation / 43
Scope / 44
Rationale / 44
Aid to Other Governmental Agencies and Private Organizations / 44
When Voter Approval of Property Taxes Is Required / 45
Other Constitutional Provisions / 48

PART II. SOURCES OF REVENUE / 49
Local Taxes / 49
Introduction / 49
The Property Tax / 49
The Local Government Sales and Use Tax / 50
Privilege License Taxes / 50
Animal Taxes / 51
State-Shared Taxes / 51
Beer and Wine Excise Tax / 51
The Intangibles Tax / 52
Real Estate Transfer Tax / 52
Revenues from Utilities and Public Enterprises / 53
Miscellaneous Revenues / 53
   ABC Profits / 53
   Miscellaneous Fees / 54
   Court Fees / 54
   Investment Income / 54
   Federal and State Grants / 54
   Federal Revenue-Sharing / 54

PART III. THE BUDGET / 54
Fund Accounting / 55
Budget Preparation and Adoption / 56
The Budget and the Budget Ordinance Defined / 56
Budget Ordinance Directions and Limitations / 57
   Requirements of Balance / 58
   Requires Appropriations / 58
   Restrictions on Interfund Transfers / 60
   Miscellaneous Directions and Limitations / 62
Budget Preparation / 64
   The Budget Officer / 64
   Administrative Procedures / 64
Submission to the Board of Commissioners / 66
Form of the Budget / Possibility of an Unbalanced **Budget** / 67
Filing and Notice / 68
The Budget Ordinance / 69
   Budget Hearing / 69
   Board Review / 69
   Budgets and the Open Meetings Law / 70
   Budget Ordinance Adoption / 70
   Form of the Budget Ordinance / 71
   Filing / 72
Levying or Collecting Taxes for Special Districts / 72
Budget Modification and Amendment / 73
Modifying the Budget / 73
Contingency Expenditures / 74
Budget Ordinance Amendments / 75
Budget Execution and Budgeting Control / 76
Expenditure Control / 77
Control of Revenues / 77
   Selection of County Depository / 77
   Daily Deposits of County Funds / 77
   Security Requirements for Deposited Funds / 77
   Investment of County Funds / 78

PART IV. DEBT / 78
Constitutional Limitations on Borrowing / 78
Authority to Incur Debt / 81
The Net Debt Limitation / 81
Use of Bond Proceeds / 82
Issuance and Sale of Bonds / 83

3 / LEGAL ASPECTS OF COUNTY FINANCE AND FISCAL CONTROL

Part I / Constitutional Limitations

PUBLIC PURPOSE

Source of the Public Purpose Limitation

All funds belonging to the county may be spent only for public purposes without regard to the source of the money. This rule is based partly on the command of the North Carolina Constitution in Article V, section 2(1), that taxes shall be levied only for public purposes and partly on decisions of the State Supreme Court handed down before the adoption of the present Constitution in 1970. The rule is also generally observed in other states of the Union and probably would be applicable in North Carolina even if the Constitution did not specifically state it in so many words.

Judicial Interpretation

The courts, ultimately the Supreme Court, decide what is and what is not a public purpose. Thus, the public purpose limitation cannot be avoided by an act of the General Assembly or even by a vote of the people. If the courts hold a particular object of expenditure to be not for a public purpose, nothing can make the expenditure legal short of a constitutional amendment. Although the Supreme Court has the final say as to what is a public purpose, it has indicated that "where the question is doubtful . . . and the legislature has decided it one way and the people to be taxed have approved the decision, . . . the will of the lawmakers, thus expressed and approved, should be allowed to prevail over any mere doubt of the courts."

Scope

In deciding whether an expenditure is for a public purpose, the courts have not tried to be specific in devising definitions of public purpose, but have relied more heavily on custom and usage—i.e., what activities are generally accepted as legitimate and proper for counties—than on any other factor. This approach implies, as the courts recognize, that changing conditions must be considered and functions that have not been considered public purposes before may be public purposes now or may become such later.

Rationale

The major reason for the public purpose limitation is to guard against the use of public funds for private benefit. The Supreme Court has said:

> . . . the objects to be attained must affect the people as a community and not merely as individuals. . . . It is not necessary, in order that a use may be regarded as public, that it should be for the use and benefit of every citizen in the community. It may be for the inhabitants of a restricted locality, but the use and benefit must be in common, and not for particular persons, interest or estates.

Aid to Other Governmental Agencies and Private Organizations

The public purpose limitation does not require the county to have full or even partial responsibility for every activity supported in part by county funds; under certain circumstances the county may lend financial support to public or private agencies to help them carry out functions that benefit the people of the county. Still, the public purpose limitation is the source of several important restrictions on county authority to support activities carried on by other governmental agencies or private groups.

The first of these is that the activity supported must be one that the county could legally undertake if it were authorized to do so. Cases decided by the State Supreme Court involving county support of the functions of other agencies do not indicate a limit imposed by the court concerning the type of agency, the nature of the contribution, or the function performed.

But several Supreme Court cases appear to lay down the rule that in giving financial support to privately controlled agencies, the county must reserve the right to control or direct the use of the funds it has contributed. For example, when a city gave money to the chamber of commerce without specifying how the money was to be used and without reserving

FINANCE AND FISCAL CONTROL 45

any right to control or direct its use, the Supreme Court expressed doubt that the expenditure could be for a public purpose under such conditions. In a later case, the court approved as a public purpose an appropriation to a chamber of commerce when the city required each expenditure from its contribution to be approved by the city council, and when the chamber of commerce was required to account periodically for the expenditure of the public funds it received. While the Supreme Court has not been entirely clear on this point, it appears that the Court believes cities and counties may not relinquish control over the disbursement of public funds to any private agency without retaining some mechanism for insuring that the funds are actually spent for public purposes, and for the purposes for which the county or city appropriated them.

A third difficulty for county support of the activity of a private agency arises when the activity in question is not one that the county is authorized to undertake itself. This is not a constitutional difficulty, assuming that the activity would be for a public purpose if authorized, but a question of statutory authority.

In summary, counties may support activities of other governmental agencies or private groups when the following conditions exist: (1) the activity in question is for a public purpose; (2) the activity in question is one that the county is authorized to undertake, or has specific statutory authorization for giving financial aid to the agency in question; and (3) through appropriate means the county retains some degree of control over the expenditure of its funds.

WHEN VOTER APPROVAL OF PROPERTY TAXES IS REQUIRED

Constitutional Provisions. Article V, section 2(5), of the Constitution provides:

> The General Assembly shall not authorize any county, city or town, special district, or other unit of local government to levy taxes on property, except for purposes authorized by general law uniformly applicable throughout the State, unless the tax is approved by a majority of the qualified voters of the unit who vote thereon.

This portion of the Constitution replaces the old "necessary expense" limitation and authorizes the General Assembly to decide for what purposes the property tax may be levied without a vote of the people. Unless the General Assembly takes affirmative action to permit the levy of property taxes for a specified purpose without a vote of the people, no property taxes may be levied for that purpose unless the voters approve.

Statutory Implementation of Article V, section 2(5). G.S. 153A-149 implements Article V, section 2(5), of the Constitution. This statute groups the functions that counties are authorized to undertake into three categories. The first category contains those functions for which property taxes may be levied without a vote and without restriction as to rate or amount. The second category includes functions for which property taxes may be levied without a vote up to a maximum rate. The third category comprises functions for which property taxes may not be levied without a vote of the people.

The purposes for which counties may levy property taxes without a vote and without limitation as to rate or amount are shown in Table 3-I.

Table 3-I

Functions for Which Property Taxes May Be Levied Without a Vote and Without Rate Limitation

Courts
Debt service[1]
Deficits[2]
Elections[3]
Jails
Schools[4]
Social services[5]
Joint undertakings[6]

1. The amount required for payment of principal of, interest on, and fiscal agency fees for general obligation bonds and notes, not including payments related to revenue bonds.
2. Including only deficits caused by unintended and unforeseeable failure of revenue collections to meet budgeted revenue estimates, except revenues associated with public service enterprises such as water and sewer systems, but not including deficits caused by overspending appropriations.
3. Including all national, state, district, and county elections, bond elections, and other county referendums.
4. Including the entire public school system from kindergarten through the community college system.
5. Including only the federal- and state-mandated "categorical" programs and social services administration. All other social services programs, such as general assistance and child protection services, are included in Table 3-II.
6. Including only joint undertakings with respect to any of the functions listed in this table.

Most of the functions that counties undertake fall into the second category. For the purposes listed in this category, counties may levy property taxes up to a maximum rate of $1.50 per $100 value of property subject to taxation, assuming a 100 per cent assessment ratio. The purposes included within this category are shown in Table 3-II.

The statute authorizes any county to hold a referendum on the levy of property taxes for any function that the county is authorized to undertake whether listed in Table 3-II or not. If such a referendum is held and the tax is approved by the voters, the tax does not count against the $1.50 rate limitation. A county may also hold a referendum on raising the $1.50 rate limitation to some higher limit.

Table 3-II
Functions for Which Property Taxes May Be Levied Without a Vote Within a $1.50 Rate Limitation

Agricultural extention	Mapping
Air pollution control	Medical examiner or coroner
Airports	Mental health
Ambulance Service	Mosquito control
Animal protection and control	Open space
Armories	Planning
Beach erosion and natural disasters	Ports and harbors
Cemeteries	Recreation
Civil defense	Register of deeds
Debts and judgments	Sewage collection and treatment
Fire protection	Social services[2]
Forest management and protection	Solid waste collection and disposal
General administration	Surveyor
Health	Veterans service
Historic preservation	Water supply and distribution
Hospitals	Water resources projects
Human relations programs	Watershed improvement projects
Jails	Joint undertakings with respect
Law enforcement	to any of the above
Libraries	

1. Debts not evidenced by general obligations bonds or notes and judgments for sums of money rendered against the county by a state or federal court, but not including revenue bonds or judgments not reduced to a sum of money.
2. All social services programs other than the "categorical" programs.

All functions not listed in either Table 3-I or Table 3-II fall into the third category, and property taxes may not be levied for these functions without an approving vote of the people. The statute does not list these functions, but the most important of them are shown in Table 3-III.

Without an approving vote of the people, no property tax revenues may be appropriated to any of the functions listed in Table 3-III, or to any other

Table 3-III
Functions for Which Property Taxes May Not Be Levied Without a Vote of the People

Armories
Cultural activities[1]
Economic development[2]
Public housing
Urban redevelopment

1. Including support for art galleries, museums, the North Carolina Symphony Society, and similar activities in support of the arts.
2. Including contributions to chambers of commerce, "industry hunting" activities, and similar efforts at economic development.

function, program, or activity of the county not found in either Table 3-I or Table 3-II. If a referendum is held and passes, any property tax approved for functions that fall within the categories summarized in Table 3-III does not count against the $1.50 rate limitation.

Status of Referendums Held Before July 1, 1973. Many counties have held tax referendums in the past in order to levy property taxes for purposes that were not "necessary expenses" under the old Constitution. If the purpose for which the referendum was held is listed in Table 3-II, the referendum is no longer valid for any purpose. The county is not subject to the old voted rate limitation for that particular purpose, and taxes levied for that purpose are not excepted from the $1.50 rate limit. If the purpose for which the referendum was held is listed in Table 3-III or does not appear in either Table 3-I or Table 3-II, the referendum is still valid and the county may continue to levy taxes pursuant to the referendum. These taxes do not count against the $1.50 rate limit. Finally, G.S. 153A-149 has no effect whatever on voted school supplemental taxes.

Effect on Other Locally Levied Taxes. The old "necessary expense" limitation applied to all locally levied and collected taxes, which included the property tax, the sales tax, privilege license taxes, dog taxes, the intangibles tax, and probably the excise stamp tax on deeds. G.S. 153A-149 applies only to the property tax and the intangibles tax (which is considered to be a part of the county property tax). None of the other local taxes mentioned above are subject to G.S. 153A-149 or Article V, section 2(2), of the Constitution and may therefore be used for any purpose that the county is authorized to undertake, unless the statute that authorizes the tax also limits its use. As of February 1, 1974, none of the local taxes mentioned above are subject to any statutory limitation as to use.

OTHER CONSTITUTIONAL PROVISIONS

Article V, section 2(7), of the Constitution authorizes the General Assembly to enact laws permitting counties (and other units of local government) to "contract with and appropriate money to any person, association, or corporation for the accomplishment of public purposes only." While this part of the Constitution has not been interpreted by the Supreme Court, it appears to enable local government, with appropriate authority from the General Assembly, to grant public money to private agencies for the accomplishment of programs or functions that would be appropriate for the county itself to undertake.

Article V, section 7(2), provides that "no money shall be drawn from the treasury of any county, city or town, or other unit of local government except by authority of law." This part of the Constitution has not been interpreted by the Supreme Court.

FINANCE AND FISCAL CONTROL

Part II / Sources of Revenue
LOCAL TAXES

Introduction

As creatures of the General Assembly, counties may levy only those taxes specifically authorized by the General Assembly. The taxes that are now authorized by the legislature are the property tax, privilege license taxes, animal taxes, and the sales tax.

The property tax is levied each year, as part of the county's budget ordinance. All other county taxes may be levied at any time during the year by a permanent ordinance that need not be readopted annually but rather stands from year to year until amended or repealed.

The Property Tax (see also Chapter 4, The Property Tax)

Property taxes are the single most important source of tax revenues to county governments, and in most counties the most important source of revenue of any sort. Property taxes are levied against particular items of real and personal property and generally are obligations of that property rather than of its owner. Thus, the normal enforcement method of this tax is to sell the property and pay the tax from the proceeds of sale; a personal judgment against the owner normally is not possible.

The Tax Base. Property is appraised for taxation by the county tax supervisor and, for the property of public service companies, by the State Department of Revenue. Certain kinds of property are or may be exempt from taxation and thus not included in the base. Only the General Assembly can exempt property from taxation, and it must do so on a statewide basis. Finally, the General Assembly is authorized to "classify" property for taxation and has used this power to exclude certain types of property from the tax base entirely or in part. This power also is restricted to the General Assembly and must be used on a statewide basis.

Statutory Limits. From 1868 through 1973, the North Carolina Constitution permitted locally levied and collected taxes to be spent only for "necessary expenses," unless the tax had been approved by the voters; and decisions on which functions were "necessary" and which were not were ultimately made by the courts. Effective July 1, 1973, this doctrine was extensively revised: The General Assembly, rather than the courts, would decide for which functions taxes may be levied without a vote. In addition, the concept of "necessary" and "nonnecessary" expense was eliminated; the legislature simply would decide for which functions a vote is unnecessary and implement this decision through enactment of statewide laws. This the 1973 General Assembly did. The implementing legislation and its rate limitation are discussed on pages 45-48.

The Local Government Sales and Use Tax

The second most important tax source for those counties that use it is the local-option sales tax. Under legislation enacted in 1971, counties are authorized to levy a local 1 per cent sales and use tax, "piggybacked" on the state's 3 per cent tax. The board of commissioners may do this by simple resolution, or it may refer the question to the county voters. If the voters approve the tax, the commissioners still have discretion as to whether to levy it; but if the tax is disapproved, it may thereafter be levied in that county only after a subsequent approval by the voters.

The tax is collected for the county by the state, along with the state's tax. After collection costs have been subtracted, the proceeds of the tax are returned to the county of collection.

A portion of these proceeds is to be distributed to each city and town in the county. The basis of distribution is either per capita (with all county citizens being counted for the county) or according to the size of each unit's tax levy (that is, the dollar amount of the levy). The decision as to which basis is to be followed in a county is first made by the board of commissioners at the time it levies the tax; this decision is binding upon the cities and towns within the county. Each April thereafter the commissioners may, in their discretion, change the basis for the next fiscal year.

Sales tax proceeds are now subject to no constitutional or statutory restrictions; they may be used for any public purpose.

Privilege License Taxes

The license tax is one imposed upon the privilege of carrying on business or engaging in certain occupations, trades, employments, or other pursuits, activities, or conduct. License taxes are commonly referred to in this state as "business license taxes," or "Schedule B taxes."

Authority to Levy. No general statutory authority has been given to counties to levy privilege license taxes. Under Schedule B of the Revenue Act (G.S. 105-113), the state imposes license taxes upon certain businesses, pursuits, and activities. Under most sections of this schedule, express provision is made as to the extent of county authority to levy a similar tax.

In some instances the county is permitted to tax only part of the activities in a particular group taxed by the state. In others, county authority may be subject to restrictions—e.g., the county may be permitted to tax only activities carried on in that portion of the county outside incorporated cities and towns. In general, the county tax may exceed the tax imposed by the state, but in a few cases the amount of the county tax is limited to one-half or one-fourth that levied by the state. The state tax is seldom imposed at a flat rate. The rate varies depending upon the subject taxed, the nature of the activity engaged in, the extent of such activity, the period of time dur-

FINANCE AND FISCAL CONTROL 51

ing which it is carried out, its location in reference to cities and towns and their population, and other factors.

Within this rather specific and limited authority, county commissioners have discretion as to which activities they will tax and the amount of tax to be imposed on each subject up to the maximums fixed by statute. The license tax is levied annually, and the license period may run from June 1 of one year to May 31 of the following year, or from July 1 of the year in which the tax is levied until June 30 of the next year, as determined by the county commissioners.

Use of Proceeds. There is no statutory restriction on the use of privilege license tax revenues.

Animal Taxes

G.S. 153A-153 authorizes counties to levy taxes on the privilege of keeping "dogs and other pets." Despite the breadth of this authorization, apparently no county has yet gone beyond a dog tax. There are no limits in the statute on the amount of such a tax and no restrictions on its use.

STATE-SHARED TAXES

A portion of the proceeds of the state-levied beer and wine tax is shared with county governments. In addition, the state levies an ad valorem tax on intangible personal property *on behalf* of local governments, and almost all the proceeds of this tax go to local governments. These two taxes are characterized as state-shared taxes.

Beer and Wine Excise Tax

The state levies a number of taxes on alcoholic beverages. These include license taxes, excise taxes on liquor, and excise taxes on beer and wine. Something less than half of the beer and wine excise taxes, which themselves account for about half of all beverage tax revenues, are shared with cities and counties. A city or county is eligible to share in beer and wine excise tax revenues if beer or wine may be legally sold within its boundaries. If only one beverage may be sold, the unit shares in the tax for only that beverage. (Under general law, beer and wine may be sold statewide. However, the statutes allow county referendums to be held to prohibit sale of either beverage in the county; the statutes also allow a city in a dry county to vote to permit sale within the city.)

The taxes are distributed on the basis of the population of eligible cities and counties; counties are given credit only for their nonmunicipal population. The beer-wine taxes may be used for any purpose without restriction.

The Intangibles Tax

Local governments levy property taxes on real property, tangible personal property, and intangible personal property that is not subject to the intangibles tax. Most intangible personal property—money on deposit, money on hand, bank accounts, shares of stock, bonds, accounts receivable, etc.—is taxed by the state, which returns the proceeds to the local governments. This arrangement began in the late 1930s as a result of local governments' difficulty in getting this type of property listed for local taxation. The tax is levied under Schedule H of the Revenue Act, beginning at G.S. 105-199.

The rate of tax is generally 25 cents per $100 value of property, although for two categories (bank deposits and funds on deposit with insurance companies) the rate is only 10 cents. All of the funds, after administrative costs of collection are removed, are paid to city and county governments—with one exception. The exception is that intangibles tax proceeds are used to pay the expenses of the State Property Tax Commission and the Ad Valorem Tax Division of the Revenue Department. The proceeds derived from property taxed at the 25-cent rate are returned to the county of collection; the proceeds derived from property taxed at the 10-cent rate are divided among the counties according to population. Once the proceeds are returned to a particular county, they are divided between the county government and the cities in the county on the basis of the ratio of the total ad valorem tax levy of all units for the preceding year to the levy of the respective units. Once the proceeds are returned to a particular city or county government, they must be distributed among the budget funds of that city or county according to the tax levy for the current year.

This tax is considered, in constitutional theory, to be a local property tax. Thus the property tax restrictions noted above also apply to intangibles tax proceeds.

Real Estate Transfer Tax

G.S. Ch. 105, Art. 8E, imposes an excise tax on the transfer of real estate in the state. The tax is levied on each deed and is measured by the price paid to the seller. Transfers by governmental units are not subject to the tax. The tax rate is 50 cents for each $500 of the sales price, excluding liens and encumbrances on the property.

The transfer tax is paid to the county in which the land is located, or, if the land lies in two or more counties, to the county in which the greater portion lies.

There are no restrictions on the use of this tax.

REVENUES FROM UTILITIES AND PUBLIC ENTERPRISES

Counties engage in a number of functions that might be characterized as utilities or public enterprises. Each of these may be financed by various charges to those who use the facility or receive the service involved. For the most part, these charges are intended only to cover the costs of operating the service or facility (including the costs of debt service and capital outlay), although part of these costs are sometimes met from tax revenues.

Water and Sewer Services. Basic charges are made for receiving county water and using a county sewerage system. These charges are not subject to the control of the State Utilities Commission. In addition, counties may levy special assessments against benefited property for laying water and sewer lines and charge a fee for tapping on to these lines.

Solid Waste Collection and Disposal. Counties may charge for the collection of solid wastes, although most finance at least a minimum level of this service through tax revenues. They may also charge for the use of a county landfill, and many do, especially for use by nonresidents. However, cities may not be charged for using a county landfill if the facility is at least partly financed by county-wide tax levies.

Airports. A county that operates an airport may impose a charge on aircraft that use the facility and may rent space in the terminal and other buildings to airlines, restaurants, aircraft maintenance firms, etc. Charges on those who leave or arrive at the airport by plane have been prohibited by Congress.

Hospitals. A county-operated hospital may charge for patient care in the same manner as would a privately operated hospital.

Recreational and Cultural Facilities. Counties may charge admission to various kinds of facilities, such as swimming pools, coliseums, etc.

MISCELLANEOUS REVENUES

Many other sources of revenues are available to counties in North Carolina. Most of them generate only small amounts of revenue, but occasionally some of the sources listed below can be significant.

Special Assessments. The installation of water and sewer lines is often paid for in part by special assessments against benefited property.

ABC Profits. Under general law, only counties may establish ABC stores and only counties may participate in the profits from the stores. However, local acts allow many cities to share in the profits of county ABC stores or to establish a city ABC system in a dry county. ABC profits can be extensive (over $1 million annually in the very largest systems), and the funds may be used for any public purpose of a county government (but sometimes local acts restrict the use of the profits).

Miscellaneous Fees. Counties may charge fees for many governmental services. Examples are inspection fees, zoning permit fees, house-moving fees, charity solicitation permit fees, etc. Another type of fee is the election filing fee, used to help meet the cost of elections.

Court Fees. Two of the costs imposed in the uniform court system go to the county. In criminal actions the unit that employs the officer who makes the arrest is entitled to a $2 arrest fee; and in any action the unit that supplies the courtroom (which may in some cases be a city) is entitled to the facilities fee, which must be used to construct or maintain the court facility. If a defendant is incarcerated in the county jail, the county also receives a jail fee. All these fees are included in the costs of court paid by the person charged and convicted.

Investment Income. Under G.S. 159-30, counties may invest idle funds in time deposits in banks or in certain kinds of income-producing securities. A well-managed investment program can realize significant revenues for a county, often the equivalent of 10 or 15 cents on the tax rate.

Federal and State Grants. For many years counties have received federal grants to help finance particular projects or activities. Increasingly the state government also has made funds available to local governments for local projects; the funds derived from the Clean Water Bond issue is a recent example.

Federal Revenue-Sharing. An important new source of revenue for all counties is the federal revenue-sharing program. The shared money is disbursed directly to the county by the United States Treasury and may be used for public safety, environmental protection, public transportation, health, recreation, libraries, social services for the poor or aged, financial administration, and capital expenditures. A detailed discussion of revenue-sharing law and administration can be found in *General Revenue Sharing: A Guide for Local Governments in North Carolina,* available from the Institute of Government.

Part III / The Budget

North Carolina counties are required by law to operate under an annual balanced budget. The current law is entitled the Local Government Budget and Fiscal Control Act (hereafter, LGBFCA) and was enacted in 1971 to take effect on July 1, 1973. Besides counties, the LGBFCA also applies to cities, special districts, public authorities, and all other local governmental agencies. In most instances, the budgetary processes of county government agencies will be a part of the county's over-all budget. However, certain kinds of regional agencies, such as councils of government and district health departments, will adopt and administer their own budgets. The LGBFCA excuses publicly owned or supported hospitals from some of its requirements.

FUND ACCOUNTING

Governmental budgeting and accounting differ from their commercial counterparts by use of the fund accounting system. A fund is simply a separate accounting entity, with its own set of accounts, having its own assets and liabilities, receipts, and disbursements. Governmental transactions are grouped into funds for various reasons. The accounting system must be structured so that proper use of earmarked revenues is both assured and demonstrable. This is accomplished by the use of funds, segregating specific revenues and related expenditures. A fund also may be used to segregate all revenues and costs attributable to a particular enterprise, to assess whether that enterprise is self-supporting. Other reasons for establishing funds will be apparent in the discussion of types of funds, below. The LGBFCA requires that certain types of funds be maintained [G.S. 159-13(a)]. Which funds, and how many, are maintained by a particular county will depend on what functions it performs and how those functions are financed. The funds required by law are as follows:

General Fund. This catch-all fund accounts for all transactions not properly accounted for in another fund.

Debt Service Fund. Such a fund (or funds) is established to account for payment of principal and interest on *general obligation* bonds and notes. Typically it also accounts for related fiscal agency fees.

School Funds. Current operating costs of the public school system are accounted for through the *school current expense fund.* Capital improvements funded by current appropriations are accounted for in the *school capital outlay fund.* (Capital improvements funded by bond proceeds are accounted for in a capital projects fund, described below.) Debt service for bonds issued for school purposes may be accounted for either in a separate *school debt service fund* or in the general debt service fund. Finally, a separate fund must be maintained to account for any *voted* supplemental school tax.

Public Assistance Funds. A county may account for public assistance programs in one of three ways: (1) as separate line items within the general fund; (2) in a single *public assistance fund;* or (3) in a separate fund for each public assistance program.

Voted Tax Funds. Proceeds from any tax levied pursuant to a vote may be used only for the function for which levied. To assure proper use, the law requires that a separate fund be established for any *function* so financed.

The fund should account not only for the revenues from the voted property tax, but for all other revenues appropriated for the purpose for which the tax is levied.

Enterprise Funds. A separate fund must be established for each enterprise owned or operated by a county. The LGBFCA does not define "enterprise," but generally the term is understood to mean any function of a commercial nature that provides services or goods to the public for a charge and attempts to be nearly or fully self-supporting—for example, a water system.

Capital Project Funds. Bond proceeds may be used only for the purpose or purposes for which the bonds were issued; to assure this use, capital project funds must be established. A county may establish a separate fund for each bond order, or it may account for several bond orders in a single fund. In the latter case, the transactions pertaining to each bond order must be strictly separated from all others.

Agency Funds. Counties frequently collect taxes on behalf of special districts, such as sanitary districts, and occasionally collect special assessments on behalf of public authorities, such as drainage districts. For each such district or authority, the collecting county must establish a separate fund to account for the collections. The money so collected belongs to the district or authority, and use of a separate fund ensures that the money is properly transferred.

Reappraisal Reserve Fund. This fund is required of counties by G.S. 153-150. It is essentially a sinking fund into which a fixed sum of money is deposited each year to assure that enough money will be on hand when needed to finance the octennial reappraisal of real property.

Service District Funds. A county must establish a separate fund to account for the financial transactions of each service district defined under the County Service District Act (G.S. Ch. 153A, Art. 16). If resources other than the proceeds of a special tax levy are used within a district, they also should be accounted for in the service district fund.

Optional Funds. The LGBFCA expressly authorizes a county to establish any additional funds it desires. Occasionally, additional funds are required by local act.

BUDGET PREPARATION AND ADOPTION

The Budget and the Budget Ordinance Defined

The LGBFCA distinguishes between the *budget* and the *budget ordinance*. The *budget* is the document submitted by the budget officer to the board of commissioners, along with any supporting data; it is the basis for the board's fiscal policy decisions for the coming year. The *budget ordinance* is the official act of the board that levies taxes and appropriates revenues for the coming fiscal year. The budget ordinance is the legal basis of the accounting system, the standard by which proposed expenditures are measured.

Because of their different purposes, the budget and the budget ordinance may, and often do, take different forms. The budget often will set forth estimated revenues and proposed expenditures in considerable detail; the budget ordinance, on the other hand, might summarize the budget figures, grouping objects of expenditure into departmental or even broader categories, and establishing summary categories for revenues.

In addition, the budget ordinance should be organized by funds, and perhaps by departments within funds, to facilitate translation to a fund accounting system. The budget, however, may well be program-oriented, cutting across departmental lines, to enable the board of commissioners to make their decisions on a program rather than a line-item basis.

Budget Ordinance—Inclusiveness. For many years, county budget ordinances did not disclose all expenditures made or revenues realized during a fiscal year. It was not by law necessary to include bond proceeds in the ordinance; by tradition other receipts, such as special assessments or federal grants or loans, were omitted as well. Such omissions are prohibited under the LGBFCA, which requires that any money expended, regardless of its source, be expended pursuant to the budget ordinance.

Budget Ordinance—Specificity. Budget ordinances exhibit great variety in their amount of detail. A very detailed ordinance might show an appropriation for each entry in the chart of accounts. separately stating for each department items as small as postage, utility bills, and even individual salaries. Such an ordinance exercises close control by the board of commissioners over departmental activities, but the cost to administrative flexibility may be substantial. On the other hand, an ordinance may be very general, showing only a total appropriation for each fund, sacrificing control for flexibility.

Practically, either extreme can be tempered by administrative arrangements. If the board adopts a detailed ordinance, the budget officer might be authorized to make certain amendments himself, as permitted by G.S. 159-15. At the other extreme, a very general ordinance might be accompanied by a resolution requiring expenditures to conform to the more detailed budget, as presented to and modified by the board.

Budget Ordinance Directions and Limitations

The LGBFCA embodies the assumption that, except as otherwise limited by law, a board of commissioners may develop fiscal policy as it judges best. Therefore, the statute sets out a number of directions and limitations that must be observed in adopting the budget ordinance. In addition, other statutes and regulations may affect a county's budgetary decisions. Once the directions and limitations and statutes and regulations are observed, however, a great deal of flexibility remains for making fiscal policy. But first, it is important to understand the requirements.

Requirements of Balance. *The budget must balance.* This is a fundamental requirement of the LGBFCA. The law requires an exact balance; it permits neither a deficit nor a surplus.

Each fund must balance. Not only must the budget ordinance as a whole be balanced, but also each fund must be balanced. This is a requirement that accords with the notion of a fund as a separate, self-contained accounting entity.

Required Appropriations. Although counties enjoy substantial discretion over what programs and services they will finance and at what level, there are limits on the discretion. The LGBFCA requires that several appropriations be made, while other statutes and regulations require that certain programs be supported at a minimum level.

1. *The full amount estimated by the finance officer to be required for debt service during the budget year must be appropriated.* During the spring, the Local Government Commission notifies each finance officer of his county's debt service obligations for the coming fiscal year. A county may select what revenues are used to meet debt service obligations, but the amount appropriated must be that reported by the Local Government Commission. If sufficient moneys are not appropriated, the Commission may order the county to make the necessary appropriation; if the county ignores this order, the Commission may levy the local tax itself.

2. *The full amount of any deficit in each fund must be appropriated.* Two types of deficits are involved in this requirement. First, despite the requirements of the LGBFCA, expenditures occasionally may be made without an appropriation, or in excess of an appropriation. If the fiscal year ends with such a circumstance, the resulting budgetary deficit must be funded. That is, the budget ordinance for the coming fiscal year must include an appropriation to cover expenditures made without or in excess of an appropriation in the fiscal year just ending, assuming that such expenditures are otherwise authorized by law.

Second, revenue estimates, *made in good faith,* sometimes turn out to be substantially low. For example, a tax might be declared illegal in the midst of the fiscal year, as the original local-option sales tax of 1969 was. In such a situation, moneys not yet collected might already be encumbered or expended. Although expenditures will not exceed revenue estimates, they may exceed revenue collections. If that occurs, then a deficit has been created in that fund and sufficient moneys must be appropriated in the next fiscal year to make up the deficit.

3. *Sufficient appropriation must be made for continuing contracts.* Continuing contracts are discussed in the section on fiscal control, below. The statute authorizing these contracts (G.S. 153A-13) requires that in each year of such a contract, the board of commissioners appropriate suf-

ficient funds to meet payments coming due that year. The LGBFCA simply repeats that requirement.

4. *Other statutes and regulations.* Other statutes establish mechanisms for directly or indirectly requiring counties to support particular programs at particular levels. Direct requirements are possible with social services, health, and education and indirect requirements with several other functions.

Social services. Counties must participate in certain social services programs. Currently, these mandated programs are Aid to Families with Dependent Children (AFDC), Medical Assistance, and Administration. Also, final authority over the amount of county appropriations for the mandated programs rests with the state's Secretary of Human Resources rather than with the board of commissioners. Basically, the budget process for mandated social service programs is as follows:

1. By March 15, the county director of social services must submit his budget estimates to the county board of social services.
2. By April 1, that board must "review, modify and approve" the estimates and transmit them to the county board of commissioners.
3. By April 15, the commissioners must review, modify, and approve the estimates and forward them to the State Director of Social Services.
4. By June 1, the Director must review the estimates and notify the county commissioners of the amount of county funds required for the coming year.
5. The county commissioners *must* levy sufficient taxes to raise the amounts reported by the State Director. If the county disputes this amount, the state Secretary of Human Resources is to make a final determination, binding on the county.

Health. Under G.S. 130-13, each county must furnish public health services—locally, through a district health department, or by contract with the state. A portion of each county's health budget is met with state and federal funds, and, as a condition of receiving those funds, the county and its appropriate health department must annually execute a contract with the State Division of Health Services. By this contract, a county is required to maintain minimum levels of health services and to appropriate specified amounts for health purposes; in addition, any unexpected and unencumbered appropriations for health services may be reappropriated the next year only for health purposes.

Education. Counties must provide for public schools, under basic policies set at the state level. As with social services, final authority over the level of county appropriations for education does not rest with the commissioners but rather, here, with the judicial system. Although the local board of education must submit its budget proposal to the county commissioners for review and approval, it need not accept the commissioners' decision. If the two boards disagree over the amount appropriated to the current expense fund, the capital outlay fund, or the debt service fund, they must meet within a week to attempt to reach agreement. If no agreement is reached, the two boards vote on the matter, each having one vote. If this does not settle the matter (and there is little reason to expect that it would), the disagreement is referred to the clerk of superior court for arbitration. His decision may be appealed to superior court, for conclusive determination. This judicial resolution is to be based on findings of fact as to the amount necessary for each of the funds. Once the determination has been made, the commissioners must levy the necessary taxes.

Indirect requirements. Also, other statutes do, or may, require units to make certain appropriations. The jail inspection law (G.S. Ch. 153A, Art. 10) authorizes the state Director of Social Services to order local confinement facilities either upgraded or closed. If a unit has been ordered to improve its jail, some appropriations will be required in the budget ordinance. Counties must conduct periodic elections, and the fees to be paid election officials are set by law and must be funded. Counties must support the operations of the sheriff and register of deeds, officers required by law. Several services and functions, once decision is made to provide them, must be provided at levels set by statute or state administrative regulation. Examples of such services and functions include: emergency medical services, sewage treatment facilities, and solid waste disposal facilities.

Restrictions on Interfund Transfers. Although funds are independent accounting entities, money may be transferred from one fund to another. If tax levies are consolidated, a number of funds might show as their primary revenue a transfer from the general fund. Some activities, especially enterprises, operate at a profit, and this profit is often transferred to other funds to finance programs unrelated to the enterprise.

The LGBFCA accepts the appropriateness of interfund transfers and simply establishes some prohibitions and restrictions, each designed to maintain the basic integrity of a fund in light of the purposes for which it was established. In addition, interfund transfers may be prohibited because moneys are earmarked for a specific program or service. For example, a county may not transfer the facilities fee from the general fund to a fund that does not account for some court-related expenditures.

1. *Public school funds.* Once money enters a school fund, it may be used only for school-related purposes. Transfers are permitted only from the capital outlay fund to a capital reserve account *for school purposes* or to a debt service fund to service *school-related* debt. Obviously, once such a transfer is made to a capital reserve fund or debt service fund, the money must be treated as earmarked for school purposes. It may not later be diverted to some other use. Transfers between current expense and capital outlay funds are not permitted.

2. *Voted tax funds.* Judicial decisions require that the revenues from property taxes levied pursuant to a vote of the people be used only for the function for which the tax was levied, and this limitation reinforces those decisions. However, a fund established to account for a voted property tax will contain *all* revenues appropriated for the function; therefore, transfer of non-property tax revenues from the fund is permitted.

Property tax proceeds in a voted tax fund may be transferred to a capital reserve fund. Once there, they are earmarked revenues, and may be used only for capital expenditures related to the functions for which the tax was levied.

3. *Agency funds.* Moneys collected for a special district belong to that district, not to the collecting unit, and moneys may not be transferred from an agency fund to any other. But if a district has ceased to function, anything left in the fund may be transferred.

4. *Public assistance funds.* G.S. 108-57 requires that moneys appropriated for mandated public assistance programs be spent for such programs. However, moneys may be transferred *between* public assistance programs if the Secretary of Human Resources approves.

5. *Bond proceeds may be transferred from a capital project fund only to the debt service fund or a capital reserve fund.* Bond proceeds may be expended only for the purposes for which the bonds were issued. Therefore the statutes permit appropriation of bond proceeds in only three circumstances: (1) directly for the purposes stated for in the bond order; (2) to a debt service fund, to pay debt service on the bonds issued to raise the proceeds (by law, their own debt service is among the purposes for which bonds are issued); (3) to a capital reserve fund for eventual expenditure for the purpose stated in the bond order (bond proceeds are earmarked revenues within a capital reserve fund).

6. *Enterprise earnings may be transferred to another fund only after all costs of the enterprise, including debt service, have been met.* This limitation reflects the policy that the first use of enterprise revenues must be to meet all costs related to the enterprise, including debt service. However, enterprise revenues are not absolutely earmarked, and once all enterprise costs have been met, any remaining moneys may be transferred to another fund.

7. *Reappraisal reserve fund.*

No appropriation may be made from a county reappraisal reserve fund except for the purposes for which the fund was established [G.S. 159-13(b) (17)].

Moneys placed in a reappraisal reserve fund may be used *only* for reappraisal purposes. If a fund balance remains following an octennial reappraisal, it must be made a part of the eight-year budget for the next such reappraisal.

8. *Service district funds may be transferred to the debt service fund or capital reserve fund.* Although a service district is not a separate government, taxes and other revenues raised within the district belong to the people of the district. Therefore, no appropriation may be made from a service district fund except for the purposes for which the district was established. Moneys may be transferred from such a fund only to service debt incurred for the district or to fund a capital reserve account for a district project. Once again, district revenues transferred to a capital reserve fund are earmarked revenues.

9. *Overhead and revenue-generation and collection costs.* Each prohibition and limitation on interfund transfers discussed above, *except those relating to capital projects funds,* is subject to the modification that any fund may be charged general administrative and overhead costs properly allocable to its activities and may be charged the costs of levying and collecting its revenues.

Miscellaneous Directions and Limitations. Six miscellaneous directions and limitations remain. One of these limits contingency appropriations, two are concerned with assuring that earmarked revenues are properly expended, and three are concerned with the integrity of revenue estimates.

1. *Contingency appropriations are limited to 5 per cent of the fund total except for public assistance.* It is impossible to anticipate in June all the needs of a unit during the coming fiscal year. Therefore, to meet emergencies or other anticipated situations, the law permits each fund to carry an appropriation for "contingencies." To guard against abuse, however, such an appropriation is limited to 5 per cent of other appropriations *in that fund.* (Thus, the general fund may not carry a contingency appropriation equivalent to 5 per cent of other appropriations in *all* funds.) The single exception to the 5 per cent limitation is in public assistance funds, which has no limit. If public assistance programs are accounted for in the general fund, presumably that fund could carry two contingency appropriations: one limited to 5 per cent of all non-public assistance appropriations in the general fund; the other, restricted to public assistance programs, is unlimited.

2. *Tax limits and earmarked revenues must be respected.* Under present statutory provisions on taxation, this limitation will be of most importance for earmarked non-property tax revenues. One example of such a revenue is the facilities fee derived from the operation of the courts, which most counties account for in the general fund. If a county shows $85,000 in facilities fees as a revenue in its general fund, this limitation requires that at least $85,000 in that fund be appropriated for court-related purposes. It

may be assumed that the appropriations were funded by the earmarked revenues.

3. *Conformance with Article V, section 2 (5)*

The total of all appropriations for purposes which require voter approval for expenditure of tax funds under Article V, § 2(5) of the Constitution shall not exceed the total of all estimated nontax revenues (not including nontax revenues required by law to be spent for specific purposes) and taxes levied for such purposes pursuant to a vote of the people [G.S. 159-13(b)(7)].

This provision offers a gross check for conformance to Article V, section 2(5), of the Constitution. That subsection, as discussed on pages 45-47, permits the levy of property taxes without a vote "for purposes authorized by general law uniformly applicable throughout the State." Since the constitutional limitation applies only to *property* taxes, the language "nontax revenues" in the quotation should be understood to refer to all non-property tax revenues.

4. *Property tax collection estimates may not exceed the prior year's experience.* It is virtually impossible to collect, within the fiscal year, 100 per cent of the property taxes levied. Therefore, revenue estimates in the budget ordinance should reflect only the amount of property taxes that is reasonably expected to be collected, not the total amount levied. The LGBFCA requires conservative collection estimates by its prohibition against estimating a collection rate greater than the rate experienced in the year just ending. That is, if on June 30, 1975, the 1974-75 levy has been 97.6 per cent collected, the *highest* percentage of collection that may be estimated in the 1975-76 budget ordinance is 97.6 per cent. Of course, it is possible to estimate collections at a lower percentage than this maximum; and to provide a margin of safety, most units do just that.

5. *Prior year's taxes must be included in estimated revenues.* At one time counties occasionally would estimate current tax collections at 100 per cent and show no estimate for collection of the prior year's taxes. Then, when actual current collections did not reach 100 per cent, the prior year's taxes were counted on to make up the difference, and the total about balanced. This practice is prohibited by combination of the requirements that property tax collection estimates not exceed the prior year's rate and that uncollected taxes from prior years that are expected to be collected be shown as estimated revenues.

6. *Non-property tax revenue estimates must be based on demonstrable facts.* This final requirement imposes a conservative bias on estimates of revenues other than the property tax. Unless the board of commissioners determines that the facts warrant a more optimistic expectation, estimates of such revenues must not exceed the amount actually realized in cash

during the preceding fiscal year. Thus, if the state beer and wine tax brought in $117,400 in 1974-75, the 1975-76 budget ordinance should show no more than that amount from that source, *unless* the facts warrant an expectation of increase.

Budget Preparation

The Budget Officer. Each county must have a budget officer, the administrative official responsible for budget preparation and budget execution (G.S. 159-9). If a county has a manager, that person is by law the budget officer. Otherwise, the board of commissioners must appoint a budget officer, to serve at its pleasure. The board may impose the duties on any county officer or employee *except* the sheriff and, in counties with a population over 7,500, the register of deeds.

Supervision of budget preparation by a single official has several advantages. It centers responsibility for seeing that departmental requests and estimates are prepared and on time. It provides a single link between the board of commissioners and department heads. It permits a technical review of departmental requests and estimates, to insure completeness and accuracy. More substantively, it permits a unified review of departmental priorities in the context of governmental priorities; the reconciliation of departmental requests with estimated revenues, leading to a balanced budget; and the mediation of conflicting claims on scarce resources. All in all, it permits submission to the board of commissioners of a budget already reviewed by someone in a position to evaluate and recommend services and priorities for the entire unit.

Administrative Procedures. The LGBFCA is simply a framework for budget preparation, and only a partial framework at that. Its provisions are simple and few, with the basic calendar as follows:

By April 30—Departmental requests to budget officer;
By June 1—Budget submitted to governing board;
By July 1—Budget ordinance adopted.

Departmental procedures. G.S. 159-10 provides that by *April 30,* the budget officer is to have in hand:

(1) Budget requests from each department for the coming year.
(2) Revenue estimates for each department for the coming year.
(3) Actual and estimated expenditures for each category of expenditure in the budget ordinance for the immediately preceding and current fiscal years.
(4) Actual and estimated amounts realized for each source of revenue for the immediately preceding and current fiscal years.
(5) Any other information he requests from the departments.

FINANCE AND FISCAL CONTROL 65

April 30, which marks the *legal* beginning of the budgetary cycle, should also mark the completion of the departmental budget preparation process, which began several months before. Although this process is of great administrative importance, the law is concerned only that it be completed in time for the budget ordinance to be adopted by July 1. Hence, April 30 ought to be understood as a guideline rather than a deadline. Many counties require that departmental requests be filed earlier than April 30 in order to provide more time for the two-stage (budget officer and governing board) review that follows.

Departmental procedures for budget preparation differ from unit to unit, in substance, in detail, and in timing, but a fairly typical procedure might follow this sequence:

(1) The budget office initiates the formal process by writing to, or meeting with, the department heads. (Normally, department heads will already have been planning for the coming year.) At this time, the budget officer often establishes ground rules for the process transmitting probable salary policy for the coming year and giving the department heads some notion of unit resources and priorities. To do this, he may already have had informal discussions with the board of commissioners.

(2) In larger counties, the budget office often prepares some sort of budget manual—including forms, instructions, and models—and provides other information useful to the department heads.

(3) Either the finance department or the department heads, depending on how records are kept, develops historical data on appropriations and revenue estimates for the current and immediately preceding fiscal years.

(4) Department heads prepare their formal budget requests, using such information as historical data, pay plans, a chart of the current cost of supplies and materials, and so on. The budget officer will have established the form for budget requests and the type and amount of supporting information required. Preparing these requests is a most important responsibility of a department head. He is the person best able to know the needs and potentialities of his department and to communicate these to the policy-makers.

(5) At the same time as budget requests are prepared, revenue estimates for the coming year should be developed. Although the LGBFCA suggests that this be done by each department head, the finance department may be in a better position to do so.

(6) All of this information—historical data, requests, estimates—is submitted to the budget officer.

Budget officer procedures. G.S. 159-11 provides that by *June 1*, the budget officer shall have prepared a budget and submitted it to the board of commissioners. Within this general direction, great variety in administrative practice may exist. The form of the budget officer's budget is prescribed by him and the board of commissioners. If the board insists, the budget officer might simply transmit departmental requests to the board, noting the rate of tax necessary to balance the budget.

This role (or non-role) for the budget officer is customary in some counties. Even here, however, the budget officer should exercise at least a technical review, checking the accuracy and completeness of departmental figures. Such a minimal role for the budget officer, while legal, does not comport with good budgetary policy. Rather, the board of commissioners should not only allow but expect the budget officer to review departmental requests substantively and submit to the board a budget already balanced and adjusted from initial requests. Such a budget could—and usually does—exhibit both the original departmental requests and the budget officer's recommendations. In this way the commissioners may know departmental wishes while enjoying the advantage of staff development of a balanced and unified budget.

The law is silent as to the procedures to be followed by the budget officer in developing his budget. Typically he meets with the department heads to discuss their requests. In many (especially smaller) counties, the board of commissioners or some of its members may participate in this process. For example, in a small county, each commissioner may have informal responsibility for one or more departments. When the budget officer meets with each department head, the appropriate board member might sit in. Some units have a board finance committee that works very closely with the budget officer in preparing of the budget. In other units, the board has no formal role until the budget is submitted to it. The point is that the law has room for a number of ways to prepare the budget. Each unit can develop budget preparation procedures that best suit its needs.

Submission to the Board of Commissioners

"Not later than *June 1"* the budget officer must submit the budget to the board of commissioners. Because the submission of the budget should be an occasion for summarizing and explaining the budget for both the board and the public, the law urges that the budget be submitted at a formal board meeting, when the explanation is most likely to reach the public. Many boards, of course, hold a regular meeting on the first Monday of each month; the first Monday in June will only rarely fall on June 1. Must such a board call a special meeting to receive the budget by June 1? Not unless it wishes to. Like April 30, June 1 is primarily a guideline, a checkpoint toward adopting the budget by July 1. Missing June 1 by a few days is not disastrous. Thus, if a board meets on the first Monday of each month and the first Monday in June is June 5, the budget might be submitted to the board in one of three ways, each complying with the spirit of the LGBFCA:

(1) The budget could be "submitted" to the board on June 1 simply by filing it with the clerk and mailing a copy to each board member. (2) The budget officer could postpone formal submission until the fifth. Missing the June 1 deadline by a few days would not impair the validity of the process. (3) The board could call a special meeting for June 1 at which the budget is submitted. Of course, it is also possible—and many units do—to submit the budget well before June 1.

Budget Message. When submitting the budget, the budget officer must include a budget message. The budget message should both introduce and summarize the budget itself:—introduce it to the board of commissioners and those members of the public who wish to study the budget, and summarize it for those who have no time to study it themselves or are perhaps intimidated by its detail. Thus the message should emphasize the major features of the budget, especially significant changes from or additions to past practice. G.S. 159-11(b) states nicely what the message should include:

> The budget message
> . . .should contain a concise explanation of the governmental goals fixed by the budget for the budget year.
> . . .should explain important features of the activities anticipated in the budget.
> . . .should set forth the reasons for stated changes from the previous year in program goals, programs, and appropriation levels.
> . . .should explain any major changes in fiscal policy.

Frequently, the message is accompanied by charts and tables summarizing the actual figures of the budget. Although a written budget is not explicitly required, a written format is preferable to a simple oral statement. The oral statement will explain the budget only to those in the immediate audience; the larger public will not benefit from the summary. Yet this larger public is the very group most dependent on the message for their information on the budget. Normally the message takes the form of a letter from the budget officer to the board of commissioners and is bound with or attached to the budget. Many managers read this letter to, and along with, the board when submitting the budget. While publication of the message is not required by law, the newspapers might be encouraged to print it as a useful summary of the budget.

When the budget officer submits the budget, many boards adopt it as the "tentative budget." Although such a step does no harm, it is neither required nor provided for by the statute.

Form of the Budget / Possibility of an Unbalanced Budget

The board of commissioners and the budget officer determine the form of the budget. The budget is often substantially more detailed than the budget ordinance and in format may be quite different from the ordinance; for example, expenditures may be organized by program rather than by department and fund. Also, the budget must comply with the same directions and limitations as the ordinance, with one exception. The budget ordinance must be balanced, and normally the budget also will be balanced, but G.S. 159-11 (c) permits the board of commissioners to allow or request submission of an unbalanced budget. For example, a county receives $200,000 in federal revenue-sharing funds, accounted for in a separate fund. The potential uses of this money might total $255,000. With the board's approval, the budget officer could present the following budget for the revenue-sharing money.

General Revenue-Sharing Trust Fund	
Revenues	
Federal Revenue-Sharing Grant	$200,000
Appropriations	
Front-end loader—landfill	30,000
Trash compactor	16,000
Library wing—land, bldg., equip.	112,000
Renovations—courthouse	37,000
School site	40,000
Additional summer recreation supervisors	20,000
Total	$255,000

Thus, the board would have before it all potential uses of the money and could choose from that list.

The *budget ordinance,* however, must be balanced. For the example given above, the ordinance would reflect the board of commissioners' decision as to where to trim $55,000 from the suggested appropriations.

Filing and Notice

On the same day he submits the budget to the board, the budget officer must file a copy with the clerk of the board (G.S. 159-12). Here it must remain, available for public inspection, until the budget ordinance has been adopted. The law also requires the clerk to make "a copy of the budget available to all news media" in the county.

Either at the meeting at which the budget is submitted to the board of commissioners or earlier, the board must schedule a public hearing on the budget for some time after the budget is submitted but before the budget ordinance is adopted. Some boards hold several meetings on various parts of the budget, at which department heads and sometimes the public are heard. Although these might be called "hearings," they do not satisfy the law. Rather, the law anticipates that there will be one hearing on the *entire* budget, pursuant to newspaper notice, primarily to allow individual citizens to speak to the board.

After the budget is filed and the date for the hearing set, the clerk must publish, in a newspaper with general circulation in the county, a legal notice stating:
—that the budget has been submitted to the board;
—that a copy is available for public inspection in the clerk's office;
—the time, date, and place of the budget hearing.

Obviously, to be effective, this notice must be published before the budget hearing is held. However, the statute requires no specific minimum number of days before the hearing. It is suggested, therefore, that the notice be published as soon as possible after the budget is filed and sereral days, perhaps at least seven, before the budget hearing is held.

The Budget Ordinance

Once the budget is before the board of commissioners, there are two prerequisites to adoption of the budget ordinance:
1. At least ten days must pass between submission of the budget and adoption of the budget ordinance [G.S. 159-13(a)].
2. The board must hold a budget hearing [G.S. 159-12(b)].

The waiting period and the hearing serve a common purpose—to permit the public to become familiar with the budget and to comment on it. The waiting period must simply be observed, and nothing more need be said about it; therefore let us turn to the budget hearing.

Budget Hearing. All that the LGBFCA requires of the budget hearing is that it be held sometime before the ordinance is adopted. However, several points should be made about the hearing. Since notice of the hearing must be included in the announcement that the budget has been submitted, the hearing necessarily will be held after the submission. To allow adequate time to study the budget, it probably should be held nearer the time of adoption than of submission. For the same reason, the board should hold the hearing at a time that permits the largest public attendance.

The board may conduct the hearing as it does any other. If attendance is large, the budget officer might begin by summarizing the proposed budget. Speakers' time may be allotted and groups of persons who hold the same position may be asked to designate spokesmen. The board might simply listen, or it might respond to points or questions raised or ask the budget officer to do so. As with most of the budget process, the law permits variety and flexibility in conducting the hearing.

Board Review. As has been noted, the budget ordinance must conform to a series of directions and limitations. Beyond that, the board of commissioners has complete discretion over the form and content of the ordinance and the fiscal policy it represents. The recommendations of the budget officer are simply that—recommendations. The board may accept them, modify them, or reject them. As the single most important policy document of any local government, the budget and the fundamental priorities it reflects should, in the end, be the work of the board itself.

Board review, as with much else in the budget process, varies from county to county. All counties, of course, must hold a budget hearing. Some boards stop there, relying on a finance committee for detailed review, or perhaps accepting with little question the recommendations of the budget officer. Such a delegation of responsibility should be carefully approached, however, lest the board find itself accepting rather than making fiscal policy. Other boards undertake an active, searching review of the budget, perhaps through a series of meetings, each given over to one segment of the budget. Department heads might be invited to the appropriate meetings, or the budget officer might answer for them. Although such a review facilitates legislative control of the budget, the board should concentrate on policies and programs rather than details.

During the period beginning with submission of the budget to the board and ending with adoption of the budget ordinance, the board may conduct its review at both regular and special meetings. During this period, special meetings for budget review may be called without compliance with normal procedural requirements. That is, the particular notice requirements of G.S. Ch. 153A and local acts may be ignored. All that is necessary is that each board member have *actual notice* of such a meeting and that only budget matters be discussed (G.S. 159-17).

Budgets and the Open Meetings Law. The North Carolina Open Meetings Law (G.S. 143-318.1 through -318.7) applies to the budget preparation and adoption process. Any legislative and executive group with power to conduct hearings, deliberate, or take official action must do so in public, unless specifically exempted from the law. There is no exemption for the local budget process.

Budget Ordinance Adoption. The budget ordinance may be adopted any time after the budget hearing, including the same day, except that at least ten days must have elapsed since the budget was submitted to the board. G.S. 159-13(a) directs that adoption take place by July 1. Each county should make every effort to meet that deadline, since having an adopted budget ordinance in hand by the beginning of the fiscal year facilitates better management. However, failure to do so does not impair the validity of the ordinance. The law has no sanction for late adoption of the budget ordinance; indeed, it provides for occasional late adoption. G.S. 159-16 directs that if the ordinance is not adopted by July 1, the board must adopt an interim budget, making "interim appropriations for the purpose of paying salaries, debt service payments, and the usual ordinary expenses" of the unit until the ordinance is adopted. Disbursements may not be made without a supporting appropriation, and an interim budget provides those appropriations after July 1. (If the budget ordinance will be adopted a few days late but before any payroll is due or other expenditures must be made, an interim budget may be unnecessary.) Any interim appropriations made must be charged against the comparable appropriations in the budget ordinance, once it is adopted.

The LGBFCA specifically provides that the budget ordinance may be adopted at any regular or special meeting at which a quorum is present by a majority of those present and voting (G.S. 159-17). Any local act with other requirements may be ignored. In addition, adoption of the budget ordinance is not subject to the normal ordinance requirements of G.S. Ch. 153A. G.S. 153A-45 specifically exempts the budget ordinance from its terms.

Form of the Budget Ordinance. By law the ordinance must contain: (1) appropriations; (2) estimated revenues; and (3) the property tax levy. Typically, a budget ordinance will devote a section to each of the three. The ordinance should be drafted, or at least approved as to form, by the county attorney.

Appropriations. The appropriations side of the ordinance was discussed above, in a comparison with the budget (see pages 56-58). To reiterate, the law requires that the ordinance show appropriations by fund and by some line items within funds. Beyond that minimum, the amount of detail is at the discretion of each unit.

Revenues. The law also requires that the ordinance show estimated revenues by fund, with greater detail within each fund when appropriate.

Tax levy. The budget ordinance must levy *property taxes* for the budget year. (Other local taxes—sales and use, privilege license, animal—need not be levied each year in the budget ordinance. They may be instituted by a permanent ordinance and simply reflected in the budget ordinance as revenue estimates, in the same manner as nontax revenues.) Commonly, the total tax rate combines several separate *levies.* How many such levies are necessary? Each county should have a general fund levy. Any taxes levied pursuant to a referendum should be stated separately. Any taxes levied for a special district or service district should be stated separately. No other separate levies are *necessary.* That is, debt service taxes, school taxes, public assistance taxes, and any other commonly separated levies may be included in the general fund levy. Separate funds may be continued for these programs, but the revenue side of such a fund would show appropriations from the general fund in place of a direct tax levy.

Frequently counties include in this section of the ordinance the assessed valuation against which taxes are levied and the expected percentage of collection. While this information may be useful, the law does not require its inclusion.

Other provisions. Although the above provisions are sufficient for a budget ordinance, others might be included. For example, the budget ordinance might include instructions as to its administration. If the ordinance states appropriations very broadly, it might direct that expenditures comply not only with the ordinance but also with the more detailed budget on which it is based. If the budget officer is to be permitted to make expenditures from contingency or to make intrafund transfers (see page 76), the authorization and any limitations upon it might be included in the ordinance. If a fund mixes earmarked revenues with general revenues, or supports a function for which property taxes may not be used, the ordinance might specify the use of the earmarked funds or direct which non-property tax revenues are to support the function.

Filing. G.S. 159-13(d) directs that the budget ordinance be entered upon the minutes of the board of commissioners and that, within five days after the ordinance is adopted, copies be filed with the budget officer, the finance officer, and the clerk to the board. Since the act itself requires that this filing take place, the ordinance need not do so.

LEVYING OR COLLECTING TAXES FOR SPECIAL DISTRICTS

A county may levy taxes on behalf of a special district or collect the district's taxes for it. The LGBFCA (in G.S. 159-14) seeks to coordinate budget-making of special districts and counties so that all budget ordinances can be adopted by July 1 and all tax bills mailed soon thereafter. The statute addresses three situations: (1) The county levies and collects taxes on behalf of the special district, *with* discretion over the rate of tax; (2) the county levies and collects taxes on behalf of the special district, *without* discretion over the rate of tax; (3) the county collects taxes levied by the special district. Let us look at each situation in turn.

1. *County levies taxes, has discretion over rate.* A number of sanitary (or water and/or sewer) districts operating under local acts and those mosquito-control districts that are congruent with a county operate within this situation. The special district must complete its own preliminary budget preparation by June 1 and by that date request the county to levy taxes on its behalf at a stated rate. The county commissioners review this request and determine the rate of tax they will approve. By June 15 the county must transmit its decision to the district; if the county does not act by June 15, it is deemed to have approved the requested rate and that rate

FINANCE AND FISCAL CONTROL 73

must be levied. Once the district knows what rate of tax will be levied, it is to complete its budget deliberations, enacting its budget ordinance by July 1.

2. *County levies taxes, no discretion over rate.* This situation applies to metropolitan sewerage districts and metropolitan water districts. The district determines the rate of tax to be levied and simply notifies the county of this amount. Notification must occur by June 15; otherwise the county need not levy the taxes.

3. *County collects taxes levied by district.* Sanitary districts established under general law and mosquito-control districts that are not congruent with a county fit this situation. The district levies its own tax; it then notifies the county of the rate levied. Notification must occur by July 15; otherwise, the county need not collect the taxes.

BUDGET MODIFICATION AND AMENDMENT

Once adopted, the budget ordinance is not merely a financial plan for the year. It also is the legal gauge against which all expenditures must be measured. An expenditure must be authorized by an appropriation in the ordinance, and sufficient moneys must remain in the appropriation to cover the expenditure. Obviously, events during a fiscal year may occasion greater spending than anticipated in some activities or entrance into new activities altogether. Needs may arise for which there is no appropriation, or for which the appropriation is exhausted. How much flexibility does the law permit in execution of the budget ordinance; may it be modified or amended, and if so, how? Modification may occur in three ways: first, the ordinance itself can be amended; second, expenditures can be made from contingency accounts; and third, the *budget* can often be modified without need to modify the *budget ordinance*. Let us look at these in reverse order.

Modifying the Budget

As has been discussed above, the budget normally will exhibit greater detail than the budget ordinance. An ordinance may make appropriations by departments within the general fund. while the budget on which it is based may well have presented departmental proposals as follows:

Recreation Department		$111,400
Personnel services	$69,000	
Nonpersonnel expense	24,250	
Capital outlay	18,150	

If only the departmental figure appears in the ordinance, it is only figure against which expenditures are, by law, judged. This is true even though the departmental figure is based on the subaccounts in the budget. To continue the example above, events during the year may result in actual recreation expenditures as follows:

Recreation Department		$110,200
Personnel services	$72,400	
Nonpersonnel expense	18,700	
Capital outlay	19,100	

Even though two of the subaccounts have been overspent, there has been no violation of the law, because the budget ordinance appropriation—the departmental total—has not been overspent. This type of adjustment within an appropriation is possible without the need to change the ordinance itself; indeed, the ability to do just this is the primary argument in favor of departmental appropriations and against greater detail in the budget ordinance. (This is not to say, of course, that a board of commissioners may not appropriate by departments and still require that the subaccounts be respected in practice. The law imposes a minimum restriction on expenditures; a county may impose greater ones on itself. However, if a board forbids modification in the subaccounts without its approval, it may find a large part of its time given over to budget execution.)

Contingency Expenditures

Contingency accounts are intended for unanticipated expenditures. Moneys may be expended from contingency funds by direct order of the board of commissioners, or if the board wishes, by order of the budget officer. The usual practice in North Carolina is for the board to retain full control over contingency expenditures, so that each such expenditure is specifically authorized by resolution of the board. The board may, however, permit the budget officer himself to authorize expenditures from a contingency account, subject to any restrictions set by the board. For example, the board might place a maximum on individual expenditures from a contingency account combined with a maximum monthly total. If the budget officer is given this power, he must report any such expenditure to the board at its next regular meeting, and the board must record the report in its minutes.

The statute provides that a board resolution approving an expenditure from contingency is "deemed an amendment to the budget ordinance setting up an appropriation for the object of expenditure authorized." That is, it is permissible to expend the money directly from the contingency account. However, many units prefer to transfer the moneys to an existing appropriation first, and then make the expenditure from that appropriation. In this way, the expenditure may be charged against the activity for which used.

Budget Ordinance Amendments

A county enjoys almost as much freedom to amend the budget ordinance as it has to adopt it. G.S. 159-15 states that the ordinance may be amended at any time during the year, so long as it continues to be balanced and continues to satisfy the other directions and limitations examined above. The only other restriction is that the board may not increase or reduce the property tax levy unless it is ordered to do so by a court or state agency.

It is important to note that the tax levy not only may not be increased but also may not be reduced during the year If, for example, a county greatly underestimates its assessed valuation in levying the tax, it may not adjust the rate downward when accurate figures become known. It will be a most unusual circumstance for a court or state agency, during the year, to order a county to amend its budget ordinance and change its tax rate. A court might do so under G.S. 115-91, at the conclusion of litigation over the amount of the school budget, if the decision is that more is needed than was appropriated. (See pages 59-60.) The Local Government Commission might do so if a unit refused to levy a sufficient debt service tax. But, to repeat, either example would be a rare occurrence.

The legal bar to altering the property tax does not apply to other taxes, although practical difficulties may be involved. The sales tax, if not in force in a county, may be levied at any time during the year; once it is levied, of course, its rate is fixed by law at 1 per cent. The privilege license tax schedule may be revised during a year but probably any changes would be instituted with the new tax year, beginning in either June or July. The same holds true of any animal tax.

Still greater flexibility is available to change any of the fees and charges levied by a county. Water rates might be adjusted at any point during the year, as might admission fees to a public golf course or permit fees in the inspection department. With these fees and charges, the primary barrier to change—at least increases—is probably political. Another change possible in the revenue side of the ordinance is the appropriation of additional fund balances. There is no practical problem to doing this, and probably little or no political problem either. Finally, if it becomes clear during the year that a particular, important revenue has been significantly *over*estimated in the ordinance, the board may wish to amend the ordinance to reflect this new information.

If revenue estimates are modified, appropriations must be adjusted so that all funds and the total ordinance remain in balance. In addition, a budget amendment may simply transfer moneys from one appropriation to another, without affecting grand totals. It is with regard to appropriations that the requirements that the ordinance continue to balance and that the other directions and limitations continue to be observed are most important. Rather than repeat the discussion of those requirements, the reader is referred to the extended discussion on pages 69-72 with the reminder that the requirements apply as much to budget ordinance amendments as they do to preparing and adopting the budget ordinance.

The usual method of amending the budget ordinance is by board action. Any such amendment should be by ordinance, which should be filed with finance officer, budget officer, and clerk of the board, each of whom has a copy of the budget ordinance itself. In amending the budget ordinance, the board enjoys the same freedom from normal procedural requirements as it has in adopting the ordinance. The amendment may be adopted at a regular or special meeting on the day it is introduced by a simple majority of those voting, a quorum being present.

As with contingency expenditures, a board of commissioners may also permit the budget officer to make certain budget ordinance amendments himself. Subject to any restrictions set by the board, the budget officer may be permitted to "transfer moneys from one appropriation to another within the same fund." Two elements of the statutory authorization should be emphasized. First, the transfer must be within the same fund; transfers *between* funds are not authorized. Second, the transfers authorized are between appropriations; changes on the revenue side, including increasing the amount of appropriated fund balance, are not authorized. If a transfer between funds is wanted, or if revenue estimates or the amount of appropriated fund balance is to be changed, the necessary amendment must be accomplished by the board. If amending power is extended to the budget officer, he must report each amendment to the board at its next regular meeting, and the board must record the report in its minutes.

The letter of the law requires that an appropriation sufficient to cover an expenditure be available at the time the expenditure is made. Therefore, if an appropriation is exhausted and an expenditure is to be charged against that appropriation, the budget ordinance should be amended *before* the expenditure is certified by the finance officer (see page 77). The practice of making an omnibus budget ordinance amendment at the close of the fiscal year, to replenish any overspent appropriations, is not consistent with the strict requirements of the law. Normally it will satisfy the post-audit, but it does not satisfy the pre-audit during the year.

BUDGET EXECUTION AND BUDGETING CONTROL

The LGBFCA leaves largely to local discretion the precise manner of accounting for county funds and ensuring conformity to the budget. This section will summarize the few, but important, practices required by the law to insure proper administration of the budget.

The LGBFCA requires each county to establish and maintain an accounting system through which all appropriations, encumbrances, expenditures, and revenues are recorded and accounted for. It requires a preaudit of every expenditure to insure that it has been authorized in the budget. It provides for basic internal reporting and reports to the public concerning the financial condition of the county. There are also procedures designed to safeguard revenue collection.

Expenditure Control

Contracts and purchase orders of the county must be in writing to be valid. In addition, there must appear on each contract or purchase order a pre-audit certificate by the county finance officer that provision for payment of the proposed obligation has been made by an appropriation in the budget. Before making this certification, the finance officer is required to determine that a sufficient unencumbered balance remains in that appropriation to meet the obligation that will arise out of the contract or purchase order during the current fiscal year.

A county is authorized to enter into a continuing contract if sufficient funds have been appropriated in the budget to meet the amounts to be paid under the contract in the fiscal year in which it is made. For continuing contracts, the accountant is required to certify only that a sufficient unencumbered balance in the appropriation exists to meet payments that will fall due in that fiscal year.

Control of Revenues

Selection of County Depository. The board of commissioners is required to select some one or more banks or trust companies in the state as the official depository or depositories of the county. The designation of the official depository is to be made by resolution adopted by the board and recorded in its minutes.

Daily Deposits of County Funds. County officers and employees who collect or receive money belonging to the county or any of its subdivisions are required to deposit these funds daily with the county finance officer or in the official depository designated by the county commissioners. Immediately after the deposit is made, the officer or employee who made the deposit must report it to the county accountant by means of a treasurer's receipt or duplicate deposit ticket signed by the depository.

Instead of requiring a daily deposit, the board of county commissioners may require that officers and employees deposit money only when they have at least $250 in their possession. A deposit must be made in any event, however, on the last business day of each month.

Security Requirements for Deposited Funds. The LGBFCA requires that adequate security for county funds on deposit in bank deposits will be provided. If the amount of such deposits exceeds the amount insured by the Federal Deposit Insurance Corporation, the county must require the depository to provide additional security for the excess.

Investment of County Funds. Collections of many revenues used by counties in financing current operations are realized early in the budget year, and frequently counties have on hand cash balances that will not be needed for some time. Increasingly, counties are investing these cash balances until they are needed.

Investment of county funds can be made only in accordance with authority granted by law. Statewide law in North Carolina authorizes the investment of specific county funds in prescribed types of investments.

All investments and deposits must be insured by a federal deposit insurance corporation; guaranteed by the federal government, the State of North Carolina, or a political subdivision of North Carolina; or secured as provided by the depository law. There is no authority to invest in stocks or bonds of private corporations or obligations of another state or political subdivision of another state.

All types of county funds are eligible for investment, including unspent proceeds of bond issues, sinking funds, capital reserve funds, and cash balances in any fund.

The law specifically requires that interest earned on investments or deposits be credited to the fund from which cash is deposited or invested. Cash of several funds may be combined for deposit or investment if this is not otherwise prohibited by law. Interest on joint deposits or investments must be prorated and credited to the various participating funds on the basis of the proportionate amounts invested, figured according to an average periodic balance or some other sound accounting principle. Interest earned on bond funds may be either used for the purpose for which the bonds were issued or applied to retirement of the bonds.

Part IV / Debt

CONSTITUTIONAL LIMITATIONS ON BORROWING

Article V, section 4, of the North Carolina Constitution forbids a county or other unit of local government "to contract debts secured by a pledge of its faith and credit" unless the debt is approved by a majority of the voters who vote on the question. There are six exceptions to this general rule, each of which is discussed later in this Part. The Constitution goes on to define the word "debt" and the phrase "pledge of its faith and credit." Debt is

FINANCE AND FISCAL CONTROL 79

limited to a borrowing of money, and a pledge of faith and credit is defined as a pledge of the taxing power. Thus, the Constitution regulates only a transaction in which the county borrows money and pledges its power to levy taxes as security for the loan. While many kinds of financial transactions could involve a borrowing of money and a direct or indirect pledge of the taxing power as security, there is statutory authority for only three kinds of such transactions: general obligation bonds, general obligation bond-anticipation notes, and tax-anticipation notes. There is no statutory authority for counties to execute promissory notes or to borrow money in any other way than mentioned, and each of the authorized means of borrowing money is subject to the complete supervision and control of the Local Government Commission.

The enumerated exceptions are as follows:

Refunding Bonds. A vote is not required for the issuance of refunding bonds. These are general obligation bonds issued for the purpose of paying off and retiring currently outstanding general obligation bonds. In other words, an existing bond issue can be refinanced through refunding bonds without a vote of the people. This is true even though the cost of the refunding bond issue may be considerably higher than the bonds being refinanced because of higher interest rates.

Revenue Deficiencies. The process through which counties make budget appropriations on the basis of estimated revenues has been described earlier in this chapter, and the possibility that actual revenue collections might not equal or exceed revenue estimates was discussed in connection with the direction in the LGBFCA that the full amount of any deficit in any fund be appropriated in the following fiscal year. If revenue collections fall below revenue estimates made in good faith, the county may issue bonds without a vote of the people to fund the resulting deficit.

Tax Anticipation. The due date of property taxes levied for a given fiscal year falls on September 1, fully sixty days after the fiscal year opens, and interest does not begin to accrue on those taxes until January 1, six months into the fiscal year. In practice, this means that the current year's tax levy is collected mostly from November through January, with very little money coming in during the first three or four months of the fiscal year. The Constitution and statutes authorize counties to borrow money without a vote of the people in anticipation of the tax levy, but the total amount of tax-anticipation notes outstanding at any one time may not exceed 50 per cent of the tax levy uncollected at the time the last note was issued.

Riots and Insurrections. Counties may issue bonds without a vote to suppress riots and insurrections. This authority has never been used by any county.

Emergencies. Counties may issue bonds without a vote "to meet emergencies immediately threatening the public health or safety, as conclusively determined in writing by the Governor." This authority became effective on July 1, 1973, and has not yet been used by any county.

The Two-Thirds Limitation. The most important of the exceptions permits counties to issue bonds for any authorized purpose without a vote of the people in an amount not exceeding two-thirds of the amount by which the county's outstanding general obligation indebtness was reduced in the preceding fiscal year. To determine what amount can be borrowed under the two-thirds limitations at any given time, it is necessary to determine the amount of reduction of outstanding debt in the preceding fiscal year and the amount of new debt already incurred in the present fiscal year. "Reduction of debt" means the net reduction of outstanding indebtness and not the gross amount retired. New debt incurred and any portion of such new debt retired during the preceding fiscal year must be taken into account in determining the net reduction of outstanding debt.

Only the net debt reduction of the *immediately preceding fiscal year* may be considered. Debt reductions of prior fiscal years may not be brought forward to increase the county's nonvoted debt-incurring power.

As a general rule in computing outstanding debt, all of the county's indebtedness should be included. The Court has defined "outstanding" to mean "undischarged, uncollected or unpaid." General obligation bonds and notes that have been issued by the county clearly constitute outstanding debt. They remain outstanding debt "until actually paid and canceled, or delivered to the county for cancellation." This is true even though sinking funds have been accumulated, earmarked, and made available at the office of the paying agent for payment of the bonds.

On the other hand, the mere passage of a bond resolution authorizing the issuance of bonds does not create any outstanding indebtedness for purposes of the two-thirds limitation.

Refunding bonds and the bonds to be refunded may be outstanding at the same time. If the refunding bonds are issued before the end of the fiscal year and the bonds to be refunded are not retired until early in the following fiscal year, do both the refunding bonds and the bonds to be refunded constitute outstanding debt? The Court has held that they do not and that the computation of outstanding debt should include only one of the bond issues.

Revenue bonds are not included in the computation of outstanding debt. Since they are payable solely from the net revenues of a revenue-producing enterprise, their issuance creates no county debt within the constitutional proscription.

AUTHORITY TO INCUR DEBT

The Local Government Bond Act is the enabling legislation authorizing counties to issue bonds. G.S. 159-48, a part of this act, enumerates thirty-one specific purposes for which counties may issue bonds and notes. In addition, the law authorizes bond issues for any authorized capital cost even though the specific purpose may not be mentioned in the enabling statute. Table 3-IV shows the authorized purposes.

Table 3-IV
Purposes for Which Bonds May Be Issued

Airports and related facilities	Museums and art galleries
Armories	Parks and recreation
Auditoriums, coliseums, and convention centers	Public buildings
Beach improvements	Real property revaluation
Cemeteries	Redevelopment
Community colleges and technical institutes	Refunding existing general obligation bonds
County home	Riot and insurrection suppression
Courthouses and jails	School buildings
Emergencies threatening health or safety	Sewer systems
Fire protection	Solid waste disposal
Funding debt other than borrowed money	Storm sewers
Hospitals	Voting machines
Judgments entered against county	Water systems
Land	Any other purpose for which counties
Law enforcement, including equipment	are authorized by general law to appropriate
Libraries	money except for current expenses.

THE NET DEBT LIMITATION

Restrictions on the amount of debt a county may incur are imposed by statute as well as by the Constitution. G.S. 159-55 provides that the net debt of a county may not exceed 8 per cent of the appraised value of property subject to taxation by the county.

All bonds and notes of the county, both those actually outstanding and those authorized but not yet issued, are included in the county's gross debt. From this figure, the statute allows deductions for funding and refunding bonds, the amount held in sinking funds for debt retirement, all bonds and notes issued for water systems, bonds and notes issued for sewer systems under certain circumstances, the amount of uncollected special assessments that will be applied to debt reduction when collected, and the estimated amount of special assessments to be levied for improvements for which part of the gross debt was incurred. The county's net debt is the figure remaining after the deductions listed above have been subtracted from gross debt (except revenue bonds and notes, tax-anticipation notes, and bond-anticipation notes issued for bonds other than funding or refunding bonds).

To insure compliance with these statutory debt limitations, a sworn statement of the county's net indebtedness must be filed with the clerk to the board of county commissioners after the introduction but before the final passage of any bond order. This sworn statement of indebtedness must remain on file in the clerk's office open to public inspection.

USE OF BOND PROCEEDS

The proceeds from the sale of bonds may be used only for the purposes specified in the order authorizing the bonds or for payment of notes issued in anticipation of the sale of the bonds. The cost of preparing, issuing, and marketing bonds is declared by statute to be one of the purposes for which bonds are issued. If any part of the bond proceeds cannot be applied to or is not necessary for the purpose for which the bonds were issued, it must be applied to the payment of the principal and interest of the bonds.

The Court has repeatedly recognized the general rule that the county commissioners may not divert bond proceeds to a use different from the purpose stated in the bond order. In applying the rule, however, the Court has said: "But [the statute] in our opinion, does not place a limitation upon the legal right to transfer or allocate funds from one project to another included within the general purpose for which the bonds were issued. The inhibition contained in the statute is to prevent funds obtained for one general purpose being transferred and used for another general purpose." In the case from which this opinion comes, both the bond order and the notice of election listed projects for which the proceeds would be used. One of the projects was a new school building in a particular school district. Because of changed conditions, the county board of education determined that repair and modification of the old school building would meet the needs of the district and proposed to reallocate part of the bond proceeds to other school buildings in the county. The proposed reallocation was upheld.

Although the county commissioners may not on their own motion use bond proceeds for purposes other than those stated in the bond order, a different use of these proceeds may be made when authorized by statute. Even here, however, the Court has indicated that when the bonds have been approved in an election, the legislature may not authorize diversion of the proceeds from the purpose stated in the bond order unless changed circumstances cause them to be no longer needed for that purpose.

ISSUANCE AND SALE OF BONDS

North Carolina is unique among the fifty states in that all local government bonds must be approved by a state agency and all such bonds are advertised and sold by the state. The state agency that has authority over local government bonds is the Local Government Commission, a division of the Department of the State Treasurer. The Local Government Commission was created in 1931 in response to the grave financial crisis existing at that time. During the 43 years since its creation, the Commission has developed an expertise in bond approval and marketing and a reputation in national financial circles that makes North Carolina local government bonds among the most attractive securities in the nation, if not in the world.

The procedures for bond and note issuance by counties are extremely complex. Among the steps are a preliminary conference with the staff of the Local Government Commission, a formal application to the Commission, approval of the application, introduction of a bond order, final passage of a bond order, a bond election in most instances, an order fixing the details of the bonds, preparation of a bond prospectus, advertisement of the issue, receipt of bids, award of the bonds, printing and delivery of the bonds, receipt of bond proceeds, disbursement of bonds proceeds to the issuing unit by the State Treasurer, local expenditure of bond proceeds, payment of the bonds, and finally destruction of paid and canceled bonds and coupons—not to mention several legal notices published in newspapers at key steps in this process.

It is an invariable practice in the financial world that local government bonds will not be traded unless each bond bears on its reverse an opinion by recognized bond counsel that the bonds are valid obligations of the issuing unit and the interest on the bonds is not subject to the federal income tax. Bond counsel will not give this opinion unless the statutory procedures for issuance of the bonds have been followed precisely, without the omission of the smallest detail. For this reason, and because of the complexity of the procedure, it is of the utmost importance that a county not begin the legal procedure for bond issuance before it contacts the Local Government Commission for a preliminary conference or before it retains nationally recognized bond counsel. The staff of the Commission and bond counsel will guide the county through the intricate procedure, thus insuring that the bonds will be issued and sold when the money is needed.

—*David M. Lawrence*
Joseph S. Ferrell

4 / The Property Tax

PART I. THE NATURE OF THE TAX / 88
Characteristics of the Property Tax / 88
Coverage: Exclusion, Exemption,
 and Preferential Treatment / 89
Real and Personal Property Defined / 90
Appraisal and Assessment Defined / 91

PART II. PROPERTY TAX LISTING AND ASSESSING / 91
The Administrative Structure / 91
The County Tax Supervisor / 92
 Appointment / 92
 Duties / 93
The List Takers / 93
 Appointment / 93
 Compensation / 93
 Duties / 93
The Board of County Commissioners / 94
 Governing Body of the County / 94
 Board of Equalization and Review / 94
The Property Tax Commission / 95
 Membership / 95
 Duties / 95
The Department of Revenue / 96
Property Tax Timetable / 97
Listing and Assessing Timetable / 97
Collection Timetable / 99
The Listing Process / 100
Listing Requirements / 100
Roles of County and City / 100
Where Property Is Taxable—A Matter of Jurisdiction / 101
Duty to List / 101
Property Not Subject to Taxation—
 Requests for Tax Relief / 101

Listing Techniques / 102
  Aids in Listing Real Property / 102
  Aids in Listing Personal Property / 102
The Valuation Process / 103
Statutory Elements of Value / 103
  General Rule / 103
  Use-Value Appraisal of Farmlands / 104
Time for Appraisal / 105
  Octennial Revaluation Schedule / 105
  Accelerating the Octennial Revaluation / 108
  Horizontal Adjustments Every Fourth Year / 108
Appraisal Techniques / 109
  Inspection of Property Being Appraised / 111
  Preparatory Work / 111
Appraisal Personnel / 112
  County Officials / 112
  Expert Appraisers / 113
Record of Valuation / 114
Powers of County Officials in Making Assessments:
  A Summary / 114
Review and Revisal of Assessments / 115
  By the Tax Supervisor / 115
  By the Board of Equalization and Review / 116
  By the Board of County Commissioners / 116
  By the Property Tax Commission / 119
Adjustment of Real Property Values in
  Non-Revaluation Years / 120
Discovered Property / 122
Discovered Real Property / 122
Discovered Personal Property / 123
Date of Discovery / 123
Listing for Prior Years / 123
Criminal Penalties for Failure to List Property for Taxes / 124

PART III. PROPERTY TAX COLLECTION / 125

The Office of Tax Collector / 125
Qualifying As Tax Collector / 126
Removing the Tax Collector / 127
Deputy Tax Collectors / 127
Collection of Prepayments and Delinquent Taxes / 128
Necessary Collection Records / 128
Reports of Collection Progress / 129
When Taxes Are Due—What Period They Cover / 130

PROPERTY TAX 87

The Order of Collection / 130
The Property Tax Lien / 131
Payment of Taxes / 133
Partial Payments / 135
Prepayments / 136
Interest for Late Payment of Taxes / 136
Release of Tax Lien Against Realty / 136
Enforcing Collection of Property Taxes / 138
Enforcing Collection Against Real Property: Lien
    Sale and Foreclosure / 138
  Report of Delinquent Taxes That Are Liens on Realty / 138
  Time and Place of Lien Sale / 138
  Minimum Bid / 139
  Collector's Report of Lien Sale / 139
  Record of Lien Sale: Tax Sale Certificates / 139
  Foreclosure / 140
Enforcing Collection Against Personal Property: Levy
    and Garnishment / 142
  Kinds of Taxes for Which Levy
    and Garnishment May Be Used / 143
  Time Limitations on Use of Levy and Garnishment / 143
  Procedure in Making Levy / 144
  Procedure in Attachment and Garnishment / 144
Collection Outside the County / 145
Reduction, Release, and Refund of Property Tax / 146
Settlements / 148
Settlement Procedure / 149
  Insolvents / 150
  Form of Settlement / 151

PART IV. SUGGESTED READING / 152

The Nature of the Tax / 152
Property Tax Listing and Assessing / 153
Property Tax Collection and Foreclosure / 155
General / 156

4 / THE PROPERTY TAX

Part I / The Nature of the Tax

CHARACTERISTICS OF THE PROPERTY TAX

The property tax is a tax on property itself. It is not a tax on the owner; it is not a tax on the privilege of owning property; it is not a tax on income from property. This tax on property is based on or measured by the value of the property as a marketable item. Thus, it is known as an ad valorem property tax.

North Carolina counties, cities, and towns derive their powers of taxation from the General Assembly; they cannot devise and impose taxes without specific legislative authorization. The General Assembly is left free by the North Carolina Constitution to choose or devise forms of taxation, and it has authority to delegate to local units of government the power to impose selected taxes within their borders. But, through the Constitution, the people have established a few important restrictions on the General Assembly's taxing powers:

> The power of taxation shall be exercised in a just and equitable manner, for public purposes only, and shall never be surrendered, suspended, or contracted away. [Art. V, § 2 (1).]

The General Assembly is left free to tax property and to select the kinds or *classes* of property to be taxed; but this power to classify cannot be delegated: "Only the General Assembly shall have the power to classify property for taxation, which power shall be exercised only on a Statewide basis and shall not be delegated" [Art. V, § 2 (2)]. Once a class of property has been chosen for taxation, it must be taxed "by a uniform rule, and every classification shall be made by general law uniformly applicable in every county, city and town, and other unit of local government" [Art. V, § 2 (2)]. If a class of property is selected for taxation, Art. V, section 2 (3), of the Constitution applies and specifies the conditions under which property in this class must be granted exemption and under which the General Assembly has discretionary authority to grant exemption on a statewide basis.

COVERAGE: EXCLUSION, EXEMPTION, AND PREFERENTIAL TREATMENT

The Constitution of the United States prohibits the taxation of property outside the jurisdiction of this state, property in transit in interstate commerce, and property imported from a foreign country so long as it maintains its character as an import. Property taxes authorized by North Carolina law are subject to these restrictions and, as already noted, to certain restrictions in the North Carolina Constitution as well.

An item of property may completely escape taxation in either of two ways: It may be excluded from the tax base through legislative exercise of the classification power granted by the North Carolina Constitution, or it may be granted exemption by the Constitution itself or by a statute enacted pursuant to constitutional authority. It should also be noted that the power to classify enables the General Assembly to provide for the taxation of a defined class of property at a rate lower than that applied to property in general or to provide for the appraisal and assessment of property according to a standard other than true or full market value; property afforded such preferential treatment thereby receives what amounts to a partial exclusion. County and municipal authorities have no power of their own to exclude property from taxation, grant it partial exemption, or grant it complete exemption, and the General Assembly has no power to delegate such authority to them. Classification and exemption decisions must be made by the General Assembly itself, and its decisions must apply throughout the state.

An attorney or tax official called upon to decide questions of exclusion, exemption, or preferential treatment inevitably finds that he must interpret the language of Constitution or statute. A good place to begin is with the plain language of the Machinery Act:

> All property, real and personal, within the jurisdiction of the State shall be subject to taxation unless it is:
>
> (1) Excluded from the tax base by a statute of statewide application ... or
>
> (2) Exempted from taxation by the Constitution or by a statute of statewide application. . . . [G.S. 105-274(a).]

The best guide to interpreting statutes that may bear on the question is found in the canons of construction adopted by the North Carolina Supreme Court:

> The general rule is liability to taxation, and that all property shall contribute its share to the support of the government which protects it. Exemption from taxation is exceptional. It needs no citation from

reiterated precedents that such exemptions should be strictly construed, and that if we had any doubts . . . they should be resolved in favor of liability to taxation. [United Brethren v. Commissioners, 115 N.C. 489, 497.]

If privately owned property qualifies for tax relief under the Machinery Act—whether by exclusion, exemption, or preferential treatment—the relief is not granted automatically. Tax officials will treat the property as though it were subject to full taxation unless the owner files a request for tax relief with the county tax supervisor annually or otherwise as specified in G.S. 105-282.1, -275(1), and -277.1 through -277.7. The taxpayer has the burden to show that his property qualifies for the benefit sought, and county officials are expected to review the requests in light of the tax immunity statutes. No request need be filed for government-owned property that is used for a public purpose or for certain other types of property, even though such property is immune from taxation.

REAL AND PERSONAL PROPERTY DEFINED

In general, all property within the county is subject to taxation. It is important, however, to understand that there are two broad categories or kinds of property: real property and personal property.

"Real property" is land, buildings, and items permanently affixed to land or buildings. It also includes rights and privileges belonging to or attached to land and buildings. Land may be owned by one individual, and a building or stand of timber on that land may be owned by another; the land is real property, and so is the building or timber. The fact that they are owned by different individuals does not change their character. When one individual owns a tract of land or building, and another has possession of the property under a lease or rental agreement, the physical assets remain real property. If a lessee erects buildings or other improvements on the premises, they are characterized as real property for tax purposes without regard to lease provisions concerning their disposal upon termination of the lease.

"Personal property" is movable as distinguished from fixed property. Within the personal property category there are two basic divisions— tangible personal property and intangible personal property. "Tangible" or *touchable* personal property includes virtually all items of visible and movable property not permanently affixed to real property. "Intangible" or *nontouchable* personal property includes stocks, bonds, notes, cash, bank deposits, accounts receivable, patents, trademarks, copyrights, and similar assets not capable of manual delivery.

APPRAISAL AND ASSESSMENT DEFINED

As used in North Carolina property tax law, the words "to appraise" mean to determine market value; the words "to assess" mean to fix tax value. The two terms represent two processes or steps in the taxing procedure: first, all property must be *appraised;* then all property must be *assessed* for taxation.

Before 1974 the distinction between appraisal values and assessed values was crucial because most counties taxed their property at assessed values, which were set at some uniform percentage of the appraisal value less than 100 per cent. Those percentages were called "assessment ratios." Since 1974, however, ratios are no longer used because the Machinery Act requires that all counties tax property at its full appraisal value. Ultimately this means that market value (as determined by the tax supervisor's appraisal) and tax value are the same, except in the few cases in which property is classified for taxation on a different basis. The difference between appraisal and assessment remains important nevertheless, because the distinction between them is maintained throughout the Machinery Act; but the two-step process—appraisal, then assessment—is no longer so centrally important in determining the value at which property is to be taxed, since property in every county must be assessed at 100 per cent of the appraisal value.

Part II / Property Tax Listing and Assessing

THE ADMINISTRATIVE STRUCTURE

In this state the county is the basic governmental unit for appraising and assessing property for taxation, not only for taxation by the county itself, but also for taxation by cities and special taxing districts within the county's borders. The policy of the North Carolina law is that property will have only one tax assessment; in brief, regardless of what taxing units are entitled to tax it, the item of property must be taxed at the same value in each unit.

Since the county has been made the responsible unit in the valuation of property for taxation, the General Assembly has prescribed a statewide standard official framework for assessment in each county. At the heart of this administrative structure stands the county tax supervisor. Above him stand the county commissioners, who name him, pay him, provide him with assistance, and—in a different capacity—sit in review on his valuation decisions. Beneath him stand his assistants (appraisers, clerks, list takers, etc.), who are selected by him and work under his direction. At the state level, over and above the county officials, stand the Department of Revenue and its component Property Tax Commission. As an administrative agency, the Department of Revenue is charged with supervising the valuation and taxation of property by local units of government and, in limited areas, with appraising property for local taxation. The Property Tax Commission, upon appeal, has power to review and change listing and valuation decisions made by local officials or the Department of Revenue.

The County Tax Supervisor

Appointment. The county tax supervisor is appointed by the board of county commissioners at the regular meeting on the first Monday in July in the odd-numbered years to serve for two years. The commissioners may remove the tax supervisor at any time for cause. Any vacancy in the position is to be filled by the commissioners by appointing a supervisor to serve for the rest of the vacating supervisor's unexpired term.

In selecting a tax supervisor, the county commissioners are required to appoint a person whose experience in the appraisal of real and personal property is satisfactory to the board and whose qualifications have been certified by the Department of Revenue. It should be noted, however, that the requirement of certification applies only to persons appointed after July 1, 1973. The law provides that anyone holding the office of tax supervisor on July 1, 1971, is deemed qualified to fill the position and need never be certified. Persons who, at the time the 1971 Machinery Act was enacted, had been appointed to fill vacancies in terms that were to expire in July, 1973, did not have to be certified in order to complete their unexpired terms but did have to be certified by the first Monday in July, 1973, in order to qualify for appointment for the term that began on that date. The Department's certification should indicate that the appointee has been instructed in the duties of the office and is qualified to appraise the kinds of real and personal property commonly found in North Carolina.

Instead of naming a separate county tax supervisor, the board of county commissioners may impose the duties and responsibilities of that position upon the county accountant, the county tax collector, or any county official other than a county commissioner. However, anyone holding the office of tax supervisor concurrently with another office is subject to the qualifications prescribed for tax supervisors, and G.S. 128-1.1 limits the number of offices that may be held concurrently by the same person to two.

PROPERTY TAX 93

Duties. In general, the tax supervisor is responsible for taking charge of the listing and appraising of all property in the county. This means that he must not only supervise the listing and appraising of property reported by its owners, but also must actively seek to discover property that is unlisted or underlisted, see that it is properly listed, and take the action necessary to prevent failures to list property. When the county board of equalization and review meets, the tax supervisor serves as its clerk, and he must be present at all its meetings and give to the board such information as he may have or can obtain with respect to the listing and valuation of taxable property in the county.

The List Takers

Appointment. The Machinery Act of 1939 required the tax supervisor to appoint, subject to the approval of the county commissioners, at least one list taker for each township. The Machinery Act of 1971 abolished that requirement; the board of county commissioners of each county is permitted to decide for itself whether it will use list takers in its property tax system. The board embodies its decision in the appropriation it makes for support of the tax supervisor's office. Thus, G.S. 105-296(6) states that "[w]ithin budgeted appropriations" the tax supervisor may appoint, without the commissioners' approval, the "list takers and assessors and clerical assistants necessary to carry out the listing, appraisal, assessing, and billing functions required by law." Under the 1971 revisal, if list takers are used, they obtain their authority by delegation from the tax supervisor, who also determines their responsibilities.

Compensation. Although the appointment of list takers is no longer subject to approval by the county commissioners, if they are used, their pay is set by the board. Each list taker is required to make out a detailed account of his daily activities, and the account must be audited by the county accountant and approved by the board of county commissioners. Before the first meeting of the county board of equalization and review, the tax supervisor must examine the abstracts turned in by each list taker; if he finds that the list taker has performed his duties satisfactorily, he must certify the list taker for compensation.

Duties. Traditionally, the list taker's responsibility has been twofold: first, to see that all taxable property is listed for taxation, and second, to see that all taxable property is fairly and uniformly appraised at its true value. Although the Machinery Act of 1971 imposes the duty to perform these functions on the county tax supervisor, and although the tax supervisor is no longer bound to use list takers in any particular place—such as townships—or for any particular type of work, the law contemplates that if list takers are used, their tasks will be much the same as under prior law.

Consequently, at some time between the date on which the list takers are appointed and January 1, the tax supervisor must call them together for the purposes of instruction "in methods of securing a complete list of all property in the county and of appraising and assessing, in accordance with law, all property that is to be appraised and assessed in the approaching listing period."

The Board of County Commissioners

Members of the board of county commissioners play a dual role in property tax administration:

Governing Body of the County. In their capacity as members of the governing body of the county, commissioners select and appoint the county tax supervisor, fix his compensation, approve his office budget (thereby passing on the number and caliber of assistants and list takers he may employ), and, if expert or professional appraisal services are required, make whatever contracts and financial arrangements may be necessary to obtain them. In short, the commissioners exercise a general supervisory and policy-making role with regard to the tax office.

Board of Equalization and Review. Each calendar year, for a limited period between the close of listing and the opening of the new fiscal year, the county commissioners assume an active role in administering the property tax. By operation of law, they are constituted a new and different agency known as the county board of equalization and review, and as members of this board they take a different oath of office. The equalization board opens its sessions not earlier than the first Monday in April and not later than the first Monday in May. It is supposed to complete its work within three weeks; upon giving proper notice, however, it may extend its sittings as required, but never later than July 1.

In this second capacity, commissioners have two responsibilities:

1. They must review the listings and valuations assigned property by the list takers and the tax supervisor, making whatever changes (within legal limitations) may be necessary to insure that the values meet the standards established by state law.

2. They must hear any property owner's appeal concerning the value assigned his property (or that of others) by the list takers and tax supervisor, and they have authority (within legal limitations) to make any adjustments, upward or downward, necessary to bring the valuation into line with the standards established by law.

In performing these two general responsibilities, the board of equalization and review has power to make investigations, employ expert assistance, and subpoena any persons and records needed to obtain information pertinent to its inquiry.

The Property Tax Commission

Membership. The Property Tax Commission is composed of five members chosen as follows: three appointed by the Governor, one by the Lieutenant-Governor, and one by the Speaker of the House of Representatives. The members serve staggered, four-year terms. Two of the gubernatorial appointments began on July 1, 1973, and the other three appointments—gubernatorial and otherwise—began on July 1, 1975. (Members of the former State Board had served out their terms in the meantime.) The chairman of the Property Tax Commission is selected by the Governor from the membership of the Commission and serves at the pleasure of the Governor. A vice-chairman is elected from and by the commission to serve for a two-year term. The Commission has no separate staff or administrative officer: "Clerical and other services required by the Commission" are supplied by the Secretary of Revenue. The Commission's work is financed from the proceeds of the intangibles tax—an arrangement unique to the Property Tax Commission and the Department of Revenue (in its property tax functions only).

Duties. The Property Tax Commission is solely an appellate body. For practical purposes its duties may be classified under three headings:

1. Review of county (and sometimes city) listing and valuation decisions: When a taxpayer makes a timely appeal from the appraisal or listing decision of a board of equalization (or board of county commissioners) or, in rare instances, a city council, the Property Tax Commission, sitting as a state board of equalization and review, must "hear and adjudicate" the appeal. In hearing such appeals, the Commission is given an option to sit as a full board or to use hearing officers, whose recommended findings of fact and conclusions of law are subject to review by the full board.

2. Review of county commissioners' orders adopting schedules, standards, and rules for use in revaluation programs and in appraising certain properties in accordance with "present use" value: When, in a revaluation year, a property owner takes timely appeal from an order of the board of county commissioners adopting a schedule of values, standards, and rules to be used in appraising real property, the Property Tax Commission is required "to hear and adjudicate" the appeal. In any year, if a property owner takes timely appeal from an order of a board of county commissioners adopting a "present use value" schedule for appraising farm, horticultural, and forest properties, the Commission is required to follow the same course. In both instances the Commission must schedule its hearing of such an appeal ahead of pending appeals from the listing and appraisal decisions of county and municipal authorities; otherwise, the Commission's procedure in hearing the appeal is the same as the one

followed when a local listing or valuation decision is appealed. The priority given appeals from orders adopting schedules is designed to facilitate the disposal of controversies arising over the schedules before actual appraisals are made under them. Based upon its findings and conclusions, the Commission may (a) affirm the local board's order for adoption, (b) modify it, or (c) require the local board to revise or modify it according to the Commission's instructions and to present the new order to the Property Tax Commission for approval.

3. Review of Department of Revenue appraisal and assessment of the property of public service companies: The Department of Revenue, discussed below, has the responsibility to appraise the property of public service companies and to allocate the value of that property among local taxing units in certain cases. Although as a matter of government organization the Property Tax Commission is a part of the Department of Revenue, the Tax Commission has "the authority to hear and decide appeals concerning the appraisal of the property of public service companies." The procedure used by the Commission in hearing appeals from appraisal and apportionment decisions by the department differs from procedures used in appeals from decisions of the county boards, but the appellate role of the Commission as a state board of equalization and review is substantially the same in both kinds of hearings.

The Department of Revenue

The Department of Revenue is responsible for all matters of property tax administration at the state level except those appellate duties assigned to the Property Tax Commission. These activities of the Department are financed from the proceeds of the intangibles tax. For practical purposes the Department's duties may be classified under two headings:

1. Appraisal of the property of public service companies: The Department has the duty to appraise certain kinds of property owned by public service companies and then to certify the appraised values to local units of government for taxation. The Machinery Act defines "public service company" to include railroad companies, pipeline companies, gas companies, electric power and electric membership companies, telephone and telegraph companies, bus and motor freight lines, airlines, and "any other company performing a public service that is regulated by the Interstate Commerce Commission, the Federal Communications Commission, the Federal Aviation Agency, or the North Carolina Utilities Commission" except water companies, radio common carrier companies, and cable television and radio or television broadcasting companies. The Department of Revenue is responsible for appraising (a) the rolling stock of bus lines, interstate motor freight carriers (except those whose home office is in North Carolina, who have no terminals outside the state and fewer than two ter-

minals inside the state, and who are not subject to property taxation in another state), and intrastate motor freight carriers operating between two or more terminals in this state; (b) the flight equipment of airlines; and (c) the value of all property *used* (whether owned or leased) by other public service companies in their public service activities. Thus, for the companies named, the only property to be appraised locally is the property of bus lines, motor freight carriers, and airlines *not* specifically mentioned in the preceding sentence. When the Department of Revenue has determined the values to be assigned the property subject to its appraisal, it must certify the appraised values to the appropriate local units (counties, cities, etc.) for taxation. A local unit must assess the valuation certified to it at the figures certified by the department, and it must "tax the assessed valuations at the rate of tax levied against other property subject to taxation therein."

2. Supervision over the valuation and taxation of property by local units: The Department of Revenue is charged to "exercise general and specific supervision over the valuation and taxation of property by counties and municipalities throughout the State." In this role, the Department is charged with providing instruction for local tax officials in regard to their work. It must also maintain a roster of expert appraisers who register with it for employment by counties, and make "continuing studies" of the ratio of appraised value to true value in each county. Since July, 1973, all persons appointed to the office of county tax supervisor must have been certified by the Department of Revenue.

PROPERTY TAX TIMETABLE

While attention has thus far been directed toward the initial steps in the total property tax process, it must be obvious that the reason for listing and valuing property is to insure that it can be taxed. Once the listing and assessing step has been completed, bills must be computed, using the rate of taxation fixed for the new fiscal year by the governing body. At that point the collection process begins. For present purposes, it is important to keep in mind that the entire taxing process is unitary, that a complete cycle must take place each year, and that the tax law is drafted to provide for completing the process each year without overlapping.

Listing and Assessing Timetable

Counties and other local units of government operate on a fiscal year that opens on July 1 and closes on June 30. Funds are appropriated to finance governmental operations for the twelve months of the fiscal year. Revenues are estimated on the basis of what will become available within the fiscal year for which expenditures have been planned. The budgetary process requires office and agency heads to prepare their requests for funds for the coming fiscal year in the last six months of the current fiscal year. Thus, from January 1 until the following June it is likely that all county agencies are estimating their financial needs for the period starting on July 1. With this brief introduction, it will be helpful to examine a typical tax cycle:

July, first Monday. In odd-numbered years the board of county commissioners appoints the county tax supervisor for a two-year term. Appointment at the opening of the fiscal year is desirable for two reasons: the listing and appraising process for the year is usually completed by that date, and the new supervisor has five or six months in which to prepare to handle the listing and appraising work for the coming year. Furthermore, if the membership of the board of county commissioners is changed drastically in a general election, the supervisor will remain in office for six months after the new board comes into office. In that time the experienced supervisor can assist and inform new board members and thereby assure some continuity in tax administration.

December, last week. If list takers are used in the county, this is the latest period in which the county tax supervisor may hold the instruction required for them. It is essential that this instruction be held before the opening of the listing period.

First business day of January. The annual period in which property owners are required to list their property for taxation opens on this day. With an exception noted in the discussion of The Valuation Process (page 103), property listed in this period will be taxed in the coming fiscal year in accordance with ownership and value as of January 1.

Thirtieth day of the listing period. The annual listing period closes on this date unless officially extended by action of the board of county commissioners.

Sixtieth day of the listing period. The annual listing period closes on this date if, in a non-revaluation year, the board of county commissioners has extended it for the permitted thirty days.

Ninetieth day of the listing period. The listing period closes on this date if, in a revaluation year, the board of county commissioners has exercised its option to extend it to this date.

March 31. Extensions of the listing period granted to individual taxpayers by the board of county commissioners may not run later than this date.

April, first Monday. This is the earliest date on which the county board of equalization and review may hold its first meeting for the year. (It may hold its first meeting on any date between the first Monday in April and the first Monday in May.)

April, fourth Monday. If the county board of equalization and review held its first meeting on the first Monday in April, this is the last date on which it is permitted to meet unless it has given proper notice of an extension.

May 1. This is the latest date on which taxpayers may apply to the tax supervisor for the property tax benefits available under G.S. 105-277.1 to elderly people with limited incomes.

May, first Monday. This is the latest date on which the county board of equalization and review may hold its first meeting for the year.

May, fourth Monday. If the county board of equalization and review held its first meeting on the first Monday in May, this is the last date on which it is permitted to meet unless it has given proper notice of an extension.

July 1. This is the first day of the new fiscal year. Even under a proper extension of time, the county board of equalization and review may not sit later than July 1 except, upon request, to review assessment changes for which notices were mailed to taxpayers after June 15.

Collection Timetable

July 1. Counties, cities, and towns must set their tax rates for the fiscal year no later than July 1, the first day of the fiscal year.

September 1. This is the date on which taxes for the fiscal year (which began on the first day of the preceding July) become legally due. The books (tax receipts, etc.) must be delivered to the tax collector by this date.

First or second business day of January. If taxes that became legally due and payable on the first day of the preceding September are paid on the first or second (see the following sentences) business day of January and before February 1, interest of 2 per cent is added to the principal. Interest is added on the *first* business day if the preceding December 31 was a business day and not a holiday. Interest is added on the *second* business day if the preceding December 31 was a Saturday or a Sunday or a holiday.

February 1. If taxes that became legally due and payable on the first day of the preceding September are paid on this date and before March 1, interest of 2¾ per cent is added to the principal.

March 1. If taxes that became legally due and payable on the first day of the preceding September are paid on this date and before April 1, interest of 3½ per cent is added to the principal.

April 1. If taxes that became legally due and payable on the first day of the preceding September are paid on this date and before May 1, interest of 4¼ per cent is added to the principal.

On and after May 1. If taxes that became legally due and payable on the first day of the preceding September are paid at any time during the month of May, interest of 5 per cent is to be added to the principal. Thereafter, interest is to be increased on the first day of each month at the rate of ¾ per cent until taxes not secured by liens against real property are paid. If the taxes are secured by liens against real property, the ¾ per cent interest is to be added on the first day of each month until the tax lien is sold. Thereafter, interest at the rate of 9 per cent per annum is to be added to the amount of the minimum legal bid at the lien sale—that is, principal, plus interest to the date of the lien sale, plus the actual advertising cost, plus the sale fee.

THE LISTING PROCESS

Unfortunately tax officials as well as property owners confuse listing and appraising; what are actually two separate processes are often treated and thought of as a single process. The listing process is equivalent to making an inventory of items of property; the appraisal process is the separate and distinct means by which value is assigned listed items.

Listing Requirements

All taxable property, both real and personal, must be listed for taxation each year, and it is the owner's legal responsibility to list what he owns. Failure to comply with the requirement serves to invoke an automatic penalty: 10 per cent of the amount of tax that will become due for the following fiscal year. Furthermore, if the owner fails to list his property, the county tax officials are required to list it in the owner's name.

Roles of County and City

Property must always be listed with county authorities, and the abstract must indicate the municipality, if any, in which it is subject to taxation. This applies to both real and personal property. The county has no option; it must provide means and personnel for taking these lists. Cities and towns may copy their listings from the county records, or, if they prefer, they may set up their own machinery for securing lists of property subject to municipal taxation. Municipalities that copy their listings from county records are nonetheless responsible for deciding whether specific property should be listed for taxation or granted immunity. This responsibility is independent of county decisions about the same property. Although a city or town may elect to do its own listing, it must accept the valuations fixed by the county authorities unless it lies in more than one county, in which case the statute grants special appraisal authority to the municipality. The requirement that municipalities accept county valuations has led most municipalities to copy county listings rather than make their own.

Where Property Is Taxable — A Matter of Jurisdiction

By its nature, real property is fixed in one location; thus the law logically provides that taxable real property must be listed in "the county in which it is situated." The one exception is the real property subject to appraisal by the Department of Revenue rather than by the counties.

On the other hand, the very essence of personal property is its movability. Thus, determining the place at which it is taxable demands more complicated rules. Stated broadly, if personal property is within the jurisdiction of the state, the Machinery Act makes the owner's North Carolina residence (or lack of residence) the key fact in determining where his tangible personal property is to be listed. *Ordinarily,* the local unit in which the owner resides has the right to tax his tangible personal property, but if the property is held or used at the owner's business premises, it must be taxed there—and, as must not be forgotten, it is essential to determine what constitutes the "residence" of a business firm as well as of an individual.

Duty to List

In general, all taxable real property and all taxable personal property must be listed in the name of the person who owned it on January 1 of the particular year, and it is the owner's duty to list it. The statute requires that "the person whose duty it is to list property for taxation" actually appear before the proper list-taking official and sign an affirmation stating that the listing, "including any accompanying statements, inventories, schedules, and other information, is true and complete." In the case of individual taxpayers residing in the county, only those who are physically or mentally incapable are exempted from this requirement; and in such cases the individual's guardian, authorized agent, "or other person having knowledge of and charged with the care of the person and property of the taxpayer" must appear. Nonresident individuals must sign the affirmation annexed to the abstract, but may elect to list property subject to taxation in the unit by mail or by an authorized agent. Corporations, partnerships, and unincorporated associations must list by the personal appearance and affirmation of a principal officer or full-time employee who has been specially designated an agent for the purpose of listing property by a principal officer. With the approval of the Department of Revenue, the board of commissioners of any county may provide for the general acceptance of listings submitted by mail.

Property Not Subject to Taxation—Requests for Tax Relief

Neither property that is exempt from taxation nor property that is classified and excluded from the tax base is required to be *listed* because neither kind of property is "subject to ad valorem taxation." Owners of such property nonetheless have the burden of demonstrating to tax authorities that their property qualifies for the tax immunity. This is done in the form of a *request* for tax relief, which will normally be filed during the regular listing period. For most of the property currently granted tax immunity by the Machinery Act, requests must be made only once, then revised thereafter when improvements or additions are made or a change in use occurs. However, for some types of exempt and classified business-related property, annual requests must be made. And in the case of government-owned property that is used for a public purpose and certain other types of property, no request at all need be made. As the requests are made or revised, tax officials are expected to review them to ensure that the property in question qualifies for the relief requested. If a request is required but has not been made, the tax supervisor will treat the property involved just as he would property for which a required listing was not made.

Listing Techniques

The tax statutes provide a number of aids or techniques for securing complete lists from property owners, and administrative experience has developed many more.

Aids in Listing Real Property. A complete set of tax maps is the most useful single instrument for the official responsible for seeing that all real property subject to taxation is placed upon the rolls. In the absence of tax maps, assessors find that other maps (recorded and unrecorded) offer valuable clues to acreage and dimension measurement. Ownership records and tract descriptions can be obtained by systematic checking and review of land transfer records. The Machinery Act recognizes the worth of this practice in its broad grant of power to enable county commissioners to regulate deed-recordation procedures. Copies of reports from building and electrical inspectors are helpful in locating new construction, and revaluation programs inevitably identify unlisted parcels and unrecorded improvements. The Machinery Act authorizes any county to adopt, with the Department of Revenue's approval, a "permanent listing system" whereby the tax supervisor is made responsible for listing all real property according to its record ownership as of January 1. Where such a system is used, the taxpayer is relieved of the duty to list his real estate except for the duty to furnish the appropriate list-taking official with certain information concerning (a) buildings and other improvements on the property, and (b) separate rights in the property—"such as mineral, quarry, timber, water power, and other rights"—owned by someone other than the taxpayer.

Aids in Listing Personal Property. The movable nature of personal property, the ease with which it is concealed, and the rapidity with which it is transferred or consumed combine to complicate the listing task. Some states have abandoned personal property taxation entirely; North Carolina, on the other hand, requires that it be taxed and has provided a number of statutory aids for those charged with the responsibility of listing it. Local tax officials have extensive powers to require owners to itemize what they own and make detailed inventories when required. After a business firm's abstract has been received, tax supervisors may, if necessary, require the firm to furnish detailed inventories, balance sheets, and statements of assets and liabilities. The county tax supervisor is allowed to inspect state income and franchise tax returns as a means of obtaining information on property subject to taxation in his unit. Warehousemen, consignees, brokers, and others "having custody of taxable tangible personal property" entrusted to them for any business purpose must furnish the tax supervisor a statement of the name of the owner of the property, a description of the property, its quantity, and the amount of money advanced against it by the custodian. Operators of mobile home parks, marinas, and aircraft storage facilities are required to furnish similar reports of property in their possession. County tax officials have developed a number of helpful techniques, perhaps the most successful of which is the training of list takers or tax office assistants who specialize in listing certain types of properties and businesses. Finally, through the State Department of Motor Vehicles each county may obtain a list of motor vehicles subject to its taxation.

THE VALUATION PROCESS

As noted earlier, property listed for taxation must be valued so that it may be taxed according to its worth; that is the essence of an ad valorem tax. It is true, however, that certain types and categories of property are commonly "listed" in terms of their "value" rather than by "item," and this has undoubtedly contributed to the general confusion. For example, a retail merchant will not list his inventory item by item; instead he will list it in terms of its value. Nevertheless, when his inventory listing is thus accepted, the dollar figure used to describe it becomes its value, and both processes have been effected in a single action.

Statutory Elements of Value

The North Carolina Constitution contains no instructions on how property is to be valued for tax purposes. It simply states that if property is taxed, the General Assembly may divide it into classes, and so long as the taxes are uniform in their application within a class, they will be upheld.

General Rule. While the General Assembly has exercised its power to tax property, until very recently it has been cautious in exercising its power to divide property into classes for differing treatment. Selecting the major varieties of intangible personal property for uniform taxation at low statewide rates, granting a $5,000 exclusion from the tax value of the property of the elderly poor, and appraising farmland according to its use value are the major illustrations of legislative classification in North Carolina. Thus, in broad terms, all other property remains in a single class and, as such, subject to a single valuation standard. That standard reads as follows:

> All property, real and personal, shall as far as practicable be appraised or valued at its true value in money.

The statute then proceeds to state that the expression "true value" means the price at which the property would change hands between a willing and able buyer and a willing seller, "neither being under any compulsion to buy or to sell and both having reasonable knowledge of all the uses to which the property is adapted and for which it is capable of being used" (G.S. 105-283). It should be noted that no distinction is permitted in the standards used in appraising real and personal property; no arbitrary standards will stand up under legal attack; all must be appraised at true value. And responsibility for this work is placed squarely on the counties—through the list takers, the tax supervisor, and the board of county commissioners. Cities and towns must accept the values fixed by the counties in which they lie, unless they happen to lie in more than one county. In this case they are permitted to establish their own valuation procedures, but such procedures must be as complete as those provided for county appraisal and assessment and must afford property owners due process of law.

Use-Value Appraisal of Farmlands. In 1973 the General Assembly enacted the only instance in the Machinery Act of a departure from the market-value standard of tax appraisal. Land used for agricultural, horticultural, or forest purposes, if it meets certain other qualifications, may be taxed on the basis of its "use value" even though it may have a greater market or "true value."[1] The Machinery Act states that "use value" means the price at which the property would change hands between a willing and able buyer and a willing seller, "neither being under any compulsion to buy or to sell, *assuming* that both of them have reasonable knowledge

---

1. N.C. GEN. STAT. §§ 105-277.2 to -277.7. The requirements for qualification—in terms of acreage, income and so forth—are different for agricultural, horticultural, and forest land; but in each case the ownership requirements are the same. The land must be the residence of the owner or it must have belonged to the owner or to members of his family for the seven years preceding the date on which application is made for classification. Furthermore, the land must be owned by a natural person or persons, not by a corporation. For a detailed explanation of the use-value appraisal legislation see *1973 Supplement to the Annotated Machinery Act of 1971,* published by the Institute of Government.

of the *capability of the property to produce income in its present use* and the *present use of the property is its highest and best use*" (G.S. 105-277.2). Market value still plays an important part in the taxation of farmlands, however. The difference between taxes paid on the use value and taxes that would have been paid on the market value—called a "deferred tax"— becomes payable for the preceding five years in a year in which the land ceases to be used for agriculture, horticulture, or forestry purposes: or if title to the land is passed to someone outside the immediate family of the owner. Furthermore, qualifying land is taxed on the basis of its use value only if the owner requests the special treatment annually. Once the owner has requested use-value appraisal, the responsibility to appraise it is placed on the counties as with market-value appraisals.

Time for Appraisal

Each year when personal property is listed for taxation, it must be appraised. The law assumes that the true value of personal property fluctuates rapidly and, therefore, insists that it be looked at annually. This annual appraisal may be a simple process—as for an automobile—or it may be highly complex—as, for example, in selecting an appropriate depreciation rate for unusual industrial machinery. In general, the day as of which the value of property is to be determined is January 1. The only exception is for "the value of inventories and other goods and materials held and used in connection with the . . . business enterprise of a taxpayer whose fiscal year closes at a date other than December 31," which values are to be determined "as of the ending date of the taxpayer's latest completed fiscal year."

Toward real property, however, the North Carolina law adopts a different attitude. It assumes that real property values fluctuate much less rapidly and, accepting some of the practical arguments against too frequent appraisal, requires that all real property be reappraised only every eight years.

Octennial Revaluation Schedule. The applicable statute states that "each county of the State, as of January 1 of the year prescribed in the schedule set out . . . below, and every eighth year thereafter, shall *reappraise* all real property," then divides the counties of the state into groups or "divisions" and establishes a base revaluation year for each division. Table 4-1 sets out a list of the counties, showing the division in which each has been placed and indicating the years as of which it is scheduled to have new real property appraisals become effective. For example, if a county is listed as being in Division VII, it must have new real property assessments ready to go into effect as of January 1, 1978, so that the unit tax rate set in 1978 may be based on the new values.

Table 4-I
Real Property Revaluation Schedule Established in 1971

NOTE: The following tabulation is based on G.S. 105-286(a) (2) and indicates the base years (for a 23-year period) in which each county is scheduled under the Machinery Act of 1971 to have real property revaluations go into effect. Counties that accelerate their positions to a different division, as explained in the text, will have to make necessary adjustments.

County	Division	Real Property Revaluations Become Effective as of January 1 of Years Listed
Alamance	VI	1977, 1985, 1993, etc.
Alexander	VII	1978, 1986, 1994, etc.
Alleghany	IV	1975, 1983, 1991, etc.
Anson	VII	1978, 1986, 1994, etc.
Ashe	III	1974, 1982, 1990, etc.
Avery	I	1972, 1980, 1988, etc.
Beaufort	VII	1978, 1986, 1994, etc.
Bertie	V	1976, 1984, 1992, etc.
Bladen	IV	1975, 1983, 1991, etc.
Brunswick	IV	1975, 1983, 1991, etc.
Buncombe	III	1974, 1982, 1990, etc.
Burke	VIII	1979, 1987, 1995, etc.
Cabarrus	IV	1975, 1983, 1991, etc.
Caldwell	II	1973, 1981, 1989, etc.
Camden	I	1972, 1980, 1988, etc.
Carteret	II	1973, 1981, 1989, etc.
Caswell	V	1976, 1984, 1992, etc.
Catawba	IV	1975, 1983, 1991, etc.
Chatham	VIII	1979, 1987, 1995, etc.
Cherokee	I	1972, 1980, 1988, etc.
Chowan	III	1974, 1982, 1990, etc.
Clay	VII	1978, 1986, 1994, etc.
Cleveland	I	1972, 1980, 1988, etc.
Columbus	II	1973, 1981, 1989, etc.
Craven	VII	1978, 1986, 1994, etc.
Cumberland	I	1972, 1980, 1988, etc.
Currituck	II	1973, 1981, 1989, etc.
Dare	IV	1975, 1983, 1991, etc.
Davidson	II	1973, 1981, 1989, etc.
Davie	VII	1978, 1986, 1994, etc.
Duplin	VII	1978, 1986, 1994, etc.
Durham	VI	1977, 1985, 1993, etc.
Edgecombe	VI	1977, 1985, 1993, etc.
Forsyth	V	1976, 1984, 1992, etc.
Franklin	III	1974, 1982, 1990, etc.
Gaston	II	1973, 1981, 1989, etc.
Gates	VI	1977, 1985, 1993, etc.
Graham	VIII	1979, 1987, 1995, etc.
Granville	VII	1978, 1986, 1994, etc.
Greene	II	1973, 1981, 1989, etc.

County	Division	Real Property Revaluations Become Effective as of January of Years Listed
Guilford	I	1972, 1980, 1988, etc.
Halifax	IV	1975, 1983, 1991, etc.
Harnett	I	1972, 1980, 1988, etc.
Haywood	I	1972, 1980, 1988, etc.
Henderson	III	1974, 1982, 1990, etc.
Hertford	VIII	1979, 1987, 1995, etc.
Hoke	III	1974, 1982, 1990, etc.
Hyde	II	1973, 1981, 1989, etc.
Iredell	V	1976, 1984, 1992, etc.
Jackson	V	1976, 1984, 1992, etc.
Johnston	VIII	1979, 1987, 1995, etc.
Jones	III	1974, 1982, 1990, etc.
Lee	I	1972, 1980, 1988, etc.
Lenoir	II	1973, 1981, 1989, etc.
Lincoln	V	1976, 1984, 1992, etc.
Macon	IV	1975, 1983, 1991, etc.
Madison	II	1973, 1981, 1989, etc.
Martin	VI	1977, 1985, 1993, etc.
McDowell	VIII	1979, 1987, 1995, etc.
Mecklenburg	VIII	1979, 1987, 1995, etc.
Mitchell	VI	1977, 1985, 1993, etc.
Montgomery	I	1972, 1980, 1988, etc.
Moore	VIII	1979, 1987, 1995, etc.
Nash	VI	1977, 1985, 1993, etc.
New Hanover	IV	1975, 1983, 1991, etc.
Northampton	I	1972, 1980, 1988, etc.
Onslow	V	1976, 1984, 1992, etc.
Orange	II	1973, 1981, 1989, etc.
Pamlico	II	1973, 1981, 1989, etc.
Pasquotank	III	1974, 1982, 1990, etc.
Pender	VIII	1979, 1987, 1995, etc.
Perquimans	V	1976, 1984, 1992, etc.
Person	V	1976, 1984, 1992, etc.
Pitt	II	1973, 1981, 1989, etc.
Polk	VI	1977, 1985, 1993, etc.
Randolph	VI	1977, 1985, 1993, etc.
Richmond	II	1973, 1981, 1989, etc.
Robeson	I	1972, 1980, 1988, etc.
Rockingham	VIII	1979, 1987, 1995, etc.
Rowan	III	1974, 1982, 1990, etc.
Rutherford	V	1976, 1984, 1992, etc.
Sampson	VIII	1979, 1987, 1995, etc.
Scotland	VIII	1979, 1987, 1995, etc.
Stanly	VI	1977, 1985, 1993, etc.
Stokes	III	1974, 1982, 1990, etc.
Surry	IV	1975, 1983, 1991, etc.
Swain	II	1973, 1981, 1989, etc.

County	Division	Real Property Revaluations Become Effective as of January 1 of Years Listed
Transylvania	II	1973, 1981, 1989, etc.
Tyrrell	IV	1975, 1983, 1991, etc.
Union	V	1976, 1984, 1992, etc.
Vance	V	1976, 1984, 1992, etc.
Wake	V	1976, 1984, 1992, etc.
Warren	VI	1977, 1985, 1993, etc.
Washington	II	1973, 1981, 1989, etc.
Watauga	VIII	1979, 1987, 1995, etc.
Wayne	VIII	1979, 1987, 1995, etc.
Wilkes	VI	1977, 1985, 1993, etc.
Wilson	V	1976, 1984, 1992, etc.
Yadkin	IV	1975, 1983, 1991, etc.
Yancey	V	1976, 1984, 1992, etc.

Accelerating the Octennial Revaluation. Some counties believe it desirable to revalue real property more frequently than every eight years, and some may desire to hold a revaluation earlier than scheduled in the state law. To meet these feelings, G.S. 105-286(a) (2) provides:

> Any county desiring to conduct a reappraisal of real property earlier than required . . . may do so upon adoption by the board of county commissioners of a resolution so providing. A copy of any such resolution shall be forwarded promptly to the Department of Revenue.

If a county follows this procedure and revalues real property earlier than scheduled, it automatically establishes for itself a new eight-year cycle. For example, if a county scheduled to revalue as of January 1, 1976, decided to revalue as of January 1, 1975, its next scheduled revaluation will be effective in 1983, rather than in 1984, subject to the county's power to revalue *earlier* if it so desires.

Horizontal Adjustments Every Fourth Year. In the fourth year after a general revaluation of all real property under the octennial schedule, each county is required to review the appraisal values that have been assigned to the real property in the county. "If it is determined that the appraised value of all real property or of defined types or categories of real property require . . . adjustment, the tax supervisor shall revise the values accordingly by horizontal adjustments rather than by actual appraisal of individual properties: That is, by uniform application of percentages of increase or reduction to the appraised values of properties within types or categories or within defined geographic areas of the county." Consider, for example, a county in Division I. It held its last revaluation as of January 1, 1972; its next scheduled octennial revaluation will become effective January 1, 1980. Assuming this county does not elect to accelerate its schedule, it is required, as of January 1, 1976, to review the market value figures that were assigned to real property in the county in 1972. It must bring these appraisal figures into line with 1976 market values, not by reappraisal of individual properties but by uniform percentages of raises or reductions applied to property valuations in general according to type, location, or any other reasonable grouping.

Appraisal Techniques

Having established "true value" as the appraisal goal,[2] the North Carolina tax statutes tend to put the county officials "on their own" in developing adequate appraisal techniques. The statutes do, however, contain some indication of what should be considered in determining the value of property. With regard to personal property, the appraiser must consider as to each item (or lot of similar items): replacement cost; sale price of similar property; age; physical condition; productivity; remaining life; obsolescence; economic utility—that is, usability and adaptability for industrial, commercial, or other purposes; and any other factor that may affect its value. Such a statement, although not entirely satisfactory, is valuable as a guide for the appraiser because, in effect, it tells him that he must employ every reasonable standard available in making his decision as to the true value of personal property.

Ordinarily, county appraising officers turn to price lists and catalogues developed for major categories of personal property as guides. Many have shown ingenuity in obtaining price data from trade sources. With useful results, standard depreciation tables have been developed in many counties for the most common types of machinery and equipment. For use in setting standards for the appraisal of household and kitchen furniture, percentage "rules" or "guides" have been found helpful in roughly half the North Carolina counties. Various "listing" techniques already mentioned also produce much information about value; but perhaps the most useful guide to appraising personal property lies in the broad powers of investigation granted appraisers under North Carolina law. These will be summarized later.

The North Carolina property tax law provides fairly explicit instructions for appraising real property in both revaluation years and non-revaluation years. The statutory instructions open with a requirement that a real property appraisal manual be developed for the county in each revaluation. The exact language of the statute on this point is important:

> In preparation for each revaluation of real property . . . it shall be the duty of the tax supervisor to see that:

---

2 Under certain circumstances land used for agricultural, horticultural, or forest purposes may be appraised at both its "true value" and its "use value." See footnote on page 104.

(1) There be developed and compiled uniform schedules of values, standards, and rules to be used in appraising real property in the county. (The schedules of values, standards, and rules shall be prepared in sufficient detail to enable those making appraisals to adhere to them in appraising the kinds of real property commonly found in the county; they shall be:
   a. Prepared *prior to each revaluation* . . .
   b. *In written or printed form;* and
   c. Available for public inspection upon request.) [G.S. 105-317(b) (1).]

The key provisions of this statute are emphasized by the italics. The written or printed schedules of value to be used in appraising real property are to be prepared before the appraisal work begins. When the board of county commissioners approves the schedules, it is required to issue an adoption order and to publish a notice of the order in a newspaper having county-wide circulation, stating in the notice that the schedules, standards, and rules have been adopted and that they are open to examination by any property owner of the county at the office of the tax supervisor for a period of 10 days from the date of publication of the notice. Any property owner who asserts that the schedules do not conform to the "true value" appraisal standard may, within 30 days after the adoption order has been published, file with the clerk of the board of county commissioners and with the Property Tax Commission a notice of appeal and statement of his grounds. "[I]n scheduling the hearing upon such an appeal, the commission shall give it priority" over appeals from listing and valuation decisions. These requirements together insure advance preparation.

In determining the true value of *land,* [the assessor shall] *consider* as to each tract, parcel, or lot separately listed *at least its advantages and disadvantages* as to

location;
zoning;
quality of soil;
water power;
water privileges;
mineral, quarry, or other valuable deposits;
fertility;
adaptability for agricultural, timber producing, commercial, industrial, or other uses;
past income;
probable future income; and
any other factors that may affect its value except growing crops of a seasonal or annual nature. [G.S. 105-317(a) (1).]

The italicized words make clear the statutory intention; the various factors that may affect true value for land must be *considered* in appraising each parcel, but the *weight* to be given each factor is left to the discretion and judgment of the appraiser. It is at this point that sales prices of comparable properties may be of greatest use in testing an appraisal.

In determining the true value of a *building* or other *improvement,* [the assessor shall] consider at least its

location;
type of construction;
age;
replacement cost;
cost;
adaptability for residence, commercial, industrial, or other uses;
past income;
probable future income; and
any other factors that may affect its value. [G.S. 105-317(a) (2).]

The factors listed for consideration encompass the three standard approaches to building appraisal: depreciated replacement cost, sales prices of comparable properties, and capitalization of income.

Inspection of Property Being Appraised. It is commonly assumed that the property owner and the tax official (list taker or supervisor) meet and agree on the listing and valuation to be assigned the items of property owned by the taxpayer. And such is the common practice; yet, the tax supervisor may require a list taker to visit any property subject to taxation in the county. Such a visit is useful for inspecting property being appraised, personal as well as real. But actual inspection of personal property is not mandatory under North Carolina law. On the other hand, when real property is being appraised, the law takes a much sterner attitude:

... [I]t shall be the duty of the tax supervisor to see that ... [e]very lot, parcel, tract, building, structure, and improvement being appraised be actually visited, observed, and appraised by a competent appraiser. ... [G.S. 105-317(b) (2).]

The purpose in visiting and observing each piece of real property being appraised is to establish a minimum inspection requirement. The "competent appraiser" who is charged with making the inspection may be an "expert" employed for the purpose (under G.S. 105-299) or one of the county officials named for that work (under G.S. 105-296).

Preparatory Work. It is generally understood that list takers and assessors, assistants to the tax supervisor, and the tax supervisor himself will appraise *personal* property at the time it is listed during the regular listing period each year. And, in non-revaluation years, it is also understood that *real* property appraisals required in such years can be made during the listing period. Nevertheless, the statute demonstrates that the legislature was aware of the magnitude of the appraisal task, especially in revaluation years. In the section setting up the annual listing period the following language appears:

> Nothing in this section shall be construed to prevent the tax supervisor, list takers, assistants, and experts . . . from conducting preparatory work. . . . [G.S. 105-307.]

This applies to both real and personal property and supports the requirement that a manual be developed *before* real property revaluation as well as the common practice of developing schedules of value and depreciation rates for appraising *personal* property before the listing period opens. But more important, the statute continues as follows: ". . . no final appraisal shall be made before the day as of which the value of property is to be determined. . . ."

Here is the legal backing for elaborate real property revaluation programs. All the appraisal work may be developed and completed before the date on which it goes into effect so long as the appraisals (and assessments) remain tentative until that date. This stipulation is imperative in view of the fact that market value *as of that date* remains the ultimate appraisal standard. The opportunity to correct an appraisal must be retained until January 1 has passed.

Appraisal Personnel

County Officials. In the eyes of the law, the tax supervisor, along with his staff, bears initial responsibility for appraising both real and personal property. Each year, when they begin their sittings as the board of equalization and review, the county commissioners take over the appraisal function from the tax supervisor; and, in limited instances, they are permitted to exercise this function until the opening of the next listing period.

In many larger counties, the tax supervisors have been able to develop appraisal staffs, sometimes with men capable of appraising both real and personal property, sometimes with real property appraisers only. This has meant that the list takers can be relieved of having to appraise real property, and with regard to certain major and more difficult types of personal property, the supervisor and his staff can take over. Unfortunately, many counties remain wholly dependent upon the list takers and the supervisor. The use of professional appraisal firms or "experts" has alleviated this problem with respect to real estate and industrial machinery and equipment, but the need for additional help in obtaining improved personal property appraisal remains acute. Under the provisions of the 1971 Machinery Act, the use of list takers may be dispensed with in any county desiring to do so, and the funds thereby saved can be used to develop more competent appraisal staffs in the tax supervisor's office.

Expert Appraisers. The need for expert assistance in property listing and appraisal was anticipated by the drafters of the North Carolina property tax law, and they turned their attention to the possibility that county tax officials may need to call on individuals with special knowledge in handling the appraisal of property. This possibility is dealt with in two separate sections of the tax law. The first considers the needs of the list takers, the tax supervisor, and the board of equalization and review:

> The board of county commissioners may employ persons having expert knowledge of the value and methods of appraising the kinds of property within the county to *aid and assist* the list takers, the tax supervisor, and the board of equalization and review in determining the true value of the property in the county. [G.S. 105-299(a).]

The second section deals solely with the needs of the members of the board of equalization and review:

> [The board of equalization and review] may appoint committees composed of its own members or other persons to assist it in making investigations necessary to its work. It may also employ expert appraisers in its discretion. [G.S. 105-322 (g) (3)a.]

The word "person" as used in these statutes is defined in the North Carolina tax laws to mean "any individual, trustee, executor, administrator, other fiduciary, corporation, unincorporated association, partnership, sole proprietorship, company, firm, or other legal entity" [G.S. 105-273 (12)]. Moreover, the statutes permit registration of appraisal experts with the Department of Revenue. The Department is required to review the qualifications and work of registered experts, and to advise county authorities with respect to the professional and financial capacity of registrants to comply with the terms of their employment.

Since expert or professional appraisers may be employed by a county for either limited or extended work, what position do those appraisers occupy? What role do they play in the valuation process? On this point the words italicized in the quoted statute—"to aid and assist"—lead to only one reasonable conclusion: Valuations for tax purposes are not to be set by an expert, professional appraiser, or anyone else not plainly required to set tax values as a part of his official duties. Thus, the experts and the professional appraisal firms, no matter how elaborate their organizations or how competent their work, can never do more than aid and assist or give advice to the list takers, the tax supervisor, and the board of equalization and review. In other words, the county officials charged with the duty of appraising and assessing property can take as much or as little of the help or advice given them by an expert as they desire, but they cannot delegate to the expert their legal duty to fix the values.

Record of Valuation

The Department of Revenue has final authority over the form and design of county tax-listing and assessment records, but both that Department and the county officials are firmly bound to insure that a separate property record be prepared for each tract, parcel, lot, or group of contiguous lots. Personal property as well as realty is to be listed so as to show the township and municipality in which it is located. More important, the records must show the assessed values of both real and personal property.

Powers of County Officials in Making Assessments: A Summary

Having charged the tax supervisor, the board of equalization and review, and the board of county commissioners with appraising property at its true value in money, the General Assembly has provided each of those agencies with a set of powers that, diligently used, will do much to provide them with the information they need to make the valuation decision.

1. The law places upon the county commissioners responsibility for selecting as tax supervisor some person with satisfactory experience in appraising real and personal property. If list takers are used, the tax supervisor must instruct them in "methods of securing a complete list of all property in the county and of appraising and assessing, in accordance with law, all property that is to be appraised and assessed. . . ."

This the tax supervisor is to back up by visiting "each list taker at least once during the listing period. . . ." And significantly, the commissioners have authority to employ appraisal experts to aid, advise, and assist county tax officials in "determining the true value of the property in the county."

2. The county tax officials have an independent responsibility to appraise each item of property listed; they may reject the value declared by the taxpayer whenever they believe it to be incorrect. This is a necessary part of the duty to *appraise* that has been assigned to the tax supervisor, the board of equalization and review, and the board of county commissioners.

3. The county tax officials have authority to inspect and investigate

property subject to taxation. This is mandatory in appraising real property; the supervisor may require it of list takers; and the board of equalization and review may perform the work itself or call on others to do so.

4. The county tax authorities have broad powers to require taxpayers to provide them with detailed inventories and itemizations of the property they own.

5. After the abstract has been received and reviewed, the county authorities may, if they need them, require statements of assets and liabilities or balance sheets from business firms whose property is subject to local taxation.

6. Upon proper application to the Department of Revenue, the county tax authorities may, on a confidential basis, examine state income and franchise tax returns filed by persons and firms owning property subject to county taxation. Intelligently used, this is an important aid in obtaining information about value.

7. When property owners and others having information pertinent to the listing and valuation of property subject to taxation in the county fail to supply needed information voluntarily, the county officials have authority to require them to appear and produce needed records. Over the signature of the chairman of the board of county commissioners, both the tax supervisor and the board of equalization and review have the power to subpoena any informed person for examination under oath and to subpoena any relevant books, papers, records, or accounts.

Review and Revisal of Assessments

Initially, property is appraised for taxation by list takers, the tax supervisor, or some member of the supervisor's office staff. Ordinarily, this initial appraisal will have been completed before the first meeting of the board of equalization and review (to be held not earlier than the first Monday in April). In this period, review and revisal jurisdiction rests with the tax supervisor; during its sessions, the board of equalization and review has exclusive review and revisal powers, subject to appeal to the Property Tax Commission; once the board of equalization has adjourned, the review and revisal power then exercisable rests with the board of county commissioners itself, but only in limited situations and in accordance with specific procedural standards. The succeeding portions of this section contain a summary of the review and revisal powers of each agency during the period in which it is authorized to exercise that jurisdiction.

By the Tax Supervisor. Before the first meeting of the board of equalization, for good cause, the tax supervisor may change the valuation placed on *personal* property by the list takers, by members of his staff, or by himself. In revaluation years, the supervisor has the same powers with respect to changing valuations on *real* property that he has in changing valuations on *personal* property. But in non-revaluation years his powers of revisal, as well as those of the board of equalization and review and the board of county commissioners, are severely limited. Those powers are described in a separate section on page 120. In making authorized changes in the valuation of either real or personal property, the supervisor must give notice of the change to the owner before the board of equalization and review holds its first meeting. Once the board of equalization and review begins its sessions for a particular year, the tax supervisor's independent power of revisal is terminated. As indicated below, the county commissioners may delegate to the supervisor certain of their nondiscretionary powers to change valuation records.

By the Board of Equalization and Review. During its brief annual life, the board of equalization and review has both the power and the duty to review and revise valuations. It exercises this responsibility in three situations: (a) on its own motion, as a result of its own review of the valuations; (b) on the request of a property owner concerning the valuation that has been assigned his property; and (c) on the request of one or more property owners relating to the valuation that has been assigned the property of others in the county. The tax supervisor serves as clerk to the board of equalization and, as such, must "be present at all meetings, . . . maintain accurate minutes of the actions of the board, and . . . give to the board such information as he may have or can obtain with respect to the listing and valuation of taxable property in the county." As for *personal* property, the board of equalization has unlimited power to make needed adjustments in **any year**. With regard to *real* property, the board has unlimited power to **make** adjustments in revaluation years, but in non-revaluation years its revisal powers, like the supervisor's, are rather severely restricted. A separate section on page 120 describes those powers.

By the Board of County Commissioners. When the board of equalization and review completes its work and the records have been corrected to reflect the results of that work, the members of the board, or at least a majority of them, must sign a statement at the end of the tax records to the effect that "these tax records constitute the fixed and permanent tax list and assessment roll and record of taxes due" for the current year, subject only to "such changes as may be allowed by law." Once that board has finished its work, "the board of county commissioners shall not authorize any changes to be made" on the tax records except as specified in G.S. 105-325. The changes that the commissioners are empowered to order under that section should be analyzed with care. Five of them are administrative or clerical in nature and involve the exercise of no appraisal discretion; thus, these may be delegated to the tax supervisor:

groups within the public board, agency, or organization; between the board and other public agencies or organizations; between the board and private agencies or organizations; and between the board and the general public. In each case, since public relations policy is determined by board members or agency administrators, the quality of decision is a primary factor in the kind and quality of performance and public acceptance.

Intra-agency Relations. Maximum morale, effort, and coordination within the board or agency are contingent upon the understanding, confidence, and cooperation of all board members and employees. No substitute has been found for taking other board members or agency employees into full confidence and letting them know the reasons underlying any decisions affecting the agency or any of its publics. The normal direction for the passage of information is from the top down; however, where membership of boards or commissions makes all communicants equals, communication may be "vertical" from the chairman or "horizontal" among members. In either case, orderly procedures for such dissemination of information should be established and followed in the interest of both efficiently spreading truth and scotching rumor and falsehood. Full disclosure of plans or facts to intra-agency personnel can be of the utmost importance. A tendency to withhold essential information has been the downfall of many a well-meaning official.

Interagency Liaison. Different public boards, agencies, and organizations have variant responsibilities. Because these responsibilities often require that one board hold the decision-making authority over other groups in matters of finance, budgeting, personnel, or authority, the existence of carefully selected and organized channels of communication is essential to effective liaison and healthy relationships. County commissioners, for example, have to deal with some authority with local boards of education, welfare, health, planning, and zoning, among others. Obviously, under such circumstances, there must be careful evaluation and balancing of needs and availabilities, together with creative thinking on ways and means to achieve desired ends. Even given a most conscientious effort to reconcile differences, challenge and conflict often will arise to handicap relationships. Workable solutions must stem from constant efforts to balance interests and see that divergent programs are worked into a cohesive framework of public law and government.

Liaison with Nongovernmental and Private Groups. Official communication with schools, colleges, civic clubs, commercial organizations, and other groups requires a willingness to give and take, to talk and listen, to exchange views, and to plan and coordinate together in the public interest. Not all ideas submitted by these groups will prove acceptable in the light of the over-all official perspective and understanding. But many a useful idea has come from fertile minds in citizen groups. Conversely, these groups and organizations, properly approached and informed, often become the spearheads for informing and persuading the remainder of the public that an official aim or proposal is desirable.

Liaison with the Mass Communication Media. Publicity and reporting remain at or near the center of useful public relations. Although federal and state agencies usually hire public information officers or set up public relations staffs in recognition of the requirements of public information, most local governments, for reasons of cost or insufficient needs, have no sources of public relations other than the public officials and employees who are directly charged with other primary responsibilities. The result is that each official is, in effect, a potential source of news or publicity. As a consequence, official relationships with the working press are vital to the knowledge and attitudes of the public at large. Cultivation of a relationship of mutual respect and understanding between officials and newsmen usually insures a well-informed public and an opportunity for a healthy functioning of the democratic process. It is well to remember that the press—consisting of newspaper, radio, and TV reporters; editorialists; and analysts—operates under the constitutional guarantee of a free press and that it is often said that the press represents "the people's right to know." It is also essential that any public official be able to correlate his responsibilities and those of his associates with those of the news media. More and more, officials are finding that mutual confidence, built through open and honest dealings, works to the advantage of all.

Liaison with the General Public. Official use of press interviews, news conferences, public statements, radio and television appearances, and even film have become standard means of extending to the widest possible public a helping hand in its quest for greater knowledge and understanding of public affairs. Such concepts as open meetings, available public records, access to proceedings, and frank and full discussion are confined to governments of free people. Others cannot afford them. Except in those cases where law or equally important considerations of public policy forbid, the rule of access deserves the respect of public officials for liaison with the general public.

No public relations program can be successful without the ultimate support of the general public. A government official, board, or agency meets the people not only through print and air lanes but in daily personal contact. To a citizen with a complaint, "red tape" resulting in undue delays or waiting is not a trivial matter. Neither is a want of courtesy on the part of a public employee or a failure to listen attentively or advise circumspectly. A grease spot on a tie or an unmatched pair of socks does not accord with the desired image of a public servant. An evidence of negligence or incompetence, even in the slightest degree, can handicap or impede public recognition of general integrity and competence. Headaches can be avoided by anticipating problems and taking steps to make certain that officials and their environment can pass public inspection. Procedure, appearance, courtesy, efficiency—these are among the touchstones of good over-all public relations. Integrity, rooted in high competence, public purpose, and personal ethics, provides the key to continuing public confidence.

GENERAL PERSPECTIVE ON PUBLIC RELATIONS

Public relations may not seem to compare in significance with the legal, quasi-legal, and formal requirements of office-holding or public service. Yet it involves both the art and science of getting along with people with honor and understanding and without undue pride or abasement. Its purposes provide a free and constant reciprocal flow of useful, reliable, and positive information between government and publics, furthering mutual understanding of public needs and directions and contributing to the maintenance of a climate in which intelligent, informed interaction between officials and publics assures both good government and good citizenship. The aim is not to homogenize thought or action but rather to provide a dynamic process through which the strengths and weaknesses of divergent views may become known and channels may be provided for proper evaluation and effective utilization. Any good public relations program has its base in information, its mortar in liaison, and its structure in analysis and interpretation. It requires direction through quality administration and dissemination through constructive relationships with the mass communication media. The requisite two-way flow of information requires an articulate, informed citizenry in constant communication with a receptive government, which uses governmental and nongovernmental publications together with oral presentations to reach into the minds and hearts of the public.

Public relations is part of everyone and belongs to no one. It tends to gain in application from a positive rather than a negative approach. It must have continuity and point. It cannot be dissociated from the obligations of personal life insofar as it relates to public obligations. Stability, honesty, fairness, competence, vision,—these are among the personal assets that can help to assure effective public relations. And, above all, there is a sense of personal and group responsibility, and attitude of servant rather than oracle, an approach of testing rather than demand, and a follow-through of care and conviction that must undergird any mutuality of meaning, understanding, and cooperation between a public body and a body public. For public relations, in the ultimate, depends upon public trust and confidence—which must be earned.

— *Elmer R. Oettinger*

9 / Records Management

Introduction / 218
Commissioners' Statutory Authority / 219
Disposition of Unneeded Records / 219
Use of Photographic Equipment / 220
Authority of the Division of Archives and History / 221
The *County Records Manual* / 221
Inventory, Repair, and Microfilming of Records / 222
Records-Management Advice and Assistance / 222

9 / RECORDS MANAGEMENT

INTRODUCTION

Taken together, the public offices of the 100 North Carolina counties constitute the largest depository of public records in the state. Much that is essential to public and governmental affairs as well as to commercial and private matters is affected by the variety of records and documents maintained by county officials. While many of the factors relating to creation, maintenance, and disposition of records are regulated directly by law, the attitude, interest, and cooperation of a board of county commissioners can have considerable influence upon the quality and general usefulness of county records. This chapter will summarize briefly some of the statutory duties and responsibilities for records management of the boards of county commissioners and describe some of the services available to counties in this regard.

Generally speaking, the county offices in which most county records are kept are those of the register of deeds, the clerk of the superior court. the local school superintendent, the county accountant, the tax supervisor, the director of social services, and the sheriff, in roughly that order, based upon volume of records. The two major county record custodians are the register of deeds and the superior court clerk. Most of the register's records are instruments and documents that affect the title to real or personal property or that relate to vital statistics (births, deaths, and marriages), while the clerk's records, although extremely varied, relate primarily to the operation of the courts or to matters that affect the administration of estates of deceased persons.

Most counties in recent years have had a great increase in the volume of public records, particularly those records of permanent or long-term value, and this trend seems likely to continue, particularly in the offices of the

---

1. The records of the clerks of superior court occupy an unusual position. Although these records are housed at the county level, they are state records and their management is under the jurisdiction of the Administrative Office of the Courts (see N.C. GEN. STAT. §§ 7A-101 and -343). But with the consent of both the Division of Archives and History and the Administrative Office of the courts, the clerk's records are included in the *County Records Manual, 1970*. The county commissioners' authority over the clerk's records extends only to the designation of office and repository space.

register of deeds and clerk of the superior court. The cost of creating and maintaining these records will therefore continue to present problems.

COMMISSIONERS' STATUTORY AUTHORITY

The statutes that relate to the authority of boards of county commissioners with respect to public records are scattered through the General Statutes, with some overlap among the various sections. The commissioners' authority is generally related to the administration and management of the county's public records and is not particularly related to the operations of any particular county office or officers. No attempt is made here to discuss the various laws that regulate the creation, filing, management, and disposition of records as applied to a specific county official or office. The records procedures in the office of the register of deeds are discussed in the *Guidebook for Registers of Deeds* published by the Institute of Government.

Disposition of Unneeded Records

Perhaps the county commissioners' most important general authority regarding county records concerns the destruction or permanent removal from county offices of records that no longer have any local official use or value. These records are generally one of two types: those that have no official use or value at the county level but have historical value, and those that have neither official nor historical value. With the increasing volume of records in many county offices, the full use of the statutory procedures for disposing of unneeded records takes on great importance. The elimination of records that have no official value has a direct bearing not only on the efficient use and management of valuable public records but also on the cost to the county of maintaining and operating the record custodians' offices. The statutes provide a procedure by which records that fall into either of the above categories may be removed from the county offices to free storage space. When a custodian of county records certifies to his board of commissioners and to the Division of Archives and History of the State Department of Cultural Resources that certain records are of no further use or value for official business of the county, the Division, if it determines that the records are of no value for historical research or reference purposes, may authorize their destruction. If the records are of historical value, it may accept them from the county or request the county to retain custody. In no case, however, should records be destroyed except as authorized by resolution of the board of county commissioners. Records legally may be transferred to the Division of Archives and History without the commissioner's consent, although some officials may prefer to secure their consent first. When records are destroyed or disposed of in accordance with this procedure, the records custodian is protected from any later liability that might otherwise be imposed as a result of the destruction or disposition of public records.

When destruction of records is authorized, they should be in fact destroyed and not permitted to fall into unauthorized hands. There are no provisions in the state laws permitting records to be removed permanently from the custodian's office except for destruction or transfer to the Division of Archives and History. County officials are frequently confronted with requests from individuals or various local historical societies or groups asking that records intended for destruction be instead turned over to them. Since records with any significant historical value may not be destroyed (but may be transferred to the Division), it is not likely that records that legally may be destroyed will be of much value to such unofficial groups, and, as noted, the law does not provide for such disposition. Nonconfidential records probably may be sold to commercial concerns as waste paper if there is reasonable assurance that they will be handled and processed carefully to destroy their identity. Otherwise, destruction should be accomplished by burning, shredding, pulping, burial, or other effective means.

A permanent account should be kept of all records destroyed or disposed of. This may be done by means of a separate record or log maintained by each records custodian, or it may be included in the minutes of the board of county commissioners. Such a record should include a description of the type and quantity in each group destroyed, the inclusive dates covered by the various types of records, and the date and method of destruction. It is also a good plan to maintain a similar log of records transferred to the Division of Archives and History.

Use of Photographic Equipment

The statutory provisions regarding photographic reproduction of county records are now contained in G.S. 153A-436. General statutory consent is given to counties to establish systems for reproducing records in the register of deeds' office and in other county offices photographically. The copies produced, however, must be legible and permanent. These copies, which are to serve as the permanent record copies, must be stored in a fire-resistant file, vault, or similar container. Once a county has established a system for photographing or microphotographing records, the original record may be removed from its regular repository for up to 24 hours for filming, and it may be removed from the county if necessary. A record may be removed from the custody of its regular repository for more than 24 hours only with permission from the county commissioners. The commissioners may authorize removal longer than 24 hours if more time is needed to reproduce the document. Once a photographic copy of a recorded instrument is made pursuant to G.S. 153A-436, the reproduction is a sufficient recording for all purposes.

AUTHORITY OF THE DIVISION OF ARCHIVES AND HISTORY

Although the Division of Archives and History of the Department of Cultural Resources has had some statutory responsibility concerning county records since 1935, only in recent years has its legal authority been broadened and sufficient funds made available to enable the Division to initiate a substantial program of assistance to the counties. The Division's primary interest is in preserving records and documents of historic value, but its services can also be helpful in the management of all local records. These services can generally be divided into three categories of programs: The *County Records Manual;* inventory, repair, and microfilming; and records-management assistance and advice.

The County Records Manual

In accordance with the statutory requirement that the Division of Archives and History administer a statewide program of local records management, the *County Records Manual* was first published in 1960 and was revised and republished in 1962 and 1970 with the help of an advisory committee composed of county officials and members of the Institute of Government staff. This publication's primary purpose is to provide a recommended retention schedule for most types of records to be found in the office of each major record custodian in the several counties. The records are grouped according to the county office or official that has custody, with a recommendation as to how long each type of record should be kept and how it should ultimately be disposed of The *Manual's* purpose is not to compel public officials to destroy records when the time periods indicated in the schedules expire. But the Division of Archives and History will routinely give permission in accordance with the record schedule to custodians who wish to dispose of unneeded records to free storage space for records that have permanent or current temporary value.

Besides the record-retention schedule, the *Manual* contains regulations and instructions concerning county records promulgated by the Division, plus an appendix of state statutes pertinent to county records and the Division's authority and responsibility in this respect. When it was first published and each time it has been revised, the *County Records Manual* has been distributed to chairmen of boards of county commissioners, the affected county offices, and the county attorneys.

Inventory, Repair, and Microfilming of Records

In 1959 the Division of Archives and History began a program of inventory, repair, and microfilming that is perhaps the nation's largest undertaking concerned with permanently preserving valuable local records. Under this program the Division visits the various offices in each county (starting with the oldest), making complete inventories of the records in each office (and preparing a schedule for each similar to those in the *County Records Manual, 1970*), repairing all records of permanent value that need repair, and microfilming all permanent records for security storage. The cost of this program, including the repair service, is borne by the state. In accordance with the requirements of law, however, the commissioners' approval is required before records may be removed from the custodian's office. Copies made from the security microfilm are available to the counties at cost and could be used to replace permanent records destroyed by disaster or other cause. The Division has finished its first visits to each county and has now begun another cycle of filming, starting with the first counties visited, microfilming the permanent records created since the first visit. Some counties are themselves microfilming their permanent records and providing the Division with a microfilm negative of each record.

Records-Management Advice and Assistance

The third aspect of the Division's records-management program involves aid and advice to individual counties or officials in connection with creating, using, maintaining, retaining, preserving, and disposing of official records. Except for the *County Records Manual*, which technically is one aspect of its duty and responsibility, the Division has not done a great deal in this area, primarily because it has lacked both trained personnel and funds. Its help is available, however, in connection with all types of local records problems. The Division may be particularly helpful in such matters as selecting the equipment that may be used in a records-management program. Many kinds of equipment are available for various purposes, and it is important to make certain that a particular machine will render the service needed before a considerable investment of county funds is made.

— *William A. Campbell*

10 / Legal Liabilities of Counties and County Commissioners

Introduction / 224
Torts: The Legal Responsibility of the County for Injuries to
    Private Persons by Public Servants / 225
The Immunity Doctrine / 225
Discretionary Immunity / 227
Governmental Immunity / Proprietary Liability / 227
The Law of Torts / 229
Intentional Torts / 229
Negligence / 231
Strict Liability / 232
Interference with Property Rights / 232
Liability Insurance / 233
Personal Civil Liability of Public Officers and Employees / 234
Policy-Makers / 234
Administrative Officials / 235
Judicial Officials / 235
Employees / 235
Statutory Liabilities of Commissioners / 236
The Civil Rights Act of 1871 / 236
**Criminal Penalties Attached to the
    Office of County Commissioner / 237**
Buying and Selling Offices / 238
Acting As Officer Before Qualifying
    As Such / 238
Failing to Make Reports / 238
Swearing Falsely to Official Reports / 238
Speculating in Claims Against Counties,
    Towns, Cities, and the State / 238
Interference with Audit / 239
Self-Dealing / 239
Motor Vehicles / 239

10 / LEGAL LIABILITIES OF COUNTIES AND COUNTY COMMISSIONERS

INTRODUCTION

The basic control retained by the people over their local governments is political. The single most effective guarantee of honesty, efficiency, and reasonable care in governmental activities is the ballot box. But elections are periodic, and many officers and employees are not elected at all. Furthermore, the electoral process does not guarantee protection to the individual, for the majority rules. For these reasons, the people have not confided absolute power in any of their elected officials. Even on the local level, government is hedged about by the system of checks and balances and separation of powers.

The major check on the exercise of power by local governments in North Carolina is the supervision of the courts. In many respects judicial supervision is inherently limited. Courts do not take the initiative. They respond only to a specific complaint by a citizen (in civil matters) or the state (in criminal cases) that a given state of affairs calls for correction. The extent and content of a particular decision is limited by the facts of the case, for judges are reluctant to stray far from the specific question, often quite narrow, before them. In a state where basic law is largely unwritten except as it may be deduced from the written opinions of judges, confident statements that the law is thus and so often cannot be made.

The nature of relief granted by the courts takes many forms. A county, through its board of commissioners, may be commanded to perform a certain act (by *mandamus);* it may be forbidden to act (by *injunction*); it may be compelled to pay a complainant a sum of money in compensation of loss (by *judgment for damages).* The members of the board in their individual capacity may incur similar liabilities, or they may be convicted of crime for malfeasance in office. This chapter will treat the major judicial remedies available to the citizen to compensate for personal loss caused by governmental action and to insure honesty in public office: the civil liability of the county in tort, civil liability of individual members of the board of commissioners, and the criminal penalties applicable to the office of county commissioner.

TORTS: THE LEGAL RESPONSIBILITY OF THE COUNTY FOR INJURIES TO PRIVATE PERSONS BY PUBLIC SERVANTS

A tort may be defined as a civil wrong for which an individual injured in person or property by the action of another may recover in the courts an award of money from the alleged wrongdoer. The primary purpose of such an award is to shift the loss from the person on whom it falls (the plaintiff) to the person who caused it (the defendant). Additional purposes are punishment and the deterrent effect of tort liability. Not all losses are, or should be, shifted. A plaintiff must be able to show that the facts of his case come within a category legally recognized as justifying a judgment compelling the defendant to pay.

Both legislatures and courts have authority to decide what common types of occurrences justify a shift of loss from plaintiff to defendant. Legislatures have seldom acted in these matters. Most tort litigation is governed by ancient rules brought to the country by English colonists. These rules, the common law of England, were declared by the judges, not Parliament. The first judges in North Carolina built on this English foundation as their successors have built on theirs, for each decision becomes a precedent for the guidance of judges in the future. Thus, for the most part we do not read a statute to determine what is tortious conduct, but examine a series of judicial decisions stretching back to medieval England and make a prediction about what judges are likely to do in the future, based on what they have done in the past.

The Immunity Doctrine

The common law of torts was developed to remedy private wrongs. The extent to which it should apply when a governmental unit is the defendant has been a perplexing problem. The state and federal governments have always enjoyed absolute immunity from any kind of lawsuit, except as they may have, by statute, consented to be sued. When such a statute is passed, it creates a new and distinctive remedy unless it adopts the common law by reference. For example, claims against the State of North Carolina are recognized only for *active negligence,* and are heard by an administrative agency, not the regular courts.

There has been no such unanimity of opinion on the tort liability of local governments. Local governments have never been immune from suits arising from contractual obligations. In regard to torts, the various states have adopted one of three alternatives governing the liability of local governments:
(1) Absolute immunity similar to the state's;
(2) Full liability;
(3) A case-by-case separation of local governmental activities into immune and nonimmune categories.

North Carolina has chosen the third alternative.

The law of torts has been developed over the centuries to compensate loss caused by private activity. It does not necessarily follow that the law can or should be applied to governmental units as if they were private corporations. The stockholders of a private corporation have voluntarily pooled their capital in a joint undertaking for private gain; the residents of a county or city stand in a different relation to their "body politic and corporate." Only recently have courts and legislatures in other states begun to realize that the problem of governmental tort liability involves more than a simple concern with immunity or no. As immunity has been abolished or restricted, the consequences of tort liability have been tried in the balances and often found wanting. If a catastrophe bankrupts a private corporation, it is fair to say that the stockholders took that risk when they invested their capital. Would it be fair to impose on the taxpayers of a city or county a tort judgment far beyond their ability to pay? Should a new activity prove so risky that a small corporation could not afford to undertake it, it is probable that either a larger corporation will, or public demand will allow the smaller corporation to charge prices high enough to cover the risk. But is it better for a local government to decline to offer its residents certain activities rather than risk liability? Is the fear of tort liability likely to improve the level of performance of public activities or curtail them through an excess of caution? These are some of the questions that must be faced and answered by policy-makers at all levels of government when dealing with governmental tort liability.

Although recent legislation in California and New York indicates a growing concern about whether special rules for governmental tort liability are desirable, the general rule is that where liability is imposed at all, the rules governing private litigation apply. In North Carolina a tort suit against a local government or a public official differs from a suit against a private individual only in the initial issue of whether the defendant may be sued at all.

Discretionary Immunity

Judicial decisions carry greater authority than any other type except acts of the legislature, and even statutes may be declared unconstitutional by the courts. As with all public officers, however, a judge's ultimate responsibility is to the people. When the people, acting in constitutional conventions or legislatures, grant power and authority to local governments, to what extent can or should the judges interfere? To illustrate, consider the case of *Hill v. Charlotte*. For many years Charlotte had had an ordinance prohibiting the use of fireworks within the city. The aldermen suspended the ordinance from Christmas to New Year's Day, 1873, to allow public celebration of the holiday season. On the evening of January 1 a group of boys set off Roman candles in the street outside Hill's warehouse. One candle fell on the roof, setting fire to the building, which was destroyed. Hill sued the city for the value of his warehouse. He claimed that the unreasonable action of the aldermen in repealing the anti-fireworks ordinance had caused his loss, and that he was entitled to compensation.

To allow Hill's claim, the Court would have had to determine that the passage and enforcement of an anti-fireworks ordinance was essential to the public welfare. But the courts are not legislatures; they were not constituted by the people to pass ordinances. Had Hill sued the boys, no question of the propriety of judicial action would have arisen, since the courts share with the legislature the power to regulate private conduct. But judicial review of the ordinance-making power in a tort context would be an unwarranted usurpation of a basic governmental function confided by the Constitution and statutes in other public officers. *The courts will not entertain a tort suit against a governmental unit based on the exercise or nonexercise of a discretionary power.*

The doctrine of "discretionary immunity" has been applied to deny recovery for damages caused by the passage of a discriminatory ordinance, failure to enforce an ordinance, failure to condemn and remove a public nuisance, wrongful refusal to issue a building permit, and negligence in granting a franchise.

Governmental Immunity / Proprietary Liability

Local government units may not be sued in tort for the manner in which a "governmental" function is carried on. They will be held fully liable for torts committed in the course of conducting "proprietary" activities. The source of confusion in local government tort liability has been the failure of the courts in North Carolina and elsewhere to formulate definitions of "governmental" and "proprietary" that will either explain their past decisions or aid in predicting future decisions.

The distinction between "proprietary" and "governmental" activities was introduced into North Carolina law by the case of *Moffitt v. Asheville,* decided in 1889. Before that time cities were treated as though they were private corporations, and they were subject to the same liabilities. Because nearly all their activities in the nineteenth century were undertaken in the furtherance of state policies, counties were accorded a legal status virtually identical with that of the state.

While writing the opinion in *Moffitt,* Justice Avery discovered the immunity doctrine, based on an 1842 New York decision and its progeny, in Professor Dillon's treatise on municipal corporations. Even though Professor Dillon devoted two pages to refuting the theoretical basis of municipal tort immunity, the Court adopted it in these words:

> The liability of cities and towns for the negligence of their officers or agents, depends upon the nature of the power that the corporation is exercising, when the damage complained of is sustained....
>
> When such municipal corporations are acting ... in their ministerial or corporate character in the management of property for their own advantage, they are impliedly liable for damage caused by the negligence of officers or agents, subject to their control, although they may be engaged in some work that will enure to the general benefit of the municipality....
>
> On the other hand, where a city or town in [*sic*] exercising a judicial, discretionary or legislative authority, conferred by its charter, or is discharging a duty, imposed solely for the benefit of the public, it incurs no liability for the negligence of its officers ... unless some statute (expressly or by necessary implication) subjects the corporation to a pecuniary responsibility for such negligence.

Subsequent decisions refined the distinction in powers to "governmental," "proprietary," and "discretionary." Included in "governmental" powers are such core activities as the court system, law enforcement, public records, the maintenance of public buildings, and the passage and enforcement of regulations for the better health, safety, and welfare of the people. "Proprietary" activities include public enterprises—activities that bear a close resemblance to, or are in actual competition with, private enterprise. The classic examples are city electric power plants, water companies, markets, and airports. Confusion has been the result of the doubtful cases. Even though garbage collection is often a private enterprise, and may even be done under a fee system, it is "governmental." A public housing authority may be created principally to provide for the general health, safety, and welfare through elimination of substandard housing, but it is "proprietary." Public hospitals often compete with private ones and charge fees intended to cover the costs of their services, yet they are "governmental." Supply of electric power to private consumers is "proprietary," but supply of the same power to street lights is "governmental."

LEGAL LIABILITIES 229

Until 1949 it could be argued that counties could never be subjected to tort liability since they were not empowered to engage in any but "governmental" activities, being mere political subdivisions of the state and not "corporations." In *Rhodes v. Asheville* the Court said:

> We fully concur in the view that a county, when acting in its governmental capacity, cannot be sued unless express authority to do so has been granted by statute.... Ordinarily a county does not undertake to perform functions except in a governmental capacity. But when it undertakes with legislative sanction, to perform an activity which is proprietary or corporate in character, such a county may be liable in tort to the same extent as a city or town would be if engaged in the same activity.

Since the Court, in recent years, has given up any serious attempt to define the limits between a city's functioning as a political entity and its enterprisory activities in the abstract, it is probable that the Court has, in the *Rhodes* opinion, discarded attempted distinctions between cities and counties as concerns tort liability. The distinction was based on an obsolete assumption: that counties function *only* as political bodies while cities undertake public enterprises. The quoted portion of the *Rhodes* opinion clearly assumes the modern fact that counties more and more are performing services formerly rendered by cities or not at all.

A ready formula to solve undecided questions of local government tort liability is impossible. Contemporary decisions in North Carolina and those states that still retain governmental immunity are being made not on legal theory but on the basis of precedent and broad considerations of sound governmental policy. Table 10-I summarizes the present liability status of local government activities in North Carolina.

THE LAW OF TORTS

Once the question of immunity is resolved against the local government in a tort action, the Court will apply general tort rules to the case. The existing body of private tort law falls into three broad divisions: the intentional torts, negligence, and strict liability. There are North Carolina decisions applying all three to local governments.

Intentional Torts

The oldest torts all involve intentional acts causing damage to another done without a valid excuse. The most common ones are assault, battery, false imprisonment, false arrest, malicious prosecution, trespass to land, trover and conversion (the unauthorized taking of another's personal property), deceit or fraud, and defamation (libel and slander). Some of these are of such serious consequences that they are also crimes. For exam-

Table 10-I
Immunity Decisions

Activity	Immunity	Case Citation
Airports	No	230 N.C. 134 (1949)
		168 N.C. 608 (1915)
City Dump and Incinerator	Yes	189 N.C. 469 (1925)
City Jail	Yes	103 N.C. 237 (1889)
Electric Power for Lighting Streets	Yes	239 N.C. 401 (1954)
Electric Power for Private Consumption	No	140 N.C. 506 (1906)
Fire Protection	Yes	130 N.C. 76 (1902)
		208 N.C. 729 (1935)
Garbage and Trash Collection	Yes	183 N.C. 630 (1922)
Hospitals	Yes	220 F.2d 716 (4th Cir. 1955)[a]
Law Enforcement	Yes	127 N.C. 146 (1900)
Maintenance and Repair of Traffic Signals	Yes	214 N.C. 737 (1939)
Mosquito Control	Yes	253 N.C. 732 (1961)
Parks	No	246 N.C. 469 (1957)[b]
Public Housing	No	249 N.C. 328 (1959)
Public Market	No	198 N.C. 180 (1930)
Streets and Sidewalks	No	90 N.C. 421 (1884)
Water Supply for Extinguishing Fires	Yes	181 N.C. 383 (1921)
Water Supply for Private Consumption	No	181 N.C. 88 (1921)

a Federal cases are not binding authority in state courts when deciding issues of state law.
b Probable liability.

ple, criminal and civil assault are virtually identical in North Carolina. Conversion may amount to the crime of larceny or one of its close relatives. Trespass may also amount to burglary, breaking and entering, or a breach of the peace, depending on the circumstances.

Since intent to injure is an essential element of the intentional torts, the courts have been reluctant to hold a governmental employer liable for intentional torts of its employees. Almost never does an employer expressly authorize his employee to damage another intentionally. In extreme cases, *implied* authority will be found.

The leading North Carolina case applying these rules to a local government is *Munick v. Durham*. Munick, an elderly gentleman, went to the office of the city water company to pay his water bill. He gave the clerk four one-dollar bills and fifty pennies, wrapped in a coin sleeve. The clerk accepted the money and gave him a receipt, and Munick prepared to leave. At this point, the superintendent of the water division came into the office, asked the clerk who had given her fifty pennies, threw the money on the floor, and ordered Munick to pick it up. Munick declined. The superintendent then locked the door and violently assaulted him. Munick sued the City of Durham for the assault of its employee. The city was held liable on the ground that a water company is a "proprietary" activity.

Forty years later the Supreme Court decided *McDonald v. Carper*. The plaintiff in that case alleged that she had been charged with embezzlement by the city manager and subjected to criminal prosecution without just cause and for improper motives. The city was held not liable since the city manager is charged with the duty of supervising city employees, a "governmental" function, which includes guarding against embezzlement.

Negligence

The second division of tort law is negligence. It is by far the most common type of tort litigation. One is under a duty to act at all times as would a reasonably prudent man under the same or similar circumstances. Thus, if (1) one's conduct falls below that of the reasonably prudent man, (2) causing injury to another (3) that is proximately rather than remotely the result of the conduct, (4) and it can be said in retrospect that some kind of injury was reasonably foreseeable in the event of such conduct, a case of actionable negligence has occurred. The negligent person must compensate his victim for the loss unless he can show other facts that the law will recognize as excusing his conduct or barring the victim's remedy.

The question whether any given set of facts constitutes negligence is usually left to the jury. In most other tort cases, the jury decides only disputed issues of fact: did the defendant actually assault the plaintiff, and if so how much damage has the latter suffered? In the negligence case, the jury measures the defendant's conduct against that of a purely fictional character: the reasonably prudent man. The judge will not tell the jury what the "reasonable man" would have done; this is for the jury to determine. Thus, in negligence cases the jury becomes both judge and jury, for it tailors the law to fit the particular case. Typically, the decisions of appellate courts in negligence cases do not tell us what is or is not negligent conduct; they decide only whether a fair-minded jury could reasonably determine that the facts of this particular case show negligent conduct.

The range of possible situations in which government employees might be found negligent is as broad as the thousands of individual acts of those employees in the day-to-day performance of their duties. It might be negligence for the driver of a garbage truck to back over a child playing in a driveway; for the courthouse janitor to allow a slippery spot of grease to remain on a hall floor; for a mosquito-fogging machine to obscure the highway without warning. The examples are infinite.

Strict Liability

The third major division of torts is the doctrine of strict liability. It is not properly a tort concept at all, for it operates on the insurance principle. Certain activities are held to be so inherently dangerous that persons who perform them must bear responsibility for resulting damage regardless of the extent of precautions against it. The most usual example is damage caused by blasting operations. In a case involving the construction of a city water and sewer line, North Carolina adopted the rule of the majority of the states that damage done by the concussion of the blast alone is recoverable. (A few states still require some actual physical invasion of the plaintiff's property, such as by falling rocks.) The Court held it not necessary to decide whether a city would enjoy immunity from ordinary tort liability in the construction rather than the operation of a sewer system, since blasting invokes the doctrine of strict liability. Had the Court proceeded to apply a pure strict liability theory, it could be said with certainty that both property damage and personal injuries would be compensable when local government engages in blasting. However, the Court preferred to place the decision on the ground of inverse condemnation: the taking of property without formal condemnation proceedings and without just compensation.

Interference with Property Rights

The doctrine of "inverse condemnation" is typically used by courts to allow recovery for property damage under circumstances in which the governmental unit would be immune from suit for personal injury. The law has always protected property rights against governmental action to a greater extent than injuries to the physical well-being of the individual. Whether the legal basis should be in tort or purely constitutional has been the subject of much debate and confusion in the cases. Because injury to property rights by governmental action cannot be analyzed as a tort consistently with the immunity rules applicable to personal injury, a separate discussion of injury to property rights is in order. The theoretical distinction is largely a lawyer's quibble, since the practical results are virtually the same.

The federal Constitution through the Fifth and Fourteenth Amendments forbids both the state and federal governments to take life, liberty, or property without "due process of law." When a taking of property is involved, due process means the payment of just compensation. The usual example of governmental taking of property is the power of eminent domain, in which title to the property is vested in the government by condemnation in a formal legal proceeding. But property may be "taken" in other ways.

For centuries the common law has recognized the tort of nuisance. A nuisance is any use of land by one person in such a manner that his neighbor's use and enjoyment of *his* land is substantially impaired. It is well established that a local government has no more right to maintain a nuisance than an individual, and is equally liable for the resulting interference. Authorized acts of a governmental character that create a nuisance are regarded as an appropriation of property to the extent of the injury inflicted. The most fertile field of litigation in the nuisance-taking area has been the operation of a sewerage system. Typically, the cases have involved a city that has been discharging sewage into a stream that overflows onto property downstream, rendering it unfit for its intended use. In recent years the mere fact that offensive odors make the property undesirable for residential purposes has rendered the city liable for decrease in land value. A peculiar case from High Point allowed recovery on allegation that the glaring silver color of a water tank constructed in a residential area made the property less valuable.

Although it is the usual theory, nuisance is not a necessary element for recovery for damage to property. When squarely confronted by a claim of interference with property rights, the Court almost always grants recovery even though there is not a nuisance. In *Prichard v. Morganton* officials of the city and county burned a private house in the mistaken belief that it was infested with smallpox and that they had authority to do so. The Court found they had no such authority. The owner lost her suit because she sued in trespass, a tort. But the Supreme Court c early intimated that had she sued for an unauthorized taking of property without compensation, she could have recovered.

The mere fact that land values are depressed by governmental action is not enough to entitle the landowner to recover compensation. There must be in addition some element of unreasonableness, or other facts that make the governmental action "wrongful."

LIABILITY INSURANCE

In 1955 the General Assembly empowered county commissioners to waive the county's tort immunity by the purchase of liability insurance. The waiver is only to the extent of indemnification by the insurance purchased. While cities may waive immunity only in connection with the operation of motor vehicles, the county authorization is general. Boards of education have been given similar authority. Bearing in mind the status of the law, boards of commissioners would be well advised to review all activities presently carried on by their county, and, in consultation with their county attorney, determine whether those activities are currently immune from tort liability.

Commissioners should also give serious thought to whether sound principles of government justify retention of tort immunity for any county activity. The clear trend of decision in other states has been toward complete abolition of the immunity either by judicial decision or statute.

Some of the advantages of the purchase of insurance are:
(1) Investigation of the claim by the insurance companies' adjusters;
(2) Out-of-court settlement of adjustment of the claim within policy limits if there is liability as determined by the investigation;
(3) Defense of the suit by attorneys hired and paid for by the insurance company;
(4) Payment of the judgment by the insurance company (There will never be a deficiency judgment against the county in an activity otherwise immune since by statute the immunity is waived only to the extent of the insurance proceeds.);
(5) Prosecution of appeal and representation of the county on appeal by the company's attorneys;
(6) Payment of all costs of court and interest on judgment by the insurance company.

PERSONAL CIVIL LIABILITY OF PUBLIC OFFICERS AND EMPLOYEES

In every tort suit the plaintiff contends that some *person* caused him injury in person or property. The tortious conduct may have been active or passive—the tortfeasor may have done those things he ought not to have done or left undone those things he ought to have done. Further, he alone may be responsible, or another person may be vicariously liable (i.e., legally liable for his conduct because of their relationship). A city or county as a "body politic and corporate" is a *legal* person, but it can act only through natural persons. A city or county is sued in tort because some natural person has committed a tortious act within the course of his employment as an officer or employee of the "body politic and corporate." But the public officer or employee does not cease to function as an individual when he performs public duties. His actions may result in liability of both himself and the governmental unit with which he is associated. In other situations the governmental unit may not be responsible for his acts, leaving him to bear the liability personally and alone. Finally, it is possible that the governmental unit may be liable when the individual causing the damage is not personally responsible. The rules of personal liability depend primarily on the nature of the individual's association with the governmental unit.

Policy-Makers

The personal liability of the members of governing boards and other policy-makers (such as administrative personnel with delegated discretionary authority) is closely interwoven with the discretionary immunity of the governmental unit itself previously discussed. The individual members of a board of county commissioners, a board of education, or a city council cannot be held civilly liable for the manner in which they in good faith perform or fail to perform duties placed on them by law as members of a governing board, just as the unit itself is not liable for their dereliction of duty. *They will be liable as individuals if they exercise their powers as public officers for corrupt or malicious motives,* but in such an event the unit will not be responsible for their actions.

Administrative Officials

The Court draws a distinction between a public officer charged with discretionary powers and one whose powers are "merely ministerial." In the latter category are most of the acts performed by such officials as the register of deeds, the clerk of the superior court, and similar officers. A public official may be held civilly liable for failure to perform ministerial duties properly. Thus, the register of deeds may be personally liable for negligence in recording documents. The line between "discretionary powers" and "ministerial duties" is often difficult to draw. The court has held that the district engineer of the Department of Transportation exercises discretionary powers while his employees perform ministerial tasks.

Judicial Officials

At the common law, a judicial officer could not be held civilly liable for any official act, even though his motives were corrupt or malicious. This rule is followed in North Carolina. Thus, a county coroner may not be sued for refusal to hold an inquest even though the plaintiff alleges his motives for refusing were to protect one of his personal employees from possible prosecution for manslaughter. For the purposes of the rule, law enforcement officers are not "judicial" officers in North Carolina.

Employees

Those who are merely employed by a city or county, subject to the direction and control of a superior, and not charged with discretion in the performance of their delegated duties, enjoy no personal immunity from the tort consequences of their acts. In *Miller v. Jones* the plaintiff alleged that the defendants, employees of the State Highway Commission, drove a road sweeper with an attached blower past his general store without giving warning. Dust and grime blown through the open doors and windows of the store ruined most of his merchandise. Justice Seawell held that

> Immunity has never been extended to a mere employee of a governmental agency . . . although employed upon public works, since

the compelling reasons for the nonliability of a public officer, clothed with discretion, are entirely absent. Of course, a mere employee doing a mechanical job, as were the defendants here, must exercise some sort of judgment in plying his shovel or driving his truck—but he is in no sense invested with a discretion which attends a public officer in the discharge of public or governmental duties, not ministerial in their character.... The mere fact that a person charged with negligence is an employee of others to whom immunity from liability is extended on grounds that public policy does not thereby excuse him from liability for negligence in the manner in which his duties are performed, or for performing a lawful act in an unlawful manner.

Statutory Liabilities of Commissioners

Commissioners are made expressly liable to civil suit by statute in only three instances: directing an illegal payment of county funds, failure to require a sufficient bond of county officers required to be bonded, and unauthorized remission of taxes. The Local Government Budget and Fiscal Control Act permits the board of commissioners to direct the payment of a bill or claim that has been disallowed by the county finance officer, but provides that the members of the board who vote to do so are personally liable for the amount disbursed if payment results in a violation of any part of the budget and fiscal control or bond laws. Commissioners may be liable as a surety on official bonds under G.S. 109-13, which provides:

> Every commissioner who approves an official bond, which he knows to be, or which by reasonable diligence he could have discovered to have been, insufficient in the penal sum, or in the security thereof, shall be liable as if he were a surety thereto, and may be sued accordingly by any person having a cause of action on said bond.

Strangely enough, there is no civil liability for failure to require any bond at all. This is made a misdemeanor, and the Court has held that attachment of a criminal penalty by implication provides that there shall be no civil cause of action. The Machinery Act prohibits a board of commissioners from releasing or compromising any property taxes owed by a taxpayer except as expressly permitted by law. It then provides that any member of the board who votes to release or compromise a tax claim in violation of law is personally liable for the tax on the suit of any resident of the county.

The Civil Rights Act of 1871

The federal Civil Rights Act of 1871 provides that

> Every person who, under color of any statute, ordinance, regulation, custom or usage of any State or Territory, subjects or causes to be subjected any citizen of the United States or other person within the

jurisdiction thereof to the deprivation of any rights, privileges or immunities secured by the constitution and laws shall be liable to the party injured in an action at law, suit in equity or other proper proceeding for redress.

Jurisdiction over this statute lies in the federal district courts, which can grant either equitable relief (usually in the form of an injunction) or an award of money damages to the person who brings the suit. The Civil Rights Act of 1871 lay dormant for many years, but it has recently been rediscovered and has become a fertile field for litigation, especially in the areas of public education and law enforcement. With regard to members of the board of county commissioners, its greatest potential use lies in personnel policies and practices that can be said to discriminate on the basis of race. A discussion of the effect of the statute on the individual liability of school board members and school administration appears in the *School Law Bulletin,* Vol. IV, No. 4, published by the Institute of Government.

CRIMINAL PENALTIES ATTACHED TO THE OFFICE OF COUNTY COMMISSIONER

The usual method employed to insure good-faith discharge of the duties of office by county commissioners is the drastic remedy of criminal conviction and, in some cases, forfeiture of office. The statutes are generally quite old and have seldom been invoked in recent years.

G.S. 14-230 provides that:

> If any . . . county commissioner . . . shall willfully omit, neglect or refuse to discharge any of the duties of his office, for default whereof it is not elsewhere provided that he shall be indicted, he shall be guilty of a misdemeanor. If it shall be proved that such officer, after his qualification, willfully and corruptly omitted, neglected or refused to discharge any of the duties of his office, or willfully and corruptly violated his oath of office according to the true intent and meaning thereof, such officer shall be guilty of misbehaviour in office, and shall be punished by removal therefrom under the sentence of the court as a part of the punishment for the offense, and shall also be fined or imprisoned in the discretion of the court

The element of willfulness or intent required by G.S. 14-230 is not necessarily a conscious evil intent. It may be inferred from extreme carelessness. Furthermore, the law presumes that a failure to discharge the duties of office is willful, and it is incumbent on the accused commissioner to prove otherwise. The statute does not speak of the corrupt *exercise* of powers of office. Corrupt or malicious motives in the exercise of a *lawful* power do not convert that exercise into either a crime or a tort.

Buying and Selling Offices

Simony, the buying and selling of public office, has been a crime in England since 1552. North Carolina has adopted the English statute unchanged. Violation is a misdemeanor and results in forfeiture of the office.

Acting As Officer Before Qualifying As Such

If an elected or appointed officer presumes to enter on the duties of his office before taking the oath or giving bond (if required), he forfeits the office and is guilty of a misdemeanor.

Failing to Make Reports

It is a misdemeanor for any county officer to refuse or neglect to file or publish any report or statement required by law, or to fail or refuse to deliver to his successor the papers, books, and money of the office. Honesty of purpose is not a full defense to a charge of violating this section, since there may be neglect without corruption. It is not necessary that there be any injurious result to any individual. But an officer will not be held liable for obeying an unconstitutional statute.

Swearing Falsely to Official Reports

It is a misdemeanor willfully to swear falsely to any report concerning county, state, or school revenue required by law to be filed.

Speculating in Claims Against Counties, Towns, Cities, and the State

> If any [county officer] shall engage in the purchasing of any county, city, town, or state claim, including teacher's salary voucher, at a less price than its full and true value or at any rate of discount thereon, or be interested in any speculation on any such claim, he shall be guilty of a misdemeanor and shall be fined or imprisoned, and shall be liable to removal from office at the discretion of the court.

This is an old statute, passed in 1868, intended to correct the then widespread abuse of speculating in the depressed prewar bonds of the state and its subdivisions. It probably does not make unlawful the purchase of state, city, or county bonds at their current market value when the issuing unit is not in default or the bonds are not depressed for some other reason. However, county commissioners should be wary of purchasing any state or municipal security at a bargain with intent to speculate on its later advance in value. The firm state of the national and state economy at this time makes the statute largely a dead letter, but a depression could revive it. There is an almost identical statute codified in G.S. 115-96 limited to speculating in the salary vouchers of school personnel.

Interference with Audit

G.S. 159-34 makes it a misdemeanor, punishable by a fine of up to $1,000 or imprisonment for up to one year, or both, for any member of the board of commissioners or other county officer or employee to impede or interfere with the annual independent audit of the county's books required by the Local Government Budget and Fiscal Control Act.

Self-Dealing

If any person, appointed or elected a commissioner or director to discharge any trust wherein the State or any county, city or town may be in any manner interested, shall become an undertaker, or make any contract for his own benefit, under such authority, or be in any manner concerned or interested in making such contract, or in the profits thereof, either privately or openly, singly or jointly with another, he shall be guilty of a misdemeanor. Provided, that this section shall not apply to public officials transacting business with banks or banking institutions in regular course of business: Provided further, that such undertaking or contracting shall be authorized by said governing board. [G.S. 14-234.]

This is an extremely important section. A county commissioner may not contract with himself, or with any firm or corporation in which he has an interest, in the name of the county. The only exception is in dealing with a bank, and then only when each transaction is specifically authorized by the full board. In the words of the Supreme Court, the General Assembly in adopting this section made the condemnation of the transactions embraced within its terms a part of the public policy of the state, so as to remove from public officials the temptation to take advantage of their official positions to "feather their own nests" by letting to themselves or to firms or corporations in which they are interested contracts for services, materials, supplies, or the like. Not only are such contracts void, but also the offending member may not recover the reasonable value of any benefits he may have conferred on the county. The fact that the transaction may have been open, fair, and free from any corrupt intent is irrelevant. However, the fact that a member of the board is merely an *employee* of one of the contracting parties does *not* invoke the statute.

Motor Vehicles

The General Assembly has closely regulated the purchase and use of motor vehicles by the state and local governments. Violation of any of the following statutes is a misdemeanor, punishable by a fine of not less than $100 or more than $1,000 or imprisonment in the discretion of the court.

G.S. 14-247. *Private use of publicly owned vehicle.* It shall be unlawful for any officer, agent or employee of . . . any county . . . to use for any private purpose whatsoever any motor vehicle of any type or description whatsoever, belonging to the . . . county. . . .

G.S. 14-248. *Obtaining repairs and supplies for private vehicles at expense of State.* It shall be unlawful for any officer, agent or employee to have any privately owned motor vehicle repaired at any garage belonging to the State or to any county, or any institution of the State, or to use any tires, oils, gasoline or other accessories purchased by the State, or any county, or any institution or agency of the State, in or on any such private car.

G.S. 14-249. *Limitation of amount expended for vehicle.* It shall be unlawful for any officer, agent, employee or department of the State of North Carolina, or of any county, or of any institution or agency of the State, to expend from the public treasury an amount in excess of two thousand five hundred dollars ($2,500) for any motor vehicle other than motor trucks, except upon the approval of the Governor and Council of State . . . . Provided further, that the limitation prescribed by this section shall not be applicable to the purchase of any motor vehicle by any county, city or town in this State, where such motor vehicle is purchased in accordance with the provisions of article 8 of chapter 143 of the General Statutes of North Carolina.

The effect of the section is to require competitive bids for the purchase of an automobile that costs more than $2,500, pursuant to procedures set out in G.S. 143-129.

G.S. 14-250. *Publicly owned vehicle to be marked.* It shall be the duty of the executive head of every department of the State government, and of any county, or of any institution or agency of the State, to have painted on every motor vehicle owned by the State, or by any county, or by any institution or agency of the State, a statement with letters of not less than three inches in height, that such car belongs to the State or to some county, or institution or agency of the State, and that such car is "For Official Use Only." Provided, however, that no automobile used by any officer or official in any county in the State for the purpose of transporting, apprehending or arresting persons charged with violations of the laws of the State of North Carolina, shall be required to be lettered. . . . Provided further, that in lieu of the above method of marking vehicles owned by any county, it shall be deemed a compliance with the law if such vehicles have painted or affixed on the side thereof a circle of not less than eight inches in diameter showing a replica of the seal of such county.

— *Joseph S. Ferrell*

11 / The Courts

The Appellate Division / 242
Supreme Court / 242
Court of Appeals / 242
The Superior Court Division / 243
Organization / 243
Judges / 245
Jurisdiction / 247
District Attorneys / 247
Clerks of Superior Court / 247
The District Court Division / 248
Organization / 248
Judges / 249
Magistrates / 249
Record-Keeping / 249
Jurisdiction / 250
Removal of Judges / 252
Reporters / 252
Juries / 253
Appeals / 253
Rules of Procedure / 253
Expenses of the Judicial Department / 253
Uniform Costs and Fees / 254
Fines and Forfeitures / 255
Representation of Indigents / The Public Defender / 255
Administrative Office of the Courts / 256
Selection of Jurors / 256
The North Carolina Courts Commission / 257

11 / THE COURTS

In 1962 the people of North Carolina adopted a new Judicial Article for the State Constitution. The new article (IV), amended in 1965 to authorize an intermediate appellate court, calls for a unified statewide and state-operated General Court of Justice (see the chart on page 244) consisting of three divisions: the Appellate Division, the Superior Court Division, and the District Court Division. The previously existing court system was changed in many respects. On the appellate, or highest, level the State Supreme Court has been joined by an intermediate Court of Appeals, activated in 1967 and designed to relieve the Supreme Court of some of its caseload, particularly the less important cases. On the highest trial level, the superior court has lost its original jurisdiction over misdemeanors and minor civil cases and over domestic relations and juvenile matters. On the next lower trial level, a variety of dissimilar city and county courts has been replaced by a new uniform district court system. At the bottom of the hierarchy, the justice of the peace and the mayor's courts have been replaced, at least in part, by the magistrate, a minor judicial official who operates within the District Court Division.

THE APPELLATE DIVISION

Supreme Court

The Appellate Division of the General Court of Justice has two branches, the Supreme Court and the Court of Appeals. The Supreme Court consists of seven justices who are elected by the people of the state as a whole for eight-year terms. The court sits in a body, in Raleigh, and hears oral arguments by attorneys representing the various parties in cases appealed from the lower courts. It does not have a jury and does not make determinations of fact; it considers cases on the written trial record only and decides questions of law. Its opinions (decisions) are printed in bound volumes and become the law of the land to the same extent as enactments of the legislature.

Court of Appeals

The Court of Appeals is composed of nine judges. All are elected in the same manner and for the same number of years as the justices of the

Supreme Court. Court of Appeals judges, however, sit and render decisions in panels of three. Individual panels may be authorized to sit in various localities throughout the state, although they usually sit only in Raleigh. Like the Supreme Court, this court decides only questions of law, including whether the trial procedure was free of error prejudicial to the appellant.

The Court of Appeals was created in 1967 to relieve the Supreme Court of a portion of its caseload, which in recent years had become more than that court could reasonably handle. The Supreme Court continues to decide, primarily, all cases involving questions of constitutional law, or legal questions of major significance to the state as a whole, or criminal cases including a sentence to death or life imprisonment. These cases may have already been decided in the Court of Appeals or may have come to the Supreme Court direct from the trial court. (For appellate routes, see the chart on page 244.) The Court of Appeals hears and decides cases in which the questions of law are less significant. No matter what the question, however, every appellant has a right to be heard by one or the other of these appellate courts, and in some cases by both, except that a defendant who pleads guilty to a criminal charge in the superior court may have his conviction reviewed only by petitioning the Court of Appeals for a writ of certiorari, which it may grant in its discretion.

The Supreme Court is located in the Justice Building at the southeast corner of the Capitol. The Court of Appeals is located across the street from the Supreme Court, at the southwest corner of the Capitol. Each court is supported by the Supreme Court Library, housed primarily in the Justice Building, and by a clerk, who is that court's administrative officer. The opinions of each court are prepared for publication by an Appellate Division reporter. Each justice or judge also has a research assistant, who must be a law school graduate. The Supreme Court librarian also serves as marshal (bailiff) to the Supreme Court; the Court of Appeals has no marshal.

When a vacancy arises—usually through death or mid-term retirement—in the membership of the Supreme Court or the Court of Appeals, the Governor is empowered to fill the vacancy by an appointment effective until the next general election. At the general election, the incumbent appointee almost always runs for the office and almost always is elected. Thus while the State Constitution provides for election of appellate judges, almost all of them attain office originally by appointment. (The same is true with respect to superior court judges.)[1]

THE SUPERIOR COURT DIVISION

Organization

The Superior Court Division consists of the superior court, which is the court with general trial jurisdiction. This court sits at least twice a year in

ROUTES OF APPEAL
General Court of Justice
1975

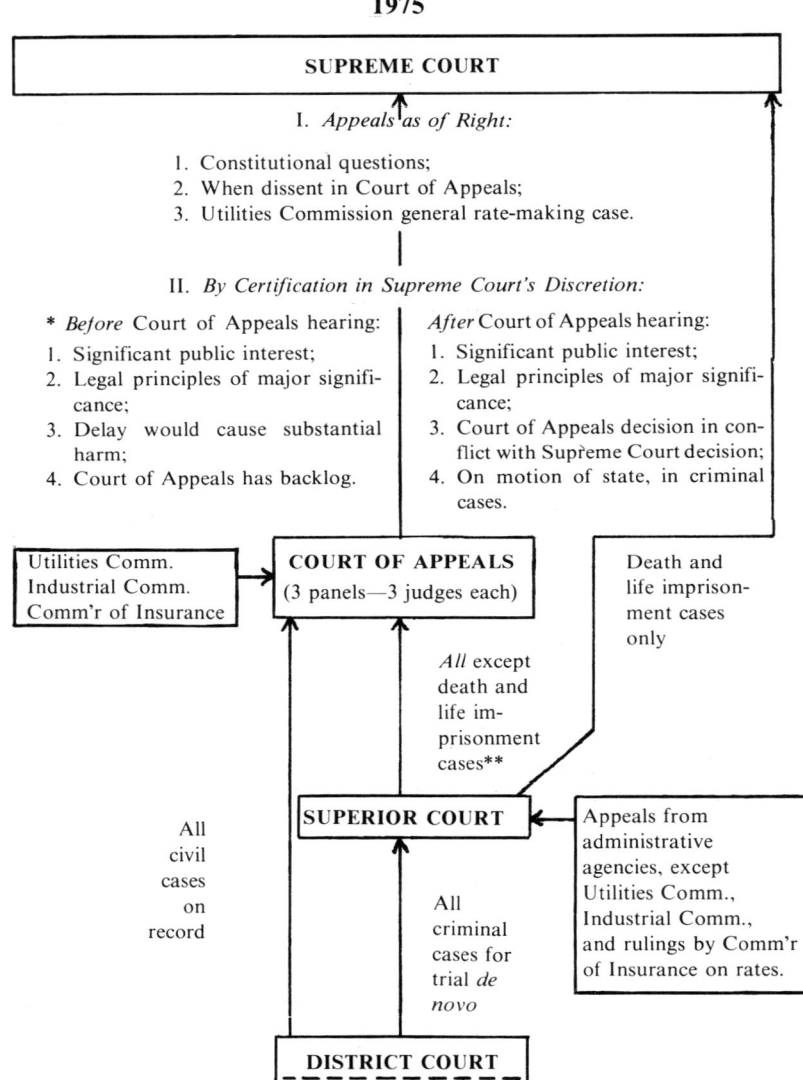

*Utilities and Industrial Commission cases *must* be heard by Court of Appeals *before* Supreme Court can hear.

**Post-conviction hearing appeals go to Court of Appeals by writ of certiorari only, and *no further*, except state may move for certification.

Approval of any settlement by the governing body does not relieve the tax collector or his bondsmen of liability for any shortage actually existing at the time of the settlement and thereafter discovered; nor does it relieve the collector of any criminal liability. [G.S. 105-373(e).]

The tax collector is supposed to settle for current taxes on the first Monday In July. This requirement fixes the time for annual settlement at a date shortly after the close of the fiscal year for which the taxes were levied, and after the annual lien sale has been held. Although the commissioners, as noted above, may require the collector to make settlement "at any other time," such other settlements as it may require must be *in addition* to the mandatory settlement to be made annually on the first Monday in July, and cannot take its place. Commissioners who permit settlements to be delayed beyond the first Monday in July should consult the following provision in G.S. 105-373(f):

> In addition to any other civil or criminal penalties provided by law, any member of a governing body ... who fails to perform any duty imposed upon him by [the settlement statute, G.S. 105-373] shall be guilty of a misdemeanor punishable by fine or imprisonment, or both, in the discretion of the court.

An administrative matter must also be kept in mind. Settlement must be made before the new tax books are turned over to the collector, and any member of the board of commissioners who votes to deliver the tax receipts to the tax collector before the collector has met the requirements prescribed (including making settlement) is individually liable for the amount of taxes charged against the tax collector for which he has not made satisfactory settlement; and any member who so votes, or who willfully fails to perform any duty imposed by the settlement law is guilty of a misdemeanor punishable by fine or imprisonment, or both, in the discretion of the court. This could become serious if the collector had not been diligent in cases in which diligence might have produced results.

Settlement Procedure

The tax collector is chosen to carry out the law as it is written; he is not a policy-maker. He is personally responsible for collecting the taxes in his hands, and the law gives him ample authority to seize any property the taxpayer may own in order to collect the county's claim. The law presumes that with this responsibility and with these remedies or weapons, the collector will do his utmost to collect, that he will, if necessary, seize whatever property of the delinquent taxpayer there may be available to him. Thus the board of commissioners rather than the collector himself has the responsibility of determining whether the collection work has been performed satisfactorily. Ultimately, it is the county commissioners that must decide in each case whether the collector has done everything he could have done to reach whatever property may have been available to him. If the unit has no lien for taxes against real property, the collector's effort to enforce collection must be the subject of the special scrutiny described below.

"*Insolvents.*" As pointed out on page 139, on the second Monday after the annual lien sale the collector is supposed to make a sworn report to the members of the governing body concerning that sale. At the same time he is supposed to present them with "a list of the persons not owning real property whose personal property taxes remain unpaid," along with his statement under oath—

(1) That he has made a diligent effort to collect these taxes out of the personal property of the taxpayers concerned.
(2) That he has made use of the "other means available to him for collection."
(3) That where applicable, he has tried to make collection outside the taxing unit.
(4) As to any information concerning these taxpayers that may be of interest to or required by board of commissioners.

This is not to be a perfunctory report. The collector is supposed to demonstrate that he has actually done everything possible under the law to collect the taxes for which the unit has no lien against real estate.

The first of the affirmations the collector must make means that he has been diligent using levy and garnishment.

The second means that he has done what he could to collect by working out partial payment schedules for taxpayers, and that he has used all the procedures available to him in collecting from estates, receivers, and bankrupts.

The third affirmation means that in appropriate instances the collector has exercised his authority to call on collectors of other units to assist him in making collections.

The fourth item listed is not itself an affirmation, but it is a reminder of two things: first, that the collector should include facts in his report to justify his failure to collect the accounts reported, and second, that when the board of commissioners desires to do so, it may *require* the collector to furnish whatever factual information is considered useful in connection with his report.

The mere fact that the collector, in making this report, swears that he has used diligence in attempting to collect from the persons listed as still owing personal property taxes is not determinative of the matter. The county commissioners have power to reject the name of any taxpayer if, in their opinion or knowledge, the taxpayer is not insolvent. In the event of a rejection, the commissioners are entitled to hold the collector liable on his bond for the uncollected tax.

Having reviewed the list submitted by the collector and having come to a

PROPERTY TAX 151

conclusion about the collector's justification in asking that he be allowed credit in his settlement for the uncollected items on the ground of the taxpayers' "insolvency," the board of commissioners must enter upon its minutes the names of the taxpayers found to be "insolvent" and designate them as the insolvent list "to be credited to the tax collector in his settlement."

Form of Settlement. A review of the North Carolina statutes will disclose that county commissioners are given every opportunity throughout the year to keep abreast of the work of the tax collector. The cornerstone of this scheme has been mentioned earlier: It is the requirement that the collector submit to the board of commissioners at each of its regular meetings a report of the amount he has collected on each year's taxes with which he is charged, the amount remaining uncollected, and the steps he is taking to encourage or enforce payment of uncollected taxes. If the collector is careful to comply with this requirement and if the county commissioners pay attention to his periodic reports, calling for additional information as desired, the annual settlement will follow in orderly culmination.

The collector's report on the lien sale having been made and the "insolvents list" approved, the time for settlement has arrived. The law specifies the items that must be charged against the collector and the items to be allowed as credits for him. They may be summarized as follows:

Charges

1. The total amount of all taxes placed in the collector's hands for collection, including taxes on discoveries, late listings, increased assessments, and values certified by the Property Tax Commission.
2. All late-listing and other penalties collected by the tax collector.
3. All interest on taxes collected by the tax collector.
4. Any other sums collected or received by the tax collector, including, for example, fees allowed in levy and garnishment.
5. Any fees that the tax collector may have taken for making "outside collections."

Credits

1. All sums deposited by the collector to the credit of the taxing unit or receipted for by the proper official.
2. Releases allowed by the governing body. (This would include rebates, reductions, refunds, etc.)
3. Discounts allowed for prepayments if the principal amounts of such accounts were collected after the books were placed in the collector's hands.

4. The principal amount of taxes constituting liens against real property, which liens were sold to the taxing unit.
5. The principal amount of taxes found by the governing body to be uncollectible in the current year because of the taxpayers who owe them are insolvent.
6. Any commissions to which the collector is entitled.

The charges and credits should balance. The collector is liable on his bond for any deficiency disclosed. In addition to this civil liability, he is subject to the criminal penalties imposed by G.S. 105-373 (f): "[A]ny . . . tax collector . . . who fails to perform any duty imposed upon him by [the settlement statute] shall be guilty of a misdemeanor punishable by fine or imprisonment, or both, in the discretion of the court."

Part IV / Suggested Reading

For those interested in pursuing the study of property taxation in North Carolina, the following publications are suggested. Unless otherwise indicated, all of them have been published by the Institute of Government. Those marked with an asterisk (*) are no longer available for sale but may be borrowed from the Institute library.

THE NATURE OF THE TAX

*BASIC LEGAL PROBLEMS IN THE TAXATION OF PROPERTY (1958), Henry W. Lewis. [This report to the 1958 Commission for the Study of the Revenue Structure of the State of North Carolina deals principally with classification, exemption, and assessment ratios. It is important for an understanding of the statutory and constitutional changes effected as a result of the Commission's Report. See the item next below.]

REPORT OF THE TAX STUDY COMMISSION OF THE STATE OF NORTH CAROLINA (published by the Commission, Raleigh, 1958). [This final report of the Commission gives valuable background for the Commission's recommendations as well as the reasons supporting those recommendations. Practically all the recommendations were adopted; thus the report has special significance. Available through the State Department of Revenue if available at all.]

REPORT OF THE COMMISSION FOR THE STUDY OF THE LOCAL AND AD VALOREM TAX STRUCTURE OF THE STATE OF NORTH CAROLINA (published by the Commission, Raleigh, 1970). [This report contains the full text of a proposed Machinery Act drafted in response to the mandate of Resolution 92, Session Laws of 1969. It also contains explanations of the points on which the proposed act differed from the Machinery Act of 1939.]

Property Tax Classification and Exemption: A Problem in North Carolina Constitutional Law, 37 NORTH CAROLINA LAW REVIEW 115-41, Henry W. Lewis (1959). [This article is an extension of a portion of the author's BASIC LEGAL PROBLEMS IN THE TAXATION OF PROPERTY and was written for lawyers.]

PROPERTY TAX LISTING AND ASSESSING

*THE LISTING AND ASSESSING OF PROPERTY FOR COUNTY AND CITY TAXES, rev. ed. (1938) with supplement (1939), Henry Brandis, Jr. [Although dated, this study by the principal author of the Machinery Act of 1939 (under which the property tax was administered in this state until July 1, 1971) will be of substantial help to county attorneys and others seeking guidance in problems of first impression.]

PROPERTY TAX EXEMPTIONS AND CLASSIFICATIONS (1970), Henry W. Lewis. [A complete analysis of every North Carolina constitutional and statutory provision on the subject of exemptions and classifications before the 1973 amendments to the Machinery Act. See PROPERTY TAX BULLETIN No. 41 for a discussion of the 1973 amendments.]

*THE ASSESSMENT OF REAL PROPERTY FOR TAXATION IN NORTH CAROLINA (1948), Henry W. Lewis. [This was an experimental effort to prepare a standard real property appraisal manual for use in North Carolina counties having limited appraisal staffs or none at all. It is for general reading, but it is not of practical use today.]

THE LIST TAKER'S GUIDE (1969), Henry W. Lewis. [Until 1971 this publication was revised and reissued following each session of the North Carolina General Assembly. In addition to simple instructions for list takers and assessors, it contains a helpful chapter on the powers and duties of the county tax supervisor.]

STATISTICS OF TAXATION (published by the State of North Carolina, 1974). [This book contains the Biennial Report of the Division of Tax Research of the Department of Revenue. Ordinarily it is published before each session of the General Assembly. While it contains information on all taxes imposed in this state, the chapters entitled "The Intangible Property Tax" and "Tax Revenue for the Local Governments" are especially relevant. The introductory statements as well as the statistics should be consulted.]

INTRASTATE TAX SITUS OF TANGIBLE PERSONAL PROPERTY (1963), Henry W. Lewis. [This publication deals with the questions of what taxing unit is entitled to tax the tangible personal property of an individual or business firm (a) when the owner lives in a unit other than that in which the property is located and (b) when the owner is not a resident of North Carolina.]

JUDICIAL REVIEW OF PROPERTY TAX APPRAISALS IN NORTH CAROLINA (1966), Donald A. Furtado and others. [This study examines the methods and grounds upon which an attorney defending or challenging a tax assessment may obtain judicial review and, once in court, what limits the court will place upon its review. Primarily for lawyers.]

MANDAMUS AND THE OCTENNIAL REVALUATION OF REAL PROPERTY (1967), William A. Campbell and others. [This publication addresses itself to these questions: If a board of county commissioners is reluctant, dilatory, or obviously ineffective in taking steps to conduct a required real property revaluation, may an interested taxpayer obtain relief from the courts? If so, by what means? It is written primarily for lawyers.]

Taxation of Movable Property of Interstate Carriers, PROPERTY TAX BULLETIN NO. 27 (1964), Henry W. Lewis. [This bulletin analyzes the problems faced by North Carolina counties in taxing the movable property of truck, bus, and air lines—both those based in this state and those based outside this state—that use the roads of this state. Although obsolete since enactment of the Machinery Act of 1971, this publication is essential to understanding the provisions of that act on this subject.]

*Taxing Private Interests on Government Land, 23 POPULAR GOVERNMENT 13-16, inside back cover (November, 1956), Henry W. Lewis. [This article is based on a significant United States Supreme Court decision and raises questions about the right of North Carolina counties to tax the value of private leaseholds of exempt lands. It should be used in connection with the article listed next below.]

*Local Taxation of Intangible Personal Property, 23 POPULAR GOVERNMENT 8-10, 18 (March, 1957), Henry W. Lewis. [This article analyzes the case of *Investment Co. v. Cumberland County* and concludes that despite the difficulties of appraisal, intangible properties not specifically taxed for the localities by the state remain subject to local taxation.]

Discovered Property: An Important Source of Tax Revenue, PROPERTY TAX BULLETIN NO. 36 (1971), Henry W. Lewis. [A survey of the dollar impact of discoveries of unlisted property made in North Carolina counties in 1970.]

*PREPARATION FOR REVALUATION (1956), Henry W. Lewis. [Although written before the octennial revaluation schedule was enacted, this book can still be useful if the reader knows its age.]

Evaluating Specifications for Revaluation Contracts, PROPERTY TAX BULLETIN NO. 21 (1960), Henry W. Lewis. [An outline analysis of provisions that a county might consider in preparing specifications for contracting for professional assistance in appraising real and personal property for tax purposes.]

Assessing Household and Kitchen Furniture—Percentage Rule, PROPERTY TAX BULLETIN NO. 25 (1962), Henry W. Lewis [An explanation of a standard technique used to bring tax values of property of this type into line with values on other kinds of taxable property.]

The Office of County Tax Supervisor, PROPERTY TAX BULLETIN NO. 33 (1968), Henry W. Lewis. [Data comparing counties with regard to the manning and operational arrangement of the tax supervisor's office, as well as the funds appropriated for operating that office—including the salaries of the supervisor and the members of his staff—all in the light of county population, area, and property valuation.]

PROPERTY TAX COLLECTION AND FORECLOSURE

PROPERTY TAX COLLECTION IN NORTH CAROLINA—Second Revised Edition (1974), William A. Campbell. [This book is the most recent, comprehensive treatment of North Carolina tax collection law and procedure available. It discusses the 1971 Machinery Act and the 1973 amendments affecting it, plus the amendments to the municipal and county government and local government finance statutes in 1971 and 1973.]

PROPERTY TAX LIEN FORECLOSURE FORMS (1972), William A. Campbell. [A guide for attorneys concerned with bringing and defending foreclosure actions for collecting county and municipal property taxes; contains fairly detailed annotations and explanations as well as suggested forms for use in both types of foreclosure authorized by North Carolina tax law.]

Property Tax Liens in Competition with Federal Claims, PROPERTY TAX BULLETIN NO. 35 (1970), William A. Campbell. [A discussion of the problems that arise when the North Carolina property tax lien is forced into a contest with the federal tax lien or the federal claim priority. Useful for collectors and attorneys attempting to collect from insolvent taxpayers.]

**Is 100% Enough?* 31 POPULAR GOVERNMENT 1-5, 21 (December, 1964), Henry W. Lewis. [A summary of the results of a study of tax collection efficiency in North Carolina counties and municipalities. Useful in measuring any unit's record in comparison with other local units.]

*THE FORECLOSURE OF CITY AND COUNTY PROPERTY TAXES AND SPECIAL ASSESSMENTS IN NORTH CAROLINA (1944), Peyton B. Abbott. [Although now largely superseded by the annotations in the 1972 publication by Campbell listed above, this book is useful in understanding the differences between foreclosure under former G.S. 105-414 and under former G.S. 105-391.]

In rem PROPERTY TAX FORECLOSURE (1959), Henry W. Lewis and Robert G. Byrd. [An analysis of *in rem* foreclosure permitted by G.S. 105-375 in the light of the judicial history of earlier North Carolina procedures as well as a long line of relevant decisions of the United States Supreme Court. Designed for attorneys engaged to defend or attack the validity of the North Carolina procedure.]

Procedure for Contesting Machinery Act Taxes, Henry W. Lewis, NORTH CAROLINA BAR ASSOCIATION: INSTITUTE ON NORTH CAROLINA TAXATION, pages II-1 through II-17 (1967). [This paper deals with the legal procedures to be used in contesting tax liability of individual properties and for contesting the valuation assigned property for tax purposes. It must be read in the light of Machinery Act changes that have been effected since 1967. Primarily for lawyers.]

GENERAL

THE ANNOTATED MACHINERY ACT OF 1971 (1971), Annotations by Henry W. Lewis. [This publication contains the text of the Machinery Act of 1971—Chapter 806, as amended by Chapters 931, 932, 1121, and 1163, Session Laws of 1971. Appended to the text of each Machinery Act section is an annotation identifying the section's source and explaining how it differs from its predecessor.]

1973 SUPPLEMENT TO THE ANNOTATED MACHINERY ACT OF 1971, Annotations by Henry W. Lewis. [A supplement to the publication listed immediately above, this publication contains the text and annotations to the 1973 amendments to the Machinery Act.]

A LEGISLATIVE HISTORY OF THE MACHINERY ACT OF 1971 (1971), Henry W. Lewis. [A complete but unofficial record of the 1971 Machinery Act's journey through the General Assembly. It contains the text of every proposal made in the General Assembly for amendment to the bill sponsored by the Local and Ad Valorem Tax Structure Commission. See the report of that Commission, above.]

Legislation Affecting Property Tax Administration, PROPERTY TAX BULLETIN NOS. 5 (1953), 11 (1955), 17 (1957), 20 (1959), 22 (1961), 25 (1963), 30 (1965), 32 (1967), 34 (1969), and 37 (1971), Henry W. Lewis and William A. Campbell; 42 (1974), Joseph S. Ferrell and William A. Campbell. [Following each session of the General Assembly a bulletin is issued to explain, catalogue, and evaluate the effect of both statewide and local legislation dealing with all phases of the property tax in North Carolina. Read together, these bulletins present a useful history of both administrative and legal developments in this field.]

— *Henry W. Lewis*

5 / Elections

Types of Elections / 160
**Relation of the County Board of Elections
  to Other Agencies / 160**
The State Board of Elections—Structure and Duties / 161
The County Board of Elections—Structure and Duties / 161
The Municipal Board of Elections / 162
Finances / 163
Relationship Between the State,
  the County Board of Elections, and the
  County Commissioners / 163
Expenses of County Elections Boards / 163
Size of County Elections Board Budgets / 165
**Registration, Qualification of Voters, and Kinds of
  Registration Systems / 167**
Who May Vote / 167
Full-time Registration Systems / 167
Office Space and Custody of Election Records / 168
Criminal Liability Arising from Elections / 168
Vacancies in Public Offices / 168
Absentee Registration and Voting / 169
Bibliography / 169

5 / ELECTIONS

TYPES OF ELECTIONS

The Declaration of Rights in the Constitution of North Carolina states, "[All] political power is vested in and derived from the people; all government of right originates from the people, is founded upon their will only, and is instituted solely for the good of the whole." The democratic method for obtaining expression of the people's will is through popular elections, which the Constitution says must be held often, be free, and be by written ballot. Three kinds of elections are held to ascertain the will of the people:

1. Party *primaries*, in which members of a political party nominate candidates to run as party representatives in elections to fill public offices. Party primaries are held on the Tuesday following the first Monday in May in each even-numbered year.

2. *General elections*, in which all qualified citizens, regardless of party affiliation, may elect persons to fill public offices. General elections are held on the Tuesday following the first Monday in November in each even-numbered year. Occasionally, an election must be held at a different time to fill a vacant office; that election, although general in nature, is usually called a *special* election.

3. *Referendums* (also commonly called *special elections*), in which qualified citizens may express their opinions for or against propositions submitted to them. Those elections may be held in regard to state, county, municipal, or special district issues. Recent statewide referenda have concerned mixed beverages (liquor by the drink) and state bond issues. Questions submitted in local referenda typically deal with the establishment of ABC stores, sale of wine and beer, creation of special districts (fire protection, sanitary, watershed, etc.), issuance of bonds, and the imposition of taxes for special purposes.

RELATION OF THE COUNTY BOARD OF ELECTIONS TO OTHER AGENCIES

The registration of all voters and the administration of all elections take place under state law, but these functions are financed by local taxes and performed by local officials. Thus, it is necessary to understand the separate responsibilities of both the State Elections Board and the local elections boards to appreciate fully the operations of the local boards and their role in county government.

The State Board of Elections—Structure and Duties

General supervision of the North Carolina election machinery rests with the five-member State Board of Elections. Its members, not more than three of whom may be members of the same political party, are appointed by the Governor on the first day of May following his inauguration—that is, every four years. The State Board has direct responsibility to:

(1) Prepare rules and regulations governing the conduct of all elections.

(2) Investigate violations of elections laws by local officials and to compel them to perform properly. (The Board hears and acts on complaints of the failure or neglect of county elections boards to comply with their duties and reports violations to the appropriate legal officers for further investigation and prosecution.)

(3) Determine the arrangement and content of registration and poll books, ballots, and other necessary election forms and records; furnish county boards of elections with registration and poll books; prepare, print, and distribute ballots used in primary and general elections for state and national offices and in referenda on constitutional amendments and other propositions of statewide concern; and instruct county boards of elections as to the printing of county and local ballots.

(4) Canvass the primary and general elections returns for national, state, and district offices and for constitutional amendments; and declare the results.

The County Board of Elections—Structure and Duties

Each county board of elections has three members, no more than two of whom may belong to same political party. The State Board appoints each county board, but the state chairman of each political party has the right to recommend to the Board the names of a number of registered voters from the county; if his recommendations are timely received by the State Board, it must appoint the county elections board members from among the names submitted. The Board makes appointments for two-year terms before the primary in each even-numbered year. Candidates, campaign managers, and elected officials may not serve on county elections boards.

The State Board may remove any member of a county elections board for incompetence, fraud, failure to perform a duty, or any other satisfactory case, but the member is entitled to notice of the charge and a chance to be heard. If a vacancy occurs, either for cause or because a member has resigned or dies, the State Board appoints his successor. If the member was removed for cause, the State Board need not consider the suggestions of the local party. But if a vacancy occurs through death or voluntary resignation, the State Board follows the same procedure as when the county board is first appointed.

The county board is responsible for supervising voter registration and conducting all elections (except some city elections) held within the county. To fulfill these responsibilities, it must:

(1) Establish election precincts, making sure that each precinct has a convenient voting place. The board may lease the space necessary to conduct the election; if necessary, the board may demand the use of any school or other state or municipal building as a voting place for the election.

(2) Appoint registrars, judges, assistants, and other election officials for each precinct.

(3) Hear appeals from those who were denied registration.

(4) Appoint any needed office personnel, including an executive secretary.

(5) Investigate any local voting irregularity or nonperformance of official duty and, if necessary, remove its appointees.

(6) Examine the sufficiency of petitions seeking to establish a new political party and petitions nominating candidates.

(7) Contract for the printing of ballots and provide adequate public notice of all elections.

(8) Prepare a budget request and submit it to the board of county commissioners.

(9) Maintain custody of all voting equipment and records when they are not in use, including all voting machines.

(10) Order and supervise new registrations of voters when required.

(11) Administer the absentee-voting law.

(12) Canvass election returns and issue certificates of elections.

The Municipal Board of Elections

Municipal elections are conducted by either the county or municipal (city) board of elections, depending on the type of election the city has. If the city election is partisan, the county board must conduct the election. If the city election is nonpartisan, the city may (1) request the county board to conduct the election, or (2) conduct it through a municipal board of elections.

All special district elections must be conducted by the county board.

If the county board conducts a city's elections, it takes on all the powers and duties necessary to conduct the elections, including voter registration. The full costs of an election, for both registering voters and conducting the election, must be paid by the city; however, the city's payment is received by the county and is not retained by the county elections board. Consequently, the costs of municipal elections must be included in the elections board's budget requests.

If a city with nonpartisan elections chooses to use a municipal elections board, the three-member board must be appointed by the city council without regard to party affiliation. Basically, the municipal board has powers similar to these of the county board, i.e. all those necessary to register voters and conduct elections.

FINANCES

Relationship Between the State, the County Board of Elections, and the County Commissioners

County boards of elections are in a sense both county and state agencies. They are often required by state law and the State Elections Board to perform certain functions and duties. The state, however, provides no financial assistance to the county elections board, which therefore must look to the county commissioners for its financial support. The elections board must submit a budget to the county commissioners at the beginning of each fiscal year. The peculiarly state-oriented nature of the elections board may require that it make unexpected expenditures to perform a duty placed upon it by the state. For example, the local board may have to conduct a special referendum on a current statewide issue, a fact that it did not know when it submitted its budget. If the state requires such special or emergency expenditures, then the elections board may need a supplemental appropriation from the county commissioners to cover the added costs.

Expenses of County Elections Boards

The following are some of the essential expenses incurred by a county board of elections:

1. *Salaries of Board Members and Office Staff.* The salaries of board members are set by statute at a per diem rate of $25 and may not be altered at the county level, except that the chairman's salary can be raised by the county. Other personnel include an executive secretary and general office staff, all of whose salaries are set at the county level. The number of office workers needed in any particular county will vary according to local needs and population, but almost all counties have executive secretaries for the board. The elections board may hire legal counsel, to be paid out of money appropriated by the county commissioners.

Board members often are required to attend state or regional workshops or conferences and are entitled to be compensated for their time on such trips at the same per diem rate applicable to other official duties. In addition, board members and executive secretaries are entitled to reimbursement for expenses that are necessarily incurred in performing their official duties.

2. *Salaries of Precinct Officials.* The elections board must appoint one registrar and two judges for each precinct; these officials are compensated at minimum per diem salaries prescribed by law. The board must appoint at least two precinct assistants for each precinct, and may appoint more than two if the number of registered voters in the precinct warrants the addition; assistants' minimum salary is also established by statute. In counties with *regular* full-time registration, special registration commissioners may be hired as needed; their salaries are not established by statute. The elections board may pay precinct officials more than the statutory minimum salaries if the county commissioners appropriate sufficient funds for this purpose.

All of these officials are entitled to pay on any election day, for being at voting places to register voters, for attending the county canvass, and for attending instructional meetings. In limited circumstances, they must be granted expense money in addition to salaries.

3. *Voting Equipment.* Each county elections board must furnish proper equipment for voters to use while voting. The law allows a certain flexibility with respect to the equipment: paper ballots only may be used, or voting machines only, or both paper ballots and voting machines.

Paper ballots. If paper ballots are used, the board will incur printing costs for sample and official ballots (including absentee ballots) for county offices and single-county legislative offices. Voting booths and ballot boxes must be made available.

Voting machines. If machines are used, the board must either buy or lease the machines. The purchase cost, though relatively high, is usually non-recurring. In addition, the board will incur costs of printing sample and official machine and paper ballots for county and single-county legislative offices; paper ballots are required, despite the use of voting machines, for absentee and curbside voters.

The ratio of voting machines to number of registered voters in the county or precinct is not fixed by statute, although most boards use a ratio of one machine for every 500 voters per precinct. In this regard, the elections board faces an annual problem in estimating how many machines it will need. After the budget is submitted to the commissioners (March or April) and before the primary (May) and general elections (November), any unusual pattern of voter registration may make the estimate too low either countywide or in a particular precinct. Given the high cost of machines, the county board must try to balance its needs for machines against the available appropriations. Consequently, the board may need to seek a supplementary appropriation to acquire more voting machines as the primary or general election approaches.

ELECTIONS 165

4. *Miscellaneous Precinct Expenses.* The elections board will incur expenses for miscellaneous items needed at the precinct voting places: locks and keys for the boxes, Bibles, flags, desks, chairs, typewriters, pencils, paper, printed voter instructions, forms on which to make abstracts of returns, and printed oaths for judges, assistants, and ballot counters. Finally, the board may have to pay for rent, utilities, maintenance, and heat at voting places.

5. *Other Election Duties and Expenses.* In addition to its regular elections, the elections board often must conduct state and local referenda or special elections. Often, the board will not know, when it submits its budget, that these elections will be scheduled, yet it must pay all costs of the special election—costs similar to those the county normally incurs in a regularly scheduled primary and general election. Also, as described above, the board may conduct municipal elections. The costs are paid by the municipality, but the elections board is not directly reimbursed for its expenditures on municipal elections. Instead, the fees paid by municipalities go into county treasury, and the elections boards includes an item in its budget request to cover the cost of municipal elections.

6. *Costs Unrelated to Voting Procedures.* Every elections board will have expenses unrelated to voting procedures. These include loose-leaf binders used on election day and office equipment, furnishings, and decorations. Also, the county elections office must have a minute book and a safe place to store registration records. Finally, it must pay postage costs.

7. *Extraordinary Expenses.* The board may have extraordinary expenses, requiring it to seek supplemental appropriations. For example, often the board is required to comply with new statutes (e.g., laws extending absentee ballots to primaries or laws directing changeovers to new registration systems). Also, when a new party seeks legal recognition by statutory procedures, the board must certify signatures on the petitions filed in the county. Finally, if a present or former member of the board is subjected to a law suit on account of orders, acts, or decisions rendered in discharging his official duties, the board may decide to provide legal counsel for his defense.

Size of County Elections Board Budgets

In 1973, the Institute of Government studied the size of county elections boards budgets, using 1972 data. Table 5-1 reflects the results.

The survey revealed that counties with comparable populations, numbers of registered voters, and assessed valuations have similar elections budgets and pay similar salaries to executive secretaries (the only local elections officials whose salaries are not fixed by state law). If skewing of the similarity occurs, it is likely to occur in the total budgets because of the costs of acquiring voting machines.

Table 5-I
Budget Statistics for County Elections Boards

No. Registered Voters	Mean Registered Voters	Mean Population	Mean Exec. Sec. Salary	Mean Assessed Valuation	Mean Budget
1,000-3,999	(1,858) 3,591 (7) (3,794)	(3,722) 6,035 (7) (7,128)	$ (750) 1,151 (6) (1,497)	$ (17,813,702) 22,135,244 (6) (28,269,072)	$ (2,750) 6,458 (4) (10,084)
4,000-5,999	(4,162) 4,719 (8) (5,710)	(7,797) 9,178 (8) (12,737)	(1,560) 1,680 (2) (1,800)	(23,993,395) 31,375,641 (6) (38,639,286)	(2,697) 5,888 (3) (8,068)
6,000-7,999	(6,525) 6,921 (8) (7,408)	(11,778) 15,240 (8) (18,947)	(1,200) 2,240 (8) (5,562)	(30,733,541) 44,756,647 (7) (56,989,094)	(6,265) 10,569 (5) (19,543)
8,000-10,999	(8,400) 9,690 (9) (10,904)	(13,393) 18,941 (9) (27,148)	(2,124) 2,914 (7) (4,300)	(28,030,900) 63,596,447 (8) (117,146,418)	(7,200) 22,829 (7) (90,500)
11,000-12,999	(11,064) 11,484 (9) (12,162)	(19,547) 23,303 (9) (26,176)	(1,323) 2,443 (8) (3,174)	(81,514,584) 107,368,069 (6) (139,858,731)	(10,000) 13,383 (8) (19,200)
13,000-14,999	(13,161) 14,005 (9) (14,659)	(23,661) 26,972 (9) (32,118)	(600) 2,453 (6) (5,100)	(63,131,575) 121,955,376 (6) (254,536,292)	(1,280) 11,543 (7) (38,645)
15,000-18,999	(15,381) 16,816 (6) (18,655)	(30,952) 35,621 (6) (41,963)	(4,188) 5,321 (6) (6,000)	(90,066,989) 110,185,385 (4) (122,097,439)	(15,400) 19,099 (3) (23,380)
19,000-20,999	(19,449) 19,850 (6) (20,405)	(33,166) 52,503 (6) (105,240)	(4,020) 4,882 (5) (5,700)	(123,558,956) 144,691,293 (5) (154,240,374)	(7,869) 17,365 (5) (22,101)
21,000-24,999	(21,230) 22,902 (9) (24,892)	(39,975) 50,514 (9) (63,027)	(4,560) 5,589 (7) (6,500)	(119,050,083) 179,910,587 (7) (238,787,698)	(19,316) 27,421 (7) (39,754)
25,000-30,999	(25,024) 27,616 (8) (30,390)	(50,054) 60,746 (8) (85,828)	(4,176) 5,285 (7) (6,000)	(125,588,739) 227,704,326 (8) (328,471,115)	(10,603) 22,367 (7) (30,279)
31,000-38,999	(31,900) 34,447 (8) (38,215)	(72,751) 73,929 (8) (84,308)	(4,800) 5,200 (8) (5,730)	(240,538,758) 296,381,213 (5) (407,285,128)	(16,000) 30,248 (8) (39,389)
39,000-51,999	(40,408) 45,422 (6) (51,520)	(84,402) 113,958 (6) (219,992)	(5,040) 6,043 (5) (7,500)	(430,116,729) 560,236,255 (4) (801,720,417)	(25,467) 44,970 (5) (74,224)
52,000-174,999	(57,516) 104,619 (7) (174,901)	(135,264) 220,777 (7) (364,975)	(6,248) 8,607 (7) (11,300)	(1,081,229,681) 1,607,960,579 (3) (2,582,862,851)	(38,889) 122,661 (7) (287,173)

The table is constructed from the following date: (1) total registered voters in a county, (2) the county's total population, (3) the executive secretary's salary, (4) the total assessed value of property within the county, and (5) the county elections board's budget during the 1971-1972 fiscal year (the year in which the 1972 primaries were held).

These data were grouped in categories according to the number of registered voters in each county. The size of the categories was chosen so as to make the number of counties in each category approximately the same.

The table shows the average for each type of data in each category. The numbers in parentheses above and below the averages are the lowest and highest values for the data of a particular type. The numbers in parentheses to the right of the averages show the number of counties in each class.

For example, the first category contains counties with 1,000 to 3,999 registered voters. The average number of registered voters in these counties is 3,591. The lowest number is 1,858 and

REGISTRATION, QUALIFICATION OF VOTERS, AND KINDS OF REGISTRATION SYSTEMS

Who May Vote

A primary function of the county elections board is registering people qualified to vote. The requirements to vote, other than the registration requirement, are that an applicant be a United States citizen, at least 18 years old by the date of the general election, and a resident of North Carolina and the precinct in which he seeks to vote for at least 30 days before the election. In addition, he must have been restored to the rights of citizenship if he has been convicted of a felony.

Full-time Registration Systems

All counties operate under a *permanent* and *full-time* registration system. Full-time registration insures that registration is available continuously throughout the year and that a person need register only once to be eligible to vote in all elections (general, primary, special, and referendum) of the state, county, city, and any special district in which he lives. Permanent registration insures that a person need not re-register unless he changes the county or city of his residence or unless the registration records are destroyed. The law sets forth elaborate procedures for accomplishing these regults; for challenging the rights of a voter to register, remain registered, or vote; and for purging the registration records of the names of people who have died or have not voted over a four-year period.

It is important to note that although all counties now have full-time registration, there are two kinds of full-time registration—*regular* and *modified*. All counties with less than 14,001 registered voters use the modified full-time system, while all other counties use the regular system. The major differences between the two are that (1) under the regular system the registration office is open at least five days a week during regular business hours, but under the modified system it is open for three full or half days per week, depending on the number of voters registered in the county; and (2) counties that use the regular system may appoint special registration commissioners, but counties that use the modified system may not. Special registration commissioners register voters.

---

the highest is 3,794. There are seven counties in this category. The average salary of the executive secretary in these counties is $1,151. Note that this is based on six of these counties because the information for one county is not available. The lowest salary is $370 and the highest is $1,497.

The study indicated that (1) as the number of registered voters increased, the average salary of the executive secretary rises, and (2) the executive secretary's salary is associated with the total assessed value of property.

Office Space and Custody of Election Records

For the full-time permanent system to operate effectively, the county board must have adequate quarters on a permanent basis. The county commissioners are responsible for providing those facilities. In addition, those quarters must provide space for keeping the registration records in a safe place; a state statute requires that these records be kept, if possible, in a fireproof vault. Administration of the absentee-ballot law lends further support to the need for office space for the elections board. The chairman is custodian of all absentee-voting records, and during the 60-day period before each general election, the board is required to meet in public session at least twice each week at the county courthouse or at the elections board office to pass upon all applications for absentee ballots.

Except when they are in the polling places, voting machines are under the custody of the county elections board chairman, who is directly responsible to the board for their safekeeping, storage, maintenance, and care. Immediately after each election the chairman is responsible for seeing that the machines are stored in a suitable place, which must be safe, dry, and securely locked so that the machines cannot be tampered with when not in use. With elections board approval, the chairman may appoint custodians to handle the maintenance, storage, and care of the voting machines and see that they are properly prepared and delivered to the voting places before an election. These custodians are paid such compensation as the elections board authorizes and the county commissioners approve.

CRIMINAL LIABILITY ARISING FROM ELECTIONS

The elections laws contain a number of provisions that make certain acts criminal offenses. These offenses, called "corrupt practices," may be committed by candidates and campaign committees and their treasurers, corporations, insurance companies, professional associations and labor unions, election officials, public officers and employees, enforcement officers, or any individual, depending on the specifics of the crime involved. Conviction (for a misdemeanor or felony) can result in the imposition of a fine or jail sentence (or both) or loss of public office, and perhaps loss of the right to vote, depending on who commits what kind of criminal act.

VACANCIES IN PUBLIC OFFICES

Simply stated, vacancies in elected public offices are filled as follows:

1. Elective state office (Council of State)—appointed by the Governor.
2. United States senator—appointed by the Governor.
3. Member of United States House of Representatives—special election.

4. State judicial offices—appointed by the Governor.
5. District Attorney—appointed by the Governor.
6. General Assembly—appointed by the Governor.
7. County commissioners—appointed by remaining commissioners.

The elections laws specify whether the appointment is for the remainder of the vacating officer's unexpired term, until the next general election, or until a special election. For county commissioners, the appointment runs until the next general election.

Vacancies in the offices of county sheriff, register of deeds, and other county elective offices are filled by the county commissioners for the remainder of the unexpired term. If the office of clerk of superior court becomes vacant, however, the senior regular resident superior court judge appoints a replacement to serve until the next general election.

ABSENTEE REGISTRATION AND VOTING

In general elections, both statewide or county, eligible voters who will be unable to come to the polling place because of illness or absence from the county on election day may vote by absentee ballot.

In state and county primary elections, those who are affiliated with a political party when they apply for absentee ballots may vote absentee. Absentee balloting is allowed in county bond elections. Absentee voting in a statewide referendum is permitted, but not in statewide bond referenda. Finally, absentee ballots are not allowed in municipal elections.

BIBLIOGRAPHY

Constitution of North Carolina. Articles I and VI.
North Carolina General Statutes, Chapter 163.
Turnbull, H. Rutherford, III. *North Carolina Primary and General Election Law and Procedure.* Chapel Hill: Institute of Government, University of North Carolina, 1974.
Turnbull, H. Rutherford, III. *Financing County Boards of Elections.* Chapel Hill: Institute of Government, University of North Carolina, 1973.

— *H. Rutherford Turnbull, III*
James C. Drennan

6 / County Property: Acquisition, Sale, and Disposition

PART I. REAL PROPERTY ACQUISITIONS / 172
Eminent Domain / 173
Purposes for Which Counties May Condemn / 174
Statutory Limitations / 175
Eminent Domain Procedures / 175
Chapter 160A Procedure / 175
Chapter 40 Procedure / 177

**PART II. SALE AND DISPOSITION OF
   COUNTY PROPERTY / 179**
Private Negotiation and Sale / 180
Advertisement for Sealed Bids / 180
Negotiated Offer, Advertisement, and Upset Bid / 180
Public Auction / 181
Exchange of Property / 181
Sale, Lease, Exchange, and Joint Use of
   Governmental Property / 182
Sale of Stocks, Bonds, and Other Securities / 182
Reconveyance of Donated Property / 182
Lease or Rental of Property / 182
Grant of Easements / 183
Warranty Deeds / 183

6 / COUNTY PROPERTY: ACQUISITION, SALE, AND DISPOSITION

Part I / Real Property Acquisitions

Counties have broad statutory power to acquire real property: the purposes for which they may acquire it are many, and the procedures they may use are varied. This chapter will emphasize the eminent domain procedures while dealing in general with the purposes and other procedures.

Under G.S. Ch. 153A, counties may acquire real property by:

— gift (a voluntary transfer of property, without cost to the county);
— grant or purchase (a voluntary transfer of property, for a price);
— devise (a voluntary gift of property by a person's last will and testament, without cost to the county);
— exchange (the voluntary transfer of property, for an equivalent piece of property);
— lease (the voluntary transfer of the use of property for a limited period of time); or
— any other lawful method, including eminent domain.

The statute specifically provides that a county may purchase property at a judicially ordered sale if the sale is ordered because the owner is in debt to the county. Also, the county is specifically authorized to acquire property that may be used in constructing buildings to be used by more than one unit of local government (cities, counties, local boards of education, etc.).

A county also may acquire real property through the operation of such legal doctrines as prescription (a method of acquiring title to rights in property, as distinguished from the property itself, as a result of a long-continued use of the property), adverse possession (a method of acquiring title to property itself, as a result of a long-continued possession of the property, under certain conditions), or dedication (a method of acquiring property when an owner designates certain land for a public purpose and the public accepts the property for that use). These and similar doctrines are outside the scope of this discussion.

EMINENT DOMAIN

Eminent domain is the power of the state or other public bodies to take private property for public use, against the owner's will, upon the payment of just compensation to the owner. The right is inherent in the state, but it may be exercised only pursuant to an act of the North Carolina General Assembly. That is to say, although the state has the right because it is a sovereign government, neither the state nor any other public body may condemn unless the General Assembly has specifically enabled it to do so.

The power of eminent domain has been extended by the legislature to certain state departments or agencies, such as the Department of Transportation, to local governments such as counties and cities, and certain private corporations operated in the public interest such as electric power companies, gas companies, and railroads.

Each time that the General Assembly delegates the power to condemn, it first determines that the condemnor would acquire the condemned property for a "public use"—that is to say, a use that enables the condemnor to furnish the public with some essential service or facility that cannot easily or readily be furnished at reasonable cost. if at all, unless the condemnor has the authority to acquire real property against the will of the owner. For example, highways, railroads, power lines, gas transmission lines, water lines, and sewer lines must follow routes that are convenient, economical, and feasible from an engineering standpoint. Schools and other public buildings must be located with the convenience of and the cost to the general public in mind. Public facilities such as sanitary landfills and jails must be located somewhere, even though they are seldom welcome neighbors. Occasionally, these considerations mean that the general public interest must override the private property rights enjoyed by a particular landowner. However, because both the United States Constitution and the North Carolina Constitution protect individuals from having their property taken without "due process of law," the entire process of eminent domain is closely supervised by the courts, which hold the government to a rigorous standard of compliance with procedural fairness to the person whose property is being taken against his will and to a requirement that the owner be fully compensated for the fair market value of the property that is to be taken from him.

Purposes for Which Counties May Condemn

Table 6-I shows the extent to which the General Assembly has granted counties the power of eminent domain, the public uses for which counties may condemn, the authority for the particular use, and the use itself.

Table 6-I
Sources of North Carolina County Governments' Eminent Domain Powers

Condemnor	Authority, G.S. Citation	Purpose
Board of County Commissioners	40-2 (5) and -6	Schools (for water supply)
	40-33	Public works projects
	77-11	Public landings
(through Boards of Education)	115-125	School sites
(through Boards of Hospital Trustees)	131-15 and 28.14	Hospitals and hospital facilities
	131-126.20 (a) and (b)	Hospital facilities
(as Watershed Improvement District)	139-41[1]	Watershed improvements
	139-44	Watershed improvements
	143-215.42	Rivers and harbors development, and flood control
	153A-159(1)	Public enterprises listed in G.S. 153A-274
	153A-159 (2) and 160A-353 (3)	Parks, playgrounds, recreation facilities
	153A-159 (4) and -263 (3)	Library facilities
	153-159 (5)	Courthouse, jail, office buildings, fire stations, and other buildings for use by county or any board, commission, or agency thereof
	153A-159 (1) and -274 (1)	Water supply and distribution systems
	153A-159 (1) and -274 (2)	Sewage collection and disposal systems
	153A-159 (1) and -274 (3)	Solid waste collection and disposal system and facilities
	153A-159 (1) and -274 (4)	Airports and air rights
	63-3, -5, -6, -36, -49 (b), and -56	
	153A-159 (1) and -274 (5)	Off-street parking facilities
(through Housing Authority or by Board of County Commissioners acting as Housing Authority)	157-34 and -50	Housing projects
(through Water and Sewer Author.)	162A-6 (10)	Water and sewer
(through Metropolitan Sewerage Districts)	162A-6 (10)	Sewerage

1. G.S. 139-41 grants county commissioners the power to exercise the powers of soil and water conservation districts. Among those powers are those of acquiring real or personal property, or interests therein, by purchase, exchange, lease, gift, grant, bequest, devise, *or otherwise* . . . [emphasis added]. It is not clear that condemnation powers exist by reason of this language.

Statutory Limitations

Though a county has a grant of power to condemn for purposes shown in Table 6-I, it is subject to three statutory limitations on its power:

1. A county may not condemn property owned by the state unless the state consents to the taking. In giving its consent, the state acts through the Council of State or the Director of Administration if the Council has delegated to him the power to consent. If the state consents, the only issue is how much the county must pay the state.

2. A county may not condemn any real property interest belonging to another unit of local government unless the property the county wants is not being used *and* is not needed for any governmental or proprietary purpose by its owner.

3. A county may not condemn any interest in property already devoted to public use and owned by a public service corporation unless the county's acquisition of the interest will not prevent or unreasonably impair the continued devotion to public use of the property or its operation by the public service corporation.

These statutory limitations are in addition to the other constitutional limitations of public use and just compensation.

EMINENT DOMAIN PROCEDURES

Counties may use either of two basic statutory procedures in condemning property—G.S. Ch. 160A, Art. 11, or G.S. Ch. 40, Art. 2. A county may also use the procedures of any other general law or local act applicable to it.

Chapter 160A Procedure

Preliminary Condemnation Resolution. Condemnation begins when the county commissioners adopt a preliminary condemnation resolution (PCR). The PCR initiates condemnation against all property described and all parties named in the resolution, but it must be limited to condemnation for a single project or purpose and to property under common ownership. The county is not required to try to buy the property before it starts condemnation procedures. The county may acquire absolute title to the property, or a lesser interest such as a right of access, a right of way, an easement, or water or air rights. Finally, in certain limited circumstances a county may acquire all of a parcel of land, or all of the improvements (buildings) on it, even though it needs only part of the parcel or part of the building. This right to acquire more property than is needed is available *only* when (1) the taking is for a proposed street or highway right of way, and (2) partial taking would leave the owner with a useless remnant of the land or building.

Notification. A copy of the PCR and any amendments to it must be served on all persons named therein as owners or parties. Also, a copy of the PCR and any amendments that change parties or affect the description of the land must be recorded in the office of the register of deeds in every county where affected land lies.

Appointment of Board of Appraisers. The property sought to be condemned must be appraised by a board of appraisers. This board consists of one person appointed by the county commissioners (who must be named in the resolution), one person appointed by the owner of the property, and one person appointed by the other two appraisers. The appraisers must be "freeholders" (real property owners) and disinterested in the rights of the parties.

Appraisal Process. The board of appraisers must meet at or near the site of the property being condemned at the time fixed by the preliminary resolution to view the property and hear evidence on what damages and benefits will result from the condemnation. If the site of the property is not a convenient place to hear evidence, the appraisers may take evidence elsewhere.

Report of Appraisers. The appraisers then determine the damages ("just compensation") to be paid to the owner by the county for the property and report their findings to the county commissioners. Their report is "sufficient" and will be submitted if it is concurred in by two of the three, but if no two of them agree or if they fail to report within the time allowed, new appraisers may be appointed in the same manner as the original appraisers. The new appointees will follow the same procedures required of the original appraisers.

Commissioners' Action on the Appraisers' Report. Within 30 days after they receive the appraisers' report, the commissioners must decide what action to take on it. They may, by resolution, either abandon or continue the proceeding. If they take no action within 80 days, the county is deemed to have abandoned the condemnation proceedings. Abandoning the proceedings, however, does not preclude the county from later instituting another proceeding to acquire the same property.

Final Condemnation Resolution. If the commissioners decide to proceed with condemnation, they adopt a final condemnation resolution. A copy of the resolution must be served on each person named therein, and a copy must be certified by the clerk to the county commissioners and then recorded in the office of the register of deeds of the county where the property is located.

Vesting of Title. Title to the property vests in the county, as between it and the persons named in the final resolution, on the date specified in the final resolution, or, if no date is specified, on the date the final resolution is adopted. As to persons not named in the final resolution, title vests in the county when the resolution is recorded and indexed by the register of deeds of the county in which the property is located. The

COUNTY PROPERTY 177

county is not entitled to possession, however, until it has paid the owners in full or deposited with the clerk of superior court the amount of damages determined by the appraisers.

Appeal. The owners may appeal the case to the superior court on any issue, but the county may appeal only on the issue of compensation. An appeal does not delay the vesting of title in the county except when the appealing condemnee is another unit of local government or a public service corporation whose property is already devoted to public use. In those cases, the vesting of the title is suspended until the court has rendered final judgment on the condemnor's right to acquire the property and the amount of compensation to be paid. An appeal results in an entirely new trial on the issue of damages.

Deposit of Award. If the owner appeals, the county may deposit with the clerk of the superior court a sum of money equal to the compensation determined by the appraisers; but if the county appeals, it may deposit a sum estimated by it to be just compensation. The owners may apply to the clerk for disbursement, and the clerk is to order that the money be paid to the persons entitled to it in accordance with the owner's application.

Interest. If the county does not make a deposit of award, the amount awarded as damages by the court is to include interest at 6 per cent per annum on the award from the date of taking to the date of judgment. If, however, the deposit is made, interest is allowed only to the date of deposit unless the court award exceeds the amount of the deposit. In that case, interest is allowed on the excess until the date of judgment.

The principal advantages of the procedure contained in G.S. Ch. 160A, Art. 11, are its speed and simplicity. It does not require the condemnor to negotiate with the owners for the purchase of the property before beginning condemnation proceedings; it has an accelerated timetable of events to insure prompt action by the parties and the appraisers; in most cases it allows a condemnor to take possession of the property despite further proceedings or appeals; in some instances it permits a county to condemn portions of land or buildings that are not strictly necessary for the public use; and it entitles a county to a lien for the cost of removing noncondemned buildings from condemned property when the owner fails to remove them.

Chapter 40 Procedure

If a county cannot agree with the owners with respect to the purchase of any property, it has the right to acquire all rights in and to the property (the fee simple title) or an easement, pursuant to the provisions of Chapter 40, Art. 2. But it may not exercise the right until it has tried and failed to purchase the property.

Initiation of Proceedings. Either the county (condemnor) or the property owner (condemnee) may begin the Chapter 40 procedure by filing a petition with the clerk of the superior court asking that appraisers be appointed.

Notification of Parties. The clerk of court will issue the summons and have it and a copy of the petition served on all condemnees (the owner or other parties who have an interest).

Answer. If the owner did not file the original petition, he has ten days in which to file an answer to it.

Hearing and Appeal. If an owner answers by denying any of the facts alleged by the county's petition or if he tries to show why the county's request for the appointment of appraisers should not be granted, the clerk is required to hold a hearing on the petition and answer. If there is no valid reason not to grant the county's request, the clerk must appoint three "commissioners" (disinterested and competent "freeholders" who reside in the county where the property lies) to appraise the property. If either party contemplates an appeal from the clerk's ruling, the party may take exception to it and appeal after the appraisers have made their report.

Appraisal Process and Report. The appraisers take an oath that they will impartially and fairly appraise the property. If the clerk thinks it necessary, he may instruct them on their duties and make any orders he deems necessary for them to fulfill the object and intent of the procedure. Regardless of whether they are specially instructed, the appraisers are required to view the premises described in the petition, hear the parties' testimony, and reduce it to writing. To do this they may meet as often as they think necessary, but before each meeting they must give both parties ten days' notice. They also have the power to issue subpoenas and administer oaths to witnesses. When a majority of the appraisers decide on a figure that they consider to be just compensation to the owner, they report it to the clerk. They must file their report no later than ten days after they are appointed, subject to extensions for cause.

Proceedings After Commissioner's Report. After the appraisers' report is filed with the court, both the owner and the county have twenty days in which to file exceptions to it. After the twenty-day period has lapsed, the clerk must decide whether to appoint new appraisers or to modify or affirm the report. If exceptions have been filed, the clerk must hold a hearing and rule on the exception. If he decides that the appraisal must be redone, he either appoints new appraisers, in which case the process begins anew, or he orders the already-named appraisers to reappraise the property. These orders cannot be appealed. But if the clerk affirms the report, either party may appeal that action to the superior court. The superior court may set aside the award, order the clerk to appoint new appraisers, amend the award, or (under G.S. 40-19) "take such orders, judgments and decrees, and issue such executions and other processes as may be necessary to carry into effect the final judgment rendered in such proceedings."

If the issue is one of fact on the damages assessed by the appraisers, either party may appeal to the superior court for a trial de novo before a jury. In this case, the appraisers' report is not admissible evidence, and the court proceeds as if the appraisers had never been appointed. Also, the damages established by the jury represent the final judgment.

Taking Possession and Final Judgment. When the appraisers have filed their report, the county may take possession of the property, notwithstanding a pending appeal. If the county does take possession, however, it must pay into court the sum fixed by the appraisers as the compensation due the owner. The court then retains the payment until it renders final judgment. Upon final judgment, the money is paid to the owner and, when the county pays the court costs and the owner's counsel fees, title vests in it. If the county takes possession and the owner appeals, he is entitled to interest on the amount of damages set by the appraisers, beginning on the date the county takes possession. After the appeal, the county has an option not to condemn the property, but the interest and costs assessed against the county must be paid to the owner.

Other provisions of G.S. Ch. 40, Art. 2, cover: payment of costs when the benefits to the land exceed the damages; acquisition of title held by infants, incompetents, and trustees without power of sale; determination of the owners' rights to the funds representing damages; appointment of attorneys to represent unknown parties; amending defects in pleadings; appointing substitute commissioners; making rules of procedure; prosecuting the case despite changes in ownership in the condemned land; curing defective title; acquiring title to state land; and limiting the quantity of land that can be acquired for certain purposes.

The principal advantage of the procedure contained in Ch. 40, Art. 2, compared with the procedure of G.S. Ch. 160A, Art. 11, is that it is time-tested and familiar to attorneys representing condemnors. It also has the advantage of containing procedures for acquiring clear title to land and for entry (for surveys, inspections, etc.) on the property before condemnation proceedings are begun. It does, however, take longer than the procedure of G.S. Ch. 160A, Art. 11.

— *H. Rutherford Turnbull, III*
James C. Drennan

Part II / Sale and Disposition of County Property

When the revision of the general law applying to counties became effective on February 1, 1974, general procedures for disposing of county property were effective for the first time. The new statute, G.S. 153A-176, provides that county governments shall dispose of property in the same manner as city governments and in accordance with the procedures set forth in G.S. 160A, Art. 12. (G.S. 160A-266 through -276). Several methods for selling or disposing of property are authorized, and procedures for using each are set forth in the statute. These methods and the procedure required with respect to each are outlined here.

Private Negotiation and Sale

This procedure may be used only for disposing of personal property valued at less than $5,000 for any one item or group of similar items.

Procedure. The board of commissioners, at a regular meeting, by resolution authorizes an appropriate official to dispose of identified property at private sale. The board may set a minimum price but is not required to do so. The resolution must be published at least ten days before the sale.

Comment. The apparent purpose of the procedure is to make public the board's intent to sell property privately, both to prevent favoritism or fraud and to give public notice that the property is available for private sale.

Advertisement for Sealed Bids

Any real or personal property may be sold by this method.

Procedure. The procedure is based on that set forth in G.S. 143-129 for purchasing property, with a special modification for real property. The advertisement for sealed bids must be published in a newspaper that has general circulation in the county one week before the bids are opened if personal property is being sold and 30 days before the bids are opened if real property is being sold. The advertisment should describe generally the property to be sold; tell where it might be examined and when and where the bids will be opened; state that a 5 per cent bid deposit is required and will be retained if the successful bidder fails to consummate the contract; and reserve the board's right to reject any and all bids. Bids are to be opened in public and recorded on the board's minutes. The award is made to the highest bidder.

Comment. This procedure appears to be designed to secure wide competition by providing public notice and good opportunity for bidders to examine the property. Invitations to bid could be mailed to prospective buyers just as invitations to bid are typically mailed to prospective vendors in the formal purchasing procedures. Minus the bid-deposit requirement, this procedure is essentially the one used by the Division of Purchase and Contract in disposing of almost all state surplus personal property.

Negotiated Offer, Advertisement, and Upset Bid

Any real or personal property may be sold by this method.

Procedure. The procedure starts when the board of commissioners receives an offer to purchase specified county property that it proposes to accept. (The offer may be either solicited or made directly by the offeror.) The board then requires the offeror to deposit with the clerk to the board a 5 per cent bid deposit and causes a notice of the offer to be published. The notice must describe the property; give the amount and terms of the offer; and give notice that the bid may be raised by not less than 10 per cent of the first $1,000 originally bid, plus 5 per cent of any amount above $1,000 of the original bid. Increased bids must also be accompanied by a 5 per cent bid deposit. Prospective bidders have 10 days from the date the notice is published to offer an upset bid. This procedure is repeated until 10 days have elapsed without receipt of an upset bid. After that time, the board may sell the property for cash. The board may at any time reject any and all offers and decide not to sell the property.

Comment. The upset bid procedure is generally considered to be especially appropriate for use in sale of real property and when several people may want to join in making an offer.

Public Auction

Any real or personal property may be sold by this method.

Procedure. Separate procedures are stipulated for real and personal property sold at public auction. For real property, the board of commissioners must adopt a resolution that authorizes the sale; describes the property to be sold; specifies the date, time, place, and terms of the sale; and states that the board must accept and confirm the successful bid. The board may require a bid deposit. A notice containing the information set out in the resolution must be published at least once and not less than 30 days before the auction. After the auction, the highest bid is reported to the board, which then has 30 days in which to accept or reject the bid.

For personal property, the same procedure is followed except that (a) the board may in the resolution authorize an appropriate county official to complete the sale at the auction, and (b) the notice must be published not less than 10 days before the auction.

Comment. Public auction is a traditional method of selling both real and personal property. Open competitive bidding may under some circumstances encourage the offering of higher prices. The possibility of immediately acquiring possession of personal property makes this approach attractive to many people.

Exchange of Property

Any real or personal property may be exchanged for other real or personal property if the county receives full and fair consideration for its property. Facilities of a county-owned enterprise may be exchanged for like facilities located either inside or outside the county.

Procedure. The terms of the exchange agreement are to be developed by private negotiation; the exchange must be authorized by the board of commissioners at a regular meeting, and a notice of intent to exchange the property must be published at least 10 days before the exchange is made. The notice must describe the properties to be exchanged, give the value of each and the value of other consideration changing hands, and cite the date of the regular meeting at which the board proposes to confirm the exchange.

Comment. The exchange procedure is probably most useful in connection with trading real property when property boundaries must be adjusted or when a single property owner has land needed by the county and wants some tract of county land.

Sale, Lease, Exchange, and Joint Use of Governmental Property

G.S. 160A-274 authorizes any governmental unit in the state, upon terms and conditions determined by the unit, to sell to, purchase from, exchange with, lease to, lease from, or enter into agreements regarding the joint use by any other government unit of any interest in real or personal property that the first unit may own. "Governmental unit" is defined to include cities, counties, the state, school units, and other state and local agencies. Bids or published notice are not required. Thus, when reaching agreements on property with another governmental unit, the county commissioners have full discretion.

Sale of Stocks, Bonds, and Other Securities

A county that owns stocks, bonds, or other securities that are traded on the stock exchanges or over the counter by brokers and securities dealers may sell them in the same way and under the same conditions as a private owner would (G.S. 153A-176 and G.S. 160A-276), and is not limited to the methods outlined above.

Reconveyance of Donated Property

If either real or personal property is donated to a county for a specific purpose and the board of commissioners later determines that it will not use the property for that purpose, the board may reconvey the property without consideration to the grantor or his heirs, assigns, or nominees. Before doing so, however, the commissioners must publish two weekly notices of their intent to reconvey the property. The resolution authorizing the reconveyance should be adopted at a regular meeting of the board.

Lease or Rental of Property

Any county property may be leased or rented if the board of commissioners finds that the property will not be needed during the term of the lease (G.S. 153A-176, G.S. 160A-272).

COUNTY PROPERTY 183

The board may, by resolution at any meeting, make leases or rentals for a period of one year or less. It may also authorize the county manager or some other county administrative officer to execute leases or rentals of county property for periods of one year or less.

The board may lease or rent county property for periods longer than one year and less than 10 years by a resolution adopted at a regular meeting after 10 days' published notice of its intention. The notice must also tell what the annual lease or rental payment will be and give the date of the meeting when the board proposes to approve the action.

A lease for longer than ten years must be treated as a sale of property and may be executed by following any procedure authorized for selling real property.

Grant of Easements

A county may grant easements over, through, under, or across any county property (G.S. 153-176 and G.S. 160A-273). The authorization for making the grant should be by resolution of the board of commissioners at a regular meeting. No published notice of intent or terms is required.

Warranty Deeds

G.S. 160A-275 authorizes the board of county commissioners to execute and deliver deeds to any governmentally owned real property with full covenants of warranty when the board determines that it is in the best interest of the county to do so. Members of the board are relieved of any personal liability arising from the issuance of warranty deeds if their actions are in good faith.

The growth of county government activities and functions has meant that the county has increased its holdings of both real and personal property and therefore more often has property to be disposed of. Perhaps as a consequence of this growth, the General Assembly has now established varying procedures for county officials to follow in selling and otherwise disposing of county property. While the statutory procedures have become more numerous and more detailed, the fundamental discretion of the officials to act has not been changed. And, in fact, most actions in selling and disposing of property in the past have been substantially in accord with one or more of the procedures that are now required.

— *Warren J. Wicker*

7 / Purchasing and Contracting

Authority to Make Purchases and Contracts / 187
Authorization for Expenditures / 187
Goals in County Purchasing / 188
Organization for Purchasing / 189
The Purchasing Process / 190
Determination of Need / 190
Specifications / 190
Buying Without Specifications / 191
  Or Equal / 191
  Approved Brand List / 191
Scheduling Purchases / 191
  Advance Requisition or Requisition Schedule / 192
  Warehouses and Stores / 192
  Price Agreements or Term Contracts / 192
Exceptional Purchases / 192
Purchase Order System / 193
Buying Under State Contracts / 193
Statutory Requirements in Purchasing and Contracting / 195
Formal Contracts / 195
  Coverage / 195
  Exceptions / 195
  Specifications / 196
  Advertising / 196
  Bid Deposit / 197
  Opening Bids / 197
  Standards in Awarding Contracts / 197
  Number of Bids Required / 198
  Procedure When Bids Exceed Funds Available / 198
  Performance and Payment Bonds / 198
Informal Contracts / 199
  Coverage / 199
  Standards in Awarding Contracts / 200
  Records of Bids / 200
Conflict of Interest / 200

Cooperative Purchasing / 202
Building Contracts / 202
State Tax Refunds / 202
Fair Trade and Collusive Bidding / 203

7 / PURCHASING AND CONTRACTING

Securing the goods and services necessary to the operation of county government is a major administrative responsibility. In a legal sense, it involves questions of proper authority, adequate authorization for the expenditure of funds, and the making of contracts in accordance with statutory requirements. Administratively, the organizational arrangements should be both efficient and legally sufficient.

AUTHORITY TO MAKE PURCHASES AND CONTRACTS

A county's power to make purchases and contracts, like other powers, is derived from the legislature and is subject to such limitations and restrictions as the legislature may impose. The basic grant of power with respect to purchasing and contracting is found in G.S. 153A-11, the statute that vests counties with general corporate powers and expressly empowers counties to enter into contracts and acquire all kinds of property. Many other statutes empower counties to perform particular functions and contain other and specific contracting powers.

AUTHORIZATION FOR EXPENDITURES

The second basic requirement with respect to all county contracts is that funds must be properly appropriated or authorized to meet the county's obligations under the contract. G.S. 159-28(b) provides:

> No contract or agreement requiring the payment of money, nor any requisition or purchase order for supplies or materials, may be made unless an appropriation therefor appears in the budget ordinance and a sufficient unencumbered balance remains in the appropriations to pay the sums to fall due thereunder during the fiscal year. No contract, agreement, requisition, or purchase order requiring the payment of money by a local government or public authority shall be valid and enforceable unless it bears on its face a certificate signed by the finance officer in substantially the following form (adding the words in brackets for continuing contracts): "Provision for the pay-

ment of moneys to fall due under this agreement [within the current fiscal year] has been made by appropriation duly authorized, as required by the Local Government Budget and Fiscal Control Act". . . .

The statute is thus quite clear. Before a contract may be entered into, funds to cover the full amount of the contract must have been appropriated. The only exception to this requirement occurs when the contract is a continuing one. G.S. 153A-13 authorizes counties to enter into continuing contracts, which are contracts "some portion or all of which are to be performed in ensuing fiscal years." In contracts of this type, the statute requires only that funds be appropriated to meet obligation arising in the fiscal year in which the contract is made. The county commissioners must later appropriate enough funds to meet the amount to be paid under the contract in ensuing fiscal years for the duration of the contract (see Chapter 3, page 58). Many service and repair contracts, for example, may be of this type. Some may extend for several years; others may simply extend into the fiscal year following the one during which the contract was made.

GOALS IN COUNTY PURCHASING

The objective in purchasing by counties is essentially the same as it is with other public agencies and with private businesses. The county purchasing organization should be designed to secure—with efficiency—what is needed, when it is needed, and at the lowest possible cost.

This goal does not suggest that every need must be anticipated in advance and the necessary goods purchased and stored for use. There are many ways other than operating warehouses to provide goods when they are needed.

Nor does the goal of low cost suggest that only the "lowest priced" goods should be purchased. The lowest cost in terms of use may result from the purchase of an item whose initial cost is not the lowest. By the same token, it does not always follow that the highest-priced item is the one with greatest quality and lowest cost in use. The job of county purchasing is to make rational decisions in buying, after considering price, quality, performance, and other relevant factors.

County purchasing officials are concerned not only with making the "right buy." They are also under obligation to buy in the proper manner— in the manner prescribed by statute. In North Carolina these statutory requirements are essentially designed to save public funds and prevent favoritism in awarding public contracts. It is these requirements that distinguish *public* buying from *private* purchasing, for public buying is *public*.

On rare occasions the two major aims of the statutory regulations may conflict. There are times when special prices might be obtained if a procedure that did not prohibit favoritism could be followed, but generally both purposes are served by the statutes. Furthermore, most of the requirements of law are also requirements that public officials would impose on themselves even in the absence of law. Awarding public contracts on any basis other than open and free competition would raise dangers that most public officials would not want to face.

ORGANIZATION FOR PURCHASING

The county commissioners, under the authority granted by G.S. 153A-76 to organize and reorganize the administration of county government, are responsible for establishing the organization for purchasing within county governments as they see fit. In practice, arrangements vary from a fair degree of centralizing with a purchasing agent to almost complete decentralization. Only a few of the larger counties have appointed full-time purchasing agents. In a number of other counties the manager, the accountant, or a board member serves as purchasing agent, the degree of centralization varying from county to county. In many small counties practically all purchasing is done by department heads.

In operations of any significant size, it is generally considered desirable to appoint a purchasing agent, either someone specifically for this position or some other officer designated to serve also as a purchasing agent. Savings through the use of a central purchasing office arise because of:

(1) Lower costs through buying in larger quantities when the needs of various departments are consolidated;
(2) Standardization of items in common use, which permits consolidation of needs and larger quantity buying;
(3) Improved specifications;
(4) Increased competition;
(5) More taking of cash discounts (where departmental buying is practiced, invoices may not be submitted for approval and payment until too late to take cash discounts);
(6) Closer check on deliveries, with respect to both quantities and condition of goods; and
(7) Improved control over expenditures.

Centralizing the purchasing function does not mean the total loss of operational control by department heads. Department and agency heads approve all requisitions for materials and usually, in consultation with the purchasing officer, develop specifications for goods to be purchased. Thus real control is not lost. On the other hand, the availability of a person who devotes his attention to developing new sources of supply, securing better prices, checking on deliveries, consolidating needs, and watching price trends should mean lower costs. The real effectiveness of centralized purchasing, of course, must depend upon the competence of the purchasing agent and the cooperation between the purchasing agent and the various agency and department heads.

Efficient buying can take place under either a centralized or a decentralized arrangement, but with equal competence among all personnel, the centralized arrangement usually results in lower costs.

THE PURCHASING PROCESS

Determination of Need

The county commissioner's role is dominant in determining needs—in deciding what goods will be purchased. Through their adoption of the budget, the commissioners have full control over what is to be purchased. Purchases of major items will probably be discussed individually at this time, especially in smaller counties. For routine supplies and minor equipment, the commissioners usually only approve appropriations and leave details of specifications to the purchasing agent and the department heads. On major purchases, involving contracts let under the formal bid procedure, commissioners also exercise control through approval action when they award the contract.

Specifications

Good purchasing practice calls for buying in accordance with carefully developed specifications, if possible. For very small purchases of fairly standard items, development of elaborate specifications is not necessary, but simple standard specifications might be needed. For example, an order for "two dozen pencils" is clearly inadequate; a better description is necessary if satisfactory results are to be obtained from their use and if the best price is to be secured in buying.

Preparing specifications also requires the buyer to determine carefully what he needs. Buying higher quality than is needed can be just as costly as buying "cheap" goods that lack the necessary quality. And if there is to be real competition—without misunderstanding as to the quality needed, so that all bidders are quoting on the same kind and quality of goods—carefully drawn specifications are essential. Finally, when specifications have been carefully prepared, the county can safely buy on a low-bid basis among those bidders who offer products in accordance with specifications.

Assistance in preparing specifications is available from a number of

PURCHASING AND CONTRACTING 191

sources. Technical personnel in many departments can often write specifications. Vendors and trade associations of various types are willing to provide specifications of their own products, or general specifications for products of their members. And other governmental units—cities, counties, the State Division of Purchase and Contract, and the federal government—all produce specifications on a wide variety of goods which may be used as guides in developing specifications. While model and sample specifications are valuable, they should not be adopted without examination. Each user should determine that the specification is suitable for his use, or modify it appropriately.

Buying Without Specifications

Although the most desirable method of buying is on specification, there are times when specifications are not available and preparing them is impractical. Two other approaches are then available.

Or Equal. In using "or equal," a particular product is named as acceptable, and bid invitations ask for quotations on this product or any other product equal to it. The named product becomes the standard of quality. Thus the invitation might be for "Two 1975 Model D Bips or equal." Each bidder, of course, is likely to insist that his product is equal to the one named. If this happens, the buyer is responsible for deciding whether it is indeed equal. Some products may be clearly eliminated by invitations in this form, but frequently there will be borderline cases.

Approved Brand List. The use of the "approval brand list" is an improvement over "or equal" in that the buyer decides in advance which products will be acceptable and will satisfy his requirements. He can then buy on price alone among those listed. Care should be taken in using this approach to see that competition is not restricted and that new products are considered. If the list were too restrictive, this approach would probably not meet the competitive-bid requirements of the statutes.

Scheduling Purchases

The materials, supplies, and equipment that a county needs during the course of a year may be bought from day to day, purchased in advance and stored awaiting use, or secured under other arrangements. The arrangement adopted will, of course, depend on a number of factors. Most counties buy a bookkeeping machine, for example, only infrequently and would likely ask for bids on the machine separately. Gasoline for automobiles, on the other hand, is needed throughout the year, and different arrangements might be made for its purchase. Office supplies could call for still another approach. The three main approaches used in the scheduling of purchases are the advance requisition, warehousing, and the term contract.

Advance Requisition or Requisition Schedule. When this approach is used, the needs for various supplies or materials are estimated for each department for some period in advance—perhaps six months to a year. Needs of the different departments are consolidated, and a single, large-quantity purchase is made for all needs for the period. Delivery of the goods may be made either to a central storeroom or to small storage cabinets or rooms of the departments. The advantages of this approach are that it usually results in lower prices because of larger-quantity buying, supplies are on hand when needed, and paper work in processing orders is reduced. Where departmental storage facilities are inadequate or permit supplies to be damaged, the advantages of the requisition schedule may be partially lost.

Warehouses and Stores. Larger counties may find that savings will be realized by establishing warehouses or stores. Such operations permit quantity buying and holding of supplies for use as needed. Departmental storage may be eliminated, with orders to the storeroom or warehouse filled on short notice. Careful establishment of re-order levels for supplies assures their availability when needed. But central stores and warehouses cannot be operated without cost; for this reason, smaller counties do not usually find them advantageous.

Price Agreement or Term Contracts. A term contract (or price agreement) is one that establishes the price at which a county may buy its needs for a given item from a contractor during the period of the contract. Usually, such contracts are let by competitive bidding and are awarded to the lowest bidder. Deliveries under the contract are made on purchase orders as county needs arise; thus the supplier becomes the warehousing agent.

In some cases, the price is not firm but tied to an established price. For example, gasoline is frequently purchased under annual term contracts with a price at a stipulated discount from tank wagon price.

Counties and other public purchasing agencies are making increased use of term contracts. Most of the buying of state agencies in North Carolina is under term contracts let by the Division of Purchase and Contract. The combination of quantity buying without warehousing costs makes term contracting adaptable to the purchase of many items in frequent use.

Exceptional Purchases

Occasionally a county official needs to make purchases on an emergency basis, usually for special needs that arise when the purchasing office is closed, or because of breakdowns or other emergency situations. Careful attention to purchasing and operating needs will reduce the emergency purchases to a minimum, but "regular" procedures for these purchases should be established for officials to follow when necessary. Too much "emergency" purchasing by departmental officials frequently indicates either that the normal purchasing arrangements are not working well or that the county's purchasing procedures are being bypassed.

Most counties find a need for limited *petty cash* funds in some offices to make payments for goods or services (freight, for example) that cannot be easily handled through regular channels. Rules should be established for handling these funds and for replenishing them on presentation of proper supporting documents.

Purchase Order System

Whether purchasing is centralized or decentralized, every county should adopt some form of purchase order system. A few counties still do not use one. Department heads give telephone orders for goods, deliveries are made, and the accountant's or commissioners' first knowledge of the purchase comes when they receive an invoice for payment. And the invoice may cover deliveries made several months previously. Such a procedure clearly fails to meet the requirements of the Local Government Budget and Fiscal Control Act and makes internal control over expenditures exceedingly difficult.

A minimum purchase order system for decentralized purchasing should provide each department with three-part prenumbered purchase order forms. The department head can then keep one carbon for departmental reference and send the original and one carbon to the accountant. After certifying the availability of funds, the accountant can send the original to the vendor and retain the other copy for his records (either as a memorandum or for encumbrance). With the necessary routing modifications, the same purchase order forms can be used for confirming orders covering emergency purchases or replenishing petty cash funds.

Assistance in establishing and revising purchasing systems is available from a number of sources, including private consulting firms, the Local Government Commission, the North Carolina Association of County Commissioners, and the Institute of Government. Also, the accounting firm employed for the annual audit can usually advise on purchasing procedures and control.

BUYING UNDER STATE CONTRACTS

Public schools in North Carolina have long been required to buy under state contracts. The 1971 revision of the statutes that control state purchasing empowered, and made it the duty of, the Department of Administration (which acts through the Division of Purchase and Contract on purchasing matters) to make its services available to the state's local governments in purchasing supplies, materials, and equipment [G.S. 143-49(6)]. The statute makes the Advisory Budget Commission responsible for adopting rules and regulations under which the services are offered to local governments.

In 1973 the Advisory Budget Commission adopted the first rules to implement the legislation, and the Division of Purchase and Contract is now instituting a program that gives local governments the opportunity to purchase under state contracts.

The Division maintains over 120 statewide term contracts, each usually covering a period of twelve months, under which some 300,000 individual items of supplies, materials, and equipment may be purchased. The Division has started the program by making a number of these contracts available to local governments. Plans of the Division call for a steady expansion of the number of contracts that are available. By 1976 local governments will have the opportunity to purchase under almost all of the 120 term contracts. Many items under state contract are not often used by local governments and will never need to be made available under plans of the Division.

The rules adopted provide, essentially, that any local government that wishes to buy under state contracts must place itself in the same position as state agencies that are required to buy under state contracts. Before each new contract is advertised, the Division will notify local governments whether that contract is to be made available to them. Units that wish to come under the contract will advise the Division of this choice and give the Division information as to their estimated needs for the contract period. The state will solicit bids, award the contract, and notify participating local governments of the award(s) at the same time state agencies and institutions are notified. Thereafter, during the contract period, a participating local government simply places orders under the contract on an as-needed basis with the vendor who has received the contract. The vendor delivers and invoices to the local government and the local government pays the vendor directly.

During the contract period, a participating local government is obligated to buy all of its needs for the items covered from the state contractor and under the contract terms and conditions. The contractor, of course, is similarly committed. A local unit may decide to participate for one contract period and then decide to buy elsewhere for the following period. It may also choose to participate in one or more contracts but not in all that are available.

The Division requires that the local unit supply, in addition to information about participation and estimated needs, a copy of each purchase order issued under a state contract. This copy will be used to obtain necessary statistical information on how the contract is used. The Division will not approve or disapprove orders by local governments. Controlling of

PURCHASING AND CONTRACTING 195

the amount of its purchasing is entirely the prerogative and responsibility of each local government.

STATUTORY REQUIREMENTS IN PURCHASING AND CONTRACTING

Public purchasing must be accomplished in accordance with law. County commissioners are responsible, either directly or indirectly, for all county expenditures and for all contracts entered into by the county. Counties have broad powers to make such contracts as are necessary to the exercise of their powers and functions. But these broad powers are limited in that other statutes prescribe the manner in which they are exercised.

Formal Contracts

While "formal" contracts are not defined in the statutes, this is the name usually applied to contracts subject to G.S. 143-129—that is, to those for which bids must be advertised, sealed bids must be received, and the contract must be awarded as prescribed by law.

Coverage. Contracts that require the use of the formal bid procedure are those (a) for ". . . construction or repair work" that requires the estimated expenditure of $10,000 or more, and (b) for the purchase of "apparatus, supplies, materials, or equipment" that requires an estimated expenditure of $2,500 or more.

It should be noted that not all contracts are covered by the statute. Only those for "construction or repair" and for the purchase of "apparatus, supplies, materials, or equipment" are covered. Professional services—such as those of engineers, auditors, or attorneys—would clearly not fall within the statute. Purchases of real property are not subject to the competitive-contracting statute. Contracts for insurance, newspaper advertising, or tax mapping also appear to be outside the statute, although good business practice might suggest that a county follow the same procedure in letting these contracts as in letting ordinary construction or repair contracts. Thus the board of commissioners is required to follow the competitive-bidding procedure in most contracts and may, under its general contracting powers, elect to follow the same procedure on other contracts.

Exceptions. In certain cases the commissioners may set aside the normal requirements. In an emergency involving the "health and safety" of the people or their property, the commissioners may let contracts as necessary and in their discretion. Such a procedure should be followed only in a real emergency—in replacing the courthouse roof damaged by a storm, for example. When following the emergency procedure, the board should probably adopt a resolution finding that an emergency exists, documenting its nature, and thus justifying contracting outside the normal procedure.

Commissioners should remember that while it is within their power to decide that an emergency exists, the courts may be called upon to review such decisions (under appropriate proceedings) to determine whether the board's discretion has been abused.

The normal requirements may also be waived for purchases of apparatus, supplies, materials, or equipment from any other governmental unit or agency. Thus county governments may buy goods directly from city, state, and federal governments without securing bids. This exception is especially important in acquiring surplus state and federal property.

The final exception is really a limitation on the amount of construction work that a county may undertake with its own forces. Construction work that will be done by county forces and will have a total cost of not more than $25,000 may be undertaken without following the competitive-bidding procedure (G.S. 143-135). Conversely, the county may not undertake projects that will cost more than $25,000 with its own forces. (A few counties, by special acts, may have different limits or requirements.)

Specifications. There are no special requirements with respect to specifications for purchases. The governing board is free to write these as it deems best, except that it cannot write specifications so as to eliminate competition and thus defeat the purpose of the statute. If there is truly only one suitable product and competition is impossible, as may happen, it is generally agreed that a single product or item may be specified.

The governing board does not have the same freedom with respect to building contracts that require the expenditure of $20,000 or more (G.S. 143-128). For building contracts of this size, the statute requires that separate specifications must be prepared for:
(1) Heating, ventilating, and/or air conditioning, and accessories;
(2) Plumbing and gas fittings and accessories;
(3) Electrical installations;
(4) Refrigeration for cold storage where the cooling load is 15 tons or more of refrigeration.

Separate bids must be received on each of these branches of work, and the contracts for each branch must be awarded to firms "regularly engaged" in such work. When any branch of work is estimated to cost less than $2,500, it may be combined with some other branch in letting the contracts.

The only exception to these requirements authorizes local units to purchase and erect relocatable or prefabricated buildings without complying with the requirements for separate specifications and contracts. These requirements continue to apply with respect to work performed at the construction site.

Advertising. Bids on work subject to the formal contracting procedure must be invited by newspaper advertisement in a paper that has general circulation in the county. The advertisement must be published once at least a full week before the bids are opened.

What should the advertisement contain? G.S. 143-129 stipulates that the advertisement shall (a) indicate ". . . the time and place where plans and specifications may be had," (b) indicate ". . . the time and place for opening of the proposals . . . ," and (c) "reserve to [the governing body] the right to reject any or all proposals. . . ." For construction contracts, the engineer or architect may need to advise prospective bidders that they must be properly licensed (G.S. 87-15).

Many bid advertisements contain much more than required by statute—often, it would appear, without merit. Advertising all contract details and specifications when it is impossible to bid from the information contained in the advertisement probably only increases costs In short, some purpose other than meeting statutory requirements should be served when long bid advertisements are used.

Bid Deposit. Each bid proposal must be accompanied "at the time of its filing" by a bid deposit equal to not less than 5 per cent of the bid. The bid deposit may be in the form of cash, a cashier's check, a certified check, or bid bond. The bid deposit is retained if the bidder is awarded the contract and fails to execute the contract and give satisfactory performance bond within 10 days after the award.

Opening Bids. Bids must be opened in public and recorded on the minutes of the board of commissioners (G.S. 143-129). The Attorney General has ruled that this provision does not necessarily require that the bids be opened and read *before* the board. They may be opened in public by an officer of the county, tabulated, and brought before the board for action and recording in its minutes.

Standards in Awarding Contracts. Contracts must be awarded to ". . . . the lowest responsible bidder, taking into consideration quality, performance and the time specified in the proposals for the performance of the contract." Thus the only ground for not considering a bid that meets specifications (a bid that does not is not properly responsive to the invitation) is a finding that the bidder is not "responsible." As used in this sense, the "responsibility" of a bidder refers to his capacity to perform the contract, and may include consideration of his experience, the training and quality of his personnel, his financial strength, other work that he is under contract to finish, and other factors that might reasonably bear on his ability to perform as proposed. For example, a bid from a small painting contractor with no construction experience to build a courthouse might be subject to questioning in this sense.

In addition to price and responsibility, a board is authorized to consider quality, performance, and completion time. While the statute is clear that these factors may be considered, such consideration must be made carefully, and if the contract is awarded to other than the low bidder on the basis of this consideration, a governing board is probably well advised to state carefully the grounds for its decision. In some cases there may be no legal problems in making an award to other than the low bidder, but political and public consequences may be another matter. As a rule, if a board has exercised its best judgment and shown no favoritism or discrimination in its decision, the courts will not disturb its discretion. [A classic statement of the discretion of the governing board may be found in *Housing Authority of Opelousas, La. v. Pittman Construction Company*, 264 F. 2d 695 (1959). In this case the court held that when a governing body exercises discretion in awarding a contract, the body has a right to be wrong, dead wrong—but not unfairly or arbitrarily wrong.]

Number of Bids Required. G.S. 143-132 requires that for construction and repair contracts for which the estimated cost is $10,000 or more, the contract shall not be awarded unless ". . . at least three competitive bids have been received from reputable and qualified contractors regularly engaged in their respective lines of endeavor." The statute does not apply to contracts for the purchase of apparatus, supplies, materials, or equipment. The statute further directs that if less than three bids are received, a second advertisement should be made. After this second advertisement, the board of commissioners may award the contract even if only one bid is received.

Procedure When Bids Exceed Funds Available. At times the lowest bid on a proposed contract may exceed the amount of funds available for the project. What may be done? May the governing board negotiate with the lowest bidder? G.S. 143-129 provides that in such cases the governing board may ". . . enter into negotiations with the lowest responsible bidder . . . making reasonable changes in the plans and specifications as may be necessary to bring the contract price within the funds available, and may award a contract to such bidder [if he will agree] to perform the work at the negotiated price within the funds available therefor." The statute offers no guidance as to what might constitute a "reasonable" change, leaving this to the discretion of the governing board.

If negotiations following "reasonable changes" fail to bring the contract within limits of available funds, the governing board is authorized to alter the plans and specifications and readvertise the contract.

Performance and Payment Bonds. The 1974 General Assembly combined the statutory procedures relating to performance and payment bonds so that the requirements and limits are now the same for both (G.S. 44A-25 to -33). All formal construction contracts involving more than $10,000 must be executed in writing, and the county must require the contractor to post a performance bond and a payment bond for 100 per cent of the contract.

The performance bond is to assure that the contract will be completed in accordance with its terms and is for the county's protection. If the contractor defaults, the surety is responsible for seeing that the work is completed.

The payment bond is taken to assure that payment is made for all labor and materials furnished or used under the public construction contract. The bond is necessary to give workmen and suppliers on public construction protection equal to what they would have automatically with laborers' and materialmen's liens in private construction.

County commissioners may waive the performance bond requirement for contracts for the purchase of apparatus, supplies, materials, or equipment. The statutes do not require a payment bond for purchasing contracts.

In lieu of posting a bond, the contractor may deposit money, a certified check, or government securities equal to the contract price. If the contractor uses some form of deposit, the county will then have funds available to complete the work if the contractor defaults, or to pay for labor and supplies if the contractor has not done so. The statutes set forth detailed procedures for making claims against bonds and for making payments by the surety or by the county from deposits.

Informal Contracts

The informal contracting statute, G.S. 143-131, requires that contracts covered by the statute be let after bids are received. By common usage, telephone quotations and written quotations are considered informal bids. A catalogue price with some evidence to indicate that it is a standing offer would probably also be considered an informal bid. An informal bid is thus one not secured by a bid deposit, but one that a buyer may nevertheless rely upon to compare with other equally reliable price indications or quotations in making a purchasing decision.

Coverage. The informal contracting procedure required by G.S. 143-131 applies to all contracts for "construction or repair work" and purchases of "apparatus, supplies, materials, or equipment" involving expenditures of $1,000 or more but less than the lower limits for formal contracts as set forth in G.S. 143-129. Under existing statutes, this means that construction and repair work costing between $1,000 and $10,000 must be let to contract after informal bids are received, and purchasing contracts that require expenditures of $1,000 to $2,500 must be let in the same manner.

The types of contracts covered by the informal requirements are the same as those covered by formal requirements. The language in G.S. 143-131 is identical with that in G.S. 143-129—both statutes cover the same types of contracts and exempt the same types. (See page 195 for a discussion of types not covered.) As with contracts in the formal-bid range, counties are free to make purchases within the informal range from other governmental units or agencies without receiving informal bids.

Standards in Awarding Contracts. The standards for awarding informal contracts are the same as those for formal contracts. (See page 197 for a discussion.) The statute directs that such contracts ". . . shall be awarded to the lowest responsible bidder, taking into consideration quality, performance, and the time specified in the bids for the performance of the contract." Since no advertisement is required for informal bids, bids are likely to be received only from those vendors who are asked to quote. The purchasing official thus has an opportunity to limit his solicitation to those bidders whom he considers responsible. The considerations in making awards (or in not making awards) to the low bidder are the same for informal contracts as for formal contracts. Most counties find it advisable to award to the low bidder unless there are clear and decisive factors of quality, performance, or delivery that justify an award to other than the low bidder.

Record of Bids. The sealed bid procedure in formal contracts assures that records of bids received will be made and that they will be recorded on the minutes of the board of commissioners. The statute does not require that informal bids appear in the board's minutes, but it does direct that a record of all such bids be kept and ". . . be subject to public inspection at any time." The officer who receives informal bids should record the date each quotation is received, from whom it is received, and for what item. Special care should also be taken to indicate why an award was made if it went to other than the low bidder.

In essence, the informal contracting procedure is designed not to avoid open competitive bidding on public contracts, but to provide an inexpensive and efficient manner of securing competitive bidding for small purchases or small construction and repair contracts.

CONFLICT OF INTEREST

That no man can serve two masters is a principle of human conduct affirmed by St. Matthew [6:24] and recognized in the English common law for centuries. The principle is widely recognized in statutes that make it unlawful for a public official to make, in his official capacity, public contracts in which he has a private interest.

The North Carolina legislature first enacted a prohibition of this type in 1825. The present statute, G.S. 14-234, is essentially the same as the original statute; it provides that any person in a position of public trust who makes a contract in which he has a private interest is guilty of a misdemeanor.

The statute makes two exceptions to the broad prohibition. With the governing board's approval, a county may do business with a bank even if one of the commissioners is an officer or stockholder of the bank. Second, a county official may in his private capacity provide personal services to clients or goods to customers even though the cost is financed through the county if the fees or prices are standard and the client or customer has a free choice in selecting who will provide his services. For example, a doctor who is a county commissioner may provide professional services to welfare recipients whose medical needs are supported by public funds if the recipient himself selects the doctor-commissioner.

Also, county commissioners are responsible for all contracts made by the county, whether the contracts are approved directly and separately by the board or made by some officer at the commissioners' direction on behalf of the county. Board members are thus a party to all county contracts and are prohibited from selling any goods or services to the county while they remain members of the board.

If a county employee purchased goods for the county from the private business of a member of the board of commissioners, and if the commissioner absented himself from the board meeting when the invoice was presented for approval, would the commissioner be in violation of the statute? The North Carolina Supreme Court has held in such a situation that the board member was guilty of a violation, even though no moral turpitude was demonstrated. The clear rule, then, is that the board member cannot do business with the county that he serves as a commissioner, and the same rule applies to any other county official who acts for the county in his official capacity; he may not contract with himself to serve a private financial interest.

The rule undoubtedly imposes hardships at times. A board member may own the only business in a county that provides certain goods the county must have. Nevertheless, the only course available is to go elsewhere for service, even though to do so may be more expensive.

A small, noncontrolling interest in a private business is generally thought not to pose a problem of conflict of interest for a board member. For example, a board member could safely act on the purchase of automobiles from a local agency if his interest was limited to ownership of stock in General Motors.

The prohibition against self-dealing also extends to the offering of personal services. Board members cannot pay themselves additional compensation for performing special services for the county, services over and above their duties as commissioners. For example, a board member who happens to be an engineer may not accept pay for supervising the construction of a county building, even though he is willing to do so at much less expense than would be incurred by employing someone else.

Commissioners may occasionally be uncertain whether a particular situation falls within the statute. They are then well advised to seek the counsel of their county attorney or the State Attorney General.

COOPERATIVE PURCHASING

Counties may join with other counties and with cities in cooperative purchasing under the authority for interlocal cooperation found in G.S. Ch. 160A, Art. 20 (see Chapter 21, page 392). Cooperative and joint purchasing actions may range from the joint purchase of a single class of items to the merger of purchasing offices. For example, Edgecombe County and the Town of Tarboro have jointly purchased gasoline and radio equipment. Guilford County vehicles are serviced in Greensboro's city garage, and Mecklenburg County and the City of Charlotte have created a joint purchasing department that serves both governments.

BUILDING CONTRACTS

A number of statutes are concerned with the special aspects of contracts for public buildings. The key statutes are these:

(1) G.S. 87-15 requires that plans and specifications inform prospective bidders that they must be licensed when the cost of the contract will be large enough to limit its undertaking to licensed contractors.
(2) G.S. 133-1.1 requires that most public buildings that will cost more than $45,000 be designed by an architect or an engineer.
(3) G.S. 133-3 requires designers of public buildings to specify in their plans at least three items of equal design, if possible, to promote competition on all goods used in constructing public buildings.
(4) G.S. 143-135 exempts counties and other political subdivisions of the state from the competitive bidding requirements on construction contracts involving less than $25,000 when the work is undertaken by officers and employers of the unit concerned.
(5) G.S. 143-128 requires that separate specifications be drawn and bids taken for the various types of work on building contracts that involved the expenditure of $20,000 or more, except for prefabricated buildings.
(6) Special authorization for the joint construction of public buildings by a county and any municipality within the county or by two or more counties is granted by G.S. 153A-164.

STATE TAX REFUNDS

G.S. 105-164.14 authorizes the refund of sales and use taxes paid by counties directly on the purchases of tangible personal property and indirectly on taxable property that may be used by contractors in erecting public buildings for counties. Refunds are made only when applications are filed as required by the Commissioner of Revenue, and within six months of the close of each fiscal year.

A refund of 8 cents of the state tax on each gallon of gasoline paid by counties is authorized by G.S. 105-446.1. Applications for these refunds are made to the Commissioner of Revenue on forms prescribed by him.

FAIR TRADE AND COLLUSIVE BIDDING

All local governments are exempted from the North Carolina Fair Trade Act by G.S. 66-57, thus preventing the enforcement of fair trade agreements if the deviation from the fair trade price is in connection with a sale to a local government. Under G.S. 75-5(b) (7), collusive bidding is unlawful.

— *Warren J. Wicker*

8 / Public Relations

Definition and Significance / 206
Adaptation and Interpretation to Publics / 207
Origins / 208
Factors Affecting Public Relations / 208
Factors Relating to Administration / 209
Factors Relating to Communication / 209
  Communication Goals / 209
  Communication Means / 209
  Communication Selection / 210
  Communication Preparation / 211
  Communication Presentation / 212
Factors Relating to Liaison / 212
  Intra-agency Relations / 213
  Interagency Liaison / 213
  Liaison with Nongovernmental and Private Groups / 213
  Liaison with the Mass Communication Media / 214
  Liaison with the General Public / 214
General Perspective on Public Relations / 215

8 / PUBLIC RELATIONS

DEFINITION AND SIGNIFICANCE

A veteran public official appearing on a Press-Government panel at the Institute of Government was asked whether he would try to hide his mistakes from press and public. "Never!" he answered promptly. "When I find I've pulled a boo-boo, I call in the press and tell them about it. I never try to sweep things under the rug. It doesn't pay."

This official was talking not only about policy but also about one aspect of public relations. So was another who said: "I always try to keep my door open to the general public." And so was a third who set up a program designed to help his public agency train employees in such matters as answering the telephone courteously, maintaining a neat appearance, and using time expeditiously.

Public relations is not just a matter of knowing the laws or office procedures, although good public relations may demand that you know both. It is primarily a matter of knowing people, including yourself, those you work with, those you live with, and those you serve and to whom you are responsible.

In fact, relations with publics, general and special, affect and are affected by everything you do.

Policies, statements, votes, reports, conduct, and participation in meetings and conferences, speeches, interviews, press statements, decisions, even manners, appearance, and home life can mean the difference between praise and criticism, success and failure in the daily functions of a public official. Public relations involves a golden rule, a public rule, and a measuring rule. That is, it concerns in varying degree one's ability and willingness to do unto others as one would have them do unto him; to recognize the publics one serves; to apply effectively one's role of service; and to evaluate the legal, logical, and emotional needs of one's position and their relationship to his public responsibility.

Specifically, for our purposes, public relations may be said to involve relations between governmental agencies and many special publics. To understand the general purpose and basic elements of public relations, however, requires mention of at least two other definitions. It has been said that "public relations have to do with the development and maintenance by any legitimate means of a favorable attitude on the part of the people with whom an agency comes into contact." In broader context, *Webster's* defines the term as follows: "1. The activities of a corporation, union, government, or other organization building and maintaining sound and productive relations with special publics such as customers, employees, or stockholders, and with the public at large, so as to adapt itself to its environment and interpret itself to society. 2. The state of such activities or the art of organizing them." Let us examine these definitions more closely.

If one recognized purpose of public relations is to encourage favorable attitudes by means of activities designed to build and keep good and useful relations inside and outside the agency, what is the significance of those other broader purposes: "To adapt itself to its environment and interpret itself to society?"

And who are these "special publics" to whom the agency must adapt and interpret?

ADAPTATION AND INTERPRETATION TO PUBLICS

Let us suppose that an agency or organization adopts speech, customs, attitudes, or procedures that are anathema to the community or region in which it functions. Its relations with the public and, consequently, its chances for success would be about those of a mole on a high wire or an ostrich in a flood. Let us suppose that the public body made no effort to understand its own basic responsibilities or goals or the needs and attitudes of the public it was called on to serve. Its acceptance likely would be the rough equivalent of that of a snake by a mongoose. The very essence of public relations, then, is derived from adaptation to environment and appropriate interpretation to society. *Webster's* definition might well have noted a step precedent: analysis of environment in order to understand it. Without this step, no adaptation or interpretation will ever meet the conditions of society.

The public at large includes every individual to whom an official has a responsibility for service. Some of these individuals also belong to special publics that may have special access to or requirements from governmental agencies in terms of public relations. These special publics include personnel of governmental agencies; the working press (representatives of newspapers, radio, television, and other mass communication media); members of civic and community service organizations; and special interest groups. So there is not just *one* public for officers of government to inform and to help understand and approve public actions. There are many, and the individual may belong both to the general public and to special publics.

Recognition of the various publics in the context of environment and interpretation requires cognizance of the complex of interests and demands that they represent and utilization of system, variety, and continuity in the functioning of any effective public relations program. Since public relations is concerned with forming and changing attitudes to achieve a desired response, its basic ideas often find root in individual and social psychology; and its practices and methods are defined and developed by persons of professional skills: educators, information specialists, statisticians, and counselors—experts in relevant facts and figures, human motivations, and advertising techniques. The result is that effective public relations requires considerable thought and planning, based on careful analysis of the agency and its publics and the intelligent formulation of policies, practices, and programs in the light of needs. This requires a two-way concept: a government official, group, or agency must both *provide* and *receive* information and understanding in constant interaction with its publics.

ORIGINS

In the beginning there was press agentry. The circus barker and patent medicine vendor of the late nineteenth century and early twentieth century presaged the fast-talking, slick-writing publicity men that enterprising commercial and industrial firms found could help market their products. Publicity was at once a vehicle and a goal of the press agent. In this century the individualistic background of tent and wagon gave way to the symbols of modern high-speed transportation and communication, the mass communications media: first newspapers and magazines, then motion pictures, radio, and television. Although the publicity aspects of public relations remained important, the concept gradually changed to embrace public service and fair play. No longer was the only technique the "hard sell" and the only goal to influence customers or clients. No government can afford to oversell the people. Now the process is more complex, the organization, agency, and individual involvement more nearly total, and the introspective or self-analytical aspects (sometimes relating to "the public image") important beyond the realm of "publicity."

Today, public relations relates to every personal contact, by officials and employees on duty and off, with any member or members of the public. In this expanded concept good public relations has become a prime asset and constant goal of business and government. Public relations policy remains a function of management or independent officialdom; public relations practice requires the awareness and cooperation of every person in any way connected with the organization, agency, or enterprise. Public good will can ride on an unbuttoned shirt, unshined shoe, discourteous remark, or broken promise.

FACTORS AFFECTING PUBLIC RELATIONS

Public relations is primarily a management function, requiring policy decisions. As a result, factors of administration and communication affect the nature and quality of public relations. Policy, for example, must be determined at the administrative or legislative level, and the wisdom and practicality of policy are keys to success or failure of public relations. Similarly, public relations can be no more effective than the chain of policy communication with employees and publics will allow.

Factors Relating to Administration

There are many hurdles to effective public relations at an administrative level. One is the very complexity of government which forces one official or set of officials to compete with others for the attention of an oversaturated public; another is the variety of publics to be served; a third, the variety of attitudes within those publics. Then there is the effect of past experience on those attitudes, resulting in understandable caution against accepting "government propaganda" or fear of pressures from "too much government." Again, there is an understandable official reluctance to use public funds for public relations purposes, thereby often denying the means for access to professional assistance, objective research and measurement, and coordinated programs. Finally, there is the failure of many officials to recognize the value inherent in public relations and their responsibility to maintain, promote, keep open, and develop the channels and currents which lead to public understanding and good will.

It must be recognized that daily decisions regarding office, interagency, and public procedures and practices do much to determine both the quality of administration and the kind of public relations. Accordingly, official judgments on matters affecting the general public or any segment of the public require groundwork and explanation. Even decisions regarding office arrangement and personal appearance can better or worsen relations. And coordination of all activities is a *sine qua non* for a superior program.

Factors Relating to Communication

Communication Goals. Good public relations depends upon effective communication. The goal of communicating is to convey facts, ideas, and opinions in such a manner as to add to the information, knowledge, and understanding of the listener, reader, or viewer. This requires that the facts, ideas, or opinions be organized and arranged in a pertinent, reliable, and meaningful pattern. Subject matter needs not only presentation but interpretation as well. Thus, communication also requires the interpretation of facts, opinions, and ideas. A good communicator learns to present and interpret a given subject with skill and clarity. Otherwise, he fails to give to his audience the necessary confidence in his own expertness and the value of his presentation.

Communication Means. Communication may be oral or written (typed, printed, etc.); personal or impersonal; individual, group, or mass; aural or visual; or a combination of means and approaches. Oral communication is verbal and demands the ability to speak clearly and effectively. That ability, in turn, requires awareness and practice of effective speech principles and techniques. *Oral* communication occurs in casual motivated conversation, interviews, meetings, conferences, lectures, forums, group and panel discussions, symposiums, public addresses, debates, stage performances, and appearances on radio, television, or film. To get the best results from most of these occasions and media, one must have some concept of their basic nature and requirements. For example, some study of techniques used in interviewing, rules of parliamentary procedure as applied to meetings, and speaking for microphone and camera can be helpful in the performance of govermental responsibilities. *Written, typed, or printed* communication is essential in the preparation and release of reports, documents, and news releases and to provide certainty of statement at meetings, occasions, and appearances on the mass communication media. Preparing material to be read rather than heard often permits the use of longer words and more complicated sentences. Yet even in written communication, conciseness is a virtue. *Physical* communication relates to the impression given by sheer presence. One needs only to have seen the old Charlie Chaplin silent films or a beautiful painting to be aware that communication does not depend upon words. Indeed, gestures and movement (even surroundings) can communicate eloquently and convincingly. The effective communicator will be aware of this and use tools of visual communication judiciously to augment and enhance his efforts.

Communication Selection. Selection of the kind of communication hinges, in part, upon the direction of communication. To communicate with other members of a board may require only a personal conversation or a telephone call. To confer with public officials or employees with different responsibilities or at other levels of government may require a letter or memorandum. Communication with personally known individuals or segments of the public at large may normally be oral. But to reach special publics or the public at large may require an oral or written press release, radio or television appearance, public address, or written report. Demands depend upon audience and occasion. *"Internal"* communication—i.e., between members of the same organization—calls for variant handling, depending upon whether the message is going "up" to persons with a higher level of responsibility, "down" to those with less status or responsibility, or "level" to persons in the same or similar position or with equal status. *"External"* communication—i.e., to individuals or groups outside of the immediate organization—must be planned with the view to best reaching the specific informational needs and backgrounds of the specific audience. In all kinds of communication there must be a recognition of a "two-way" process between speaker and audience and an awareness of the qualifications and relationships of both. There must be a further awareness that no worthwhile presentation is possible without adequate preparation. These two processes—preparation and presentation—represent complementary sides of the coin of communication as it passes in the marketplace of human relations.

Communication Preparation. One should use every resource at his command to prepare himself for the occasion: research, experience, analysis, discussion with knowledgeable persons, and organization of material. Here are some keys to preparation.

(1) Identify and analyze the occasion, publics, purpose, and your own qualifications. Apply the results of your analysis to your preparation.

(2) Decide upon a specific purpose or goal. Be aware of the techniques of reporting, inquiry, persuasion, and inspiration, and use these rhetorical objectives singly or in combination, as appropriate.

(3) Cast and limit your concept to make certain you have or obtain a perspective on your subject.

(4) Do careful and thorough research, using library and personal resources.

(5) Outline and organize your material. The following divisions are applicable to oral and written preparation:

- (a) *Introduction.* Determine whether the subject matter may be approached directly or whether the publics to be reached require some preliminary explanatory matter or motivation.
- (b) *Discussion.* This is the heart of the presentation. Here is written or stated the purpose of the presentation—main points, development of ideas, and illustrations.
- (c) *Conclusion.* All publics tend to remember best that which is heard or read last. Thus, no preparation is complete that does not provide for a summary or, at least, a statement in perspective of the substance of the presentation. The conclusion is designed to win acceptance of and, in some cases, action on, the ideas presented. In other words, it is important not only that the public understand and perhaps come to agree with the communicator, but sometimes that it vote, abstain, confirm, or otherwise act in furtherance of its understanding or agreement.

(6) Be aware of the two-way relationship between officials and publics. Recognize principles of listening or reading as well as those of speaking and writing. Make necessary distinctions in publics so that each segment as well as the totality may be best served. This requires making an allowance for different backgrounds, needs, viewpoints, and so on. Mold preparation to these backgrounds, interests, and needs.

(7) Decide upon the appropriate media and method for presentation. Decisions must be carefully reached on such alternative possibilities as

speaking or writing to individuals, groups, or the entire public; preparing news releases or holding news conferences; appearing for speeches, interviews, forums, group discussions, panels, debates, and symposiums; speaking impromptu (off the cuff), extemporaneously, or from memory; editing manuscripts, or reading prepared materials; using newspapers, radio, television, films, slides, tapes, graphs, charts, or blackboards; place and timing; and maintaining silence.

(8) Strive for appropriate language and style. Avoid clichés ("old hat" ways of speaking and writing). Language can be vivid, symbolic, and exciting. Work to achieve clear, concise, and cogent style as an aid to understanding. Stay within the bounds of taste and reason.

(9) Arrange facts, opinions, and ideas in patterns that combine to permit fair and reliable interpretation. Interpret through the use of comparison and contrast, cause and effect, and other established methods.

These guides to preparation, if followed, will help eliminate such barriers to effective presentation as "stage fright" or poor organization.

Communication Presentation. Once preparation is thorough and complete, the job of presentation can be seen in proportion. It involves speaking, writing, or otherwise communicating in terms of *meaning* and *feeling* rather than mere words. A direct approach, using eye contact in oral presentation, helps to win public attention. Appropriate gestures and pauses in speaking, and underlining, spacing, and paragraphing in writing, are necessary to a rounded approach. Both writing and speaking call for vitality. In speaking, body action augments sound. Good posture and appropriate body movement are vital factors in oral presentation; so are gestures to denote emphasis, approval, disapproval, size, designation, and various shadings and nuances. An acceptable speaking voice can be assured, in part, by the proper use of resonance, pitch, pace, and quality. Diction also is important. In writing there are equally essential factors: cohesion, style, word usage, etc. In speech or writing, qualities of sincerity, fairness, dignity, humor, and integrity are to be established as prerequisites to getting results. No communication occurs in a vacuum. Inevitably, such things as reputation, choices, and attitudes will enter into the over-all impression. Generally the best approach is realistic and affirmative, but there is no paradox in the fact that imagination is an important element in any effective communication. The presentation must build in a manner comparable to a good story or play. This means that a conclusion, when read or voiced, must have a vigor and freshness to bring the presentation to a convincing culmination.

Factors Relating to Liaison

Public relations requires effective liaison between individuals and groups within the public board, agency, or organization; between the board and other public agencies or organizations; between the board and private agencies or organizations; and between the board and the general public. In each case, since public relations policy is determined by board members or agency administrators, the quality of decision is a primary factor in the kind and quality of performance and public acceptance.

Intra-agency Relations. Maximum morale, effort, and coordination within the board or agency are contingent upon the understanding, confidence, and cooperation of all board members and employees. No substitute has been found for taking other board members or agency employees into full confidence and letting them know the reasons underlying any decisions affecting the agency or any of its publics. The normal direction for the passage of information is from the top down; however, where membership of boards or commissions makes all communicants equals, communication may be "vertical" from the chairman or "horizontal" among members. In either case, orderly procedures for such dissemination of information should be established and followed in the interest of both efficiently spreading truth and scotching rumor and falsehood. Full disclosure of plans or facts to intra-agency personnel can be of the utmost importance. A tendency to withhold essential information has been the downfall of many a well-meaning official.

Interagency Liaison. Different public boards, agencies, and organizations have variant responsibilities. Because these responsibilities often require that one board hold the decision-making authority over other groups in matters of finance, budgeting, personnel, or authority, the existence of carefully selected and organized channels of communication is essential to effective liaison and healthy relationships. County commissioners, for example, have to deal with some authority with local boards of education, welfare, health, planning, and zoning, among others. Obviously, under such circumstances, there must be careful evaluation and balancing of needs and availabilities, together with creative thinking on ways and means to achieve desired ends. Even given a most conscientious effort to reconcile differences, challenge and conflict often will arise to handicap relationships. Workable solutions must stem from constant efforts to balance interests and see that divergent programs are worked into a cohesive framework of public law and government.

Liaison with Nongovernmental and Private Groups. Official communication with schools, colleges, civic clubs, commercial organizations, and other groups requires a willingness to give and take, to talk and listen, to exchange views, and to plan and coordinate together in the public interest. Not all ideas submitted by these groups will prove acceptable in the light of the over-all official perspective and understanding. But many a useful idea has come from fertile minds in citizen groups. Conversely, these groups and organizations, properly approached and informed, often become the spearheads for informing and persuading the remainder of the public that an official aim or proposal is desirable.

Liaison with the Mass Communication Media. Publicity and reporting remain at or near the center of useful public relations. Although federal and state agencies usually hire public information officers or set up public relations staffs in recognition of the requirements of public information, most local governments, for reasons of cost or insufficient needs, have no sources of public relations other than the public officials and employees who are directly charged with other primary responsibilities. The result is that each official is, in effect, a potential source of news or publicity. As a consequence, official relationships with the working press are vital to the knowledge and attitudes of the public at large. Cultivation of a relationship of mutual respect and understanding between officials and newsmen usually insures a well-informed public and an opportunity for a healthy functioning of the democratic process. It is well to remember that the press—consisting of newspaper, radio, and TV reporters; editorialists; and analysts—operates under the constitutional guarantee of a free press and that it is often said that the press represents "the people's right to know." It is also essential that any public official be able to correlate his responsibilities and those of his associates with those of the news media. More and more, officials are finding that mutual confidence, built through open and honest dealings, works to the advantage of all.

Liaison with the General Public. Official use of press interviews, news conferences, public statements, radio and television appearances, and even film have become standard means of extending to the widest possible public a helping hand in its quest for greater knowledge and understanding of public affairs. Such concepts as open meetings, available public records, access to proceedings, and frank and full discussion are confined to governments of free people. Others cannot afford them. Except in those cases where law or equally important considerations of public policy forbid, the rule of access deserves the respect of public officials for liaison with the general public.

No public relations program can be successful without the ultimate support of the general public. A government official, board, or agency meets the people not only through print and air lanes but in daily personal contact. To a citizen with a complaint, "red tape" resulting in undue delays or waiting is not a trivial matter. Neither is a want of courtesy on the part of a public employee or a failure to listen attentively or advise circumspectly. A grease spot on a tie or an unmatched pair of socks does not accord with the desired image of a public servant. An evidence of negligence or incompetence, even in the slightest degree, can handicap or impede public recognition of general integrity and competence. Headaches can be avoided by anticipating problems and taking steps to make certain that officials and their environment can pass public inspection. Procedure, appearance, courtesy, efficiency—these are among the touchstones of good over-all public relations. Integrity, rooted in high competence, public purpose, and personal ethics, provides the key to continuing public confidence.

GENERAL PERSPECTIVE ON PUBLIC RELATIONS

Public relations may not seem to compare in significance with the legal, quasi-legal, and formal requirements of office-holding or public service. Yet it involves both the art and science of getting along with people with honor and understanding and without undue pride or abasement. Its purposes provide a free and constant reciprocal flow of useful, reliable, and positive information between government and publics, furthering mutual understanding of public needs and directions and contributing to the maintenance of a climate in which intelligent, informed interaction between officials and publics assures both good government and good citizenship. The aim is not to homogenize thought or action but rather to provide a dynamic process through which the strengths and weaknesses of divergent views may become known and channels may be provided for proper evaluation and effective utilization. Any good public relations program has its base in information, its mortar in liaison, and its structure in analysis and interpretation. It requires direction through quality administration and dissemination through constructive relationships with the mass communication media. The requisite two-way flow of information requires an articulate, informed citizenry in constant communication with a receptive government, which uses governmental and nongovernmental publications together with oral presentations to reach into the minds and hearts of the public.

Public relations is part of everyone and belongs to no one. It tends to gain in application from a positive rather than a negative approach. It must have continuity and point. It cannot be dissociated from the obligations of personal life insofar as it relates to public obligations. Stability, honesty, fairness, competence, vision,—these are among the personal assets that can help to assure effective public relations. And, above all, there is a sense of personal and group responsibility, and attitude of servant rather than oracle, an approach of testing rather than demand, and a follow-through of care and conviction that must undergird any mutuality of meaning, understanding, and cooperation between a public body and a body public. For public relations, in the ultimate, depends upon public trust and confidence—which must be earned.

— *Elmer R. Oettinger*

9 / Records Management

Introduction / 218
Commissioners' Statutory Authority / 219
Disposition of Unneeded Records / 219
Use of Photographic Equipment / 220
Authority of the Division of Archives and History / 221
The *County Records Manual* / 221
Inventory, Repair, and Microfilming of Records / 222
Records-Management Advice and Assistance / 222

9 / RECORDS MANAGEMENT

INTRODUCTION

Taken together, the public offices of the 100 North Carolina counties constitute the largest depository of public records in the state. Much that is essential to public and governmental affairs as well as to commercial and private matters is affected by the variety of records and documents maintained by county officials. While many of the factors relating to creation, maintenance, and disposition of records are regulated directly by law, the attitude, interest, and cooperation of a board of county commissioners can have considerable influence upon the quality and general usefulness of county records. This chapter will summarize briefly some of the statutory duties and responsibilities for records management of the boards of county commissioners and describe some of the services available to counties in this regard.

Generally speaking, the county offices in which most county records are kept are those of the register of deeds, the clerk of the superior court. the local school superintendent, the county accountant, the tax supervisor, the director of social services, and the sheriff, in roughly that order, based upon volume of records. The two major county record custodians are the register of deeds and the superior court clerk. Most of the register's records are instruments and documents that affect the title to real or personal property or that relate to vital statistics (births, deaths, and marriages), while the clerk's records, although extremely varied, relate primarily to the operation of the courts or to matters that affect the administration of estates of deceased persons.[1]

Most counties in recent years have had a great increase in the volume of public records, particularly those records of permanent or long-term value, and this trend seems likely to continue, particularly in the offices of the

---

1. The records of the clerks of superior court occupy an unusual position. Although these records are housed at the county level, they are state records and their management is under the jurisdiction of the Administrative Office of the Courts (see N.C. GEN. STAT. §§ 7A-101 and -343). But with the consent of both the Division of Archives and History and the Administrative Office of the courts, the clerk's records are included in the *County Records Manual, 1970*. The county commissioners' authority over the clerk's records extends only to the designation of office and repository space.

register of deeds and clerk of the superior court. The cost of creating and maintaining these records will therefore continue to present problems.

COMMISSIONERS' STATUTORY AUTHORITY

The statutes that relate to the authority of boards of county commissioners with respect to public records are scattered through the General Statutes, with some overlap among the various sections. The commissioners' authority is generally related to the administration and management of the county's public records and is not particularly related to the operations of any particular county office or officers. No attempt is made here to discuss the various laws that regulate the creation, filing, management, and disposition of records as applied to a specific county official or office. The records procedures in the office of the register of deeds are discussed in the *Guidebook for Registers of Deeds* published by the Institute of Government.

Disposition of Unneeded Records

Perhaps the county commissioners' most important general authority regarding county records concerns the destruction or permanent removal from county offices of records that no longer have any local official use or value. These records are generally one of two types those that have no official use or value at the county level but have historical value, and those that have neither official nor historical value. With the increasing volume of records in many county offices, the full use of the statutory procedures for disposing of unneeded records takes on great importance. The elimination of records that have no official value has a direct bearing not only on the efficient use and management of valuable public records but also on the cost to the county of maintaining and operating the record custodians' offices. The statutes provide a procedure by which records that fall into either of the above categories may be removed from the county offices to free storage space. When a custodian of county records certifies to his board of commissioners and to the Division of Archives and History of the State Department of Cultural Resources that certain records are of no further use or value for official business of the county, the Division, if it determines that the records are of no value for historical research or reference purposes, may authorize their destruction. If the records are of historical value, it may accept them from the county or request the county to retain custody. In no case, however, should records be destroyed except as authorized by resolution of the board of county commissioners. Records legally may be transferred to the Division of Archives and History without the commissioner's consent, although some officials may prefer to secure their consent first. When records are destroyed or disposed of in accordance with this procedure, the records custodian is protected from any later liability that might otherwise be imposed as a result of the destruction or disposition of public records.

When destruction of records is authorized, they should be in fact destroyed and not permitted to fall into unauthorized hands. There are no provisions in the state laws permitting records to be removed permanently from the custodian's office except for destruction or transfer to the Division of Archives and History. County officials are frequently confronted with requests from individuals or various local historical societies or groups asking that records intended for destruction be instead turned over to them. Since records with any significant historical value may not be destroyed (but may be transferred to the Division), it is not likely that records that legally may be destroyed will be of much value to such unofficial groups, and, as noted, the law does not provide for such disposition. Nonconfidential records probably may be sold to commercial concerns as waste paper if there is reasonable assurance that they will be handled and processed carefully to destroy their identity. Otherwise, destruction should be accomplished by burning, shredding, pulping, burial, or other effective means.

A permanent account should be kept of all records destroyed or disposed of. This may be done by means of a separate record or log maintained by each records custodian, or it may be included in the minutes of the board of county commissioners. Such a record should include a description of the type and quantity in each group destroyed, the inclusive dates covered by the various types of records, and the date and method of destruction. It is also a good plan to maintain a similar log of records transferred to the Division of Archives and History.

Use of Photographic Equipment

The statutory provisions regarding photographic reproduction of county records are now contained in G.S. 153A-436. General statutory consent is given to counties to establish systems for reproducing records in the register of deeds' office and in other county offices photographically. The copies produced, however, must be legible and permanent. These copies, which are to serve as the permanent record copies, must be stored in a fire-resistant file, vault, or similar container. Once a county has established a system for photographing or microphotographing records, the original record may be removed from its regular repository for up to 24 hours for filming, and it may be removed from the county if necessary. A record may be removed from the custody of its regular repository for more than 24 hours only with permission from the county commissioners. The commissioners may authorize removal longer than 24 hours if more time is needed to reproduce the document. Once a photographic copy of a recorded instrument is made pursuant to G.S. 153A-436, the reproduction is a sufficient recording for all purposes.

AUTHORITY OF THE DIVISION OF ARCHIVES AND HISTORY

Although the Division of Archives and History of the Department of Cultural Resources has had some statutory responsibility concerning county records since 1935, only in recent years has its legal authority been broadened and sufficient funds made available to enable the Division to initiate a substantial program of assistance to the counties. The Division's primary interest is in preserving records and documents of historic value, but its services can also be helpful in the management of all local records. These services can generally be divided into three categories of programs: The *County Records Manual;* inventory, repair, and microfilming; and records-management assistance and advice.

The County Records Manual

In accordance with the statutory requirement that the Division of Archives and History administer a statewide program of local records management, the *County Records Manual* was first published in 1960 and was revised and republished in 1962 and 1970 with the help of an advisory committee composed of county officials and members of the Institute of Government staff. This publication's primary purpose is to provide a recommended retention schedule for most types of records to be found in the office of each major record custodian in the several counties. The records are grouped according to the county office or official that has custody, with a recommendation as to how long each type of record should be kept and how it should ultimately be disposed of. The *Manual's* purpose is not to compel public officials to destroy records when the time periods indicated in the schedules expire. But the Division of Archives and History will routinely give permission in accordance with the record schedule to custodians who wish to dispose of unneeded records to free storage space for records that have permanent or current temporary value.

Besides the record-retention schedule, the *Manual* contains regulations and instructions concerning county records promulgated by the Division, plus an appendix of state statutes pertinent to county records and the Division's authority and responsibility in this respect. When it was first published and each time it has been revised, the *County Records Manual* has been distributed to chairmen of boards of county commissioners, the affected county offices, and the county attorneys.

Inventory, Repair, and Microfilming of Records

In 1959 the Division of Archives and History began a program of inventory, repair, and microfilming that is perhaps the nation's largest undertaking concerned with permanently preserving valuable local records. Under this program the Division visits the various offices in each county (starting with the oldest), making complete inventories of the records in each office (and preparing a schedule for each similar to those in the *County Records Manual, 1970*), repairing all records of permanent value that need repair, and microfilming all permanent records for security storage. The cost of this program, including the repair service, is borne by the state. In accordance with the requirements of law, however, the commissioners' approval is required before records may be removed from the custodian's office. Copies made from the security microfilm are available to the counties at cost and could be used to replace permanent records destroyed by disaster or other cause. The Division has finished its first visits to each county and has now begun another cycle of filming, starting with the first counties visited, microfilming the permanent records created since the first visit. Some counties are themselves microfilming their permanent records and providing the Division with a microfilm negative of each record.

Records-Management Advice and Assistance

The third aspect of the Division's records-management program involves aid and advice to individual counties or officials in connection with creating, using, maintaining, retaining, preserving, and disposing of official records. Except for the *County Records Manual,* which technically is one aspect of its duty and responsibility, the Division has not done a great deal in this area, primarily because it has lacked both trained personnel and funds. Its help is available, however, in connection with all types of local records problems. The Division may be particularly helpful in such matters as selecting the equipment that may be used in a records-management program. Many kinds of equipment are available for various purposes, and it is important to make certain that a particular machine will render the service needed before a considerable investment of county funds is made.

— *William A. Campbell*

10 / Legal Liabilities of Counties and County Commissioners

Introduction / 224
Torts: The Legal Responsibility of the County for Injuries to
    Private Persons by Public Servants / 225
The Immunity Doctrine / 225
Discretionary Immunity / 227
Governmental Immunity / Proprietary Liability / 227
The Law of Torts / 229
Intentional Torts / 229
Negligence / 231
Strict Liability / 232
Interference with Property Rights / 232
Liability Insurance / 233
Personal Civil Liability of Public Officers and Employees / 234
Policy-Makers / 234
Administrative Officials / 235
Judicial Officials / 235
Employees / 235
Statutory Liabilities of Commissioners / 236
The Civil Rights Act of 1871 / 236
Criminal Penalties Attached to the
    Office of County Commissioner / 237
Buying and Selling Offices / 238
Acting As Officer Before Qualifying
    As Such / 238
Failing to Make Reports / 238
Swearing Falsely to Official Reports / 238
Speculating in Claims Against Counties,
    Towns, Cities, and the State / 238
Interference with Audit / 239
Self-Dealing / 239
Motor Vehicles / 239

10 / LEGAL LIABILITIES OF COUNTIES AND COUNTY COMMISSIONERS

INTRODUCTION

The basic control retained by the people over their local governments is political. The single most effective guarantee of honesty, efficiency, and reasonable care in governmental activities is the ballot box. But elections are periodic, and many officers and employees are not elected at all. Furthermore, the electoral process does not guarantee protection to the individual, for the majority rules. For these reasons, the people have not confided absolute power in any of their elected officials. Even on the local level, government is hedged about by the system of checks and balances and separation of powers.

The major check on the exercise of power by local governments in North Carolina is the supervision of the courts. In many respects judicial supervision is inherently limited. Courts do not take the initiative. They respond only to a specific complaint by a citizen (in civil matters) or the state (in criminal cases) that a given state of affairs calls for correction. The extent and content of a particular decision is limited by the facts of the case, for judges are reluctant to stray far from the specific question, often quite narrow, before them. In a state where basic law is largely unwritten except as it may be deduced from the written opinions of judges, confident statements that the law is thus and so often cannot be made.

The nature of relief granted by the courts takes many forms. A county, through its board of commissioners, may be commanded to perform a certain act (by *mandamus);* it may be forbidden to act (by *injunction*); it may be compelled to pay a complainant a sum of money in compensation of loss (by *judgment for damages).* The members of the board in their individual capacity may incur similar liabilities, or they may be convicted of crime for malfeasance in office. This chapter will treat the major judicial remedies available to the citizen to compensate for personal loss caused by governmental action and to insure honesty in public office: the civil liability of the county in tort, civil liability of individual members of the board of commissioners, and the criminal penalties applicable to the office of county commissioner.

TORTS: THE LEGAL RESPONSIBILITY OF THE COUNTY FOR INJURIES TO PRIVATE PERSONS BY PUBLIC SERVANTS

A tort may be defined as a civil wrong for which an individual injured in person or property by the action of another may recover in the courts an award of money from the alleged wrongdoer. The primary purpose of such an award is to shift the loss from the person on whom it falls (the plaintiff) to the person who caused it (the defendant). Additional purposes are punishment and the deterrent effect of tort liability. Not all losses are, or should be, shifted. A plaintiff must be able to show that the facts of his case come within a category legally recognized as justifying a judgment compelling the defendant to pay.

Both legislatures and courts have authority to decide what common types of occurrences justify a shift of loss from plaintiff to defendant. Legislatures have seldom acted in these matters. Most tort litigation is governed by ancient rules brought to the country by English colonists. These rules, the common law of England, were declared by the judges, not Parliament. The first judges in North Carolina built on this English foundation as their successors have built on theirs, for each decision becomes a precedent for the guidance of judges in the future. Thus, for the most part we do not read a statute to determine what is tortious conduct, but examine a series of judicial decisions stretching back to medieval England and make a prediction about what judges are likely to do in the future, based on what they have done in the past.

The Immunity Doctrine

The common law of torts was developed to remedy private wrongs. The extent to which it should apply when a governmental unit is the defendant has been a perplexing problem. The state and federal governments have always enjoyed absolute immunity from any kind of lawsuit, except as they may have, by statute, consented to be sued. When such a statute is passed, it creates a new and distinctive remedy unless it adopts the common law by reference. For example, claims against the State of North Carolina are recognized only for *active negligence,* and are heard by an administrative agency, not the regular courts.

There has been no such unanimity of opinion on the tort liability of local governments. Local governments have never been immune from suits arising from contractual obligations. In regard to torts, the various states have adopted one of three alternatives governing the liability of local governments:
(1) Absolute immunity similar to the state's;
(2) Full liability;
(3) A case-by-case separation of local governmental activities into immune and nonimmune categories.

North Carolina has chosen the third alternative.

The law of torts has been developed over the centuries to compensate loss caused by private activity. It does not necessarily follow that the law can or should be applied to governmental units as if they were private corporations. The stockholders of a private corporation have voluntarily pooled their capital in a joint undertaking for private gain; the residents of a county or city stand in a different relation to their "body politic and corporate." Only recently have courts and legislatures in other states begun to realize that the problem of governmental tort liability involves more than a simple concern with immunity or no. As immunity has been abolished or restricted, the consequences of tort liability have been tried in the balances and often found wanting. If a catastrophe bankrupts a private corporation, it is fair to say that the stockholders took that risk when they invested their capital. Would it be fair to impose on the taxpayers of a city or county a tort judgment far beyond their ability to pay? Should a new activity prove so risky that a small corporation could not afford to undertake it, it is probable that either a larger corporation will, or public demand will allow the smaller corporation to charge prices high enough to cover the risk. But is it better for a local government to decline to offer its residents certain activities rather than risk liability? Is the fear of tort liability likely to improve the level of performance of public activities or curtail them through an excess of caution? These are some of the questions that must be faced and answered by policy-makers at all levels of government when dealing with governmental tort liability.

Although recent legislation in California and New York indicates a growing concern about whether special rules for governmental tort liability are desirable, the general rule is that where liability is imposed at all, the rules governing private litigation apply. In North Carolina a tort suit against a local government or a public official differs from a suit against a private individual only in the initial issue of whether the defendant may be sued at all.

Discretionary Immunity

Judicial decisions carry greater authority than any other type except acts of the legislature, and even statutes may be declared unconstitutional by the courts. As with all public officers, however, a judge's ultimate responsibility is to the people. When the people, acting in constitutional conventions or legislatures, grant power and authority to local governments, to what extent can or should the judges interfere? To illustrate, consider the case of *Hill v. Charlotte*. For many years Charlotte had had an ordinance prohibiting the use of fireworks within the city. The aldermen suspended the ordinance from Christmas to New Year's Day, 1873, to allow public celebration of the holiday season. On the evening of January 1 a group of boys set off Roman candles in the street outside Hill's warehouse. One candle fell on the roof, setting fire to the building, which was destroyed. Hill sued the city for the value of his warehouse. He claimed that the unreasonable action of the aldermen in repealing the anti-fireworks ordinance had caused his loss, and that he was entitled to compensation.

To allow Hill's claim, the Court would have had to determine that the passage and enforcement of an anti-fireworks ordinance was essential to the public welfare. But the courts are not legislatures; they were not constituted by the people to pass ordinances. Had Hill sued the boys, no question of the propriety of judicial action would have arisen, since the courts share with the legislature the power to regulate private conduct. But judicial review of the ordinance-making power in a tort context would be an unwarranted usurpation of a basic governmental function confided by the Constitution and statutes in other public officers. *The courts will not entertain a tort suit against a governmental unit based on the exercise or nonexercise of a discretionary power.*

The doctrine of "discretionary immunity" has been applied to deny recovery for damages caused by the passage of a discriminatory ordinance, failure to enforce an ordinance, failure to condemn and remove a public nuisance, wrongful refusal to issue a building permit, and negligence in granting a franchise.

Governmental Immunity / Proprietary Liability

Local government units may not be sued in tort for the manner in which a "governmental" function is carried on. They will be held fully liable for torts committed in the course of conducting "proprietary" activities. The source of confusion in local government tort liability has been the failure of the courts in North Carolina and elsewhere to formulate definitions of "governmental" and "proprietary" that will either explain their past decisions or aid in predicting future decisions.

The distinction between "proprietary" and "governmental" activities was introduced into North Carolina law by the case of *Moffitt v. Asheville,* decided in 1889. Before that time cities were treated as though they were private corporations, and they were subject to the same liabilities. Because nearly all their activities in the nineteenth century were undertaken in the furtherance of state policies, counties were accorded a legal status virtually identical with that of the state.

While writing the opinion in *Moffitt,* Justice Avery discovered the immunity doctrine, based on an 1842 New York decision and its progeny, in Professor Dillon's treatise on municipal corporations. Even though Professor Dillon devoted two pages to refuting the theoretical basis of municipal tort immunity, the Court adopted it in these words:

> The liability of cities and towns for the negligence of their officers or agents, depends upon the nature of the power that the corporation is exercising, when the damage complained of is sustained. . . .
> When such municipal corporations are acting . . . in their ministerial or corporate character in the management of property for their own advantage, they are impliedly liable for damage caused by the negligence of officers or agents, subject to their control, although they may be engaged in some work that will enure to the general benefit of the municipality. . . .
> On the other hand, where a city or town in [*sic*] exercising a judicial, discretionary or legislative authority, conferred by its charter, or is discharging a duty, imposed solely for the benefit of the public, it incurs no liability for the negligence of its officers . . . unless some statute (expressly or by necessary implication) subjects the corporation to a pecuniary responsibility for such negligence.

Subsequent decisions refined the distinction in powers to "governmental," "proprietary," and "discretionary." Included in "governmental" powers are such core activities as the court system, law enforcement, public records, the maintenance of public buildings, and the passage and enforcement of regulations for the better health, safety, and welfare of the people. "Proprietary" activities include public enterprises—activities that bear a close resemblance to, or are in actual competition with, private enterprise. The classic examples are city electric power plants, water companies, markets, and airports. Confusion has been the result of the doubtful cases. Even though garbage collection is often a private enterprise, and may even be done under a fee system, it is "governmental." A public housing authority may be created principally to provide for the general health, safety, and welfare through elimination of substandard housing, but it is "proprietary." Public hospitals often compete with private ones and charge fees intended to cover the costs of their services, yet they are "governmental." Supply of electric power to private consumers is "proprietary," but supply of the same power to street lights is "governmental."

LEGAL LIABILITIES 229

Until 1949 it could be argued that counties could never be subjected to tort liability since they were not empowered to engage in any but "governmental" activities, being mere political subdivisions of the state and not "corporations." In *Rhodes v. Asheville* the Court said:

> We fully concur in the view that a county, when acting in its governmental capacity, cannot be sued unless express authority to do so has been granted by statute.... Ordinarily a county does not undertake to perform functions except in a governmental capacity. But when it undertakes with legislative sanction, to perform an activity which is proprietary or corporate in character, such a county may be liable in tort to the same extent as a city or town would be if engaged in the same activity.

Since the Court, in recent years, has given up any serious attempt to define the limits between a city's functioning as a political entity and its enterprisory activities in the abstract, it is probable that the Court has, in the *Rhodes* opinion, discarded attempted distinctions between cities and counties as concerns tort liability. The distinction was based on an obsolete assumption: that counties function *only* as political bodies while cities undertake public enterprises. The quoted portion of the *Rhodes* opinion clearly assumes the modern fact that counties more and more are performing services formerly rendered by cities or not at all.

A ready formula to solve undecided questions of local government tort liability is impossible. Contemporary decisions in North Carolina and those states that still retain governmental immunity are being made not on legal theory but on the basis of precedent and broad considerations of sound governmental policy. Table 10-I summarizes the present liability status of local government activities in North Carolina.

THE LAW OF TORTS

Once the question of immunity is resolved against the local government in a tort action, the Court will apply general tort rules to the case. The existing body of private tort law falls into three broad divisions: the intentional torts, negligence, and strict liability. There are North Carolina decisions applying all three to local governments.

Intentional Torts

The oldest torts all involve intentional acts causing damage to another done without a valid excuse. The most common ones are assault, battery, false imprisonment, false arrest, malicious prosecution, trespass to land, trover and conversion (the unauthorized taking of another's personal property), deceit or fraud, and defamation (libel and slander). Some of these are of such serious consequences that they are also crimes. For exam-

Table 10-I
Immunity Decisions

Activity	Immunity	Case Citation
Airports	No	230 N.C. 134 (1949)
		168 N.C. 608 (1915)
City Dump and Incinerator	Yes	189 N.C. 469 (1925)
City Jail	Yes	103 N.C. 237 (1889)
Electric Power for Lighting Streets	Yes	239 N.C. 401 (1954)
Electric Power for Private Consumption	No	140 N.C. 506 (1906)
Fire Protection	Yes	130 N.C. 76 (1902)
		208 N.C. 729 (1935)
Garbage and Trash Collection	Yes	183 N.C. 630 (1922)
Hospitals	Yes	220 F.2d 716 (4th Cir. 1955)[a]
Law Enforcement	Yes	127 N.C. 146 (1900)
Maintenance and Repair of Traffic Signals	Yes	214 N.C. 737 (1939)
Mosquito Control	Yes	253 N.C. 732 (1961)
Parks	No	246 N.C. 469 (1957)[b]
Public Housing	No	249 N.C. 328 (1959)
Public Market	No	198 N.C. 180 (1930)
Streets and Sidewalks	No	90 N.C. 421 (1884)
Water Supply for Extinguishing Fires	Yes	181 N.C. 383 (1921)
Water Supply for Private Consumption	No	181 N.C. 88 (1921)

a Federal cases are not binding authority in state courts when deciding issues of state law.
b Probable liability.

ple, criminal and civil assault are virtually identical in North Carolina. Conversion may amount to the crime of larceny or one of its close relatives. Trespass may also amount to burglary, breaking and entering, or a breach of the peace, depending on the circumstances.

Since intent to injure is an essential element of the intentional torts, the courts have been reluctant to hold a governmental employer liable for intentional torts of its employees. Almost never does an employer expressly authorize his employee to damage another intentionally. In extreme cases, *implied* authority will be found.

The leading North Carolina case applying these rules to a local government is *Munick v. Durham.* Munick, an elderly gentleman, went to the office of the city water company to pay his water bill. He gave the clerk four one-dollar bills and fifty pennies, wrapped in a coin sleeve. The clerk accepted the money and gave him a receipt, and Munick prepared to leave. At this point, the superintendent of the water division came into the office, asked the clerk who had given her fifty pennies, threw the money on the floor, and ordered Munick to pick it up Munick declined. The superintendent then locked the door and violently assaulted him. Munick sued the City of Durham for the assault of its employee. The city was held liable on the ground that a water company is a "proprietary" activity.

Forty years later the Supreme Court decided *McDonald v. Carper*. The plaintiff in that case alleged that she had been charged with embezzlement by the city manager and subjected to criminal prosecution without just cause and for improper motives. The city was held not liable since the city manager is charged with the duty of supervising city employees, a "governmental" function, which includes guarding against embezzlement.

Negligence

The second division of tort law is negligence. It is by far the most common type of tort litigation. One is under a duty to act at all times as would a reasonably prudent man under the same or similar circumstances. Thus, if (1) one's conduct falls below that of the reasonably prudent man, (2) causing injury to another (3) that is proximately rather than remotely the result of the conduct, (4) and it can be said in retrospect that some kind of injury was reasonably foreseeable in the event of such conduct, a case of actionable negligence has occurred. The negligent person must compensate his victim for the loss unless he can show other facts that the law will recognize as excusing his conduct or barring the victim's remedy.

The question whether any given set of facts constitutes negligence is usually left to the jury. In most other tort cases, the jury decides only disputed issues of fact: did the defendant actually assault the plaintiff, and if so how much damage has the latter suffered? In the negligence case, the jury measures the defendant's conduct against that of a purely fictional character: the reasonably prudent man. The judge will not tell the jury what the "reasonable man" would have done; this is for the jury to determine. Thus, in negligence cases the jury becomes both judge and jury, for it tailors the law to fit the particular case. Typically, the decisions of appellate courts in negligence cases do not tell us what is or is not negligent conduct; they decide only whether a fair-minded jury could reasonably determine that the facts of this particular case show negligent conduct.

The range of possible situations in which government employees might be found negligent is as broad as the thousands of individual acts of those employees in the day-to-day performance of their duties. It might be negligence for the driver of a garbage truck to back over a child playing in a driveway; for the courthouse janitor to allow a slippery spot of grease to remain on a hall floor; for a mosquito-fogging machine to obscure the highway without warning. The examples are infinite.

Strict Liability

The third major division of torts is the doctrine of strict liability. It is not properly a tort concept at all, for it operates on the insurance principle. Certain activities are held to be so inherently dangerous that persons who perform them must bear responsibility for resulting damage regardless of the extent of precautions against it. The most usual example is damage caused by blasting operations. In a case involving the construction of a city water and sewer line, North Carolina adopted the rule of the majority of the states that damage done by the concussion of the blast alone is recoverable. (A few states still require some actual physical invasion of the plaintiff's property, such as by falling rocks.) The Court held it not necessary to decide whether a city would enjoy immunity from ordinary tort liability in the construction rather than the operation of a sewer system, since blasting invokes the doctrine of strict liability. Had the Court proceeded to apply a pure strict liability theory, it could be said with certainty that both property damage and personal injuries would be compensable when local government engages in blasting. However, the Court preferred to place the decision on the ground of inverse condemnation: the taking of property without formal condemnation proceedings and without just compensation.

Interference with Property Rights

The doctrine of "inverse condemnation" is typically used by courts to allow recovery for property damage under circumstances in which the governmental unit would be immune from suit for personal injury. The law has always protected property rights against governmental action to a greater extent than injuries to the physical well-being of the individual. Whether the legal basis should be in tort or purely constitutional has been the subject of much debate and confusion in the cases. Because injury to property rights by governmental action cannot be analyzed as a tort consistently with the immunity rules applicable to personal injury, a separate discussion of injury to property rights is in order. The theoretical distinction is largely a lawyer's quibble, since the practical results are virtually the same.

The federal Constitution through the Fifth and Fourteenth Amendments forbids both the state and federal governments to take life, liberty, or property without "due process of law." When a taking of property is involved, due process means the payment of just compensation. The usual example of governmental taking of property is the power of eminent domain, in which title to the property is vested in the government by condemnation in a formal legal proceeding. But property may be "taken" in other ways.

LEGAL LIABILITIES 233

For centuries the common law has recognized the tort of nuisance. A nuisance is any use of land by one person in such a manner that his neighbor's use and enjoyment of *his* land is substantially impaired. It is well established that a local government has no more right to maintain a nuisance than an individual, and is equally liable for the resulting interference. Authorized acts of a governmental character that create a nuisance are regarded as an appropriation of property to the extent of the injury inflicted. The most fertile field of litigation in the nuisance-taking area has been the operation of a sewerage system. Typically, the cases have involved a city that has been discharging sewage into a stream that overflows onto property downstream, rendering it unfit for its intended use. In recent years the mere fact that offensive odors make the property undesirable for residential purposes has rendered the city liable for decrease in land value. A peculiar case from High Point allowed recovery on allegation that the glaring silver color of a water tank constructed in a residential area made the property less valuable.

Although it is the usual theory, nuisance is not a necessary element for recovery for damage to property. When squarely confronted by a claim of interference with property rights, the Court almost always grants recovery even though there is not a nuisance. In *Prichard v. Morganton* officials of the city and county burned a private house in the mistaken belief that it was infested with smallpox and that they had authority to do so. The Court found they had no such authority. The owner lost her suit because she sued in trespass, a tort. But the Supreme Court clearly intimated that had she sued for an unauthorized taking of property without compensation, she could have recovered.

The mere fact that land values are depressed by governmental action is not enough to entitle the landowner to recover compensation. There must be in addition some element of unreasonableness, or other facts that make the governmental action "wrongful."

LIABILITY INSURANCE

In 1955 the General Assembly empowered county commissioners to waive the county's tort immunity by the purchase of liability insurance. The waiver is only to the extent of indemnification by the insurance purchased. While cities may waive immunity only in connection with the operation of motor vehicles, the county authorization is general. Boards of education have been given similar authority. Bearing in mind the status of the law, boards of commissioners would be well advised to review all activities presently carried on by their county, and, in consultation with their county attorney, determine whether those activities are currently immune from tort liability.

Commissioners should also give serious thought to whether sound principles of government justify retention of tort immunity for any county activity. The clear trend of decision in other states has been toward complete abolition of the immunity either by judicial decision or statute.

Some of the advantages of the purchase of insurance are:
(1) Investigation of the claim by the insurance companies' adjusters;
(2) Out-of-court settlement of adjustment of the claim within policy limits if there is liability as determined by the investigation;
(3) Defense of the suit by attorneys hired and paid for by the insurance company;
(4) Payment of the judgment by the insurance company (There will never be a deficiency judgment against the county in an activity otherwise immune since by statute the immunity is waived only to the extent of the insurance proceeds.);
(5) Prosecution of appeal and representation of the county on appeal by the company's attorneys;
(6) Payment of all costs of court and interest on judgment by the insurance company.

PERSONAL CIVIL LIABILITY OF PUBLIC OFFICERS AND EMPLOYEES

In every tort suit the plaintiff contends that some *person* caused him injury in person or property. The tortious conduct may have been active or passive—the tortfeasor may have done those things he ought not to have done or left undone those things he ought to have done. Further, he alone may be responsible, or another person may be vicariously liable (i.e., legally liable for his conduct because of their relationship). A city or county as a "body politic and corporate" is a *legal* person, but it can act only through natural persons. A city or county is sued in tort because some natural person has committed a tortious act within the course of his employment as an officer or employee of the "body politic and corporate." But the public officer or employee does not cease to function as an individual when he performs public duties. His actions may result in liability of both himself and the governmental unit with which he is associated. In other situations the governmental unit may not be responsible for his acts, leaving him to bear the liability personally and alone. Finally, it is possible that the governmental unit may be liable when the individual causing the damage is not personally responsible. The rules of personal liability depend primarily on the nature of the individual's association with the governmental unit.

Policy-Makers

The personal liability of the members of governing boards and other policy-makers (such as administrative personnel with delegated discretionary authority) is closely interwoven with the discretionary immunity of the governmental unit itself previously discussed. The individual members of a board of county commissioners, a board of education, or a city council cannot be held civilly liable for the manner in which they in good faith perform or fail to perform duties placed on them by law as members of a governing board, just as the unit itself is not liable for their dereliction of duty. *They will be liable as individuals if they exercise their powers as public officers for corrupt or malicious motives,* but in such an event the unit will not be responsible for their actions.

Administrative Officials

The Court draws a distinction between a public officer charged with discretionary powers and one whose powers are "merely ministerial." In the latter category are most of the acts performed by such officials as the register of deeds, the clerk of the superior court, and similar officers. A public official may be held civilly liable for failure to perform ministerial duties properly. Thus, the register of deeds may be personally liable for negligence in recording documents. The line between "discretionary powers" and "ministerial duties" is often difficult to draw. The court has held that the district engineer of the Department of Transportation exercises discretionary powers while his employees perform ministerial tasks.

Judicial Officials

At the common law, a judicial officer could not be held civilly liable for any official act, even though his motives were corrupt or malicious. This rule is followed in North Carolina. Thus, a county coroner may not be sued for refusal to hold an inquest even though the plaintiff alleges his motives for refusing were to protect one of his personal employees from possible prosecution for manslaughter. For the purposes of the rule, law enforcement officers are not "judicial" officers in North Carolina.

Employees

Those who are merely employed by a city or county, subject to the direction and control of a superior, and not charged with discretion in the performance of their delegated duties, enjoy no personal immunity from the tort consequences of their acts. In *Miller v. Jones* the plaintiff alleged that the defendants, employees of the State Highway Commission, drove a road sweeper with an attached blower past his general store without giving warning. Dust and grime blown through the open doors and windows of the store ruined most of his merchandise. Justice Seawell held that

> Immunity has never been extended to a mere employee of a governmental agency ... although employed upon public works, since

the compelling reasons for the nonliability of a public officer, clothed with discretion, are entirely absent. Of course, a mere employee doing a mechanical job, as were the defendants here, must exercise some sort of judgment in plying his shovel or driving his truck—but he is in no sense invested with a discretion which attends a public officer in the discharge of public or governmental duties, not ministerial in their character.... The mere fact that a person charged with negligence is an employee of others to whom immunity from liability is extended on grounds that public policy does not thereby excuse him from liability for negligence in the manner in which his duties are performed, or for performing a lawful act in an unlawful manner.

Statutory Liabilities of Commissioners

Commissioners are made expressly liable to civil suit by statute in only three instances: directing an illegal payment of county funds, failure to require a sufficient bond of county officers required to be bonded, and unauthorized remission of taxes. The Local Government Budget and Fiscal Control Act permits the board of commissioners to direct the payment of a bill or claim that has been disallowed by the county finance officer, but provides that the members of the board who vote to do so are personally liable for the amount disbursed if payment results in a violation of any part of the budget and fiscal control or bond laws. Commissioners may be liable as a surety on official bonds under G.S. 109-13, which provides:

> Every commissioner who approves an official bond, which he knows to be, or which by reasonable diligence he could have discovered to have been, insufficient in the penal sum, or in the security thereof, shall be liable as if he were a surety thereto, and may be sued accordingly by any person having a cause of action on said bond.

Strangely enough, there is no civil liability for failure to require any bond at all. This is made a misdemeanor, and the Court has held that attachment of a criminal penalty by implication provides that there shall be no civil cause of action. The Machinery Act prohibits a board of commissioners from releasing or compromising any property taxes owed by a taxpayer except as expressly permitted by law. It then provides that any member of the board who votes to release or compromise a tax claim in violation of law is personally liable for the tax on the suit of any resident of the county.

The Civil Rights Act of 1871

The federal Civil Rights Act of 1871 provides that

> Every person who, under color of any statute, ordinance, regulation, custom or usage of any State or Territory, subjects or causes to be subjected any citizen of the United States or other person within the

jurisdiction thereof to the deprivation of any rights, privileges or immunities secured by the constitution and laws shall be liable to the party injured in an action at law, suit in equity or other proper proceeding for redress.

Jurisdiction over this statute lies in the federal district courts, which can grant either equitable relief (usually in the form of an injunction) or an award of money damages to the person who brings the suit. The Civil Rights Act of 1871 lay dormant for many years, but it has recently been rediscovered and has become a fertile field for litigation, especially in the areas of public education and law enforcement. With regard to members of the board of county commissioners, its greatest potential use lies in personnel policies and practices that can be said to discriminate on the basis of race. A discussion of the effect of the statute on the individual liability of school board members and school administration appears in the *School Law Bulletin,* Vol. IV, No. 4, published by the Institute of Government.

CRIMINAL PENALTIES ATTACHED TO THE OFFICE OF COUNTY COMMISSIONER

The usual method employed to insure good-faith discharge of the duties of office by county commissioners is the drastic remedy of criminal conviction and, in some cases, forfeiture of office. The statutes are generally quite old and have seldom been invoked in recent years.

G.S. 14-230 provides that:

> If any . . . county commissioner . . . shall willfully omit, neglect or refuse to discharge any of the duties of his office, for default whereof it is not elsewhere provided that he shall be indicted, he shall be guilty of a misdemeanor. If it shall be proved that such officer, after his qualification, willfully and corruptly omitted, neglected or refused to discharge any of the duties of his office, or willfully and corruptly violated his oath of office according to the true intent and meaning thereof, such officer shall be guilty of misbehaviour in office, and shall be punished by removal therefrom under the sentence of the court as a part of the punishment for the offense, and shall also be fined or imprisoned in the discretion of the court.

The element of willfulness or intent required by G.S. 14-230 is not necessarily a conscious evil intent. It may be inferred from extreme carelessness. Furthermore, the law presumes that a failure to discharge the duties of office is willful, and it is incumbent on the accused commissioner to prove otherwise. The statute does not speak of the corrupt *exercise* of powers of office. Corrupt or malicious motives in the exercise of a *lawful* power do not convert that exercise into either a crime or a tort.

Buying and Selling Offices

Simony, the buying and selling of public office, has been a crime in England since 1552. North Carolina has adopted the English statute unchanged. Violation is a misdemeanor and results in forfeiture of the office.

Acting As Officer Before Qualifying As Such

If an elected or appointed officer presumes to enter on the duties of his office before taking the oath or giving bond (if required), he forfeits the office and is guilty of a misdemeanor.

Failing to Make Reports

It is a misdemeanor for any county officer to refuse or neglect to file or publish any report or statement required by law, or to fail or refuse to deliver to his successor the papers, books, and money of the office. Honesty of purpose is not a full defense to a charge of violating this section, since there may be neglect without corruption. It is not necessary that there be any injurious result to any individual. But an officer will not be held liable for obeying an unconstitutional statute.

Swearing Falsely to Official Reports

It is a misdemeanor willfully to swear falsely to any report concerning county, state, or school revenue required by law to be filed.

Speculating in Claims Against Counties, Towns, Cities, and the State

If any [county officer] shall engage in the purchasing of any county, city, town, or state claim, including teacher's salary voucher, at a less price than its full and true value or at any rate of discount thereon, or be interested in any speculation on any such claim, he shall be guilty of a misdemeanor and shall be fined or imprisoned, and shall be liable to removal from office at the discretion of the court.

This is an old statute, passed in 1868, intended to correct the then widespread abuse of speculating in the depressed prewar bonds of the state and its subdivisions. It probably does not make unlawful the purchase of state, city, or county bonds at their current market value when the issuing unit is not in default or the bonds are not depressed for some other reason. However, county commissioners should be wary of purchasing any state or municipal security at a bargain with intent to speculate on its later advance in value. The firm state of the national and state economy at this time makes the statute largely a dead letter, but a depression could revive it. There is an almost identical statute codified in G.S. 115-96 limited to speculating in the salary vouchers of school personnel.

Interference with Audit

G.S. 159-34 makes it a misdemeanor, punishable by a fine of up to $1,000 or imprisonment for up to one year, or both, for any member of the board of commissioners or other county officer or employee to impede or interfere with the annual independent audit of the county's books required by the Local Government Budget and Fiscal Control Act.

Self-Dealing

If any person, appointed or elected a commissioner or director to discharge any trust wherein the State or any county, city or town may be in any manner interested, shall become an undertaker, or make any contract for his own benefit, under such authority, or be in any manner concerned or interested in making such contract, or in the profits thereof, either privately or openly, singly or jointly with another, he shall be guilty of a misdemeanor. Provided, that this section shall not apply to public officials transacting business with banks or banking institutions in regular course of business: Provided further, that such undertaking or contracting shall be authorized by said governing board. [G.S. 14-234.]

This is an extremely important section. A county commissioner may not contract with himself, or with any firm or corporation in which he has an interest, in the name of the county. The only exception is in dealing with a bank, and then only when each transaction is specifically authorized by the full board. In the words of the Supreme Court, the General Assembly in adopting this section made the condemnation of the transactions embraced within its terms a part of the public policy of the state, so as to remove from public officials the temptation to take advantage of their official positions to "feather their own nests" by letting to themselves or to firms or corporations in which they are interested contracts for services, materials, supplies, or the like. Not only are such contracts void, but also the offending member may not recover the reasonable value of any benefits he may have conferred on the county. The fact that the transaction may have been open, fair, and free from any corrupt intent is irrelevant. However, the fact that a member of the board is merely an *employee* of one of the contracting parties does *not* invoke the statute.

Motor Vehicles

The General Assembly has closely regulated the purchase and use of motor vehicles by the state and local governments. Violation of any of the following statutes is a misdemeanor, punishable by a fine of not less than $100 or more than $1,000 or imprisonment in the discretion of the court.

G.S. 14-247. *Private use of publicly owned vehicle.* It shall be unlawful for any officer, agent or employee of . . . any county . . . to use for any private purpose whatsoever any motor vehicle of any type or description whatsoever, belonging to the . . . county. . . .

G.S. 14-248. *Obtaining repairs and supplies for private vehicles at expense of State.* It shall be unlawful for any officer, agent or employee to have any privately owned motor vehicle repaired at any garage belonging to the State or to any county, or any institution of the State, or to use any tires, oils, gasoline or other accessories purchased by the State, or any county, or any institution or agency of the State, in or on any such private car.

G.S. 14-249. *Limitation of amount expended for vehicle.* It shall be unlawful for any officer, agent, employee or department of the State of North Carolina, or of any county, or of any institution or agency of the State, to expend from the public treasury an amount in excess of two thousand five hundred dollars ($2,500) for any motor vehicle other than motor trucks, except upon the approval of the Governor and Council of State . . . . Provided further, that the limitation prescribed by this section shall not be applicable to the purchase of any motor vehicle by any county, city or town in this State, where such motor vehicle is purchased in accordance with the provisions of article 8 of chapter 143 of the General Statutes of North Carolina.

The effect of the section is to require competitive bids for the purchase of an automobile that costs more than $2,500, pursuant to procedures set out in G.S. 143-129.

G.S. 14-250. *Publicly owned vehicle to be marked.* It shall be the duty of the executive head of every department of the State government, and of any county, or of any institution or agency of the State, to have painted on every motor vehicle owned by the State, or by any county, or by any institution or agency of the State, a statement with letters of not less than three inches in height, that such car belongs to the State or to some county, or institution or agency of the State, and that such car is "For Official Use Only." Provided, however, that no automobile used by any officer or official in any county in the State for the purpose of transporting, apprehending or arresting persons charged with violations of the laws of the State of North Carolina, shall be required to be lettered. . . . Provided further, that in lieu of the above method of marking vehicles owned by any county, it shall be deemed a compliance with the law if such vehicles have painted or affixed on the side thereof a circle of not less than eight inches in diameter showing a replica of the seal of such county.

— *Joseph S. Ferrell*

11 / The Courts

The Appellate Division / 242
Supreme Court / 242
Court of Appeals / 242
The Superior Court Division / 243
Organization / 243
Judges / 245
Jurisdiction / 247
District Attorneys / 247
Clerks of Superior Court / 247
The District Court Division / 248
Organization / 248
Judges / 249
Magistrates / 249
Record-Keeping / 249
Jurisdiction / 250
Removal of Judges / 252
Reporters / 252
Juries / 253
Appeals / 253
Rules of Procedure / 253
Expenses of the Judicial Department / 253
Uniform Costs and Fees / 254
Fines and Forfeitures / 255
Representation of Indigents / The Public Defender / 255
Administrative Office of the Courts / 256
Selection of Jurors / 256
The North Carolina Courts Commission / 257

11 / THE COURTS

In 1962 the people of North Carolina adopted a new Judicial Article for the State Constitution. The new article (IV), amended in 1965 to authorize an intermediate appellate court, calls for a unified statewide and state-operated General Court of Justice (see the chart on page 244) consisting of three divisions: the Appellate Division, the Superior Court Division, and the District Court Division. The previously existing court system was changed in many respects. On the appellate, or highest, level the State Supreme Court has been joined by an intermediate Court of Appeals, activated in 1967 and designed to relieve the Supreme Court of some of its caseload, particularly the less important cases. On the highest trial level, the superior court has lost its original jurisdiction over misdemeanors and minor civil cases and over domestic relations and juvenile matters. On the next lower trial level, a variety of dissimilar city and county courts has been replaced by a new uniform district court system. At the bottom of the hierarchy, the justice of the peace and the mayor's courts have been replaced, at least in part, by the magistrate, a minor judicial official who operates within the District Court Division.

THE APPELLATE DIVISION

Supreme Court

The Appellate Division of the General Court of Justice has two branches, the Supreme Court and the Court of Appeals. The Supreme Court consists of seven justices who are elected by the people of the state as a whole for eight-year terms. The court sits in a body, in Raleigh, and hears oral arguments by attorneys representing the various parties in cases appealed from the lower courts. It does not have a jury and does not make determinations of fact; it considers cases on the written trial record only and decides questions of law. Its opinions (decisions) are printed in bound volumes and become the law of the land to the same extent as enactments of the legislature.

Court of Appeals

The Court of Appeals is composed of nine judges. All are elected in the same manner and for the same number of years as the justices of the

Supreme Court. Court of Appeals judges, however, sit and render decisions in panels of three. Individual panels may be authorized to sit in various localities throughout the state, although they usually sit only in Raleigh. Like the Supreme Court, this court decides only questions of law, including whether the trial procedure was free of error prejudicial to the appellant.

The Court of Appeals was created in 1967 to relieve the Supreme Court of a portion of its caseload, which in recent years had become more than that court could reasonably handle. The Supreme Court continues to decide, primarily, all cases involving questions of constitutional law, or legal questions of major significance to the state as a whole, or criminal cases including a sentence to death or life imprisonment. These cases may have already been decided in the Court of Appeals or may have come to the Supreme Court direct from the trial court. (For appellate routes, see the chart on page 244.) The Court of Appeals hears and decides cases in which the questions of law are less significant. No matter what the question, however, every appellant has a right to be heard by one or the other of these appellate courts, and in some cases by both, except that a defendant who pleads guilty to a criminal charge in the superior court may have his conviction reviewed only by petitioning the Court of Appeals for a writ of certiorari, which it may grant in its discretion.

The Supreme Court is located in the Justice Building at the southeast corner of the Capitol. The Court of Appeals is located across the street from the Supreme Court, at the southwest corner of the Capitol. Each court is supported by the Supreme Court Library, housed primarily in the Justice Building, and by a clerk, who is that court's administrative officer. The opinions of each court are prepared for publication by an Appellate Division reporter. Each justice or judge also has a research assistant, who must be a law school graduate. The Supreme Court librarian also serves as marshal (bailiff) to the Supreme Court; the Court of Appeals has no marshal.

When a vacancy arises—usually through death or mid-term retirement—in the membership of the Supreme Court or the Court of Appeals, the Governor is empowered to fill the vacancy by an appointment effective until the next general election. At the general election, the incumbent appointee almost always runs for the office and almost always is elected. Thus while the State Constitution provides for election of appellate judges, almost all of them attain office originally by appointment. (The same is true with respect to superior court judges.)

THE SUPERIOR COURT DIVISION

Organization

The Superior Court Division consists of the superior court, which is the court with general trial jurisdiction. This court sits at least twice a year in

ROUTES OF APPEAL
General Court of Justice
1975

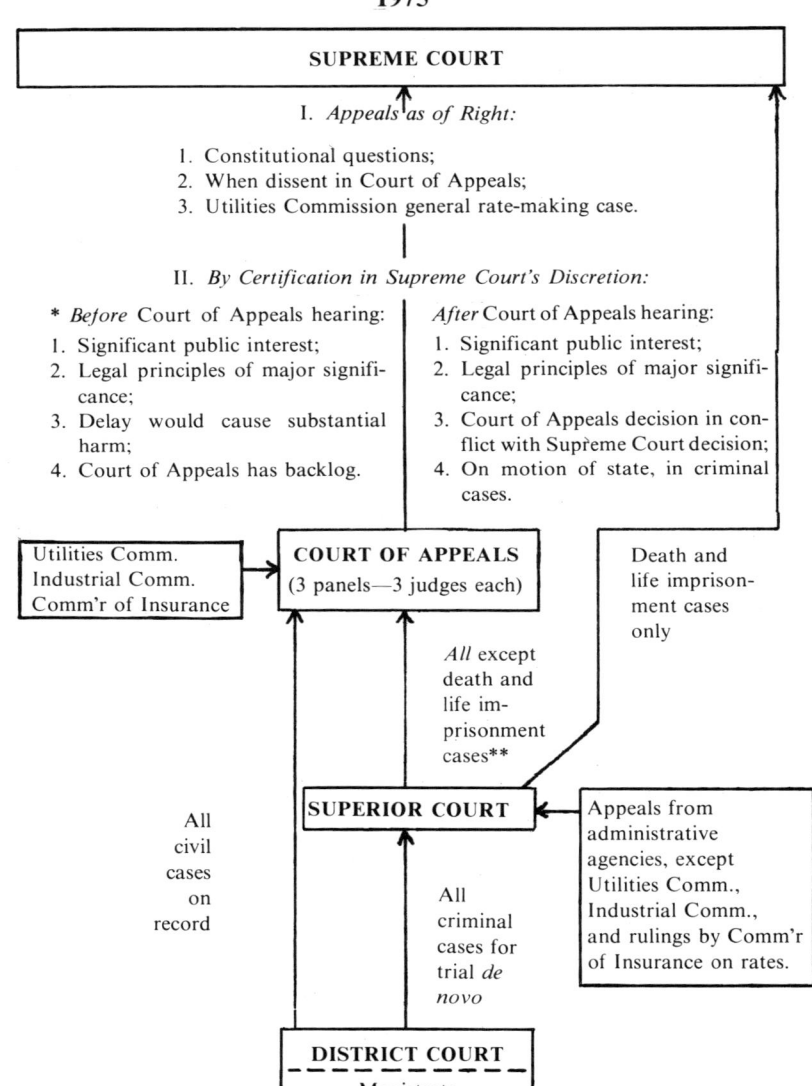

*Utilities and Industrial Commission cases *must* be heard by Court of Appeals *before* Supreme Court can hear.

**Post-conviction hearing appeals go to Court of Appeals by writ of certiorari only, and *no further*, except state may move for certification.

THE COURTS 245

each county of the state; in the busiest counties, several sittings or sessions may be held concurrently each week. The state is divided into thirty *judicial districts,* each of which has from one to seven counties and one, two, three, or four regular superior court judges. The thirty judicial districts are grouped into four divisions, each of which represents roughly one-quarter (seven or eight judicial districts) of the state.

Judges

There are forty-seven regular superior court judges who are nominated by the voters of the district in which they live but elected for eight-year terms by the voters of the state as a whole. There are also eight special superior court judges who are appointed by the Governor for four-year terms. The number of judges is specified by the General Assembly and is based on the volume of judicial business. (See the map on page 246 for the locations of the judicial districts.)

North Carolina's Constitution requires regular superior court judges to rotate, or "ride circuit," from one district to another within their divisions. Each regular judge holds court six months in his district of residence and then six months in another district and so on until he has presided for six months in each district of his division. When he rotates to a district that has two, three, or four resident judges, his rotation period in that district is lengthened accordingly, to twelve, eighteen, or twenty-four months served in six-months segments. A regular judge, therefore, spends only six months in every five to six years holding court in his district of residence. Many regular judges thus spend months or years holding court as far as 200 miles or more away from their homes, commuting on weekends or, in some instances, establishing a second home in the district to which temporarily assigned. North Carolina is unique among the states in the extent to which it carries rotation of the judges of its major trial courts.

Special superior court judges are assigned by the Chief Justice of the Supreme Court to hold sessions of court in any county of the state where they may be needed, without regard to district of residence or rotation requirements. Theoretically, therefore, a special judge over the years could sit in each of the 100 counties of the state. In practice, they are usually assigned to those counties closest to their residences.

Superior court judges who have retired—usually at age sixty-five or older—and who are physically fit are called upon from time to time by the Chief Justice to hold special sessions of superior court. In such capacity they are known as emergency superior court judges. While holding court, they receive $100 per week and expenses, in addition to their retirement compensation.

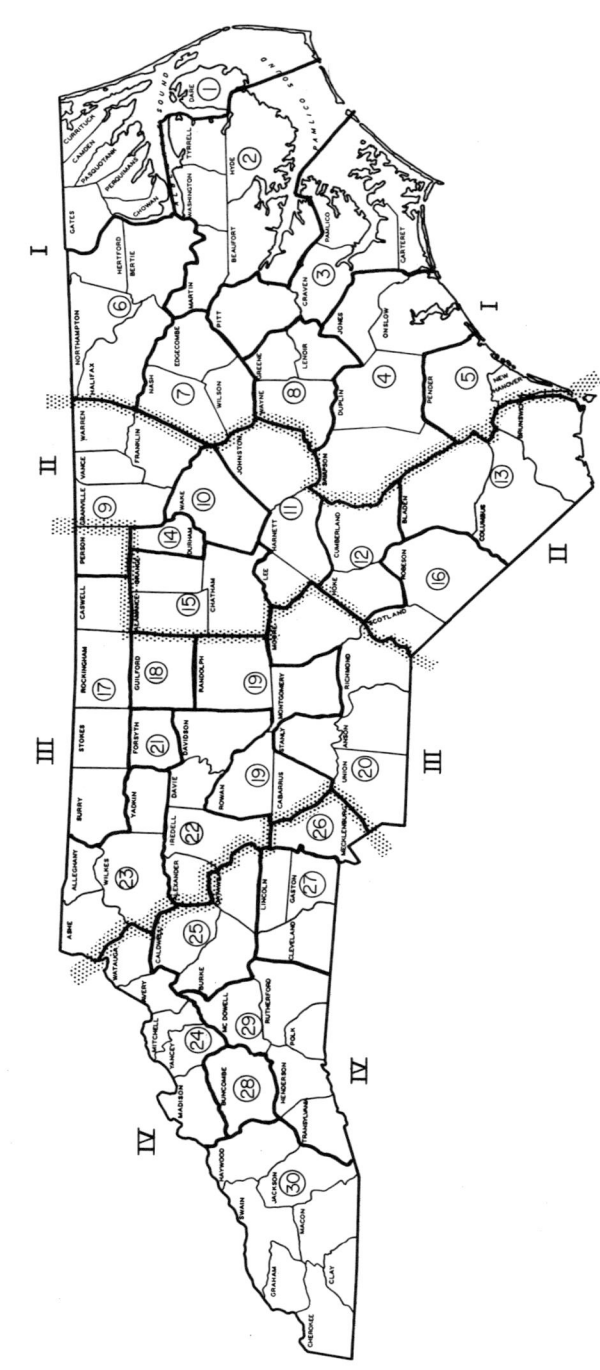

Jurisdiction

With one exception noted on page 250, the civil jurisdiction (power) of the superior court is concurrent with that of the district court. But cases involving $5,000 or more in money (or the equivalent of money), plus a few special categories of cases (injunctions, constitutional issues, eminent domain actions, corporate receiverships), are usually tried in the superior court. The flexibility in choice of forum is not needed ordinarily, but it can be used to prevent an accumulation of untried cases in one court or the other and thus expedite the administration of justice. A twelve-man jury is available in civil cases. For more details on civil jurisdiction, see this topic under the District Court Division, page 250.

As to criminal jurisdiction, the superior court has exclusive original jurisdiction over all felonies (major crimes) and appellate jurisdiction over misdemeanors (crimes for which the sentence cannot exceed two years' confinement) in which conviction was had in the district court. Felony trials are by a jury of twelve, preceded by indictment by a grand jury of eighteen. The grand jury indictment can be waived, except in capital (potential death sentence) cases, but the trial jury cannot, unless the defendant chooses to dispense with trial altogether and plead guilty. Trial of appealed misdemeanors is de novo—that is, anew, without regard to the proceedings in the original trial court.

District Attorneys

In criminal matters the *district attorney* represents the state in the superior court. The district attorney is elected for a four-year term by the voters of his district. In each district, depending on the caseload, one or more full-time assistant district attorneys, paid by the state, are authorized, to serve at the pleasure of the district attorney. In those districts where, due to caseload or geography, part-time assistant district attorneys are needed, the state provides them, and they are compensated by the state at a daily rate.

The primary duty of the district attorney and his assistants is to prosecute all crimes in the superior and district court divisions of the General Court of Justice.

A district attorney may be removed from office for misconduct after a due-process hearing before a superior court judge.

Clerks of Superior Court

The clerk of superior court is elected for a four-year term by the voters of his county. He is paid by the state, his salary depending on the population of his county. The clerk is responsible for all clerical and record-keeping functions of the superior court. To these duties have been added the identical functions of the district court, so that there is in each county only one trial court clerk's office. The clerk's former function as judge of juvenile court has been transferred to the district court, but he is empowered to issue arrest and search warrants and to exercise the same powers as a magistrate with respect to minor traffic offenses. The clerk is ex officio judge of probate—that is, he has exclusive original jurisdiction over matters relating to the probate of wills and the administration of estates of decedents, minors, and incompetents. Finally, he has authority to hear a variety of special proceedings such as adoptions, condemnation of private lands for public use, and sales of land for partition or to create cash assets. Depending on the volume of business, the clerk has a number of assistants and deputies employed by him and paid by the state in accordance with a schedule fixed by the Administrative Office of the Courts (see page 256).

The clerk's books and accounts are subject to annual audit by the State Auditor, and the clerk is bonded by a blanket state bond. In the event of a clerk's misconduct or mental or physical incapacity, the senior regular resident superior court judge serving the clerk's county is empowered, after notice and hearing, to remove him.

THE DISTRICT COURT DIVISION

The most far-reaching changes in North Carolina's system of courts have taken place on the level of the courts of limited jurisdiction, that is, below the superior court. All of these former courts—city or county recorder's court, domestic relations court, juvenile court, mayor's court, justice of the peace court, and various others—have been abolished. In the place of this confusing hodgepodge of local courts, no two of which were quite alike, the uniform district court system has been created.

Organization

As it is for the superior court division, the state is divided into thirty district court districts, and for simplicity and convenience the numbers and boundaries of the districts are the same as the superior court judicial districts. Like the superior court, the district court sits in the county seat of each county. It may also sit in certain other cities and towns specifically authorized by the General Assembly. Most counties have no additional seats of court, but a few counties have several; the present number of additional seats is thirty-seven.

District court judges and assistant solicitors serve in each district. Magistrates, as officers of the district court, serve each county within a district, in accordance with a minimum-maximum quota per county established by statute. The clerk of superior court performs the clerical functions of the district court in each county; there is no separate clerk of district court.

Judges

District court judges, in the number authorized by the General Assembly, are elected by judicial districts for four-year terms. Currently there are 118 of these. They serve full time and are forbidden to practice law. Each district has from two to seven judges, depending on population and geography. The Chief Justice of the State Supreme Court appoints one of them as chief district judge. The responsibilities of the chief district judge include assigning himself and the other judges of his district to sessions of court, prescribing the times and places at which magistrates will discharge their duties, assigning civil ("small claims") cases to magistrates for trial, and promulgating a schedule of minor traffic offenses for which magistrates and clerks of court may accept written appearances, waivers of trial, and pleas of guilty. Chief district judges are required to get together at least once a year to discuss mutual problems and make recommendations concerning the improvement of the administration of justice. Specialization by judges is encouraged by law but can be achieved to a significant degree only in those districts with four or more judges.

Vacancies in the office of district court judge are filled by the Governor, for the unexpired term, from nominations submitted by the district bar (if submitted within two weeks after the vacancy occurs).

Magistrates

Magistrates for each county are appointed for two-year terms by the senior regular resident superior court judge, on nomination of the clerk of superior court. The number of magistrates allowed each county is fixed by law. Magistrates are officers of the district court, and they are subject to the supervision of the judge in nondiscretionary judicial matters and to the clerk in clerical matters. They are full-time or part-time officials, as determined by the chief district judge, and their salaries, paid by the state, vary in accordance with their duties. If the minimum quota (never less than one) of magistrates in a county proves to be inadequate, additional magistrates within a maximum quota per county may be authorized by the Administrative Office, on recommendation of the chief district judge. A vacancy in the office of magistrate is filled, for the unexpired term, in the same manner as the original appointment. A magistrate can be removed from office, for cause, after a hearing before a superior court judge, with right of appeal to the Court of Appeals.

Record-Keeping

The clerk of superior court operates a consolidated clerk's office for both the superior and district court divisions of the General Court of Justice. In counties in which additional seats of district court are authorized, the clerk furnishes assistants and deputies as needed to serve at the additional seats, but the clerk's office at the county seat remains the permanent depository for all official records.

Jurisdiction

The jurisdiction of the district court is somewhat complicated and can be explained clearly only by reference to both trial court divisions, including the magistrate. In addition, for convenience the subject should be treated in four categories: civil, criminal, juvenile, and magisterial.

Except for the clerk of superior court's exclusive original jurisdiction over the probate of will and the administration of decedents' estates, civil jurisdiction is concurrent between the trial divisions (superior and district) of the General Court of Justice. The *proper* division, however, for cases involving amounts in controversy of $5,000 or less is the District Court Division; for cases involving amounts in controversy of over $5,000, the proper division is the Superior Court Division. Normally this $5,000 dividing line will be followed, but by consent of the parties, for reasons of speed or convenience, cases may be filed and tried in the "improper" division. No case is ever "thrown out," therefore, for lack of jurisdiction, although a case, on motion before a superior court judge, may be transferred to the proper division.

Exceptions to the general rule that the amount in controversy determines the proper forum arise in certain specific subject-matter categories. For example, civil domestic relations matters (divorce, custody and support of children, etc.) are properly the business of the district court, and the superior court is the proper forum for constitutional issues, special proceedings, corporate receiverships, and reviews of certain administrative agency rulings. Civil cases involving amounts not over $500 may, under certain conditions, be assigned to a magistrate for trial.

The criminal jurisdiction of the district court is somewhat less complicated. Since felony cases must be tried in the superior court, the district court has authority in these cases only to conduct preliminary hearings to determine whether there is probable cause to bind the defendant over (require giving an appearance bond in lieu of which the defendant remains in jail pending trial) to the superior court for trial. In misdemeanor cases, the district court has exclusive original jurisdiction that, with respect to very minor offenses, it shares with the magistrate.

The district court also has jurisdiction over juvenile matters. These cases concern children under the age of sixteen (eighteen for undisciplined children) who are delinquent, undisciplined, dependent, or neglected. Delinquents are children who have committed acts that, if committed by adults, would be crimes. Undisciplined children are primarily those who are beyond parental control, or truant from school, or both. The dependent and neglected categories are self-explanatory. Proceedings against children who may be found by the court to belong in one of these categories are initiated by petition (as distinguished from the arrest warrant used in adult cases) and the hearing conducted by the judge is informal, although children charged with actions that might result in their being transferred to the superior court for trial (this can happen in felony cases only) or to confinement in a state institution are entitled to the services of an attorney at the hearing. Before a hearing to determine either the child's status or what disposition should be made of his case, a court counselor (juvenile probation officer) may investigate both the matter alleged in the petition and the child's background and makes his findings available to the judge. The judge's authority ranges from placing a child on probation to confining him in a state institution and includes, in a suitable case, appointing a guardian and terminating parental rights.

In 1973 the district court was given jurisdiction over the involuntary commitment of mentally ill and inebriate persons to mental health treatment facilities, and in 1974 the district court was given jurisdiction over sterilization proceedings.

Magisterial jurisdiction is both civil and criminal. The magistrate's authority in criminal matters is limited to trying worthless check cases in which the check is for $50 or less, to accepting guilty pleas to other minor misdemeanors for which the maximum punishment is thirty days' confinement or a $50 fine, to issuing arrest or search warrants, and to fixing bail. For minor traffic offenses—a high percentage of all misdemeanors—the fine for each offense is fixed in advance by a uniform statewide schedule promulgated by the chief district judges, so that the magistrate has neither trial nor sentencing discretion in these cases.

In civil cases, the magistrate is authorized to try small claims involving up to $500 in money value, including summary ejectment (landlord's action to oust a tenant) cases, on assignment of the chief district judge. The plaintiff must request assignment of the small claim to a magistrate, and the defendant (or one of them) must reside in the same county as the magistrate. The typical small claim is for recovery of personal property, or for money for goods sold or services rendered, or for summary ejectment, and the parties are not usually represented by attorneys. Simplified trial procedures are followed. Often the claim is uncontested. The magistrate's judgment has the same efficacy as that of a district judge and is recorded by the clerk of superior court. If the chief district judge fails to assign a small claim to a magistrate within five days of the request for assignment, the claim is tried in district court as a regular civil case.

Besides small claims, the magistrate is authorized to perform various quasi-judicial or administrative functions formerly discharged by justices of the peace. Of these, performance of the marriage ceremony is the most common. Other authorized functions include administering oaths, verifying pleadings, and taking acknowledgments (notarizing) of instruments.

REMOVAL OF JUDGES

The traditional methods for removing judges—legislative action (impeachment and joint resolution)—have never been successfully used in North Carolina. While leaving these procedures in the Constitution, the people by amendment to the Constitution in 1972 authorized the General Assembly to prescribe another procedure. Effective January 1, 1973, the General Assembly created a Judicial Standards Commission composed of judges, lawyers, and laymen. The Commission is authorized to conduct a confidential due-process hearing in the case of a judge charged with willful misconduct in office, failure to perform his duties, habitual intemperance, conviction of a crime involving moral turpitude, or conduct prejudicial to the administration of justice that brings the judicial office into disrepute. If it feels that the evidence warrants, the Commission can recommend removal of the judge to the Supreme Court, which takes final action. The Commission may also recommend censure of a judge, and removal or retirement for physical or mental incapacity. This new procedure for the discipline, removal, and retirement of judges has proved itself in recent years in many states as a reliable and fair method of removing incompetent or corrupt judges.

In North Carolina in 1973 two judges vacated their offices while under investigation by the new Judicial Standards Commission, and one judge accepted a private reprimand in lieu of a formal investigation.

The grounds for removing a magistrate are the same as for a judge.

REPORTERS

Court reporters are appointed by the senior regular resident judge for the superior court and by the chief district judge for the district court. Compensation is set by the appointing judge, within limits fixed by the Administrative Office. Reporters are required to record verbatim such courtroom proceedings as testimony of witnesses and orders, judgments, and jury instructions of the judge. Transcripts of courtroom proceedings are required when an appeal is taken, and reporters receive a fee in addition to their salaries for preparing transcripts for appellants. A reporter is not required in district court criminal sessions since, on appeal, trial is de novo—that is, anew. The reporter's original notes are state property and are preserved by the clerk.

If a reporter is not available, on request of the senior regular resident superior court judge or the chief district judge, the state will furnish elec-

THE COURTS 253

tronic recording equipment. The clerk of superior court is responsible for operating such equipment and for preserving and transcribing the record thus produced.

JURIES

In criminal cases there is no jury in district court or before the magistrate. In civil cases, there is no jury before the magistrate, but there is a twelve-man jury in district court, on demand. The superior court has a twelve-man jury in both civil and criminal cases. The Appellate Division has no jury.

A *grand jury* of 18 persons is utilized in superior court to indict (find probable cause) persons accused of felonies. Indictment is a necessary prerequisite to trial, unless the accused waives it.

APPEALS

On appeal from the magistrate to the district judge or from the district court to the superior court, trial in criminal cases is de novo (anew). In civil cases, appeals from the magistrates are to the district court for trial de novo; appeals from the district court are on the record (matters of law) to the Court of Appeals. Appeals from the superior court go to the Court of Appeals also, except for capital and life imprisonment cases, which go directly to the Supreme Court. See the chart on page 244.

RULES OF PROCEDURE

Except as incidentally affected by the shift to a system of district courts and the advent of the magistrate as an officer of the district court, the civil and criminal procedure set out in Chapters 1, 1A, and 15 (primarily) of the General Statutes was not changed by the court reorganization movement. As an independent project, however, the rules of civil procedure have been substantially revised. The revision replaces the code-pleading concept of the last century with "notice pleading" based in many major respects on the federal civil rules. Procedures in juvenile matters have also been modernized, in response primarily to federal case-law developments. An overhaul of the rules of criminal procedure is to take effect in July 1975.

Appellate procedure is prescribed by the State Supreme Court.

EXPENSES OF THE JUDICIAL DEPARTMENT

All operating expenses of the Judicial Department are borne by the state. These include salaries and travel expenses of all judges, solicitors, clerks and their assistants, magistrates, court counselors, and reporters. They also include the books, supplies, records, and equipment in the clerk's office and the fees of all jurors and of witnesses for whom the government is responsible. Counties and cities retain responsibility for providing physical facilities for the courts, such as courtrooms and offices for judges, the clerk of superior court and his staff, solicitors, and magistrates. In a number of counties the physical facilities are inadequate. Many of these counties have undertaken construction or renovation programs to overcome these defects. A similar situation exists in some of the noncounty-seat cities that have been designated as additional seats of district court.

Financially, counties have benefited substantially from the shift to the state of responsibility for support of the court system. The burden assumed by the state has not been fully met by revenues generated by the courts.

UNIFORM COSTS AND FEES

The former detailed, itemized system of billing costs and fees has been abandoned in favor of a lump-sum averaging of costs (per type of case and court) system. In civil actions, special proceedings, and administration of estates, there are only two cost items: a General Court of Justice fee, which accrues to the state for support of the courts generally, and a facilities fee, which accrues to the county or city supplying the physical facilities and is earmarked for support of court facilities only. The amount of the fee in each case may vary with the nature of the action or proceeding and with the court in which it is tried.

In criminal actions, there are four items in the uniform bill of costs. In addition to the General Court of Justice fee and the facilities fee, a law enforcement officers' fee of $2 is chargeable for each arrest or personal service of criminal process and payable to the county or city whose officer performed the service. (Fees for arrests made by state officials accrue to the county where the arrest was made.) The fourth item is a $3 Law Enforcement Officers' Benefit and Retirement Fund fee.

Uniform Basic Costs Bill

Type of Case	Magistrate	District Court	Superior Court
Criminal	$16	$16	$40
Civil	$7	$10-15*	$25

*Varies with money value sued for

Besides these four basic costs items, in any particular case additional expenses—such as fees of witnesses, court-appointed guardians, referees, interpreters, commissioners, etc.—may be incurred. These charges are assessable against the party liable therefor along with the basic costs.

Witness fees are fixed at $5 per day, plus mileage if the witness comes from outside the county, and juror fees—paid by the state—are set at $8 per day, with no mileage allowance. A short costs bill for the miscellaneous services rendered by magistrates and clerks is also authorized, and the civil process and related costs chargeable by sheriffs are lumped into five all-inclusive, uniform categories. No charges of any kind other than those specified in the law may be imposed. All costs charged by clerks, magistrates, and sheriffs accrue to the governmental unit concerned; none accrues to individuals.

FINES AND FORFEITURES

Fines and forfeitures are to be distinguished from costs and fees. A fine is the money penalty imposed by the sentencing judge as part or all of the punishment upon conviction of a crime. A forfeiture occurs when the judge orders a bond (usually an appearance bond) forfeited when a defendant, at liberty under bond, fails to meet the conditions of the bond (usually a court appearance). Fines and forfeitures, by constitutional mandate, accrue to the county school fund and cannot be used to support either the court system generally, its physical facilities, or law enforcement activities.

REPRESENTATION OF INDIGENTS/ THE PUBLIC DEFENDER

Defendants accused of crimes for which confinement is likely and who are financially unable to employ counsel to represent them are entitled to the services of counsel at state expense. The trial judge makes the determination as to whether the accused is indigent and, if the determination is affirmative, assigns a local attorney to represent him. Fees and necessary expenses of counsel so assigned are paid by the state.

In two judicial districts—the twelfth (Cumberland and Hoke counties) and the eighteenth (Guilford County)—this assigned counsel system has recently been replaced by the public defender system. The defender is a full-time state-paid attorney whose sole function is to represent indigents. These two defenders are appointed by the Governor on written nomination of the district bars for four-year terms. The defender system is designed to provide uniformly higher-quality professional services than are sometimes available under an assigned-counsel system that may make use of attorneys with little or no experience in criminal law. Also, the defender system may prove more economical. If it proves in practice to be more efficient than the assigned-counsel system, it will probably eventually replace the assigned-counsel system in a number of the urban districts of the state. Due to insufficient volume of cases, the defender is not likely to replace the assigned-counsel system in rural districts.

In 1973 the General Assembly provided a public defender for the twenty-eighth judicial district (Buncombe County). This defender is appointed by the senior regular resident superior court judge.

ADMINISTRATIVE OFFICE OF THE COURTS

A Director of an Administrative Office of the Courts is appointed by the Chief Justice. The Director is a nonjudicial housekeeping officer, responsible for a variety of administrative functions of the Judicial Department. His major duties include preparing the budget for the Judicial Department; fixing the number of employees in the clerks' offices and setting their salary schedules; determining the salaries of magistrates, after consultation with the chief district judges; supervising a statewide system of court counselors, who assist district court judges in juvenile cases; prescribing uniform forms, records, and business methods for the offices of clerks; keeping statistics; and assisting the Chief Justice in assigning superior court judges and the Supreme Court in scheduling sessions of superior court.

The Administrative Officer is ex officio a nonvoting member of the Courts Commission (see page 257), thus assuring valuable liaison between judicial policy-makers and judicial administrators.

SELECTION OF JURORS

While not a part of court reorganization as such, a 1967 juror-selection law has an important effect on court operations. This law provides for selection of prospective jurors in each county by a jury commission. The commission uses the tax rolls and voter-registration lists as raw material for compiling jury lists. Selection is by a random process with no opportunity for favoritism or discrimination because of race, sex, or any other constitutionally prohibited reason. All former statutory exemptions from jury duty are abolished; all qualified citizens, if summoned for jury duty, are expected to serve. Excuses can be granted only by a trial judge, and then only for reasons of compelling personal hardship or because service would be contrary to the public health, safety, or welfare.

For a civil or criminal session of superior court, or for a civil session of district court, a panel of 36 to 48 prospective jurors is ordinarily summoned. When more than one jury session of court is sitting at a time, pooling of jurors in the interests of economy and the saving of jurors' time is authorized.

Petty (trial) jurors usually serve only one week. Grand jurors serve for a year, but their service is restricted to the first day, usually, of a session of superior court for the trial of criminal cases. There may be as few as two or as many as fifty criminal sessions of superior court a year in a particular county.

THE NORTH CAROLINA COURTS COMMISSION

By joint resolution, the 1963 General Assembly created a temporary Courts Commission and charged it with the responsibility of recommending legislation to implement the new Judicial Article that had been adopted by vote of the people in November, 1962. Since the General Court of Justice was sketchily outlined in the Judicial Article, a vast amount of detail was left to the legislative policy-makers, who directed the Courts Commission to recommend the necessary machinery to make the General Court of Justice a modern and efficient judicial organization. The Commission worked diligently, and over a period of six years—including three regular sessions of the General Assembly—produced a number of major bills that received legislative approval almost without change. The most basic of these was the Judicial Department Act of 1965, which established the District Court Division of the General Court of Justice and the Administrative Office of the Courts. Other major proposals of the Commission included an act creating the Court of Appeals; an appellate jurisdiction statute; a new juror-selection law; a revision of the superior court prosecutorial machinery; a rewriting of the laws regarding juvenile offenders; a revamping of the laws dealing with the representation of indigents; establishment of two experimental public defender districts; overhaul of the retirement laws affecting judges; and creation of a judicial standards commission.

This record of accomplishment convinced the General Assembly of 1969 that the Courts Commission should be a permanent body charged with continuing oversight over the organization, jurisdiction, procedures, and personnel of the Judicial Department. The Commission created by the joint resolution of 1963, which was scheduled to expire in 1970, was accordingly superseded on July 1, 1969, by the North Carolina Courts Commission, a body designed to be permanent in nature. The new Commission, like the old, has fifteen regular members appointed by the President of the Senate and the Speaker of the House and consisting primarily of lawyers and people with legislative experience. The Administrative Officer of the Courts and representatives of the North Carolina State Bar and the North Carolina Bar Association are members ex officio.

The duties of the North Carolina Courts Commission, by definition, will never be completed. Its task of continuous supervision of the judicial system assures that problems that arise in the administration of justice will be faced promptly.

— *C. E. Hinsdale*

12 / The Criminal Justice System

Introduction / 260
Sheriffs and Policing / 261
Courts and Adjudication / 264
Correctional Activities / 265
County Control of Civil Disorders / 266

12 / THE CRIMINAL JUSTICE SYSTEM

INTRODUCTION

A principal means by which government may influence how citizens act is by enacting and enforcing the criminal law. Of course this method of regulating behavior is not the only way—other ways include subjecting a citizen to civil penalties[1] or giving other citizens a right of action against him if he acts in a way that he is not supposed to, or rewarding the citizen for behaving in a manner that the government deems to be worthwhile. Through much of American history, the criminal law has been reserved largely for use against behavior that carries some moral stigma, although now many kinds of merely regulatory "crimes," such as traffic offenses, are found in the statutes. Thus, not everything called a crime carries a possibility of social disgrace and loss of personal freedom for the offender. As a practical matter, the use of the criminal law as a means of regulating behavior is distinguished by the various special procedures a defendant can claim before any criminal sanction can be imposed on him. These include provision of counsel to the defendant, trial by jury, a heavy burden of proof upon the state, and so on.

The apparatus for enforcing criminal law in the United States has three main components. The first component is sheriffs, police departments, and other "law enforcement agencies," which investigate reported crimes and apprehend those believed to have committed them. The second is the courts, which process the arrested defendant to determine whether he is to be convicted for the crime with which he has been charged and then pronounce a judgment that specifies what penalty is to be imposed. The third component is "correctional agencies," which execute whatever sentence the court has imposed upon a convicted defendant.

The operation of this apparatus, sometimes called the "criminal justice system," has several objectives. First, it makes the defendant "pay for his

---

1. A civil penalty resembles the fine that is often imposed in a criminal case. It differs from the fine in that it can be collected only by bringing a civil suit against the citizen.

crime"—that is, it permits society to exact some kind of retribution from the offender for the offense. The criminal justice system also helps prevent further crimes through deterrence of potential offenders by apprehending and convicting an offender and through reinforcing citizens' notions of right and wrong. Another aim of the criminal justice system is the rehabilitation of those convicted of crime—that is, to treat them in such a way that they will be less likely to commit further criminal acts. The criminal justice system also puts the offender out of harm's way; the convicted offender who might otherwise repeat his criminal activity may be locked away or supervised so closely that he is unable, during that period of custody, to repeat his crimes.

The county's principal role in criminal justice is to investigate and apprehend criminals (activities that have traditionally fallen to sheriffs' departments and police departments) and to provide custody or control for arrested defendants between the time of the arrest and the time that guilt or innocence is determined and sentence imposed. Though this is now the county's primary role in the criminal justice system, the county also has minor responsibilities in almost all components of the system. (Before unification of the court system, counties had much wider responsibilities in its courts and employed many judicial officials, including lower court judges and justices of the peace.)

SHERIFFS AND POLICING

County government's activity in enforcing the criminal law traditionally has been focused on "law enforcement," which is carried on through the sheriff's department or, occasionally, through a county police department. Although this realm of activity is usually thought of largely as investigating crimes and apprehending offenders, a closer look reveals that most law enforcement officers spend a majority of their time on matters that are not intended to lead to an arrest and in many cases are not even associated with crimes. For example, an officer is expected to intervene in domestic fights, disperse trouble-making youths, direct traffic, investigate accidents, subdue and transport those who are dangerous and mentally ill, and help in emergencies around citizens' homes. Furthermore sheriffs' deputies may spend a great deal of time serving civil process. Nevertheless, investigating crimes and arresting suspects is the law enforcement officer's basic and most widely recognized job.

Specific demands of the law mold the activities of a sheriff's department or county police department. Not only is an officer limited in his enforcement role to focusing upon activities that are precisely defined as illegal, but also the methods he may use to detect offenses are very closely regulated by both state law and the United States Constitution. Therefore, sometimes an activity that is generally regarded as undesirable may be beyond the reach of law enforcement activities because the law does not make that activity a crime, or it may happen that a law enforcement agency cannot arrest anyone for a crime that "everybody knows" is happening because there is no lawful way to obtain evidence that would justify the arrest.

Although the state generally exercises little control over the way in which local law enforcement operates (except by enacting the substantive and procedural laws that guide the officers), the state does attempt to control the quantity and quality of training that local officers receive. This is done through the North Carolina Criminal Justice Training and Standards Council, which operates from the state Department of Justice and is guided in its policy by a 21-member council that includes sheriffs, police officers, state agency representatives, and a number of others. In general, the council can specify that no one except an elected sheriff may serve as a law enforcement officer beyond a probationary period unless he completes an approved training program. This requirement does not apply to officers serving under permanent appointments on July 1, 1971.

A few state-level agencies are in a position to aid a county's law enforcement effort. The State Bureau of Investigation exists to investigate crimes and has specialized equipment and facilities for scientific analysis of evidence. Except for a few special crimes listed in the statutes, the State Bureau of Investigation may not investigate or assist in investigating a crime without a specific request from the local enforcement agency with jurisdiction. Some assistance also is available from the state medical examiner. The part played by the medical examiner is discussed in Chapter 13, page 273.

The State Division of Law and Order can provide some financial assistance to local law enforcement capabilities. This agency disburses money, primarily derived from federal funding, to state and local government. At the local level, this money is handled through regional planning boards, which usually serve more than one county.

Another source of assistance is a state fund to help local governments meet minimum salary requirements for the 1973-74 and 1974-75 fiscal years. An act passed in the 1973 General Assembly required certain minimum salaries for all law enforcement officers and appropriated $2,-000,000 to help local governments meet these requirements.

Counties may also be able to take advantage of a state criminal justice education and training system, which is now being developed within the Department of Justice and has its headquarters in Salemburg, North

CRIMINAL JUSTICE 263

Carolina. This program will help assure that adequate training is provided for both state and local law enforcement agencies.

The state also plays a part in arresting defendants when they are in another state. On application by the district attorney, the Governor must take steps to extradite the defendant and have him returned to the county in which he is charged. Local law enforcement officers may be sent to pick up the defendant, but the state pays the cost when the defendant is charged with a felony. The costs of extraditing a misdemeanant must be paid by the county.

In most North Carolina counties the sheriff is the principal law enforcement officer. Although the sheriff has jurisdiction to enforce the criminal law within the boundaries of cities, as a practical matter sheriffs generally confine their law enforcement activities to territory within the county but outside the boundaries of those municipalities with their own police departments. The sheriff is charged with general enforcement of the criminal law and also is specifically authorized by statute to enforce within his county the motor vehicle laws, the game and fish laws, and certain laws of the state pertaining to the manufacture, possession, transportation, and sale of non-taxpaid liquor. The sheriff has general legal powers of arrest, search, and seizure and can "call upon the aid of the county" (call together a posse) whenever he believes it necessary to the discharge of his duties.

In some counties, county police departments have been established and thus have removed the burden of criminal law enforcement from the sheriff. Mecklenburg County established the first county police department in 1917. Since then county police departments have appeared also in Durham, Cumberland, Gaston, and Columbus counties, although the departments in Durham and Cumberland no longer exist. Burke County was given authority in 1973 to create a county police department, but had not done so as of July 1, 1974.

When a county police department is created, it assumes the responsibilities of the sheriff for enforcement of the criminal laws outside the municipalities of the county. Although county policemen sometimes have authority to execute civil process issuing from the courts, this responsibility usually remains with the sheriff. Members of the county departments have the same powers of law enforcement as sheriffs and their deputies.

Counties can also seek cooperative arrangements with other jurisdictions for the use of law enforcement officers. G.S. 160A-283 permits an auxiliary force of law enforcement officers to be shared among a county and one or more other jurisdictions. G.S. 160A-288 permits counties to send to or request from another jurisdiction officers to help out during an emergency. In order to do this, the county must have had a prior agreement to do so recorded in its minutes, and must record the details of the assistance in the minutes of its next meeting after the officers were used under the agreement.

COURTS AND ADJUDICATION

The county plays a limited role in the criminal justice process that occurs after a defendant is arrested and before his case is disposed of by the courts. The primary contribution of a county to that part of the process is ensuring that the defendant is present at the trial and that adequate facilities for conducting the trial and housing court officials are provided. All other costs of the court system are met by the state. (See Chapter 11, page 253).

The county jail has historically been the means by which the county ensures that an arrested defendant is present when he must appear in court. A defendant who cannot pay the cost of a bond, post his own security, secure the help of a friend who can post that security, or obtain unsecured release spends the time between his arrest and his appearance in court in the county jail.

Responsibility for county jails is divided between the sheriff and the board of commissioners. The commissioners build, maintain, and finance the jail, and the sheriff administers it. However, with the sheriff's consent, the county commissioners may take over the administration of the county jail by appointing a jailer who is not subject to the sheriff's supervisory authority. Also, two or more units of local government may jointly operate a district jail.

How the jails are run is not entirely within the discretion of county officials. The state develops and publishes minimum jail standards to assure secure custody of prisoners and to protect their health and welfare. These standards govern both the physical condition of confinement facilities and the care given prisoners. A jail inspection service within the Department of Human Resources inspects jails to see that the standards are met. If they receive notification from the Secretary of Human Resources that the standards have not been met, the county commissioners must call a special public meeting to consider the inspection report and initiate corrective action within 30 days after the report is received. If they do not correct the unsuitable conditions within a reasonable period of time, the Secretary can order the county jail closed. The commissioners may appeal from the Secretary's order to the senior regular resident superior court judge.

North Carolina law makes special provision for the health and safety of jail inmates. The county commissioners must provide sufficient jail personnel, who must be continuously present and available to supervise prisoners. In addition, they must develop a plan for providing medical care for prisoners, including the services of licensed physicians specifically responsible for medical services for prisoners. The plan must be approved by the county health director, who determines whether it is adequate to protect the health and welfare of the jail prisoners.

Recently some counties have become interested in another approach to providing pretrial control of arrested defendants through pretrial release programs. Under North Carolina law, a judge or magistrate may release an arrested defendant even when he posts no security to assure his return for trial if the judicial official determines that the defendant is a good risk and will return to trial upon his promise. An alternative now operating in Mecklenburg County is a program in which county employees interview arrestees to determine whether they have firm enough roots in the community to indicate that they will probably return for trial. If the interviewer is satisfied that the defendant has strong community ties, he can recommend to judicial officials that the defendant be released on his own promise to return. This program hopes to identify and reach persons who do not need to be taken into custody since they are highly likely to return to the trial, thus saving money for the county and unnecessary inconvenience and penalty for the defendant who may be found not guilty on trial.

In the adjudication of criminal cases, the county plays a very limited role. All personnel involved in the adjudication of criminal cases, except the court's bailiff, who is traditionally the sheriff or his deputy, are state officers or employees. The county, however, is responsible for providing courtrooms and related facilities, including furniture.

CORRECTIONAL ACTIVITIES

If a defendant is convicted of a criminal offense, three general types of penalties, or a combination of them, usually await him. These are imprisonment, fines, or probation.[2] Of these three alternatives, the county plays a significant part only in imprisonment. Fines are collected almost entirely by the court's own officers and thus the county's only contribution in this area is through its general support for court facilities. Similarly, probation is a state-operated function for which the county's only responsibility is to provide facilities, similar to its responsibility in regard to courts. In imprisonment, however, the counties are at least theoretically capable of playing a substantial part—although in practice this part is limited. In sentencing offenders to imprisonment, judges have the option of sentencing either to the state Department of Correction (which operates the state's prison system) or to local jails, regardless of the length of the sentence imposed. Thus, an offender convicted for almost any kind of

---

2. The suspension of sentence, with conditions that the defendant must meet in order to avoid activation of the sentence, is much like probation.

crime could be sentenced to serve his term of imprisonment in the county jail. As a matter of practice, however, offenders who are sentenced to terms of 30 days or greater are almost always sentenced to the state prison system. Shorter sentences—many of which are for public drunkenness—are usually served in the county jail; but occasionally an offender with a longer sentence is assigned to a county jail when the judge wants him to keep his job in the community, spending his days on the job and his nights at the jail.

COUNTY CONTROL OF CIVIL DISORDERS

One aspect of the county's role in enforcing criminal laws deserves special mention because it involves an extraordinary power in this area; counties have special powers to deal with riots and civil disorders. Under these powers, granted by G.S. 14-288.13, boards of county commissioners are authorized to enact ordinances that permit the county to impose, during a state of emergency, special prohibitions and restrictions. When the county has such an ordinance, the chairman of the board of commissioners may have the authority to declare a state of emergency and, having done so, to restrict the movements of people in public places, the operation of offices and other facilities, the possession and sale of intoxicating liquors and dangerous weapons and gasoline, and other activities that need to be controlled in dealing with a state of emergency. Furthermore, whether the county has such an ordinance or not, the chairman of the board of commissioners, upon request of a city or town in the county, may extend any similar prohibitions that have been put into effect within the city or town throughout any areas of the county that the chairman believes need extraordinary measures to control a state of emergency.

— *Douglas R. Gill*

13 / Coroners and Medical Examiners

Coroners / 268
Powers and Duties / 268
Performance of Duties in Place of the Sheriff / 269
Issuing and Serving Warrants / 269
Election and Qualification / 270
Special Coroners / Vacancies / Assistants / 270
Bond / 270
Compensation / 270
The Future of the Office / 271
Medical Examiners / 273
Background / 273
General Organization of the System / 274
Chief Medical Examiner / 274
County Medical Examiners / 274
Financing the System / 275
Powers and Responsibilities of the County Medical Examiner / 275
Relationship with the Coroner / 275
Autopsy, Burial, and Cremation Authorization / 275
Death Certificates / Reports / 276
The Future of the Medical Examiner System / 276

13 / CORONERS AND MEDICAL EXAMINERS

CORONERS

Historically, the office of coroner is an ancient one, rooted in medieval English law, and the coroner was one of North Carolina's earliest county officials. The office of coroner is essentially judicial, with the primary duty of investigating criminal deaths. It was a constitutional office until 1962, when the North Carolina Constitution was amended to make the office subject to the control of the legislature. Not every county now has a coroner, since local legislation has eliminated the office in more than a quarter of the counties, including most of the populous ones. The laws affecting coroners are set out in G.S. Ch. 152.

Powers and Duties

The principal powers and duties of the coroner arise when an unattended or questionable death within the county is reported to him. It then becomes his duty to make a preliminary investigation to determine whether the death probably resulted from a criminal act or default on the part of another person. It is the responsibility of the coroner to decide in the first instance whether an act of criminal homicide may have occurred. If he decides that it did not, he closes the case without further investigation. If he decides that there may have been an act of homicide, he is required to continue his investigation to whatever extent is necessary to assist in making the determination or in apprehending the person or persons criminally responsible. He may order the arrest of, set bail for, or commit to jail any persons found to be probably guilty of any crime in connection with the homicide.

Though he is responsible for reaching a determination as to when, how, and by what means a person met his death, the coroner's powers are in some respects limited. First, the coroner or his jury may *not* order an autopsy; only the medical examiner may do so. Second, unless he is a licensed physician or has been designated by the Chief Medical examiner as *acting* county medical examiner to complete and sign death certificates in cases investigated by him, the coroner cannot lawfully certify to cause of death. For deaths without medical attendance, the county medical examiner is the only local official empowered to sign the death certificate. Other deaths must be certified to by the attending physician.

Performance of Duties in Place of the Sheriff

Although the coroner is in many ways concerned with enforcement of the criminal laws, he is not an enforcement officer in the general sense. He is more properly called an investigative officer, with certain judicial powers in connection with inquests and preliminary hearings. Nevertheless, at any time when there is no person properly qualified to act as sheriff, the statutes provide for the coroner to perform the duties of the sheriff (they also provide that the clerk of court may instead appoint any other person to carry out particular functions of the sheriff). The need for the coroner to act in place of the sheriff may occur when the sheriff dies in office or is incapacitated by illness and provisions for such an emergency have not been made by the county.

In addition, the coroner may be responsible for serving process on behalf of the sheriff in one other special situation. Since the sheriff may not serve process upon himself or upon any other parties to an action in which he has an interest, the coroner may act for the sheriff in any case in which the sheriff is an interested or affected party. Hence, the old rule that the coroner may arrest the sheriff is still true, although it is limited to the situations in which the sheriff would be faced with the problem of arresting himself or having his deputy do so.

Issuing and Serving Warrants

Aside from exercising law enforcement powers when acting as sheriff (such occasions now being very rare), the coroner seldom acts as an enforcement officer. Ordinarily he performs duties of investigating criminal deaths, holding inquests and preliminary hearings, and issuing criminal process in homicide cases. Thus he acts first as an investigative officer and second as a judicial officer. A coroner cannot issue a search warrant or warrants generally. He can issue arrest warrants only for persons to appear before the coroner or his jury when he has reasonable grounds to suspect such persons are "culpable" in the matter of a death under investigation by the coroner. He can subpoena witnesses to appear before him for inquests or investigations. Although the coroner was for many years considered a law enforcement officer, he does not now have specific authority, as law enforcement officers do, to make arrests *without* a warrant.

Election and Qualification

Coroners are elected in each county for a term of four years, or until a successor is elected and qualified. There are no special qualifications as to experience or education. It is necessary only that he be a voter and not subject to the disqualifications that apply to public offices generally. Since the coroner is an elected office, he may be appointed to one other public office but may not hold any other elected office. Several coroners have been appointed as acting county medical examiners.

Special Coroners / Vacancies / Assistants

When the coroner is absent from the county or otherwise unable to perform his duties in a particular case, the clerk of superior court may appoint a special coroner. When the office becomes permanently vacant during a term, the board of county commissioners appoints a qualified person to fill the office for the unexpired term and until the election and qualification of a successor.

There is no general authority for the appointment or election of assistant or deputy coroners. Special authority for such an appointment or election may be given by the General Assembly, and several counties have this local legislation.

Bond

Unless affected by local act, before the coroner-elect or a specially appointed coroner may take his oath and assume his duties, he must post a bond in the sum of $2,000 conditioned on the faithful discharge of the duties of his office. The coroner's bond must be approved by the board of county commissioners and made payable to the state. As with the bonds and sureties of the sheriff, the coroner's bond must be examined and its sufficiency determined by the board of county commissioners on the first Monday in December of each year of his term. Failure on the part of the coroner to provide sufficient bond with good sureties, or his failure to strengthen his bonds upon annual examination when directed to do so, will result in his disqualification. As with the sheriff and other public officials in the county required to give bonds, the premiums on the coroner's bond may be paid by the county.

Compensation

The general law provides for payment to the coroner of such fees as are allowed for sheriffs in similar cases, and specifically, $5 for each inquest plus an additional $5 for each additional day necessarily spent in conducting the inquest. The same statute authorizes reimbursement to the coroner for actual and necessary expenses incurred in burying a pauper over whose body an inquest was held. Payment is also authorized by the county to any physician upon whom the coroner calls to help him investigate a death. The general law does not provide for payment of mileage or other travel expenses incurred by the coroner in performing his duties. However, many local acts have been passed increasing the amount of fees payable to the coroner, authorizing travel expenses, and changing the method by which he is compensated. Boards of county commissioners have authority to fix the compensation and expense allowances of all county officers and employees, including coroners.

The Future of the Office

It has become apparent that the coroner of modern times is only a shadow of the coroner in old England. In those days he was an officer of the Crown; he was required to be a knight to qualify and had a long list of responsibilities. In North Carolina the powers and duties of the coroner have been reduced by statute and court decision over the years so that today the office is no longer prescribed by the Constitution and has been eliminated in some counties by statute; his jurisdiction is limited to investigation of only those deaths probably involving some criminal act; he has no power to order an autopsy; he cannot execute a search warrant; he can no longer sign death certificates; there is no requirement that the coroner be notified of deaths other than by the medical examiner; funeral directors must obtain permission from the medical examiner (not the coroner) before embalming a body when any suspicion of crime exists; and the coroner has no power to prohibit a body from being removed from the scene of death. In short, while the coroner is still responsible for making a determination about probable criminal culpability in connection with deaths that come to his attention, many other officials (police, medical examiners, district attorneys, sheriffs, judges) are actually required by statute and policy to be principally involved with homicides, suicides, and accidental deaths.

The question has arisen in a number of counties about whether a county is compelled by statute to continue the office of coroner. The following discussion is on the procedural question of how a coroner may be replaced and does not consider the substantive issue of whether to abolish the office.

Can the coroner be fired? In any county in which the office of coroner is filled, he may be removed only in certain cases, such as for misconduct in office or for improper assumption of the office (no bond posted or oath taken). The county commissioners are required to check the sufficiency of the bond annually; and if it is unacceptable, they can in their discretion declare the office to be vacant and proceed to fill it by appointment. What constitutes abuse of this discretion is difficult to predict. Thus, removal is not an easy matter.

Can someone else replace the coroner? In many counties local legislation permits the county commissioners to appoint an assistant coroner who may act when the coroner is unavailable. A special or acting coroner may be appointed by the clerk of superior court on a case-by-case basis when the coroner is unavailable or otherwise unable to perform. In neither of these instances, however, is the coroner actually replaced by the commissioners.

Can a coroner resign? A coroner can voluntarily resign from office at any time. Then three possibilities concerning the vacancy arise under G.S. 152-1:
(1) The county commissioners can fill the office by appointment;
(2) The county commissioners can delay in filling the office for the remainder of the term, if they so choose;
(3) The clerk of superior court can, upon request, appoint an acting coroner as each coroner's case is reported.

Can the functions of the coroner's office be ignored? The local medical examiner is required to notify the coroner about every case that comes before him, and the coroner is required to hold an inquest and preliminary hearing in all instances specified in G.S.152-7. In most cases the coroner's duty to make a personal investigation is actually discretionary (exceptions: when a citizen files an affidavit indicating blame and perhaps when a district attorney requests an investigation), depending on whether he feels that the situation is within his purview. If a law enforcement official or medical examiner conducts an investigation, the coroner is necessarily relieved of the duty to investigate, although he may use the results. His duty to hold an inquest or to call a jury is also discretionary, depending on whether he feels that there is sufficient evidence of a criminal act. His duty to hold a preliminary hearing is discretionary (exception: when a coroner's jury, if one is called, makes a positive finding), depending on whether the coroner feels there is probable culpability of a particular person. In any event, if some other official holds a preliminary hearing for the accused, the coroner does not do so. As noted above, the coroner is directed to act as sheriff in certain cases, but the clerk of superior court can instead appoint a person especially for this occasion. Since his functions are essentially discretionary, the coroner cannot be forced to perform them even if an action for mandamus is brought by some citizen. Thus, the basic duties of a coroner need not actually be performed, although the law of course contemplates that they will be performed.

Can the office be eliminated or quieted by fiscal means? Under the general law coroners are entitled to certain fees, but the commissioners of every county are authorized to set the coroner's compensation. The compensation cannot be reduced, without the coroner's consent, during his term of office or after fourteen days before the filing date in an election year. Thus, the commissioners could diminish the activity of the office by setting a salary of $1 per year, but not as to the present or an immediately prospective occupant of the office.

What if the incumbent coroner has not run again and no one else runs for the office? Unless the incumbent coroner resigns, he remains coroner even though no name appears on the ballot for coroner. The statutes provide that he shall hold office "until his successor is elected and qualified."

What action could the General Assembly take in regard to the office of coroner? The General Assembly could abolish the office (since it is no longer a constitutional office) in any or all counties. It has already done so in about two dozen counties by individual special acts. This action could be effective upon ratification of the act (even if it means immediate removal of present officeholders) or at any future date—for example, upon expiration of the term of the incumbent coroner. Or the General Assembly could authorize the county commissioners to abolish the office in their discretion or at the expiration of a term or by a certain date.

It appears, then, that if the medical examiner system is to replace the office of coroner, the only satisfactory way to accomplish the changeover is by state legislation.

MEDICAL EXAMINERS

Background

Across the country physicians are increasingly being used as official medical examiners to investigate cause of death when the circumstances surrounding the death are unnatural, unusual, or suspicious. Enabling legislation has existed in North Carolina since 1955 for the appointment of local medical examiners in every county. Fewer than two dozen counties implemented this act, which also provided for a system of district pathological services. In some counties that utilized the medical examiner legislation, the elected coroner (if he was an M.D.) was also named as the medical examiner by appointment of the county commissioners.

The 1965 General Assembly passed another enabling act that gave nineteen counties the option to abolish the office of coroner and have only a medical examiner. Only a few of the authorized counties used this option.

In 1967 legislation was enacted (G.S. 130-97) that established the present statewide system of medical examiners and replaced the previous enabling acts.

General Organization of the System

The current system is statewide in scope, requiring at least one medical examiner to serve each county. It is supervised and largely financed at the state level. A Chief Medical Examiner is the administrative officer and has primary responsibility for the conduct of all medicolegal post-mortem examinations in the state.

The boards of county commissioners have little responsibility under the state medical examiner system, except for financing part of the county medical examiner's functions, but the local medical examiner is expected to cooperate with county officials. Coordination, as well as cooperation, with the coroner and local law enforcement officials and with the district attorney and the clerk of the superior court is necessary for effective local handling of death cases in which the cause is questionable.

Not every death comes under the jurisdiction of the medical examiner. Only about 20 per cent of the deaths in the state are cases for the medical examiner, and of these, about 36 percent are autopsied either locally or at the central laboratories. In 1973 medical examiners handled 9,890 cases, of which 836 were homicides and 1,927 were related to motor vehicle accidents. About 90 per cent of all homicide cases are autopsied.

Various administrative details and guidelines for handling cases and making reports are contained in the "Medical Examiner System Rules and Regulations" adopted by the State Commission for Health Services.

Chief Medical Examiner

The Secretary of Human Resources appoints an experienced pathologist as Chief Medical Examiner for a four-year term to administer a coordinated system of post-mortem medicolegal examinations throughout the state. A central office and laboratory are located in Chapel Hill, where the University of North Carolina Medical School provides space and services. Other public and private laboratories are used for additional services. The Chief Medical Examiner appoints all his staff and employees.

County Medical Examiners

The Chief Medical Examiner chooses one or more local medical examiners for each county from a list of physicians submitted by the county or district medical society. When no local physician is willing or available, the coroner may be appointed as *acting* medical examiner. The term of the county medical examiner is three years.

There are about 600 county medical examiners in the state; most of them serve part-time. Customarily several practicing physicians are appointed in each county so that a rotation system can be arranged among them.

Financing the System

The central services of the medical examiner system are financed entirely by the state, but the counties finance a large part of the services performed by county medical examiners. The county commissioners are responsible for both the $25 fee paid to the county medical examiner for each investigation of a deceased who was a local resident and the $150 fee for any autopsy in such a case. The state pays the fees for all other investigations as well as the $10 fee for each cremation ordered. In 1973 the state appropriation for the medical examiner system was $843,000; in addition, about 80 per cent of the local costs were paid by the counties, or approximately $600,000.

Powers and Responsibilities of the County Medical Examiner

The medical examiner must be notified "upon the death of any person, apparently by criminal act or default, or apparently by suicide, or while an inmate of any penal or correctional institution, or under any suspicious, unusual or unnatural circumstances." In those situations the body must not be disturbed without authorization by the county medical examiner.

The medical examiner then takes charge of the body, makes an investigation, and submits a report form to the Chief Medical Examiner. He gives copies to the district attorney and upon request to any party in a court action.

Relationship with the Coroner

Unless the office of coroner has been abolished in a county, the coroner is still directed to make an investigation under existing laws whenever it appears that the deceased probably came to his death by the criminal act or default of some person. The statutes contemplate close cooperation between the coroner and medical examiner in such cases. The medical examiner is to notify the coroner of deaths, so that the coroner may hold an inquest and preliminary hearing when appropriate. The coroner is to submit his reports to the medical examiner as well as to the district attorney. Both the medical examiner and the coroner have the power of subpoena.

Autopsy, Burial, and Cremation Authorization

Autopsies are ordered by the Chief Medical Examiner or by the local medical examiner whenever "it is advisable and in the public interest" or when requested by a superior court judge or district attorney. When there is any suspicion of crime, no dead body shall be embalmed or buried, and no burial permit issued, without the written permission of the medical examiner. No cremation of any dead body (except a still-born delivered in a hospital) is permitted without the written authorization of the medical examiner. Upon notification by the medical examiner of any burial in any medical examiner case without investigation or of any cremation without authorization, a superior court judge may order the remains exhumed and examined.

Death Certificates / Reports

For deaths without medical attendance, the death certificate may be signed only by the medical examiner or, in his absence, by the Chief Medical Examiner. In other cases the certificate is signed by the attending physician.

Reports of the medical examiner's investigations and autopsies may be received as corroborative evidence, if otherwise admissible, in any court or other proceeding.

The Future of the Medical Examiner System

The full effect of the new system may not be appreciated for several more years, but uniformity and medical involvement in cause of death investigations has already proved essential to lawyers, courts, health officials, and law enforcement officials. In addition, the Office of Chief Medical Examiner has developed a data collection and analysis capability to deal with traffic deaths, deaths caused by drugs and alcohol, and other types of deaths poorly documented in the past. The system is a unique blending of state government's responsibility for vital information and private medicine's concern for scientific determination of death. The result is that some of the painful confusion surrounding many deaths is being increasingly eliminated.

—*David G. Warren*

14 / Alcoholic Beverage Control

Introduction / 278
Alcoholic Beverages / 279
ABC Store Elections / 279
County ABC Boards / 279
Transportation and Possession of Alcoholic Beverages / 280
Malt Beverages and Unfortified Wine / 281
Malt Beverage and Unfortified Wine Elections / 281
Permits and Licenses / 282
Transportation and Possession of Malt Beverages and
   Unfortified Wine / 282

14 / ALCOHOLIC BEVERAGE CONTROL

INTRODUCTION

The relevant history of North Carolina liquor legislation dates from the passage of the Turlington Act in 1923. This was a prohibition statute designed to make state law conform to federal law as expressed in the Volstead Act and in the Eighteenth Amendment to the Constitution of the United States. The Turlington Act made it unlawful for any person to manufacture, transport, purchase, or sell any beverage containing one-half of 1 per cent or more of alcohol.

In 1937, some four years after repeal of the Eighteenth Amendment, the North Carolina General Assembly passed the Alcoholic Beverage Control Act (ABC Act), which provided for the establishment, on a local-option basis, of county liquor stores (ABC stores) where alcoholic beverages could be legally purchased. The ABC Act defined "alcoholic beverage" to include only those beverages that contain more than 14 per cent of alcohol by volume (hard liquor and fortified wine). Malt beverages and unfortified wine have an alcoholic content of less than 14 per cent and are therefore not sold in ABC stores.

Beer and all wines, other than those that have been fortified by the addition of brandy, are sold only in private establishments (i.e., grocery stores and restaurants) that have been issued a permit by the State Board of Alcoholic Control (State ABC Board). These beverages were originally legalized and regulated by the Beverage Control Act rather than by the ABC Act.

Enactment of the Turlington Act, the ABC Act of 1937, and the Beverage Control Act of 1939 was followed by the passage of several statutes that were more limited in scope. In each instance, however, previous acts were left on the books unamended. The Turlington Act, for example, still prohibited the sale of whiskey, beer, or wine; but all three could be sold pursuant to subsequently enacted statutes. Eventually the result was legal and administrative chaos. The 1971 General Assembly, in an effort to eliminate the statutory ambiguities, repealed all of the liquor legislation then existing and enacted a new G.S. Ch. 18A. The primary purpose of the new act was to clarify and consolidate statutes rather than to make substantive changes in the law. Those provisions of the 1971 liquor control act that are likely to be of interest to county government officials are outlined in the material to follow.

ALCOHOLIC BEVERAGES

No ABC store may be operated in any county of this state until a county-wide election has been held in which a majority votes in favor of establishing such stores. The general law, as contained in G.S. Ch. 18A, does not provide for city-wide ABC store elections. Nevertheless over 70 municipalities have established ABC systems pursuant to special local legislation. By way of comparison, only 44 of North Carolina's 100 counties have voted in liquor stores on a county-wide basis.

ABC Store Elections

A county ABC store election is called by the county board of elections upon the written request of the county commissioners or upon a petition signed by at least 20 per cent of the registered voters. The number of registered voters in the county is determined by the board of elections as of the date the petition is presented to the board. The board of elections also fixes the date for the ABC store election, but it may not be held on the same day as a biennial election for county officers or within 45 days thereof.

County ABC Boards

When an ABC store election is successful, the first order of business is to select a county board of alcoholic control to operate the system. The ABC board consists of a chairman and two other members who are selected in a joint meeting of the county boards of commissioners, health, and education. Salaries of the ABC board members are set by the three appointing boards. While county boards of alcoholic control are subject to the general supervision of the State ABC Board, they have the following statutory powers and duties:
(1) To control the sale of alcoholic beverages within the county;
(2) To buy, possess, and sell alcoholic beverages;
(3) To adopt rules and regulations governing the operation of county ABC stores;
(4) To prescribe and direct the duties of all board (store) employees;
(5) To fix the hours of operation for the stores (but all stores must remain closed from 9:00 p.m. until 9:00 a.m.);

(6) To require stores to close on days designated by the board (but all stores must remain closed on Sundays, New Year's Day, Fourth of July, Labor Day, Thanksgiving, Christmas, and statewide election days);
(7) To import, transport, receive, and deliver alcoholic beverages;
(8) To purchase or lease property and furnish or equip buildings required for the storage and sale of alcoholic beverages;
(9) To sell at public auction any real or personal property that the board deems unnecessary for the operation of its stores;
(10) To borrow money and to issue checks and promissory notes;
(11) To investigate and aid in the prosecuting of liquor law violations;
(12) To require ABC stores to sell alcoholic beverages at prices fixed by the State ABC Board;
(13) To select the location for ABC stores and to employ a manager for each store;
(14) To spend from 5 to 15 per cent of total profits for law enforcement purposes (at least one county ABC officer must be employed by each board). In addition, not less than 7 per cent of total profits must be spent for education on the excessive use of alcohol or for the rehabilitation of alcholics.
(15) To discontinue the operation of any store that is not profitable enough or is inimical to the morals or welfare of the community;
(16) To invest funds temporarily held in U.S. government obligations, savings and loan shares, or certificates of deposit or savings accounts of banks.

G.S. Ch. 18A requires all net profits derived from the operation of ABC stores to be paid on a quarterly basis into the general fund of the county wherein the store is located. Since municipal stores are all established pursuant to special acts, their profits are distributed in accord with such special acts. The profits of some county ABC systems are also divided pursuant to local legislation, rather than being placed in the general fund.

Transportation and Possession of Alcoholic Beverages

Provisions governing the transportation, possession, and consumption of alcoholic beverages are set forth in detail in Article 3 of G.S. Ch. 18A. Briefly, the rules are as follows:

Transportation. A person who is at least 21 years of age may transport up to one gallon of alcoholic beverages (or five gallons with a permit) to and from any place in the state. But a bottle that has been opened must be carried in a place other than the passenger area of a motor vehicle (i.e., the trunk).

Possession. The possession and consumption by persons over 21 of

alcoholic beverages (hard liquor and fortified wine) is lawful in certain designated places. Among these places are:
(1) A private residence.
(2) A hotel or motel room.
(3) A private club that has a "social establishment permit" issued by the State ABC Board.
(4) A restaurant that has an appropriate permit issued by the State ABC Board.

G.S. 18A-30 expressly prohibits consumption of alcoholic beverages on a public street or on the premises of an ABC store.

MALT BEVERAGES AND UNFORTIFIED WINE

Malt beverages and unfortified wine are not statutorily defined as alcoholic beverages; they have a lower alcoholic content than alcoholic beverages; and under the general law they may not be sold in ABC stores. The laws pertaining to malt beverages and unfortified wine are quite different from those regulating alcoholic beverages and are summarized below.

Malt Beverage and Unfortified Wine Elections

Malt beverage and unfortified wine elections are called by a board of elections upon the written request of a city or county governing board or upon receipt of a petition signed by at least 20 per cent of the registered voters of a city or county. A municipal election may not be held unless the sale of the beverage to be voted on is prohibited in the county as a whole. One to six questions may be presented at any given election, as follows:
(1) Whether to permit "on-premises" sales of unfortified wine by Grade A hotels and restaurants and "off-premises" sales by other licensees. (An "on-premises" license permits the beverage to be consumed where purchased.)
(2) Whether to permit "off-premises" sales only of unfortified wine.
(3) Whether to permit both "on-premises" and "off-premises" sales of malt beverages.
(4) Whether to permit "on-premises" sales only of malt beverages.
(5) Whether to permit "off-premises" sales only of malt beverages.
(6) Whether to permit the "on-premises" sale of malt beverages in Grade A hotels and restaurants and "off-premises" sales by other licensees.

At present 54 counties and 45 cities located in dry counties permit retail sales of malt beverages. Unfortified wine may be sold at retail in 53 counties and in 35 municipalities.

Permits and Licenses

No place of business may sell beer or wine, whether for on-premises or off-premises consumption, until the appropriate permits and licenses have been acquired. Permits are issued by the State ABC Board in Raleigh following a comprehensive investigation of both the applicant and the premises to be licensed. All retail permits must be renewed annually.

Licenses are of three general types: state, county, and city. All establishments that wish to sell alcoholic beverages must obtain a state license from the North Carolina Department of Revenue. They must also acquire a county license; and, if they are located inside a city, then also a municipal license. The authority to issue local licenses is vested by statute in governing boards of cities and in boards of county commissioners. Usually, however, the granting of a permit to a particular establishment by the State ABC Board indicates that all legal requirements have been met, and state and local licenses are subsequently issued as a matter of course. The annual county license fee is $25 for an on-premises beer license, $5 for an off-premises beer license, and $25 for an on- or off-premises unfortified wine license.

Transportation and Possession of Malt Beverages and Unfortified Wine

G.S. Ch. 18A contains no limitation on the quantity of malt beverages or unfortified wine that a person may transport for his own use. It should be noted, however, that the possession of over 20 gallons of beer or more than five gallons of wine constitutes *prima facie* evidence of "unlawful possession for the purpose of sale." Also, there is no statewide law indicating exactly where these beverages may or may not be possessed and consumed. Absent a local ordinance, malt beverages and unfortified wine can probably be possessed and consumed anywhere; and a recent State Supreme Court decision has cast doubt on the validity of local ordinances prohibiting possession and consumption in certain designated places.

— *Ben F. Loeb, Jr.*

15 / Health Organization and Services

PART I. PUBLIC HEALTH / 286
History / 286
State Organization / 287
State Commission for Health Services / 287
State Division of Health Services / 288
State Rules and Regulations / 288
State-Local Relationship / 289
Local Organization / 289
New Developments / 289
County Health Departments / 290
District Health Departments / 290
State-Operated Local Health Departments / 291
Local Boards / 291
   Per Diem / Expenses / 291
   Meetings / 291
   Vacancies and Removals / 291
   Officers / 291
   Powers and Duties / 291
Local Regulations / 292
Fees / 293
Local Department Administration / 293
Local Health Director / 293
Other Agencies Allied to Public Health / 294
Sanitary Districts / 294
Mosquito Control Districts / 294
Finances / 295
State Policies Governing Allocation of Funds / 296
The Contract Between the State Division of Health Services and
   Local Governing Boards / 297
Health Department Programs / 298
Public Health Laws Relating to Specific Local Functions / 299
County Physicians / 299
Local Confinement Facilities / 299
Vital Statistics / 299
Immunization / 300

PART II. MENTAL HEALTH / 300
History / 300
State Mental Health Organization / 301
Local Mental Health Programs / 301
Organization of Local Mental Health Services / 301
Financing Local Mental Health Services / 302
Community Alcoholism and Drug-Abuse Programs / 303

15 / HEALTH ORGANIZATION AND SERVICES

> Public Health is the science and the art of preventing disease, prolonging life, and promoting physical and mental health and efficiency through organized community effort.
> Dr. C. E. A. Winslow

Public health, with its early objective of preventing communicable diseases, has long been a concern of community life. More recently mental health came to be recognized as an area of the public's health that requires special attention. Nearly everyone today accepts the idea that organized public health and mental health service is one of the fundamental responsibilities of government in our society. Government at every level is now engaged in some part of the work—the *federal government* through the United States Public Health Service, National Institutes of Health, categorical disease programs, and a number of other agencies; the *state governments* through their state boards of health and mental health, health professions and health facilities licensing boards, and health planning agencies; and the *local governments* through district and county health departments, community mental health centers, alcoholic information centers, and special health programs and projects.

Increased governmental emphasis has been placed on both personal and environmental health in recent years. There are new federal programs relating to general health care for the poor, for the aged, and for persons in depressed areas and regions. There have been federal legislation pertaining to controls on air and water pollution; grants for solid waste disposal projects; development of local mental health facilities and area health education centers; and programs to stimulate state and regional health planning. This is in addition to individual state and local legislation for a wide variety of new health programs.

Part I / Public Health

HISTORY

The first substantial piece of health legislation applicable to the territory that is now North Carolina was a maritime quarantine law, enacted in 1712 by the General Assembly of the Province of Carolina. From this beginning, state governmental responsibility for public health grew slowly, while municipalities took some responsibility for promoting the public health through various health and nuisance ordinances.

Not until the years shortly after the Civil War did state boards of health in roughly the modern pattern begin to be established throughout the country. North Carolina joined the move in 1877 by enacting a law designating the entire membership of the State Medical Society as a State Board of Health, to act through a health committee established by the Society, with an annual state appropriation of $100 for its expenses. Two years later this statute was repealed and another enacted creating a nine-member State Board of Health that became a regular department of state government. In 1973 the Board was changed to the Commission for Health Services in the Department of Human Resources, pursuant to state government reorganization.

In 1911 the State Board of Health acquired the services of its first full-time health officer, thus beginning the development of a state health department staffed by professional men and women working under the general direction of the Board of Health. Between 1911 and 1957 a wide range of public health statutes was passed by the General Assembly. In 1957 the General Assembly completely rewrote the public health laws of the state, clarifying and organizing them. Most of the state laws pertaining to public health are compiled in G.S. Ch. 130.

North Carolina was an early leader in local health department organization. In 1879 the General Assembly provided for the semblance of a statewide local public health system by declaring that each county should have a county board of health composed of all the practicing physicians in the county, plus the chairman of the board of county commissioners, the mayor of the county town, and the county surveyor. This board functioned in practice as something in the nature of a medical "vigilante committee." It was organized to deal with epidemics, nuisances, and similar urgent threats to the community's health, usually after they had already begun. The need for an agency administering laws and regulations aimed at preventing health disasters soon became apparent.

In 1911 a statute was enacted that gave local regulatory authority to a county board of health composed of both medical and lay members. Under this act several counties soon established health departments. Guilford was the first county in the state to offer full-time county health services; its health department was the second in the nation at the local level. Robeson County is credited with having the first *rural* health department, which resulted from an intensive demonstration campaign by teams from the Rockefeller Foundation to eradicate hookworm disease and build sanitary privies. By 1949 the state had full-time local health services in all its counties, served by either county or district health departments.

Although cities in North Carolina have had statutory authority since 1893 (and under particular town charter provisions since colonial days) to tax and spend money to provide for the public health, most of the state's municipalities have left organized health work to the counties and districts. While several cities have had health departments at one time or another, none now has a separate health department, Rocky Mount in 1974 being the last to dissolve. In 1973 a special legislative study commission made numerous recommendations about the statutory basis for local public health services.

STATE ORGANIZATION

State Commission for Health Services

The statutes create a State Commission for Health Services within the Department of Human Resources. The Commission consists of twelve members, four of whom are elected by the Medical Society of the State of North Carolina. The remaining eight members, who are appointed by the Governor, must include a pharmacist, optometrist, nurse, dairyman, dentist, veterinarian, and two other persons. The members serve four-year, staggered terms.

The Commission has the responsibility to establish general policies to be followed in carrying out public health programs. It has authority to adopt rules and regulations necessary to enable its administrative staff to administer and enforce the public health laws of the state. The State Department of Human Resources is authorized to accept and allocate or spend grants-in-aid for public health purposes that are made available by the state and federal legislative bodies; the Commission may advise the Secretary of Human Resources on policies relating to these programs.

State Division of Health Services

Administration of the state public health program is the responsibility of the Director of the Division of Health Services (previously called the State Health Director) and his staff. The Director must be a licensed physician with training and experience in public health work. Others on the staff have special training as required by the various programs they administer. The variety of programs and staff consultants is indicated by the sections: Research and Development, Sanitary Engineering, Personal Health, Dental Health, Epidemiology, Laboratory, and Administrative. Several sections have particular relevance to county health departments.

Under the Assistant Director for Local Services, the Health Services Regional Offices in Black Mountain, Winston-Salem, Fayetteville, and Greenville work very closely with local health departments in advising on financial and program matters and administering the federal and state money allocations. The Laboratory Section furnishes immunization material and laboratory services, such as rabies analyses. The Sanitary Engineering Section trains and certifies sanitarians for local departments and provides advice on food-handling facility inspections, septic tank regulation, and other sanitation problems.

State Rules and Regulations

The State Commission for Health Services (previously called the State Board of Health; most of the printed rules and regulations still carry this name) has adopted rules and regulations controlling the sanitation aspects of a wide range of places and activities:

Restaurants and other food-handling establishments
Private hospitals, nursing and rest homes, sanitoriums
Meat markets, abattoirs, frozen-food locker plants and poultry-processing plants
Hotels, motels, inns, and tourist homes
Mass gatherings (such as rock festivals)
Local confinement facilities
Child day-care facilities
Summer camps
Solid waste disposal sites
Sewage disposal
Water supplies

There are still other rules and regulations that affect these diverse subjects: sale of turtles, radiation equipment, milk processing, breath alcohol testing, nursing home administrators, communicable diseases, transportation of migratory farm workers, shellfish and crustacea processing and scallops.

The Division of Health Services has also issued advisory or informational bulletins on acceptable public health practice in regard to privy and septic tank construction, insect control, impoundment of dogs, immunization of children, and other matters.

Commission regulations have the force of law, and violations carry a maximum penalty of a $50 fine or 30 days' imprisonment. The Secretary of Human Resources may also institute injunctive actions. The regulations are statewide in application and are enforced by employees of both the Division of Health Services and the respective county boards of health. For example, most of the restaurant sanitation inspections are made by local department sanitarians, who sign a grade certificate bearing the imprinted name of the Division Director. The local sanitarians are certified and supervised in this work by state regional sanitarians.

State-Local Relationship

The State Division of Health Services does not directly control or supervise the work of the local health departments. However, the Commission and its administrative staff do indirectly exercise considerable influence on local health work:

(1) By providing consultative and advisory services, and conducting training and certification programs for the various specialities in local health departments;
(2) By supervising the enforcement of state rules and regulations by local health department employees; and
(3) By allocating federal and state funds to the counties, such grants being conditioned on an agreement by local authorities to meet certain requirements set out in a contract entered into by the State Commission for Health Services and each board of county commissioners.

LOCAL ORGANIZATION

New Developments

Following the recommendations of a special Public Health Study Commission, the 1973 General Assembly of North Carolina enacted several significant statutes designed to enhance the ability of local health departments to carry out their role "to protect and advance the public health" as described in G.S. 130-17. Among these are new provisions to

(a) Require, not merely authorize, counties to provide public health services [G.S. 130-13(a)];

(b) Revise the composition of local boards of health to allow greater citizen participation [G.S. 130-13(b) and -14(c)];
(c) Establish statewide standards for local public health services [G.S. 130-9(g)];
(d) Provide local health services directly from the state to appropriate counties [G.S. 130-14.2];
(e) Appoint local health directors only after consultation with the State Director of Health Services and the county commissioners [G.S. 130-18];
(f) Permit local health departments to charge fees (and therefore collect from third-party payers) for voluntary services rendered to citizens [G.S. 130-17]; and,
(g) Increase state financial support of local public health services, including a special $2 million appropriation for district departments and state-provided local services and for local salary increases.

Perhaps more than any other legislation since the creation of local health departments sixty years ago, these changes will dramatically affect the organization and effectiveness of local health activities in North Carolina counties.

County Health Departments

Each county is required to make public health services available to its citizens. This may be accomplished in one of three ways: (a) by operating a county health department, (b) by contracting with the state for provision of services, or (c) by operating a district health department jointly with other counties. When the county has a county health department, the policy-making body is a county board of health composed of nine members appointed by the board of county commissioners, upon consultation with the local health director. The board includes five persons appointed from the general public in addition to one representative each from the professions of medicine, dentistry, and pharmacy, and a county commissioner. The statutory requirement that the board "reasonably reflect the population makeup of the entire county" is intended to insure that some consumers of the health department services are appointed to the board. Members serve three-year terms; three consecutive terms is the maximum allowed. Employees of a county health department are considered to be county employees.

In 1974 there were sixty-seven single-county health departments.

District Health Departments

Either upon agreement of the county commissioners and the boards of health of several counties or upon request of the state (after determining that the public interest would be better served), a district health department may be formed. The district may have health department offices and employees in each component county, but it will have only one board of health. The board will consist of one county commissioner from each county, plus a physician, dentist, pharmacist, and enough persons from the general public to bring the number to fifteen. As with county boards of health, the composition must reasonably reflect the population makeup of the entire district. Terms are three years, with a three-term limit.

There were eleven districts covering thirty-three counties in 1974.

State-Operated Local Health Departments

If all of the boards of commissioners of the affected counties approve, the state may enter into contracts with county and district boards of health for the state to provide local public health services. This is similar to the arrangement in other states, including neighboring Virginia. Under this arrangement, the local board of health continues to be the policy-making body and is appointed in the same way as the county or district board is appointed in the conventional arrangement.

In 1974, one county health department and one district health department (composed of five counties) were scheduled to begin operating under this arrangement with the state providing services directly. In practice, the chief distinction in this new system is that the department personnel are state employees rather than county employees.

Local Boards

Per Diem / Expenses. Members of local boards of health may receive up to the $20 per diem ($25 for chairmen) plus travel expenses allowed for state board members generally, but only as authorized by the board of county commissioners.

Meetings. Local boards of health must meet at least quarterly, and special meetings may be called. Vacancies arising during the term are filled at a special or regular meeting.

Vacancies and Removals. If the statutory requirement for any of the required health professionals—a physician, dentist, or pharmacist—cannot be met, a 1974 law permits members of the general public to replace that professional. Any member may be removed from office by the board for cause.

Officers. The full board of health elects its chairman. The health director serves as secretary.

Powers and Duties. The local board of health is the policy-making body within its jurisdiction for all matters pertaining to public health. While the board of county commissioners does have secondary rule-making authority for health, sanitation, and nuisance activities, the statutes give local boards of health the primary authority to "make such rules and regulations . . . as are necessary to protect and advance the public health.

Local Regulations

These regulations are subject to the fundamental court-imposed requirement that they be reasonable and that their purposes and provisions bear a substantial relationship to legitimate public health goals.

When there is an emergency or peculiar local condition or circumstance, these regulations may be more stringent than the Commission for Health Services regulations, if any, for the same activity. Otherwise the state regulations prevail.

A district board of health generally adopts district-wide regulations. When there are peculiar local circumstances and a reasonable basis for differences, the board may make different regulations for different counties within the district.

Local boards of health may adopt national or state codes or standards, or portions thereof, as part of their local regulations. They may be adopted by reference—that is, by citation only, without setting them out in full. Copies of the codes or standards must be filed in the office of the clerk of superior court. Additions or changes in the national or state codes are not effective unless the local board expressly adopts them. Many county health departments have adopted by reference the United States Public Health Service milk sanitation standards.

The broad power to regulate and control activities affecting the public health has been exercised differently by each board, varying because of local needs and capability to enforce them. The most common local regulations concern septic tank installation and mobile home park sanitation. Others cover air pollution control, garbage collection and disposal, swimming pools, water supply, and miscellaneous nuisances.

All health departments are directed to enforce the statewide public health nuisance law, which provides procedures for notifying the responsible persons to abate the nuisance and for court action if necessary. Local departments also enforce several of the Commission for Health Services regulations, including those governing sanitation of restaurants and lodging places, nursing home licensing, local confinement facilities standards, and meat market and processing plant standards.

Notice of Regulations. Before any local regulations or amendments thereto can become effective, they must be posted at the courthouse for two weeks. Also, a notice that the regulations have been posted and are on file in the health department must be published in a local newspaper once each week for two weeks.

HEALTH SERVICES 293

Violation of Regulations. Local regulations have the force and effect of law. Penalty for their violation, upon conviction by a court of competent jurisdiction, is a maximum of a $50 fine or thirty days' imprisonment. In addition, a local health director or his representative may bring an action in the superior court to obtain an injunction against any person who either is violating or threatens to violate health laws or regulations.

Fees

Local departments may charge fees for services rendered, unless the fee is one specifically prohibited by law or regulation. Even when a fee is permissible, the services may be rendered without charge to persons who are medically indigent, as determined by the local health director. The fees charged are set by the health director with the approval of the board of health and the county commissioners but must not exceed actual costs.

Local Department Administration

The statutes do not prescribe how local departments are to be organized or administered. But in 1973 for the first time the state was empowered to set standards governing the nature and scope of public health services rendered by local health departments. State funds can be denied those counties that do not comply with the standards. The standards are established after consultation with an advisory committee composed of three local health directors, three local board of health chairmen, and three county commissioners. In addition, the State Division of Health Services advises on organization through its published policy guidelines, in local contracts for state financial aid, and by periodic consultation. The State Personnel Department regulations determine qualifications, salary ranges, leave, and other personnel matters. The county board of commissioners exercises review of the health department organization and programs when it annually reviews and approves the budget request. The ongoing organization and administration of the department is the responsibility of the local health director, with the approval of the local board of health.

Local Health Director

A local health director who meets the State Personnel Department qualifications is chosen by the local board of health after consultation with the State Director of Health Services and serves as the administrative head of the department. By statute he has general quarantine and sanitation authority within the county or district. He is directed to disseminate public health information and promote the general public health, particularly in the public schools with the cooperation of school officials.

The statutes direct that the health director should devote his full time to public health work. However, the state has approved some part-time health director positions in counties where financial and personnel circumstances require this arrangement.

The personnel classification description of health director requires him to be either a physician or a health administrator with a Master of Public Health (M.P.H.) degree and training in public health but no medical degree. Some counties have health administrators as assistants to the health director. When a health administrator is appointed to run a local department, he will use physicians as consultants for aspects of the department work that require medical advice or practice. In 1974 there were forty-three physicians and eighteen administrators serving as local health directors in North Carolina.

OTHER AGENCIES ALLIED TO PUBLIC HEALTH

Sanitary Districts

Sanitary districts have been established in several parts of the state to provide water and sewerage services to citizens not served by municipal services. The State of Commission for Health Services is authorized to create sanitary districts without regard for municipal or county boundaries but in strict accordance with the statutory procedures. The general law also describes the authority of the sanitary district boards and contains procedures for issuing bonds and levying taxes; provisions for extending, dissolving, and merging sanitary districts; and other details related to sanitary districts. Because counties now have all the powers that sanitary districts possess as well as numerous other powers, sanitary districts are not as useful a device for providing rural water and sewerage services as they have been in the past.

Mosquito Control Districts

A political subdivision called a mosquito-control district may be formed for the limited purpose of controlling mosquitoes and other dangerous or undesirable arthropods.

The district is created after a petition by 10 per cent of the resident freeholders, a public hearing, approval by both the Commission for Health Services and the board of county commissioners, and a favorable vote of the residents of the proposed district at a special election. A five-member board is appointed by the county commissioners, the Director of Health Services, and the Director of the Wildlife Resources

Commission. The district board has the authority to issue bonds and to levy and collect taxes (not to exceed a rate of 35 cents per $100 assessed valuation). The board may finance and conduct mosquito-control programs within the district, upon approval of the plan of operation by the Secretary of Human Resources. The statutes provide procedures for dissolving a district when it has no outstanding indebtedness.

FINANCES

The local board of health has no power to tax. But the statutes authorize the board of county commissioners to levy a special purpose tax, without a vote of the people, for the preservation and promotion of the public health. Proceeds from this tax or from a general tax may be used for the construction of a health department as well as for its operation and maintenance.

A capital reserve fund may be established by the boards of county commissioners for the purpose of financing the purchase, erection, repair, or alteration of public health or mental health facilities. These procedures were established by 1965 legislation to provide for anticipating future needs and to facilitate the utilization of federal matching grants.

Besides the funds made available from local property tax revenues, additional financial support is received from the state and federal governments. (See Table 15-I.) Previously only a very small amount was received from fees, but under Medicaid and Medicare, fee receipts have tremendously increased. All expenditures must be made under the provisions of the Local Government Budget and Fiscal Control Act.

The table shows the relationship between the sources of funds for all local programs. The increases in expenditures in the past decades are striking.

Table 15-I
Support of Local Public Health Programs by Level of Government

Fiscal year	Local	State	Federal	Total
1943-44	$ 1,230,046	$ 150,000	$754,004	$ 2,134,051
1953-54	3,873,002	1,132,000	296,110	5,301,112
1963-64	7,610,791	1,527,268	200,000	9,338,059
1967-68	10,497,061	2,028,824	120,000	12,645,885
1973-74	21,492,412	4,586,441	504,095*	26,582,853

Source: North Carolina Local Health Service Budget, Fiscal Year 1973-74 and Other Pertinent Information on Local Health Departments (North Carolina State Division of Health Services, Raleigh, 1974).

*Fees only. No other federal participation.

While the 1967-68 ratio was about 83 per cent local funds, 16 per cent state funds, and 1 per cent federal funds, the 1973-74 ratio was 80.8 per cent local funds, 17.2 per cent state funds, and 2 per cent federal funds. The 1973-74 cost per capita for the state—based on all funds and a population of 5,000,000, was about $5.23—more than twice the 1967-68 amount. Mecklenburg County had the largest total budget with $3,114,804, and Clay the smallest with $26,118, but both budgets have doubled in the last six years.

State Policies Governing Allocation of Funds

Funds appropriated by the General Assembly to local health departments are administered through the State Division of Health Services. Each year the Division prepares a written policy governing the distribution of state funds. The current method of allocating funds involves three categories of distribution: regular annual support of local health departments, new appropriations for local distribution, and specially earmarked appropriations for local programs. The regular annual support has remained constant for each county since fiscal year 1970-71 and is called the base allocation.

A county's base allocation is the sum of (a) an amount (not more than $1,000) equal to half of the county's cost of providing benefits in the Local Governmental Employees' Retirement System for county health department employees, plus (b) a flat amount of $4,000, plus (c) a share of the remaining funds on a per capita basis according to the latest decennial census (or approximately 33 cents per capita). The total amount annually distributed is $2,028,824 as the base allocation.

New money appropriated by the 1971 General Assembly and succeeding legislatures is allocated according to population, appraised property value, and the health appropriation by the county for the prior fiscal year using this formula:

$$\left(\frac{\frac{\text{County health appropriation}}{\text{County property value}} \times \text{County population}}{\text{Sum of the above for all counties}} \right) \times \begin{array}{l} \text{Additional} \\ \text{state funds} \\ \text{available} \end{array}$$

For the fiscal year 1974-75, the amount of new money distributed was $200,000.

In 1974, $2 million in specially earmarked new money was made available to be distributed on a discretionary basis by the Division of Health Services to local departments to improve salaries, promote multi-county districts, and provide for direct provision of services by the state in counties that agree to shift the administration of the local health department to the State Division of Health Services. In addition, there are other federal and state categorical funding programs: home health services, cancer, multiphasic screening, glaucoma screening, kidney, neurosensory, tuberculosis, maternal and child health, mosquito control, and crippled children.

The Contract Between the State Division of Health Services and Local Governing Boards

The practice of the State Division of Health Services each fiscal year has been to allocate state and federal funds to local health departments on the condition that certain standards and procedures be complied with as set out in a written contract. This contract is signed by the chairman of each board of county commissioners and by the Division's Assistant Director for Local Services. It generally includes the following principal provisions;

(1) Stipulation of the amount of state and federal funds being allocated and the amount of local financial support appropriated by the county commissioners;
(2) The requirement that the local health department furnish some minimum period of dental services depending on the population of the county (if there is no program, the state withholds a certain amount of funds);
(3) Agreement that the local board of health employ a qualified health director and that full-time employees not engage in the practice of medicine or related activities other than in the discharge of official duties;
(4) Agreement that the local health director has sole authority to employ, direct, and replace department employees, subject to the requirements of the State Personnel Department regulations;
(5) Agreement that salaries of the health department staff must be approved by the State Division of Health Services, and salaries and leave must be in accord with State Personnel regulations:
(6) Requirements for reporting and recording, including submission of the following reports: annual budget, annual contract, monthly budget report, memorandum of June payroll, bill for consulting physicians' services in clinics, monthly vital statistics, restaurant and lodging inspection sheets of sanitarians, monthly report of sanitation activities, and State Personnel Department reports.

Besides these provisions, the contract sets out the payment schedule for all funds (local appropriations are paid monthly; state and federal, quarterly), provisions for supplemental fund applications, provisions relating to a district health department disbursing agent, a choice of methods for paying travel allowances, and a choice of monthly or annual audit procedures.

If the terms of the contract are not complied with, thirty days' written notice of cancellation of the contract (and any state and federal funds) is required.

HEALTH DEPARTMENT PROGRAMS

Public health programs carried on by the county and district health departments vary considerably, depending on population and other factors, but many departments have the following programs:

Administration. Program planning, supervision of services, and clerical services.

Sanitation. Sanitation inspections and regulation of milk, restaurants, meat markets, hotels, motels, hospitals, schools, ambulances, local detention facilities, child day-care facilities, water and sewerage facilities, agricultural labor camps, swimming pools, and other public places.

Public Health Nursing. Programs for the prevention and control of disease, care of the sick in the home, family health guidance, school health services, and clinic services.

Public Health Dentistry. Educational programs and corrective services either in clinics or in schools.

School Health. Pre-school and in-school examinations, demonstrations and special classes, and cooperation with medical and dental professions in correction of defects.

Nutrition. Services in schools and maternity classes, group demonstrations, and distribution of educational literature.

Veterinary. Animal and meat inspections, cooperation with veterinaries in rabies control, and testing for Bangs' disease and tuberculosis.

Mental Health. Mental health prevention services (where there is no local mental health clinic), child guidance in schools, and cooperation with official and nonofficial agencies.

Venereal Disease. Educational programs, diagnostic proof-finding, contact investigation, and treatment.

Health Education. Interpretation of public health programs to the community and correlation of school health, sanitation, nutritional, nursing, venereal disease, and other services.

Clinical. Tuberculosis and X-ray, venereal disease, prenatal, preschool, family planning, orthopedic, diagnostic, cancer, food-handling, immunization, and other clinics.

Laboratory. Serologic tests, blood and differential counts, water and milk analysis, smears and cultures for communicable disease control.

Rodent and Fly Control. Various programs for the control of rodents and flies, including traps, sprays, fogs, landfills, and civic clean-up promotions.

Air Pollution Control. Monitoring and sampling of air quality; restricting the emission of some contaminants, including dense smoke, into the air.

Vital Statistics. The preparation and preservation of birth and death reports and records.

PUBLIC HEALTH LAWS RELATING TO SPECIFIC LOCAL FUNCTIONS

County Physicians

A board of county commissioners is authorized to employ a county physician to perform such duties as the board directs. The principal duty usually assigned the county physician is to provide medical care to the inmates of county confinement facilities. If no other physician is available for this position, the commissioners may permit but not require the local health director to serve as county physician.

Local Confinement Facilities

Legislation requires the board of county commissioners to develop a plan for providing medical care for prisoners. The plan must be designed to protect the health and welfare of prisoners and to avoid the spread of contagious diseases. It must be reviewed by the local health director for adequacy. The county physician, the sheriff, and the local medical society must be consulted on this matter, both for advice and for cooperative participation in the plan.

Local health department sanitarians are also required to inspect jails under State Commission for Health Services jail sanitation regulations and to report disapproved facilities to the Commissioner of Social Services, who, as over-all supervisor of jail inspection services, may then order the jail closed.

Vital Statistics

The State Division of Health Services has responsibility for registering births and deaths. The Secretary of Human Resources is designated as the State Registrar of Vital Statistics and has general supervisory responsibility for the uniform enforcement of the vital statistics laws.

The state is divided into local registration districts that generally follow county lines. The State Registrar appoints local health directors as local registrars. Each local registrar must appoint a deputy and may appoint subregistrars. If a vacancy occurs in the position of health director, the deputy continues to carry out the responsibilities of the local registrar.

Among the duties of the local registrar are the registration of fetal deaths, examination and filing of birth and death certificates upon forms prescribed by the State Registrar, and the issuance of disposal permits authorizing the burial or other disposition of dead bodies. The local registrar makes a copy of birth, death, and fetal death certificates and sends the original certificates and a summary report each month to the State Registrar. Reports of contagious diseases made by physicians in the community to the local health director are also transmitted to the State Registrar.

Other vital statistics reports to the State Registrar are required from clerks of superior court (for divorces) and registers of deeds (for marriages).

Immunization

All children in the state are required to be immunized against diphtheria, tetanus, whooping cough, poliomyelitis (infantile paralysis), and red measles (rubeola). The Department of Human Resources determines the various children's ages and doses for administration and also whether smallpox immunization should be given. It is the legal obligation of the parent or guardian of the child to see that the immunizations are administered to his child by either a private physician or the local health department. Failure to do so within thirty days after the child first enters school may result in criminal liability for the parent. Children with a certificate from a physician to the effect that such immunization would be detrimental to their health are exempted from these immunization requirements. Children whose parents belong to a recognized religious organization whose teachings are contrary to the specified immunization practices are also exempted.

Part II / Mental Health

HISTORY

Governmental involvement in its citizens' mental health problems dates back to the inglorious days of witch trials and public-furnished cages for indigent mental cases. Reform in the commitment laws and financial support of mental health facilities came slowly all across the country. In recent years, however, much progress has been made in mental health services, administration, and support.

Mental health organization and responsibility in North Carolina is now directed primarily toward rendering individual and community services. Unlike public health organization, mental health organization has little responsibility for regulatory measures. The admission of patients to mental hospitals is controlled by mental health authorities, but commitment is the responsibility of the courts. Both admission and commitment procedures are described in detail in the statutes. Voluntary use of mental health services is generally considered desirable.

For many years the state mental hospital system was operated by the State Hospitals Board of Control. The mental health programs at both the state and community level were the responsibility generally of the old State Board of Health and local health departments. The Mental Health Section of the State Board of Health allocated state and federal funds to the county and regional mental health clinics. It also encouraged mental health services and education through public health nurses in local health departments.

Significantly increased attention was given to mental health by the General Assembly when it created the State Department of Mental Health in 1963. The new Department was given authority and responsibility over all phases of mental health in North Carolina, including jurisdiction over all the state's existing mental health services and programs. In 1973 the Department was renamed the Division of Mental Health Services in the Department of Human Resources.

STATE MENTAL HEALTH ORGANIZATION

The mental health policies of the state are determined by a fifteen-member State Commission for Mental Health Services. The Commission adopts the necessary rules and regulations to govern both the policies of the Division and the employment of professional and staff personnel. The policies are administered by the Director of the Division of Mental Health Services (previously called the Commissioner of Mental Health) and his staff.

The Division carries out a wide variety of educational, training, and service programs in mental health at both the state and local level. It administers the state's mental hospitals and residential centers for the retarded. It provides special programs for alcoholics and emotionally disturbed children. Private psychiatric facilities must be licensed by the Division. Research and education in mental health is a continuing responsibility of the Division.

LOCAL MENTAL HEALTH PROGRAMS

Organization of Local Mental Health Services

Until 1971 all local mental health programs were conducted by a local mental health authority that was established by a county, city, or community agency with state approval. Generally, the authority was either a single-county or multi-county board consisting of county commissioners. The authority received state and federal funds under a Memorandum of Understanding with the State Division of Mental Health

Services (previously called the Department of Mental Health). Some local mental health services continue to be provided under such an arrangement.

The present policy of the state is to provide mental health services through approximately thirty-five area health programs including services and activities for diagnosis, treatment, care, and rehabilitation of mentally impaired persons and for the promotion of mental health in the area, using a combination of state and community resources.

Each area has a fifteen-member board that meets at least six times each year. The board consists of six categories of persons and must be equitably representative of the entire area. Specifically, there must be at least one commissioner from each county; these members appoint the rest of the members: two physicians; one representative from psychology, social work, nursing, or religion; three representatives from local citizen organizations; one hospital or area planning organization representative; and one attorney. The board is responsible for reviewing and evaluating the area needs and programs in mental health, mental impairment, mental retardation, alcoholism, drug dependence, and related fields. The board must develop jointly with the Division an annual plan for the effective development, use, and control of both state and local facilities and resources in a comprehensive program of mental health services for the residents of the area.

An area mental health director is appointed by the area board with the approval of the Secretary of Human Resources. He is responsible to the board for carrying out the policies and programs of the board and the rules and regulations of the Commission for Mental Health Services.

Financing Local Mental Health Services

The State Division of Mental Health Services in the state's mental health authority for the purpose of administering federal funds allotted to North Carolina under the National Mental Health Act and other federal legislation. The Division establishes standards and conditions for participation by local communities in federal and state grant programs.

Boards of county commissioners are authorized to appropriate funds for the support of mental health clinics or programs whether they are located within or outside the county, using general tax funds or other revenues. When clinics or services are jointly sponsored by two or more counties, the costs are shared on the basis of population.

Land, buildings, and equipment are not financed by state funds; local or federal funds may be used for this purpose. A capital reserve fund may be established by boards of county commissioners to finance the purchase, erection, repair, or alteration of mental health facilities.

Under current federal grant programs, a local mental health center must be designed ultimately to include (1) consultation, education, and prevention services; (2) outpatient clinic services in various locations in the county or counties; (3) emergency services; (4) partial hospitalization services; and (5) inpatient hospitalization services. The program may also include, but is not limited to, diagnostic services, rehabilitation services, research, training, and pre-care and after-care services.

Appropriations are made annually by the Department of Human Resources to area mental health programs for the provision of community-based services. Allocations are in the form of a base grant computed on the basis of $500 per 1,000 population within the area. Additional allocations may be made to the area program according to a formula based on the area's relative ability to fund mental health services, but the statutes provide that the formula shall be not less than 1:1 state matching funds and not more than 9:1.

When local mental health programs are under a single-county local mental health authority, appropriations are allocated on the basis of two-thirds of the first $30,000 of the approved budget and half of the remainder of the budget.

Community Alcoholism and Drug-Abuse Programs

Community-based drug-abuse programs are authorized by the statutes to be established by the Secretary of Human Resources. Such programs may be as comprehensive as fiscal limitations permit and include the following services relative to treating and preventing drug abuse: inpatient and outpatient services, diagnostic services, rehabilitation services, partial hospitalization, emergency services, consultation and education services, pre-care and after-care services, training, and research and evaluation. Counties are also authorized to form single-county or multi-county agencies for sponsoring alcoholism programs. Local mental health authorities participating in such programs must comply with the rules and regulations of the Commission for Mental Health Services.

Related to such a program may be a "hot line" telephone answering service for the purpose of crisis intervention. These telephone service programs must be licensed by the North Carolina Drug Authority.

State funds for both community alcoholism and drug-abuse programs are distributed on the same formula basis as prescribed by statute for area mental health programs and for local health mental authorities.

— *David G. Warren*

16 / Public Education

Introduction / 307
Public Education As a State Function / 308
The Legal Structure of Public Education in North Carolina / 308
State Structure / 308
  State Board of Education / 308
  State Superintendent of Public Instruction / 309
  Controller / 309
  Department of Community Colleges / 309
  Private Organizations / 311
Local Structure of Education / 311
  Administrative Units and Their Boards of Education / 311
  Local School Superintendents / 311
  District School Committees and Advisory Councils / 312
  Boards of County Commissioners / 313
  Boards of Trustees of Community College Institutions / 313
The Local Board of Education / 314
Selection of Board Members / 314
Organization of the Board / 314
Special School Elections / 315
School Consolidation / 316
Property / 317
  Acquisition of Property / 317
  Eminent Domain / 318
  Disposition of Property / 319
  Control and Management / 319
  Insurance / 320
  Nonschool Use of Property / 320
Tort Claims Against School Boards / 320
Desegregation / 321
Finance / 324
Brief History of School Finance / 324
Sources of Revenue / 325
State Financial Support / 327
Local Financial Support / 331
Federal Financial Support / 334

The Budget-Making Process / 334
Introduction / 334
Relationship of the Board of County Commissioners to the
  Board of Education / 334
School Budgets / 336
  Current Expense Budget / 336
  Capital Outlay Budget / 337
  Debt Service Budget / 337
  Supplemental Tax Current Expense Budget / 338
  Operating Budget / 339
Procedure for Resolving Disputes / 339
Apportionment of Local School Funds
  Among Administrative Units / 340
Capital Reserve Fund / 341
Disbursement of School Funds / 341
Financial Records, Reports, and Audits / 342

16 / PUBLIC EDUCATION

INTRODUCTION

No responsibility of a democratic government is more important than the education of its citizens. This fact is confirmed by the North Carolina Constitution, which states: "Religion, morality, and knowledge being necessary to good government and the happiness of mankind, schools, libraries, and the means of education shall forever be encouraged." The Constitution also states: "The people have a right to the privilege of education, and it is the duty of the State to guard and maintain that right." Thus, education is recognized as the foundation for a viable democratic society and a service that the state is obligated to promote and protect for its citizens. To carry out these constitutional mandates, the State of North Carolina maintains a system of elementary and secondary schools; a system of community colleges and technical institutes; and the University of North Carolina, which consists of sixteen senior institutions of higher education.

Though the state assumed primary responsibility for financing the state's system of elementary and secondary schools in the 1930s, the General Assembly has delegated financial responsibility for certain areas of public education to the counties. Public schools receive from half to three-quarters of a county's entire budget. Thus schools are a major concern for the board of county commissioners for two reasons: their importance to communities and their high cost, which the commissioners must meet from county revenues. To give a better idea of how schools are operated and administered, this chapter will review the basic legal structure for operating the public schools, the major issues in school operation, and the means used to finance and budget for schools. However, information about specific problems of particular school systems can be obtained only from the local school boards and local school officials. County officials who have a responsibility for schools should seek opportunities to meet with their school boards, to visit schools, and to talk with school administrators about school problems and plans.

PUBLIC EDUCATION AS A STATE FUNCTION

Public education is a function and responsibility of state government. The Tenth Amendment to the United States Constitution reserves to the states or to the people those powers not delegated to the United States. The federal Constitution makes no mention of education; therefore, the organization and operation of the public school system is left to the state and its political subdivisions.

The State of North Carolina did not accept the responsibility for a public school system early in its history. Originally, education was considered a local matter, and the state's first schools were financed and operated by church groups. Gradually, however, the education of its citizens came to be considered a fundamental obligation of government, but an obligation to be met primarily at the local level. In time, the state began adding its resources to the support of public schools, and in 1933, during the hard days of the Depression, it took over most of the financial responsibility for the schools. Recognition of education as a responsibility of state government is indicated today in the North Carolina constitutional provisions that require the General Assembly to provide "for a general and uniform system of free public schools." The Constitution further provides that these schools shall be maintained for at least nine months in every year and that every child of appropriate age and sufficient mental and physical ability shall attend public schools, unless educated by other means. Thus the public school system in North Carolina is now considered both an obligation and a function of state government. School operation today is largely determined by state statutes and state policies adopted by the State Board of Education. School officials and teachers are employees of the state, and school funds and assets belong to the state. School boards are agents of the state and their power is only as broad as the state chooses to make it. The public school system is clearly a state school system.

THE LEGAL STRUCTURE OF PUBLIC EDUCATION IN NORTH CAROLINA

State Structure

State Board of Education. The State Board of Education is a constitutional body. It has thirteen members, two of whom are ex officio—the Lieutenant Governor and the State Treasurer. The remaining eleven are appointed by the Governor for staggered, eight-year terms subject to confirmation by the General Assembly.

PUBLIC EDUCATION   309

The State Constitution makes the Board responsible for supervising and administering the state's free public school system and the educational funds provided for its support, except for the county school fund. The Board has the power to make all rules and regulations, subject to the laws enacted by the General Assembly, that are necessary to carry out this responsibility. The statutory duties of the State Board of Education are set out in G.S. 115-11. In general, the state school board is vested with full authority to maintain and operate North Carolina's schools.

State Superintendent of Public Instruction. The State Superintendent of Public Instruction is a constitutional officer. In most states the Superintendent is appointed by the Governor or selected by the state school board; in North Carolina, he is popularly elected for a four-year term. The State Constitution makes the Superintendent the secretary and chief administrative officer of the State Board of Education. As such, he is responsible for keeping the State Board of Education and the public informed of the problems and needs of the public schools and recommending needed changes to deal with these problems and needs. He is also responsible for organizing and administering a Department of Public Instruction that is to provide supervision and assistance to the public school system. For a breakdown of the department, see Chart 16-1.

Controller. The Controller is the State Board of Education's administrator in supervising and managing the public schools' fiscal affairs. The General Assembly created the office in 1945 in an attempt to clarify and separate the duties of the State Board of Education from those of the State Superintendent of Public Instruction. The Controller is appointed by the State Board of Education and serves at its will. The General Statutes require the Controller to supervise and manage the fiscal affairs of the State Board of Education. Fiscal affairs are defined as "all matters pertaining to the budgeting, allocation, accounting, auditing, certification, and disbursing of public school funds" administered by the Board.

These board duties are set out more specifically by the school statutes. They provide that the Controller shall prepare, administer, and account for the state school budgets, which include all funds appropriated to the State Board for maintaining and operating the public schools and the institutions of the community college system. The Controller's office has such responsibilities as auditing all school accounts, administering the school insurance fund, making the allotment of teachers to local school units, administering the state's textbook program, administering federal funds, and supervising the state school transportation system.

Department of Community Colleges. The Community College Act of 1963, which is codified as G.S. Ch. 115A, authorized the establishment of a comprehensive system of educational institutions throughout the state to offer courses of instruction in one or more of the general areas of

Chart 16-1
NORTH CAROLINA DEPARTMENT OF PUBLIC EDUCATION

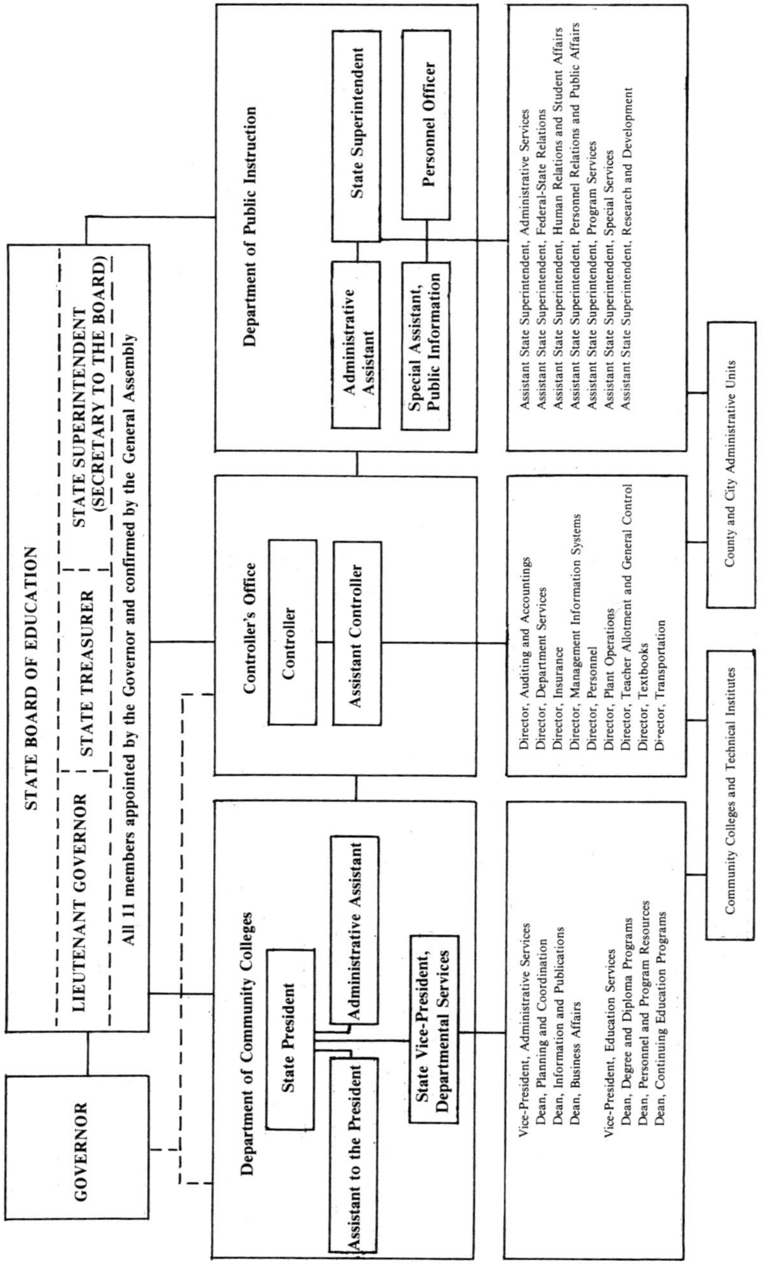

PUBLIC EDUCATION   311

two-year college-parallel, technical, vocational, and adult education programs. It also authorized a Department of Community Colleges to be established by and operated under the authority of the State Board of Education. The Department carries out Board policies in providing state-level administration for the system of community colleges. That system now includes 17 community colleges and 40 technical institutions, all of which are separate from the state's public school system.

Private Organizations. Besides the educational bodies created by the law, a number of important private educational organizations operate within the state. The North Carolina Association of Educators (NCAE), with a membership of over 51,000, is the largest and most powerful of these groups. Other educational organizations include the North Carolina School Boards Association, the professional organization for school boards, and the state Parent-Teachers Association.

Local Structure of Education

Administrative Units and Their Boards of Education. The county or city school administrative unit is the legal structure that operates directly below the State Department of Public Instruction in the public school organizational hierarchy. By statute, each county of the state is classified as a school administrative unit; the schools of this unit are under the general supervision and control of a county board of education. City administrative units are areas within a county or adjacent parts of two or more contiguous counties that have been approved to operate as separate school units by the General Assembly. The schools of a city unit are under the control of a city board of education established by the special legislative act that created the unit.

During the 1974-75 school year there were 100 county and 49 city administrative units in North Carolina. They ranged from 700 to 81,000 pupils in average daily attendance. Each of these units has a board of education that is responsible for directing, supervising, and planning for the public schools of that unit. The board is a corporate body, and G.S. 115-27 gives it "all powers and duties conferred and imposed by law respecting public schools, which are not expressly conferred and imposed upon some other official. . . ." Among the specific duties imposed upon the board by the General Statutes are the appointment of the superintendent; the appointment of teachers, principals, and other professional employees; the preparation of the school budget; and the promulgation of all rules and regulations necessary to govern enrollment of pupils. School boards in most other states have the authority to levy taxes to support the schools they administer; North Carolina school boards do not. The tax-levying authority for school administrative units in this state is the board of county commissioners.

Local School Superintendents. The superintendent of schools is the school administrator at the local level. He is the school system's chief executive officer, and his relationship to the local board is comparable with the relationship of the State Superintendent to the State Board of Education. In exercising the duties and powers granted to him by the statutes, he serves as ex officio secretary for his board of education; recommends teachers, principals, and other personnel to the board for approval; and approves and signs state and local vouchers. The superintendent is appointed by the board of education for a term of two or four years, subject to the approval of the State Superintendent and the State Board of Education. G.S. 115-39 requires that the superintendent have a written contract stating the term of office and the conditions of the agreement.

District School Committees and Advisory Councils. The third and lowest unit in the legal framework for administering the public schools is the district school committee or the advisory council. At one time all county units were divided into districts, each with a school committee to help operate the schools under the county school board. Improved communications and transportation have reduced the need for school committees. In 1965, G.S. 115-70, the statute providing for appointment of district committees, was amended so that county school units that have chosen to organize as one district need not appoint school committees. Since the State Board of Education creates county administrative units upon the recommendation of the county board of education, the county school board decides whether its unit will have district school committees.

In many counties the school district and its committee has been replaced by an advisory council. Unless the county board chooses to grant the advisory council specific powers, it can only advise the county board; it does not have the powers formerly enjoyed by the school district committee.

Ten or fifteen counties still have district school committees. These committees have three to five members who are appointed by the county board of education for terms of either two or three years. The principal statutory duties of a district school committee are: (1) to appoint principals upon recommendation of the superintendent and subject to approval of the county board of education; (2) to elect the teachers and auxiliary personnel upon nomination of the principal and subject to approval of the county board of education and the superintendent; (3) to protect all school property in the district in accordance with the rules and regulations of the board of education. The committee may also have authority to adopt policies and rules for the operation of the schools in the district, if the county school board has elected to convey such power. In the few counties where school committees remain, however, their powers have been substantially reduced, both by the General Assembly and by county school boards themselves.

Boards of County Commissioners. The board of county commissioners is an integral part of the legal structure of public education. Although county commissioners are seldom thought of as educational policy-makers, they in fact influence and at times determine school policy. These occasions arise most frequently in the budget process. The board of commissioners is the tax-levying authority for the schools, except in those few situations in which the governing body of a municipality levies a supplemental tax for a city administrative unit. It provides the local tax money and therefore influences and at times even substitutes its judgment for that of the school board on basic educational issues.

The already substantial role played by the county commissioners in the school area may be increased if or when collective bargaining by teacher groups becomes a reality in North Carolina. This point is illustrated by an episode in which a labor organizer who had come to a North Carolina city to talk with a teacher group accompanied them to a school board meeting. From the discussion, the organizer soon realized that the school board had no fiscal authority but was dependent upon the county commissioners for the school tax levy. Turning to the teachers, he said: "We are wasting our time here. We need to be talking to the people with the tax power — the board of commissioners." It is reasonable to expect that teacher groups seeking more money for schools at the local level will agree with this logic and will put most of their pressure on the governmental board that has the power—the county commissioners. Thus the issue of collective bargaining by teachers, a subject of proposed legislation to the last several sessions of the General Assembly, becomes an important issue for county commissioners.

Boards of Trustees of Community College Institutions. The General Statutes authorize three types of institutions within the Department of Community Colleges: community colleges, technical institutes, and industrial education centers. At present only the first two exist. The local administrative authority for any of these institutions is vested in a board of trustees. That board's duties and responsibilities are similar to those of the local school board. It is a corporate body with all the powers usually conferred on such bodies and has such other rights and privileges as are necessary for the management and administration of the institution. Like the school board, it is dependent upon the local tax-levying authority (or authorities) for local financial support.

Both the community college and the technical institute have a twelve-member board of trustees. Four members are appointed jointly by the local boards of education within the administrative area of the institution, four are appointed jointly by the board or boards of county commissioners of the administrative area, and four by the Governor. The trustees serve for eight-year, overlapping terms and must be residents of either the county or counties comprising the administrative area of the institution or counties contiguous to that area. Vacancies are filled by the agency that appointed the member who caused the vacancy. If a vacancy is not filled within sixty days, the Governor has the authority to appoint a replacement for the unexpired term.

THE LOCAL BOARD OF EDUCATION

Selection of Board Members

The general law for selecting county school board members was rewritten by the 1969 General Assembly to require them to be elected on a nonpartisan basis. The general law, however, does not apply to city school units or to county units with local acts that provide for a different selection procedure. The two key statutes governing school board elections are G.S. 115-18 and G.S. 115-19. G.S. 115-18 provides: "The county board of education in each county shall consist of five members elected by the voters of the county at large for terms of four years." Note that all voters in the county, including voters in the city administrative units, vote for the county school board members under this statute.

G.S. 115-19 provides that: "The county boards of education shall be elected on a nonpartisan basis at the time of the primary. . . ." Some boards are elected on a partisan basis because the unit has a local act excepting it from this general statute. G.S. 115-19 also provides that the board shall have four-year staggered terms, half of which expire every two years. With five-member boards, two of the terms will expire in one year and the other three two years later.

The boards of city administrative units are creatures of special acts, and the general law does not apply to such a board in any particular unless it is incorporated by the special act. Many different methods of selecting city boards of education are now provided. A slight majority of city administrative units have appointed boards, but the trend in recent years has been toward nonpartisan elections. In general, the residents of city administrative units have the right to vote for the county board of education, but there are several exceptions to this—Burlington in Alamance County, Chapel Hill in Orange County, Mount Airy in Surry County, and Raleigh in Wake County.

Organization of the Board

The General Statutes give very little guidance for organizing the school board. G.S. 115-26 provides that county boards appointed by the General Assembly are to "organize" at the first board meeting in April by electing a chairman. This statute was adopted during the time when the legislature appointed county school board members, who took office in April. The statute should be changed, since elected board members take office in December. Nevertheless, county school boards are still required to organize in April.

The superintendent of schools is the ex officio secretary of his board. As such, he keeps a record of all board proceedings and issues all notices and orders of the board.

G.S. 115-28 requires meetings on the first Monday of each quarter, but the board may hold regular monthly meetings and meet in special sessions upon the call of the chairman or secretary as often as school business requires.

Since the statutes make no mention of such matters as proper notice for meetings, what constitutes a quorum, and what is required in voting, the law in this area has been made by the courts. A quorum has been held to be a majority of the whole membership, notice to members a requirement of a legal meeting, and method of voting a matter for the board to decide.

A city school board is created by special legislation and thus is not bound by the general law when its local act differs from general law. Local acts should always be checked when a question concerning organization arises.

SPECIAL SCHOOL ELECTIONS

Article 14, which contains most of the law on special school elections, is hard to understand. The purposes for which school elections may be called are primarily set out in G.S. 115-116. Elections may be held to vote upon proposals to:

(1) Authorize a local supplemental tax;
(2) Increase the supplemental tax rate in a school area that has previously voted a supplemental tax for less than the maximum rate;
(3) Enlarge a city administrative unit by extending a supplemental tax into areas of a county unit and consolidating such areas into the city school unit;
(4) Abolish a supplemental school tax;
(5) Authorize school bonds;
(6) Provide a supplemental tax on a county-wide basis pursuant to merger of all administrative units within a county; and
(7) Annex or consolidate school areas, including areas from contiguous counties, and provide a supplemental school tax in such annexed or consolidated areas.

If an election is held on any of these issues and the proposition is rejected, G.S. 115-117 provides that another election on the same issue in the same area may not be called until six months after the preceding election. Elections on whether to abolish a local tax district may not be held sooner than one year after an election that has established a district or an election on the question of revoking the local tax district. Also, G.S. 115-120 provides that no election may be held on whether to abolish a local tax district when the district is in debt or has obligated or committed its resources in any contractual manner.

The county commissioners' role in the school election procedure begins when they receive a petition from a county or city school board requesting a special school election. The petition, which must be approved and submitted by the school board to the board of county commissioners, need not originate with the school board itself. A school committee or committees or a majority of the qualified voters in a school area may initiate a petition and submit it to the county board of education for any of the purposes set out above. If a petition is approved by the school board and is submitted to the county commissioners, G.S. 155-121 requires the board "to call an election and fix the date for the same." The North Carolina Supreme Court has held that if the petition is properly presented, the duty of the board of commissioners is ministerial and not discretionary; they are obliged to call the election. The only exceptions to this rule occur when the school board withdraws the petition and when other laws, such as the limits on bonded indebtedness, would be violated and thus justify a refusal to call the special school election.

Legislation passed in 1971 provides that all school elections, whether for county or city school administrative units, shall be conducted, canvassed, and certified by the county board of elections. Heretofore, the board of county commissioners rather than the board of elections have conducted special school elections.

SCHOOL CONSOLIDATION

Most of North Carolina's county-wide school systems have always been one school unit and did not obtain their unity through a consolidation procedure. The others, however, resulted from a consolidation of separate school units—a growing trend throughout the country. In the 1966-67 school year, North Carolina had 169 separate school units; in 1974-75, only 149.

School consolidation has never been simply a matter of getting school boards to consolidate into one unit. For many years, a special legislative act and usually voter approval were required for consolidation. Some of the restrictive legal requirements for consolidation, however, were removed in 1967. The legislature rewrote G.S. 115-11(11) to give the State Board of Education new powers in approving school consolidation plans. It also amended the former consolidation statute, G.S. 115-74, and added a new section, G.S. 115-74.1. The new statute provides that when the boards of education of two or more school administrative units within a county agree that the units should be consolidated, the boards shall work out together the problems of the merger, setting out the procedures that are to be followed. When a plan of consolidation has been written and mutually agreed upon by the boards of education and approved by the county commissioners, it is submitted to the State Board of Education. If approved, the plan of consolidation and merger becomes final and cannot be changed or amended except by an act of the General Assembly. Submission of the plan to the voters of the geographic area affected by the consolidation is permitted but not required.

G.S. 115-74.2 authorizes consolidation of adjoining county-wide units, and any city unit located within the counties that chooses to join the consolidation, into a single unit. Consolidation may be accomplished by adoption of a merger plan by the school units involved. The plan must be approved by the board of commissioners in each county and by the State Board of Education. North Carolina has not yet had a merger of two or more county units into a single unit.

PROPERTY

The modern school district holds title to real property and personal property that, in both number of items and total value, make the one-room schoolhouse doubly distant and naive in retrospect. Any school district's physical plant represents an enormous investment by the state and the district.

The school district's personal property, such as textbooks and classroom furniture, has a limited life expectancy and may be entirely superseded as a result of technological developments. Consequently, there is little litigation over a school district's management of such property. But the school district's real property—land and the school buildings erected thereon—raise many legal questions, some of which produce litigation.

Acquisition of Property. The authority of a school district to acquire and manage property is statutory. G.S. 115-27 gives boards of education the power to purchase and hold real and personal property for school purposes. G.S. 115-125 empowers the local board of education to acquire real or personal property by purchase, transfer, or gift or, if land cannot be otherwise obtained, through the power of eminent domain. This authority extends to taking land sufficient not only for present needs, but also for future needs even though the statute does not specifically permit acquisitions for future needs. When the property is acquired,

G.S. 115-27 provides that the school district holds legal title to the property as the agent of the state, but the state has the final authority over the use and disposition of all school property.

Eminent Domain. The power of eminent domain is the authority of the state or its delegated agent to take private property for a public purpose upon the payment to the owner of just compensation. G.S. 115-125 provides that:

> Whenever any such board is unable to acquire or enlarge a suitable site for a school, . . . condemnation proceedings to acquire same may be instituted by such board under the provisions of article 2, chapter 40 of the General Statutes, and the determination of the county or city board of education of the land necessary for such purposes shall be conclusive. . . .

The procedure for condemnation is the general procedure used by most of the state's governmental units, and the property interest the school acquires from the condemnation is fee simple title—i.e., the owner is entitled to the entire property with unconditional power of disposition. Thus there is no possibility that the property may revert to its original owner when the land is no longer needed for school purposes.

The decision of a school district to take lands for a school purpose is solely within its discretion, subject only to the requirements that the land taken be for a school use and that the taking not deprive the owner of his property without due process of law. The question what constitutes a permissible school use has been answered by the courts broadly. A permissible use has been held to be any function that furthers a general school purpose. The courts have upheld the right to condemn for a playground, athletic field, or gymnasium.

In general, the district may anticipate future needs and may take as much land as is reasonably required for the purpose intended, except that G.S. 115-125 limits the amount of property that may be condemned for school purposes to not more than fifty acres.

Though the authority of a school board to take land by eminent domain is conclusively recognized today, problems relating to the procedural aspects of a condemnation action may still arise. The issue that most often creates conflict is the amount of compensation that should be awarded for the property condemned. Just compensation is usually considered to be the fair market value of the property. The general rule is that the compensation due includes "everything which affects the value of the property and its relation to the entire property affected." Though the rule sounds simple, its application is often difficult. Determination of a money value for all the variables that may affect a tract of land is the most litigated issue in public condemnation.

If a school board engaged in a condemnation proceeding is unhappy with the amount of compensation awarded by the court and wishes to drop the action, it usually may do so.

Disposition of Property. School districts, like all other property owners, at times will find it necessary to dispose of their property or agree to its being used for nonschool purposes. The need may result from a school population shift that makes a present school location undesirable or from the need to replace an existing building when building on a new site is cheaper than tearing down the present structure and building anew. G.S. 115-126 authorizes the board to sell, exchange, or lease school property, both real and personal, and to grant easements and rights-of-way on school property. These actions must be taken by the board itself and may not be delegated to a member of its property committee. The procedures for accomplishing these transactions are also set out in the statute; they require, for example, that all real property be sold at public auction, although personal property may be sold either at public auction or through the state's Division of Purchase and Contract.

A requirement that real property be sold only at public auction makes the sale process longer and usually more expensive. G.S. 160A-274 permits an exception to this procedure when the school is dealing with another governmental unit. It authorizes local school boards, upon such terms and conditions as it deems wise, to "exchange with, lease to, lease from, sell to, purchase from, or enter into agreements regarding the joint use by any . . . governmental unit of any interest in real or personal property that it may own." The only requirement for such real property transactions is that it be taken after a public hearing and with proper notice.

A school district may find that leasing its property is more profitable or prudent than selling it. Since leasing property suggests the possibility of making a profit, G.S. 115-126(e) limits the term of a lease to one year. Generally a school district may not enter into a lease agreement that amounts to a gift of the property, regardless of the board's motive or the validity of the purpose. Even when the lease is to another governmental unit, payment reflecting the value received is required.

The exchange and joint use of property held by a school district with another governmental unit is becoming more common. Libraries, administration offices, and recreational grounds are facilities that are frequently shared by the school with another unit of the county or city. As already noted, G.S. 160A-274 permits both the exchange and joint use of such property by governmental units.

Control and Management. A major duty of the school board, its employees, and the board of commissioners with respect to school property is to see that it is properly protected, repaired, and maintained. The common law's great concern for the sanctity of property is reflected in our statutes. G.S. 115-80(a) makes it the "first duty" of the board of education, in preparing the school budget, to provide "adequate funds for the maintenance of plant in order to protect and preserve the investment . . . in the school plant." Other statutes further demonstrate the concern for the proper protection of property. G.S. 115-149 makes it the duty of every teacher and principal to instruct students in the proper care of school property, to protect school property from damage, and to report damage to the parents of any student who damages school property. G.S. 115-133 makes principals, teachers, and janitors responsible for damage to school buildings resulting from "lack of proper discipline of pupils." G.S. 115-133.2 authorizes school boards to offer rewards of up to $300 for information leading to the arrest and conviction of persons who vandalize, steal, or damage school property.

Insurance. G.S. 115-133.1 requires each school board to insure at least 75 per cent of the insurable value of its school buildings. The method of insurance is up to the board, but most school districts insure their property under the state Public School Insurance Fund, a form of self-insurance that results in lower premium rates but may not offer coverage that is adequate for the district's needs. The insurance fund procedures are set out in G.S. 115-134 through -141.

Nonschool Use of School Property. The use of school property by other governmental units and persons not connected with the school is frequently a problem for the board of education. If the board chooses, it may deny all nonschool groups the use of school facilities. Often, however, the board will want to let groups in the community—such as city or county recreation departments, civic groups, and even churches—use the property when it is not needed for school functions. If the school board is to permit this outside use, it should adopt regulations that clearly cover such things as the conditions under which the property may be used, the rent or deposit to be paid, and the liability for damage or personal injury. G.S. 115-133 provides that county and city boards of education shall have authority to adopt rules and regulations by which school buildings, including cafeterias and lunchrooms, may be used for other than school purposes so long as such use is consistent with the proper preservation and care of the public school property. The board regulations should clearly state that no liability shall attach to the board of education or any member of the board as an individual or any school employee for personal injury suffered by reason of the use of such school property by nonschool groups.

TORT CLAIMS AGAINST SCHOOL BOARDS

Except for school bus accidents, which are covered by the State Tort Claims Act [G.S. 143-300.1 (c)], school boards generally are not liable for the negligent acts of their employees. They can defend actions against them by pleading governmental immunity, the ancient common law concept based on the proposition that the king can do no wrong. The school board can waive its governmental immunity defense by purchasing liability insurance. It is authorized to purchase this insurance by G.S. 115-53, and its waiver of immunity is only to the extent of its insurance coverage. Chapter 10 contains a discussion of tort actions against governmental units.

DESEGREGATION

In 1954 the United States Supreme Court in *Brown v. Board of Education of Topeka,* 347 U.S. 483 (1954), declared segregation to be unlawful. Separate school systems are inherently unequal, the Court said, and thus they deny equal protection of the law to the children of the minority group in violation of the Fourteenth Amendment of the federal Constitution.

During the first decade after the *Brown* decision, desegregation was achieved primarily in the courts on a case-by-case basis. This approach proved inadequate to cope with the mammoth task of desegregating the over 2,000 legally segregated school districts of the South. The Civil Rights Act of 1964, however, provided the legal mechanism to accelerate school desegregation. Title VI of the act provided that discrimination in federally assisted programs must cease or those programs would no longer receive federal assistance. It was a declaration of national policy in civil rights, and also the basis for a new approach to school desegregation.

The 1964 Civil Rights Act required each federal department or agency that extends federal financial assistance to any program to issue regulations for carrying out the provisions of Title VI. Accordingly, the Secretary of Health, Education, and Welfare issued a regulation requiring programs eligible to receive federal funds administered by HEW to be free of discriminatory practices. The regulation considered those systems to be qualified that either comply with a final court order to desegregate or submit and comply with a voluntary desegregation plan that the United States Commissioner of Education has determined to be adequate. In reviewing this regulation, the Fifth Circuit Court declared that it set "only minimum standards of general application."

In the spring of 1965, the Commissioner of Education issued a "Statement of Policies for School Desegregation Plans under Title VI" to indicate to school officials what steps would be necessary to bring their districts into compliance with the Civil Rights Act. These guidelines, as the "Statement of Policies" came to be called, were the first of several that would be issued in the next few years.

The act and the guidelines raised some new issues for the courts. One was the relationship to be established between the desegregation procedures prescribed in the guidelines and the procedures required by the courts to satisfy the mandate of the Constitution as interpreted in *Brown*. Generally, the courts have adopted the executive department's standards as an important but not limiting consideration in setting judicial standards.

A second question raised by the guidelines and the act hinged on the applicability of the prohibition in Section 401(b) of the Civil Rights Act against pupil assignments to overcome racial imbalance. The Fifth Circuit Court of Appeals in *United States v. Jefferson County Board of Education,* 372 F. 2d 836 (5th Cir. 1966), held that the provision applied only to de facto situations, and in any event it did not mean that such assignments were unlawful. This view was recently affirmed by the United States Supreme Court in *Swann v. Charlotte-Mecklenburg Board of Education,* 402 U.S. 1 (1971).

The most recently litigated issue concerning the Civil Rights Act concerns enforcement under Title VI. In *Adams v. Richardson,* 351 F. Supp. 636 (D.D.C. 1972), a suit brought by the NAACP against the Secretary of HEW and the HEW Office of Civil Rights, the federal district court for the District of Columbia held that HEW's discretion to enforce compliance with the act's racial discrimination prohibition is limited and may be used only if HEW has grounds to believe that voluntary compliance can be achieved. In five areas where school systems were found to be or were assumed to be in violation of Title VI, the Court issued injunctive orders compelling action by specified dates. The Court said that the time permitted for discretion had passed and HEW could not permit further federal assistance to districts that are not in compliance with, but must enforce the statute. The opinion, which affects several North Carolina school districts, was affirmed with only slight modification by the federal court of appeals.

Another question that arose from the act concerned the duty of school districts to integrate rather than simply desegregate. Many courts had interpreted *Brown* as imposing no duty to achieve any particular racial mix in the schools. Freedom-of-choice plans were adopted throughout the South. The issue was whether these plans, conducted on a nondiscriminatory basis, satisfied constitutional requirements even though they produced only token integration. The Fifth Circuit Court held in *United States v. Jefferson County Board of Education,* 372 F. 2d 836 (5th Cir. 1966), that a freedom-of-choice plan was insufficient if it did not achieve more than token integration. The United States Supreme Court declined to hear that case, but a little over a year later it agreed to hear three cases in which other circuit courts upheld freedom-of-choice plans regardless of the amount of resulting integration. In all three cases the Court found that the school boards had not fulfilled their constitutional requirement to desegregate schools. The principal case is *Green v. New Kent County School Board*, 391 U.S. 430 (1968). A year later the Court reaffirmed its position in *Green* in a case from Mississippi, *Alexander v. Holmes County Board of Education*, 396 U.S. 19 (1969). It said that the remedy must be implemented forthwith.

Two years later the Supreme Court issued its next school desegregation opinion, *Swann v. Charlotte-Mecklenburg Board of Education*, 402 U.S. 1 (1971), which dealt with the volatile issues of busing and the constitutionality of all-black schools. The opinion makes no attempt to define a "unitary school system." As it points out, "conditions in different localities will vary so widely that no rigid rules can be laid down to govern all situations." It reinforced this point in discussing the scope of permissible busing of students: "No rigid guidelines as to student transportation can be given for application to the infinite variety of problems presented in thousands of situations."

To deal with the uniqueness that each school community presents, the Court emphasized the broad powers and affirmative duty of school boards to eliminate school segregation. It also stressed the broad "equitable" powers of the federal district courts in fashioning a remedy to assure a unitary school system. These powers include (1) altering attendance zones to allow pairing or grouping of noncontiguous zones on a racially based mathematical ratio of students as a starting point in shaping a remedy, and (2) adopting an optional majority-to-minority transfer plan.

The next issue to come before the Supreme Court concerned the consolidation or creation of school units as a means to desegregate or to avoid desegregating. The Supreme Court decided two cases on the relationship of the creation of new school districts to school desegregation. The basic rule that emerged is that school districts that were created without intent to segregate but have a racial imbalance due to demographic patterns are constitutionally permissible. However, newly established school districts that increase the racial imbalance are not permissible and can be overturned by federal courts.

In *United States v. Scotland Neck*, 407 U.S. 474 (1972), the Court declared unconstitutional a special legislative act of the North Carolina General Assembly that would have allowed the City of Scotland Neck to withdraw from the Halifax County school district, a district that had just agreed to a Justice Department desegregation plan. The Court concluded that the separate district would result in greater racial imbalance, with more whites attending the city schools and more blacks the county schools. Justice Stewart, writing for the majority, said that the courts would look at the effect of such plans in determining whether they are permissible.

A related issue is the power of the court to order the merger of two or more separate school systems when the court thinks such a merger is necessary to desegregate schools. In *Bradley v. Richmond,* 41 U.S.L.W. 4685 (U.S. May 22, 1973), an equally divided Court affirmed the Fourth Circuit's decision not to merge the City of Richmond schools with those of the two counties surrounding it when the racial imbalance in the schools could not be substantially altered without disregarding the county lines. So many whites had moved from the City of Richmond to suburban Henrico and Chesterfield counties that the city schools had become largely black while the county schools had become more white. Even though the Virginia legislature had the power to alter school districts, the Court did not find that the racial imbalance had been the product of deliberate state action.

The issue of court-ordered merger to accomplish school desegregation is still not settled, nor are several other desegregation issues, such as discrimination in employment. Public school systems will continue to deal with desegregation issues.

FINANCE

Brief History of School Finance

North Carolina has basically a state system of school finance, but state support for public education is fairly recent. During the depression years of the early thirties, many local governments were in default of their financial responsibilities. In one of several actions to stabilize the state's fiscal situation, the General Assembly passed the School Machinery Act of 1933. This legislation embodied a principle of complete state support for the operational costs of the public schools. (The change effected by this law is illustrated in Table 16-I.) As a result, the state assumed responsibility for providing and administering financial support for the schools.

The basic structure of school finance in North Carolina has not changed since 1933. As new programs were adopted, new line items were added in the state budget. Except for capital improvements and maintenance of plant, which are primarily paid for at the local level, the state pays for maintaining a statewide, nine-month school system. In this way it tries to guarantee a minimum level of educational opportunity to each child in the state regardless of where he lives or the school he attends.

Sources of Revenue

North Carolina's approach to financing its public schools differs in three respects from that of most other states. These three differences have been cited as the basis for both the strength and the weakness of North Carolina's public school system.

First, the basic financial support for the system comes from state rather than local revenues, as Chart 16-2 shows. Thus state income and sales taxes rather than the locally levied ad valorem property tax are the primary revenue sources for financing the state's schools.

Second, state support is basically a flat grant to a school system based on the number of students enrolled and the general cost of operation. Operation costs will vary from system to system because of differences in such factors as heating and transportation needs. North Carolina differs from most other states in that it does not allocate some state money on the basis of the local unit's financial ability to support schools. Most states have equalizing grants that compensate poorer districts with fewer resources per student required to be educated. North Carolina makes no such grants, and to the extent that local school systems must appropriate money for specified parts of their school programs, such as buildings and maintenance, this state does not equalize the financial burden of the local units.

Third, the local school board has no authority to levy taxes for the schools in its unit; it must rely upon the board of county commissioners for the tax levy.

Table 16-I
1970-71 Financial Expenditures for the North Carolina Public Schools*
(in millions of dollars)

	State	Local	Federal	Total
Current Operating Expenditures	$493.5	$130.2**	$115.1	$738.8
Capital Outlay Expenditures	$ 6.3	$ 66.0	$ 3.1	$ 75.4
Debt Service Expenditures	—	$ 36.7	—	$ 36.7
Total Contributions	$499.8	$232.9	$118.2	$850.9

*This information was taken from the annual financial report for 1970-71 of the North Carolina public school system. The report was prepared by the Division of Management Information Systems of the North Carolina State Board of Education. The totals for current operating expenses shown above are higher than those shown in the publication *Current Expense Disbursements by Source of Funds, 1970-71*, because expenditures for such items as summer school and adult education are included here that are not included in that publication.

**Student collections included here are only those that flow through the superintendent's books. Other student collections—such as instructional fees, e.g., chemistry lab, band, typing; gym and locker fees; and parking fees—are not included.

Chart 16-2

Current Operating Expense Funds by Governmental Unit
for Selected years

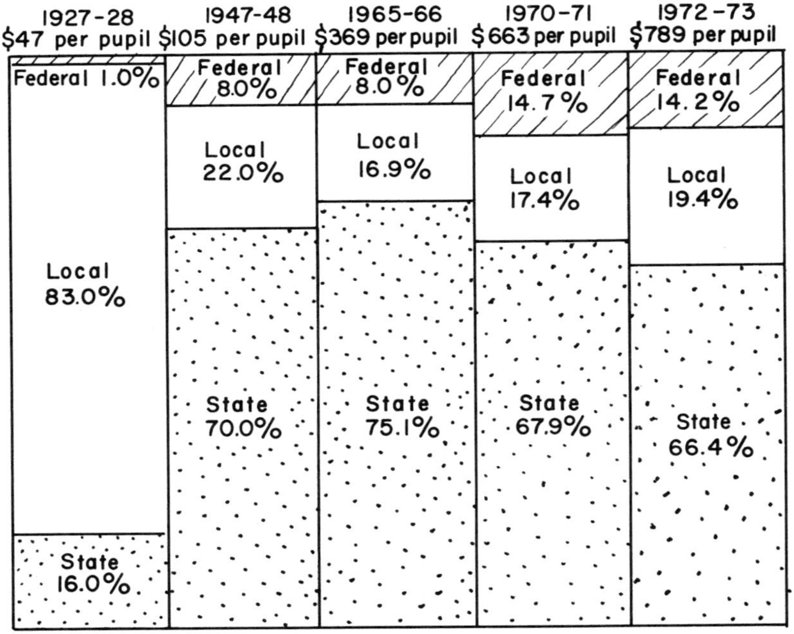

1927-28 $47 per pupil	1947-48 $105 per pupil	1965-66 $369 per pupil	1970-71 $663 per pupil	1972-73 $789 per pupil
Federal 1.0%	Federal 8.0%	Federal 8.0%	Federal 14.7%	Federal 14.2%
Local 83.0%	Local 22.0%	Local 16.9%	Local 17.4%	Local 19.4%
State 16.0%	State 70.0%	State 75.1%	State 67.9%	State 66.4%

The state-financed basic support of the nine- or ten-month school term is supplemented by both the local and federal governments. As Table 16-1 shows, during the 1970-71 school year 58.7 per cent of the total public school support (current expense, capital outlay, and debt service costs) was paid by state appropriations. During the same school year, local governments contributed 27.4 per cent and the federal government 13.9 per cent. The proportions of state, local, and federal support in the various school units of course varied. In percentage of total support for current operating expenses (omitting capital outlay and debt service), administrative units ranged in support from local sources from a high of 35.1 per cent (Charlotte/Mecklenburg) to a low of 3.4 per cent (Graham County). Similarly, federal support varied from a high of 31.7 per cent (Maxton City) to 6.0 per cent (Charlotte/Mecklenburg). State support varied from 80.8 per cent (Randolph County) to 57.1 per cent (Durham City). The average per-pupil current expense expenditure from all sources was $789 during the 1972-73 school year, a 9 per cent increase over that for the preceding year.

State Financial Support

The North Carolina General Assembly appropriated $789 million for operating the public schools for the 1974-75 school year. (This total includes social security and retirement payments.) Most of the state money comes from the state income tax and sales and use taxes, with franchise, beverage, insurance, and other taxes contributing to a lesser degree.

State appropriations for schools are provided through these ten funds:

State Public School Fund
Vocational Education Fund
Retirement and Social Security Fund
Trainable Children Fund
Driver Education Fund
Planning Research and Development Fund
Professional Improvement of Teachers Fund
Elementary Textbook Fund
High School and Supplementary Textbook Fund
Textbook Clerical Fund

Of the ten funds, the State Public School Fund contributes over 90 per cent of the state money. It provides the basic support for the public school program and is disbursed on the basis of these thirty-seven categorical allotments, each with a different allocation formula.

(1) Salary: Superintendent
(2) Salary: Assistant Superintendent
(3) Travel: Superintendent

(4) Salary: Clerical Assistance
(5) Salary: Property and Cost Clerks
(6) Office Expenses
(7) County Boards of Education: Per Diem, Travel
(8) Salary: Attendance Counselors
(9) Salary: Elementary Teachers
(10) Salary: High School Teachers
(11) Salary: Elementary Principals
(12) Salary: High School Principals
(13) Instructional Supplies—General
(14) Instructional Supplies—Film
(15) Salary: Supervisors
(16) Clerical Assistance in Schools
(17) Wages: Janitors
(18) Fuel
(19) Water, Lights, Power
(20) Janitors' Supplies
(21) Telephones
(22) Compensation to Injured School Employees
(23) Reimbursement for Injured School Children
(24) Tort Claims
(25) Wages: Drivers
(26) Gas, Oil, Grease
(27) Gas Storage Equipment
(28) Salary: Mechanics
(29) Repair Parts, Batteries
(30) Tires and Tubes
(31) License and Title Fees
(32) Garage Equipment
(33) Contract Transportation
(34) Replacement of Major Items
(35) Principals' Bus Travel
(36) Libraries—Supplies, Repairs
(37) Child Health Program

The state financial support provided through the ten funds, as noted earlier, is primarily for current operating expenses. The objects of expenditure of state-appropriated funds are itemized by G.S. 115-79. The statute breaks the state school expenditures into the following five categories: general control, instructional service, operation of plant, fixed charges, and auxiliary agencies. Included in these categories are such major educational costs as salaries of administrative and teaching personnel, employees' social security and retirement costs, operation of plant, and pupil transportation (see Table 16-II). State funds may be used for only an instructional period of 180 days; thus summer school programs are paid for with local funds.

PUBLIC EDUCATION 329

Table 16-II
Expenditures to Be Included in School Current Expense Fund
(X indicates expenditures made substantially (over 50%) from state funds.)

GENERAL CONTROL

Salaries of superintendent	X
Salaries of assistant superintendent	X
Travel of superintendents	—
Salaries and travel of business manager	—
Salaries and travel of attendance officer—local	—
Salaries of clerical assistants	—
Salaries of property-cost clerks	X
Salaries of treasurers, including cost of their bonds	—
Per diem and travel of county board of education (state share limited to total of $100 per annum)	—
Office expenses	—
Cost of audit	—
Elections	—
Attorneys' fees	—
Other necessary expenses of general control	—

INSTRUCTIONAL SERVICES

Salaries of elementary and high school teachers	X
Salaries of elementary and high school principals	X
Salaries of supervisors	—
Travel and office expense of supervisors	—
Salaries and travel of vocational education teachers (agriculture, home economics, trades and industries, and distributive education; see G.S. Ch. 115, art. 27)	X
Clerical and travel expenses of principals	—
Commencement expenses	—
Instructional supplies	—
Textbooks	X

OPERATION OF PLANT

Wages of janitors	X
Cost of fuel	X
Water, light, power	—
Janitors' supplies	—
Telephone	—

MAINTENANCE OF PLANT

Cost of repairs to buildings and grounds and teacherages (including salary of superintendent of grounds)	—
Repairs and replacements of furniture and instructional apparatus	—
Repairs and replacements of heating, electrical, and plumbing equipment	—

FIXED CHARGES

Health and disability Insurance	X
Social security	X
Cost of rents, insurance on buildings and equipment	—

Workmen's compensation (on other than bus drivers)	—
Compensation to injured employees	X
Payment for injuries to school children	—
Retirement	X
Tort claims (as covered in G.S. 143-300.1)	X

AUXILIARY AGENCIES

Transportation of pupils	X
Insurance on activity buses (see G.S. 115-53)	—
Library supplies, repairs, and replacements	—
Other costs of operation and maintenance of school libraries	—
Child health programs	—
Aid to indigent pupils	—
Night schools	—
Summer schools	—
Adult education	—
Lunchrooms	—
Veterans' training	—
Interest on temporary loans	—

The individual school unit's share of the state appropriations is determined by the State Board of Education, which is empowered by the State Constitution to supervise and administer the state's public school system and state educational funds. The allocations to the 149 school units are based on standards set by the State Board, the most important of which are the number of pupils in average daily attendance and the salary schedules for various classes of personnel employed by the school unit to fill the state-allocated positions.

The state salary payments for school personnel usually represent over half of a school unit's current operating budget. The professional staff is paid on the basis of state salary schedules that are explained in a publication of the State Controller. Separate salary schedules are used for the following personnel: superintendents, associate and assistant superintendents, classified principals, building principals, supervisors, teachers, and vocational teachers. The index scale used in these schedules for teachers and supervisors is based on two factors—level of education and years of experience. The index in the superintendents' schedule also includes the number of students in the unit in computing salary payments. The principals' schedule includes the number of teachers supervised in addition to experience and education. Superintendents, principals, and supervisors are employed on a twelve-month basis, and teachers are employed for ten months.

Each of the ten funds listed above has its own distribution procedures, some of which require intricate accounting techniques. In most instances state funds are disbursed on a monthly basis. G.S. 115-84 requires a monthly deposit of state funds in the state treasury to the credit of the local school administrative unit to meet the needs of the nine-month school term. Before the monthly deposit is made, the local school board must file with the State Controller a certified statement of all expenditures and salaries and other obligations that may be payable in the following month. The state funds are then, according to G.S. 115-90, released on warrants drawn on the State Treasurer and signed by the chairman and secretary of the school board.

Besides providing funds for current operating expenses, the state has helped local units in their responsibility for capital outlay expenditures. The General Assembly authorized bond issues of $25 million (plus an appropriation of $25 million) in 1949; $50 million in 1953; $100 million in 1963; and $300 million in 1973 for acquiring school sites, constructing school facilities, and improving and maintaining the school plant. These funds are distributed to school units primarily on the basis of the per capita average daily membership in the particular unit.

Another source of state support for school capital outlay is the State Literary Fund. Established in 1825 as a state endowment for education, this fund became, early in this century, a permanent loan fund for local school units for constructing and equipping school plants. The fund is maintained by the State Board of Education, which lends this money for ten years at a rate of interest not to exceed 6 per cent per year. The borrowing procedure is set out in Article 11 of Chapter 115 of the General Statutes and the rules of the State Board of Education.

Local Financial Support

Although North Carolina's school system is primarily supported by state funds, the average county allocates from 50 to 75 per cent of its funds for the operation of the public schools. These locally raised revenues, amounting to 27.4 per cent of the total school budget in the 1970-71 school year, are used to support the public schools in two major ways. First, they provide, equip, and maintain the physical plant for the schools in the administrative unit. Second, they supplement the state's minimum level of support for operating the schools.

It is important to note the areas of school operation that local school districts, and thus the county commissioners, are required by statute to finance. North Carolina General Statutes specify approximately fifteen items that must be supported from local revenues because either inadequate or no state money is appropriated for them:

Attorneys Fees
Audits [G.S. 115-97(d), (e)]
Fidelity Bonds [G.S. 115-85; G.S. 115-91]
Furniture and Apparatus [G.S. 115-129]

Garage and Maintenance Equipment for School Buses [G.S. 115-188(e)]
Insurance [G.S. 115-133.1; G.S. 115-80(a)]
Maintenance of Plant [G.S. 115-80(a); G.S. 115-133]
Matching Retirement and Social Security of Locally Paid Employees [G.S. 115-80(a)]
Necessary Operating Expenses [G.S. 115-89]
Rents [G.S. 115-80(a)]
Sites and Buildings [G.S. 115-129]
Superintendent's Office Adequately Furnished [G.S. 115-40]
Supplies for School Buildings, e.g., books and other instructional supplies [G.S. 115-132]
Water Supply and Sewerage Facilities [G.S. 115-40]
Workman's Compensation for Locally Paid Employees [G.S. 115-80(a); G.S. 115-60]

Local revenue for school support comes from at least twenty different sources that are usually characterized as tax revenues or nontax revenues, classifications stemming from a former constitutional restriction on the use of local tax revenues. Although the Constitution no longer contains this restriction, the tax and nontax dichotomy makes a convenient division for looking more closely at local revenues available to finance the public school system.

Almost 90 per cent of the total local revenues used for schools comes from taxes. (Table 16-III lists the local taxes used for schools and their relative importance to school financing.) The ad valorem tax on personal and real property is the most important local revenue source. It accounts for approximately 95 per cent of the local tax revenues devoted to school finance, including most of the local current operating expense funds and the revenue to retire capital improvement bonds.

Table 16-III
Major Sources of Local Tax Revenues Used for Schools, 1970-71

Source	Amount Received	Percentage
Property Tax[a]	$172.2 million	93.5%
Intangibles Tax	7.2 million	4.0
Poll and Dog Taxes[b]	.9 million	.5
Sales Tax	3.8 million	2.0
TOTAL	$184.1 million	100.0%

a. Property tax includes debt service payments and payments into capital reserve and sinking funds. Revenue from bonds, loans and sinking funds, which amounted to $37.1 million in 1970-71, are not shown in this table. Bond and loan revenues will be paid back in future years from property tax levies.

b. Poll tax is no longer levied.

PUBLIC EDUCATION 333

The second most important tax source is the intangibles tax. Unlike the other local taxes, it is neither levied nor collected by the governmental unit that receives its proceeds. The state performs these functions and returns the proceeds, minus collection costs, to the counties and municipalities. The other local tax sources contribute little revenue.

Nontax revenues are a less important finance source in terms of the amounts collected. They include such moneys as donations, profits from county-operated alcoholic beverage control stores; the county share of the state beer and wine tax; interest on deposits; sales of property; proceeds from fines, penalties, and forfeitures; surpluses from the operation of government-owned public utilities and other proprietary operations of the county; and collections from students (see Table 16-IV). A significant nontax revenue source is proceeds from fines, penalties, and forfeitures. This revenue source is guaranteed to the schools by Article IX, section 7, of the State Constitution, which provides:

> [T]he clear proceeds of all penalties and forfeitures and of all fines collected in the several counties for any breach of the penal laws of the State, shall belong to and remain in the several counties, and shall be faithfully appropriated and used exclusively for maintaining free public schools.

Although not so significant in terms of amount collected, several other nontax revenues are legally required to be used to finance schools. Among these are the proceeds from the sale of seized, tax-paid whiskey, which are paid into "the school fund of the county in which the seizure was made," and the proceeds from the sale of cars used in prearranged racing.

Table 16-IV
Major Sources of Nontax Local Revenues, 1970-71

Source	Amount Received	Percentage
Fines, Forfeitures, and Penalties	$10.6 million	31%
Donations and Miscellany	14.8 million	44
Student Collections (tuition and fees)[a]	1.1 million	3
Interest	3.9 million	12
Sale and Rental of Property	2.8 million	8
Profits from ABC, Beer, and Wine Sales	.8 million	2
Total	$34.0 million	100%

a. The student collections shown here are only those that flow through the superintendent's books. Other student collections—such as instructional fees, e.g., chemistry lab, band, typing; gym and locker fees; and parking fees—are not shown. If total student collections averaged $5 per student, the total contribution would be between $5 million and $8 million.

Federal Financial Support

Federal financial support for public schools in the last fifteen years represents a major new impact on public school operations. Until very recently public schools had been financed almost exclusively by state and local government. With the passage of the National Defense Education Act in 1958 and the Elementary and Secondary Education Act of 1965, federal money for North Carolina schools has increased from practically nothing to $196 million in the 1970-71 school year.

Most federal funds are categorical funds, which means that they are appropriated to the states by Congress for specific educational purposes. Thus federal financial support is earmarked for such school programs as vocational education, school lunchrooms, instruction and guidance services, school library resources, textbooks, and other instructional materials, and special programs for educationally deprived children. Most of this money is for programs to support the current operation of the school system. It is channeled through the State Board of Education for distribution to the local units, but the State Board has little control over the programs for which it may be spent, since the funds are designated for specific programs.

THE BUDGET-MAKING PROCESS

Introduction

Budgeting for schools is a complex and sometimes uncertain process. The complexity and uncertainty exist for two reasons. First, two sets of statutes contain detailed procedures and requirements for school budgeting—the Local Government Budget and Fiscal Control Act of Chapter 159 and the school budgeting law of Chapter 115. Since both laws apply to schools, questions arise about when the provisions of which law apply. The second complicating factor in school budgeting exists because school boards are dependent upon the county commissioners for local financial support. The school boards have no power to levy for taxes to supplement state financial support. In effect, school boards have responsibility for operating schools, yet the appropriation of local funds to provide for a "general and uniform system of free public schools" when state funds are not sufficient and to supplement that minimum rests within the discretion of the county commissioners. In this circumstance, conflicts sometimes arise.

Relationship of the Board of County Commissioners to the Board of Education

The State Board of Education is responsible for the over-all supervision and administration of the state school system, but the county or city school board is chiefly responsible for the operation of the schools within the particular board's administrative unit. The General Statutes grant the local school board substantial authority over such areas of school operation as personnel, property, organization, and program. Nevertheless, the school board has no power to provide the funds to support school needs above the level provided by the state or to finance activities not paid for by the state. This power, with its attendant responsibility, lies with the board of county commissioners, which is designated by the school law as the "tax-levying authority" for schools. As such, it must provide funds to maintain the constitutional school term.

The school law requires local boards of education to make the initial determination of what expenditures are needed for operating the schools and then file budget requests with the county commissioners in the same manner as other county departments and agencies. Except for the supplemental school budget, however, which the commissioners may accept or reject in whole or in part, the school law does not clearly define the commissioners' authority and role in acting upon school budget requests. Nevertheless, it is clear that the commissioners have less power with respect to the school budget than they have in adopting budgets for other county agencies. Their power is limited because the General Assembly has set out by statute, and the State Board of Education by rules and regulations, the general educational program of the state. These statutes and regulations impose specific obligations upon county commissioners and boards of education that must be met. It is the duty of the local board of education to implement this general program; it is the duty of the county commissioners to provide funds to finance the program. In providing local funds to pay for school programs fixed by law, the commissioners' review of the school budgets is limited to determining whether the requested funds are necessary to provide such programs. In discretionary areas of school operation, such as adult education programs, the commissioners' review of the budget is less restricted, and they have a general power to approve or disapprove recommendations for such programs.

This division of authority and the absence of clear guidelines for either the school board or the board of commissioners create uncertainty as to the role of each board. On several occasions the two boards have reached an impasse that resulted in court litigation. The clearest definition of the relationship between the two boards emerged from a conflict carried to the North Carolina Supreme Court. In its decision, the Court said:

> The basic philosophy with respect to the operation of our school system remains. It is the duty of the board of education to evaluate their needs, apply to the board of county commissioners for funds

to supply the needs, and when funds are appropriated, to spend the same within the designated classification, current expenses and capital outlay, as will best serve school needs. It is the duty of county commissioners to study the requests for funds filed with them by the board of education and to provide by taxation such funds, and only such funds, as may be needed for economical administration of schools. . . . When disagreement arises, the county commissioners cannot be required to provide funds beyond their estimate of needs until the controversy has been resolved in the manner provided by statute. . . .

School Budgets

The school finance and budgeting statutes divide expenditures for school operations into three main categories: current operating, capital outlay, and debt service. The school board must prepare and maintain separate budgets for each of these categories. A supplemental tax current expense budget is required if the unit has a special supplemental school tax. Preparing these budgets is the responsibility of the local board of education, which must submit them to the county commissioners on forms provided by the State Board of Education on or before June 1 preceding the fiscal year for which the budget requests are made.

Current Expense Budget. G.S. 115-80(a) provides that the first duty of boards of education and county commissioners in providing funds for current operations is to assure adequate funds for items of expenditure under maintenance-of-plant and fixed charges not provided for by state funds. The purpose of this statutory requirement is to preserve and protect the investment in the school plant. Expenditures that come under this primary duty include: repair to buildings and grounds; repairs and replacement of furniture and instructional apparatus and of heating, electrical, and plumbing equipment; and rent and insurance on buildings and equipment.

The current expense budget is divided into two parts—revenues and expenditures. The revenue portion must show and total all funds requested for the current operation of the schools, whether from state or local sources.

The expenditure portion of the budget lists the expenditures to be made. Six broad categories of expenditure to be included in the current expense budget, with detailed objects of expenditure under each, are set forth in G.S. 115-78. Most of these items are funded by the state. Table 16-II shows the categories and objects of expenditure under each, and also indicates those items that are financed substantially from state funds.

Capital Outlay Budget. The capital outlay budget is filed with the current expense budget. It includes requests for the purchase of sites; the erection of school buildings; improvements of new school grounds; alteration of and addition to buildings; and purchase of furniture, equipment, trucks, automobiles, and school buses. G.S. 115-78(c) arranges these items into three categories—(1) new buildings and grounds, (2) old buildings and grounds, and (3) auxiliary agencies—and describes what items are to be included under each category. These items are primarily paid for by local funds, although the 1973 state bond authorization will increase the amount of state funds for school construction.

The major difficulty with the capital outlay budget is in distinguishing those items that might be included in the maintenance-of-plant section of the current expense budget. Generally a distinction is made between repairs and replacements, which are classified as current expense items, and new acquisitions, which are classified as capital outlay items. For example, replacing a boiler is a current expense item, but converting from coal to oil heat is a capital outlay expenditure.

The capital outlay budget may also include requests for appropriations for a capital reserve fund. This fund allows the school board to accumulate funds for buildings and other items of major expense that will have to be purchased in the future.

Debt Service Budget. Two limitations on the issuance of county bonds for school purposes should be noted before considering the preparation of the debt service budget. One is the "two-thirds limitation," a restriction set out in Article V, section 4(1), of the North Carolina Constitution, which prohibits counties and municipalities from contracting debts during any fiscal year in an amount that exceeds "two-thirds of the amount by which the outstanding indebtedness of the particular county . . . shall have been reduced during the next preceding fiscal year, unless the subject is submitted to a vote of the people of the particular county . . . ." The second limitation is contained in amended G.S. 159-55, which provides that the net county indebtedness may not exceed 8 per cent of the appraised valuation of taxable property.

The debt service budget includes payments of principal and interest on indebtedness incurred for school purposes and the payment of moneys into sinking funds. It is prepared and submitted by the county school board for all separate school tax districts and city administrative units for which the county commissioners are the tax-levying authority. This budget is submitted with the other school budgets by the June 1 deadline.

The key to the debt service budget is the county accountant. G.S. 115-80(d) requires him to examine all county debt service requests and to determine their accuracy. In actual practice, the county accountant prepares this budget and determines what requests are sufficient to meet debt service payments in the budget year. Once he sets this figure or approves these budget items as adequate, the amounts cannot be reduced by the county commissioners. The commissioners must adopt his recommendation and provide sufficient funds to pay for it. In general, it can be said that the commissioners must provide those funds needed for payments of principal and interest on debt and for payments into sinking funds. Their only area of discretion is whether to combine the school debt service fund with the county debt service fund, as G.S. 159-13(a) (3) permits them to do.

Supplemental Tax Current Expense Budget. City and county school boards with jurisdiction over areas for which supplemental school taxes have been approved by the voters file a supplemental tax current expense budget as required by G.S. 115-80(b). (Many school boards do not actually file a separate budget but instead integrate the supplemental tax line items into the current expense budget.) This proposed budget seeks appropriations to operate the schools at a higher level than would otherwise be provided. These appropriations may supplement items financed from state funds, such as teacher salaries, or they may add completely new items, such as additional personnel not allotted and paid for by the state.

Certain limits on the availability of funds from voter-approved supplemental taxes should be noted. First, they are available only to supplement current expense items, such as kindergartens, adult education, summer schools, teacher supplements, additional teachers, or nearly any other program in the school that can be considered part of the educational process. They may not be used to finance items in the capital outlay or debt service budget. Second, G.S. 115-117 limits the amount of the voter-approved supplemental tax that may be levied. The tax may not exceed 50 cents on the $100 valuation of taxable property unless the administrative unit, district, or other area has a population greater than 100,000, in which case a maximum levy of 60 cents is authorized. (Some units have been given legislative authority through local acts to exceed these limits.) If the voters in an area approve a rate below the statutory maximum, only a tax up to the voter-approved rate may be levied. Third, G.S. 115-80(b) and G.S. 115-124 give the commissioners the authority to determine whether a supplemental tax shall be levied, even though the tax levy has been approved by the voters and requested by the board of education. Once the budget is approved, however, the commissioners are obliged to levy the supplement to fund the budget, subject only to the limit set by the voters.

Although at one time the only way to supplement the school program was by the use of a voter-approved supplement, G.S. 115-80(a) now per-

PUBLIC EDUCATION 339

mits the county commissioners to levy taxes for funds to add to or supplement any item of expenditure in the current expense budget upon a showing by the school board that necessity or peculiar local conditions justify the expenditure. A referendum to approve this use of local funds is no longer necessary. Specifically included in this statute as items of expenditure for which local taxes may be levied are additional personnel and supplements to teacher salaries. The State Supreme Court has upheld the constitutionality of this authority, which has become an important factor in school board requests for local funds to pay for items in the current operating budget. The new State Constitution also recognizes this new authority. Article IX, section 2(2), provides that:

> The governing boards of units of local government with financial responsibility for public education may use local revenues to add to or supplement any public school or post-secondary school program.

Operating Budget. All of the budgets submitted to the county commissioners in June must be returned to the school boards on or before July 1. The returned budgets are seldom actually approved budgets. The county commissioners normally scale down the school board's requests and ask that the budgets be resubmitted when they have been drawn within the limits placed on them by the commissioners. If the school board accepts these modifications, the budgets are then approved. Approved budgets are filed with the State Board of Education.

In early July the State Controller notifies the school board of its tentative allotment of state funds for operating the schools. The board also receives notification from the state whether its local budgets, including supplements for operating schools at a higher standard, are acceptable.

Procedure for Resolving Disputes

The school statutes contain special provisions for resolving any conflict between the school board and the county commissioners as to what is adequate financing for the public schools. If the school board is unwilling to accept the commissioners' reduction or change of a budget it has proposed, it may invoke the statutory dispute procedure of G.S. 115-87 and G.S. 115-88. This procedure begins with a joint meeting of the two boards, which the two chairmen must arrange within one week of the disagreement. At this meeting, the controversial budget or budgets must be considered "carefully and judiciously item by item." If the boards cannot reach agreement, each board has one vote on the question in dispute; the majority of each board determines its vote. If the boards remain deadlocked, the issue goes to the clerk of the superior court, who must render a decision within five days. If either board is dissatisfied with the clerk's finding, it may appeal within ten days to the superior court. Here the judge must "find the facts," unless one of the boards has requested a jury trial, and enter judgment requiring a tax levy to provide the funds necessary to maintain the schools.

Either board may appeal the superior court decision. If such an appeal would delay final determination of school appropriations until after the time for levying taxes for the schools, the superior court judge is required to order the commissioners to levy for the ensuing year a tax rate sufficient to pay the debt service fund and to provide, together with what is received from the state's Public School Fund, an amount for current expense and capital outlay equal to the funds available for these purposes in the previous year.

Apportionment of Local School Funds Among Administrative Units

In the thirty-six counties that contain a city administrative school unit, the statutes require that most of the locally raised revenue for schools be apportioned among the administrative units in the county on a per capita enrollment basis. Included among funds that must be apportioned are all county-wide current expense funds (G.S. 115-86) and supplemental taxes levied county-wide [G.S. 115-116(a)]. Capital outlay funds for new school sites, initial bus purchases, additions to present school sites, new school buildings, new additional construction at existing buildings, and equipment for new buildings are apportioned to the various school units on the basis of budgets approved for each administrative unit. Most other capital outlay school funds are apportioned on a per capita enrollment basis in the same manner as the current expense funds are apportioned. (In practice this statutory mandate is sometimes ignored; for example the law requires that current operating costs of school transportation be apportioned, but this is rarely, if ever, done.)

The per capita enrollment of each school unit is determined by the State Board of Education. Every year the State Board certifies to each unit the enrollment figure for that school system. On the basis of these enrollment figures and the approved budget, the county remits to the school units, on a monthly basis, funds for current expense and capital outlay. If a greater amount is collected and paid to any unit than is authorized to be spent in the unit's approved budget, the surplus becomes an unencumbered balance to be credited to the fund to which it was deposited for the coming fiscal year.

Revenue collections for debt service funds are handled differently. Instead of being paid to the administrative units, they are deposited to the

PUBLIC EDUCATION 341

credit of a county debt service fund or a district debt service fund, the indebtedness of which is payable from county funds. Funds are then paid out when principal and interest payments become due.

Capital Reserve Fund

The basic purpose of a capital reserve fund—also known as a pay-as-you-go plan—is to permit local boards of education to anticipate future school capital outlay needs before they arise and to build up capital that will pay for at least part of the facility. The school law had provided a special school capital outlay procedure, but it was replaced in 1973 with a general county procedure. This procedure is codified as G.S. 159-18 through -22.

Disbursement of School Funds

G.S. 115-89 makes the local school board responsible for paying promptly and when due all obligations incurred in the operation for the public schools. The procedure for disbursing state funds was described briefly at pages 327-31. The disbursement of local money varies depending upon whether it is a city or county school administrative unit, a school district within a county administrative unit, or an individual school that withdraws the fund. In general, however, school funds are disbursed by warrants signed by the chairman and secretary of the school board; for local school funds, G.S. 115-90 requires that the warrant be countersigned by the county accountant or the treasurer of the city unit. Warrants usually are drawn monthly and must be accompanied, if state funds are being used, with certified statements of expenditures and obligations due and payable in the succeeding month. Local funds are disbursed on the basis of an invoice or voucher that will show that the warrant is proper. Thus the type of proposed expenditure must be identified and be requested by a statement or voucher signed by proper school officials. For payment of salaries, the monthly payroll, prepared on forms provided by the State Board of Education, is the only proper authority for obtaining funds.

School boards must pay their obligations "promptly and when due." To facilitate meeting this responsibility, the statutes require the school board to inform the county commissioners of any anticipated expenditures that will exceed the current collection of taxes and any balance on hand. If the expenditure is for an expense that the board of commissioners is obligated to pay by virtue of the school budget approved by it, the board is required to make the necessary funds available, even if it must borrow the money. But if a school board or its members willfully create a debt that results in an obligation exceeding the amount authorized by the budget, and without approval of the board of commissioners, the members of the school board responsible for the debt are personally liable for it.

Financial Records, Reports, and Audits

Both the Local Government Budget and Fiscal Control Act and the school law require numerous records and accounts of school financial transactions to be maintained. The school law, G.S. 115-60, which duplicates in part the record-keeping required of the county accountant by the Fiscal Control Act, requires the superintendent of schools, who is the secretary of the school board, to keep a complete and detailed record of all financial transactions of that board. Besides this record-keeping for the board, the county superintendent has other duties. He must record all fines, forfeitures, and penalties due to the school fund (G.S. 115-62); keep separate financial records for special taxing districts (G.S. 115-61); and examine yearly the county records to see that all funds accruing to the school fund are correctly and promptly accounted to it (G.S. 115-100).

Many reports must be made from the records kept. Most of them go to the State Board of Education or the State Department of Public Instruction. An example is the annual treasurer's report of the year's receipts and disbursements during the preceding fiscal year. Also, the United States Office of Education requires an increasing number of reports in accounting for federally financed school programs.

Besides the records and reports that must be kept, G.S. 115-97 requires an annual audit of all school funds. The State Board of Education, in cooperation with the State Auditor, must audit state school funds disbursed by county and city administrative units. The local boards of education are responsible for auditing all county, city, and district school funds for which they are responsible. The audit report must be filed not later than October 1. On or before that date, a summary statement of the audit report must be published in a county newspaper, or, if no paper is published within the county, the statement must be posted at the courthouse door.

— *Robert E. Phay*

17 / Social Services

Introduction / 344
History of Social Services in North Carolina / 345
The Social Security Act / 346
State and County Agencies in Social Services / 347
Department of Human Resources / 347
Social Services Commission / 348
Division of Social Services / 349
Personnel / 349
Board of County Commissioners / 349
County Social Services Board / 350
County Department of Social Services / 351
Relationship Among the County Commissioners,
    the Social Services Board, and the County Director / 351
A Summary of Basic Social Services Programs / 352
AFDC / 352
SSI and State-County General Assistance / 353
Food Stamps / 353
County General Assistance / 353
Medicaid / 353
Services / 353
Financing Social Services / 354
Federal Funds / 354
State Funds / 354
County Funds / 355

17 / SOCIAL SERVICES

INTRODUCTION

The social services program is one of the human services programs provided through county government. It is complex and hard to understand, and professionals in that field tend to compound the difficulty by using unfamiliar language when referring to it.

Social services include public assistance payments to families with dependent children, food stamps to eligible persons, medical care and services, and other services to persons and families that do not involve money payments. The program involves three levels of government—federal, state, and county—in financing and administration.

The basic laws and policies of the federally supported public assistance programs are determined by the federal government. The federal Social Security legislation offers federal funds to states on a matching basis if the state meets certain requirements. Within this basic federal framework, the state and county have areas of discretion.

The federal welfare program has recently been changed by amendments to the Social Security Act. For example, public assistance payments through county departments of social services to needy aged, blind, and disabled persons—which were formerly called aid to the aged, aid to the blind, and aid to the disabled—are now abolished. Instead, a new federal program of Supplemental Security Income (SSI) is federally administered through the Social Security system. However, counties remain responsible for certain medical care and services to SSI recipients.

Recent state government reorganization legislation has changed the names of state agencies and levels of responsibility in state government for social services programs. The state agency responsible for state-level services is an umbrella agency with broad responsibilities in other human services areas—the Department of Human Resources. The Secretary of Human Resources is legally responsible for state supervision of county departments of social services in administering the program. In general, the Secretary delegates much of this state-level responsibility to the Division of Social Services within the Department of Human Resources.

HISTORY OF SOCIAL SERVICES IN NORTH CAROLINA

The North Carolina Constitution of 1868 provided the framework for the development of a welfare program in North Carolina. It required that the General Assembly appoint a board of public charities, which was done by legislation enacted in 1868-69. This State Board of Public Charities was responsible for supervising charitable and penal institutions of the state, investigating conditions in county jails and almshouses, and obtaining reports from the boards of county commissioners on jails, almshouses, and "outside paupers" cared for. This Board was basically a group of state leaders who volunteered their time, and during many of these early years state funds were not appropriated for the Board to carry out its responsibilities.

The General Assemblies of 1917 and 1919 revised the public welfare laws to establish a county-administered welfare program under the supervision of the state. The name of the state-level board was changed to the State Board of Charities and Public Welfare. The welfare program during this period consisted primarily of operating a county home, providing "outside relief" consisting of money or goods to needy persons, and mother's aid—a limited public assistance program to needy, widowed, divorced, or deserted women with children under 14 years of age. The state and the participating counties shared equally in the cost of the mother's aid program.

The depression of the 1930s brought economic programs beyond the financial capacity of the state and county governments to help those caught in the calamity. The response from Washington was the Social Security Act of 1935, which offered federal funds to states on a matching basis to provide public assistance to specified categories of needy persons and certain child welfare programs.

North Carolina adopted legislation in conformity with the requirements of the Social Security Act in 1937, thus making the state eligible for federal financial participation. This legislation provided for a statewide plan for county administration of the welfare program through a county board in each of the 100 counties. The state-level board, then called the State Board of Charities and Public Welfare, was renamed the State Board of Public Welfare in 1945.

The 1969 General Assembly rewrote Chapter 108 of the North Carolina General Statutes, which contains the basic legal authority for the welfare program. One result of this legislative interest was the new name for the program—social services. The 1973 General Assembly enacted legislation to re-organize state government that affected social services; it abolished the State Board of Social Services and replaced it with the Social Services Commission in the Department of Human Resources.

THE SOCIAL SECURITY ACT

Under the Social Security Act as amended, federal funds are available on a matching basis under specified formulas to pay a portion of the cost of aid to families with dependent children, medical care for eligible needy persons, family and children's services, and administration of these programs. To qualify for matching federal funds, a state must have both implementing legislation and state policies that meet federal requirements as outlined in federal law and implementing federal policy. Seven of these federal requirements follow, with an explanation of how North Carolina complies:

1. The federally supported public assistance program (primarily AFDC) must be statewide and uniform throughout the state. This means that each of North Carolina's 100 counties must offer the same program to eligible families. Unlike many states that have state-level administration, North Carolina has a county-administered social services program that is state-supervised by the Department of Human Resources. Each county has a county board of social services that must follow the state plan in administering AFDC.

2. Federal law requires that the state participate financially in the AFDC Program. State law requires that the counties pay a share of the costs. Since 1937, each successive General Assembly has appropriated state funds for the social services program based upon a budget request submitted by the state agency, now the Department of Human Resources. The state budget does not cover the entire cost of the program, and the board of county commissioners in each county appropriates funds annually for that county's share of the costs of social services.

3. A single state agency must administer or supervise administration of the state plan. In North Carolina, this agency is the Department of Human Resources, which supervises the 100 county departments that administer the program under state law and policies of the Social Services Commission within the funds appropriated by the General Assembly.

4. Any person whose application for federally supported public assistance is denied must have the right to appeal this decision for a fair hearing before a state agency. This state agency in North Carolina is the Department of Human Resources. The right of appeal is to the Secretary of Human Resources, who may delegate his decision-making authority regarding appeals. This authority has been delegated to the Director of the Division of Social Services in the Department of Human Resources.

5. The state agency that supervises administration of the federally supported public assistance programs must have legal authority to provide for methods of administration that are considered by federal authorities to be

necessary for the "proper and efficient" operation of the state plan. Under North Carolina law, the Services Services Commission has authority to adopt such rules and regulations as may be required by the federal government for federal grants-in-aid for social services purposes.

Federal law also requires that the state establish and maintain personnel standards on a merit basis. The provision for merit appointments is designed to protect the program from staff appointments for political purposes. The North Carolina Personnel Board classifies positions in the social services program at the state and county levels and establishes appropriate qualifications and salary ranges. Job applicants must qualify by passing a merit examination for a classified position.

6. Information concerning assistance recipients may be used only for purposes directly connected with the administration of the program, but a state may prescribe conditions under which the public may have access to information concerning disbursement to recipients. Under North Carolina law, each month the Department of Human Resources must furnish the county auditor of each county with a copy of the register showing who received public assistance checks, their addresses, and the amounts of the monthly payment. This check register is a public record open to public inspection, but it may not be used for any commercial or political purpose.

7. Recent amendments to the Social Security laws contain a "hold harmless" provision applicable to the states regarding payments to needy aged, blind and disabled persons. Three federally supported public assistance programs (aid to the aged, aid to the blind, aid to the disabled) were absorbed by the federal government into the Social Security system. Therefore, since January 1, 1974, these three public assistance programs will no longer be administered through county departments of social services in North Carolina. However, federal law requires that previous recipients of these three public assistance programs may not receive less than they had under the new program, which is called Supplemental Security Income (SSI). In order to meet this federal requirement, North Carolina adopted legislation establishing the State-County General Assistance program (see page 353).

STATE AND COUNTY AGENCIES IN SOCIAL SERVICES

Department of Human Resources

The Department of Human Resources is the state-level umbrella department that is responsible for a number of human services, including health, mental health, social services, services to older persons, vocational rehabilitation services, child advocacy, various licensing and inspection functions, and others. The head of the Department of Human Resources is the Secretary of Human Resources, who is appointed by the Governor. The Secretary has all management functions of the Department, which include planning, organizing, staffing, directing, coordinating, reporting, and budgeting.

Within the Department of Human Resources, there is a fifteen-member Board of Human Resources, which is advisory to the Secretary on any matter that the Secretary may refer to it. This Board is to assist the Secretary in developing major programs and to recommmend priorities for programs within the Department. It includes seven members who are chairmen of commissions or councils within the Department, eight members appointed by the Governor, and the Secretary of Human Resources, who is chairman ex officio.

Social Services Commission

The Social Services Commission of the Department of Human Resources consists of seven members appointed by the Governor for six-year staggered terms. This is one of five commissions created by statute within the Department of Human Resources. A commission is defined by general law to be "a collective body which adopts rules and regulations in a quasi-legislative manner and which acts in a quasi-judicial capacity in rendering findings or decisions involving differing interests." In general, the powers, duties, and functions of a commission are not subject to the approval, review, or control of the Secretary or the Governor.

The Social Services Commission has a chairman and a vice-chairman. The chairman is appointed by the Governor from among the members of the Commission. The vice-chairman is elected by the Commission members.

The Social Services Commission has policy-making authority at the state level as authorized for social services programs. The Commission also has authority to adopt standards for licensing certain types of facilities or homes. Thus it has the authority to adopt rules and regulations as follows: for federally supported public assistance, to achieve cooperation between state and federal agencies; to strengthen family life and to help people be self-supporting; for placement of dependent and delinquent children and payment of necessary costs for foster care.

The Commission also has authority to establish and adopt standards for licensing maternity homes, boarding homes, rest homes, private child-care institutions; for inspecting jails and juvenile detention homes; for paying the cost of day care for needy children; and for licensing charitable solicitation. It is important to remember that the actual licensing is done by another division of the Department of Human Resources—the Division of Facilities Services.

Division of Social Services

The Division of Social Services is the subunit within the Department of Human Resources that carries the state-level responsibility of the Secretary for supervising county departments of social services in administering the social services program. This division is headed by a director, who is administratively responsible to the Secretary of Human Resources.

The Director of the Division of Social Services has no specified legal authority. The legal authority for all management functions of the Department of Human Resources is with the Secretary, but in actual practice, the Secretary delegates much of the state-level responsibility for social services to the Director of the Division of Social Services.

Personnel

Federal and state law requires that personnel employed in the social services program at the state and county level be appointed on a merit basis. Under state law, the merit system is administered by the Personnel Division of the Department of Administration.

County social services departments may employ personnel who meet personnel standards for various positions under the classification system of the State Personnel Board. The Personnel Division conducts merit examinations on a regular basis and maintains a register of persons who are eligible for appointment to the various classified positions in county departments. The salaries offered for the various positions must be within the salary ranges approved by the Personnel Board.

As in most pay plans, there are minimum and a maximum salaries allowable for each classified position. Ordinarily county social services departments are required to pay at least the minimum salary set by the classification plan. In some cases, the State Personnel Board may allow a county to pay salaries that are below the minimum salary established by the standard pay plan. These exceptions are arranged on an individual yearly basis between the State Personnel Division and the designated county.

Board of County Commissioners

The county commissioners are the elected representatives of the people of the county, with responsibility for the county's governmental operations and the power to levy taxes. Social services is one of the programs that compete for tax funds at the county level.

The county director, the county board of social services, and the board of county commissioners share responsibility for developing the social services budget at the county level. Financing may be the most important role of the board of county commissioners in relation to the social services program. The board of county commissioners is subject to certain state-level control in the amount of funds that it must appropriate for the social services program. Its decision about this appropriation is therefore made differently from decisions concerning appropriations for other county departments. A county commissioner must understand the law and the social services program in order to assess the program's funding needs.

The law gives the board of county commissioners other responsibilities related to the social services program as follows:
(1) The commissioners decide whether the county social services board will consist of three or five members;
(2) The commissioners appoint one or two of the county social services board members, depending upon the size of the board;
(3) With the approval of the county board of social services, the commissioners may appoint a special county attorney for social services matters to advise the director, the county board of social services, and the board of commissioners on social services matters, or they may designate the county attorney to perform these duties;
(4) The commissioners may review any public assistance payment approved by the county board of social services, provided that the recipient of the disputed grant is notified of the time and place of the commissioners' review. If the board of county commissioners determines that a grant was improperly allowed under the policies of the Social Services Commission, the board may order that proper action be taken, with notice being given to the recipient and a copy of the order to the county board of social services and the Secretary of Human Resources. If a board of county commissioners modifies any payment, this action is subject to review by the Secretary of Human Resources.

County Social Services Board

Each county has a county social services board of either three or five members. The board of county commissioners in each county decides whether there will be three or five. If the social services board is to have three members, one is appointed by the Social Services Commission and one by the board of county commissioners, and these two members select the third. If the social services board is to have five members, two are appointed by the Social Services Commission and two by county commissioners, and these four select the fifth. The board members serve for three-year terms. At their July meeting each year, they elect a chairman who serves a term of one year or until a new chairman is elected.

The social services board has six primary legal responsibilities:
(1) To select the county director of social services according to the merit system rules of the State Personnel Board;

SOCIAL SERVICES

(2) To advise county and municipal authorities in developing policies and plans to improve the social conditions of the community.
(3) To consult with the director of social services about problems relating to his office and to help him plan budgets for the county department of social services;
(4) To transmit or present the budget of the county department of social services to the board of county commissioners;
(5) To have such other duties and responsibilities as the General Assembly or the Social Services Commission or the board of county commissioners may assign to it.
(6) To approve and review public assistance cases.

County Department of Social Services

Each county has a county department of social services that is responsible for administering the social services program in the county. The department's administrative head is the county director of social services, who is appointed by the county board of social services.

The county director of social services has a number of legal duties, which include:

(1) To serve as executive officer and secretary of the county board of social services;
(2) To appoint the personnel of the county department under the merit system;
(3) To administer public assistance programs;
(4) To act as agent for the Social Services Commission in the county;
(5) To investigate adoption applications and supervise adoption placements;
(6) To issue employment certificates to children;
(7) To supervise boarding homes, rest homes, and convalescent homes under the rules and regulations of the Social Services Commission;
(8) To investigate reports of abuse or neglect to children or elderly persons;
(9) To accept children for placement in foster homes and to supervise such placements.

Relationship Among the County Commissioners, the Social Services Board, and the County Director

A good working relationship among the county commissioners, the county social services board, and the director of social services is the key to successful local administration of the social services program. While the social services board and the county director are directly responsible for local administration of the social services program, they should work closely with the board of county commissioners in developing new programs, particularly on matters that might require additional county funding.

Frequently one county commissioner also serves on the social services board, which increases effective communication between the two boards: The commissioner has an opportunity to learn about the details of the social services program so that he can serve as a link between the commissioners, the social services board, and the director on matters of program, policy, and finances.

A SUMMARY OF BASIC SOCIAL SERVICES PROGRAMS

The Social Security Act as amended provides for two federally supported public assistance programs: (1) Aid to Families with Dependent Children (AFDC); and (2) Supplemental Security Income (SSI). AFDC is administered by the county under federal and state law through county departments of social services. SSI is federally administered through the Social Security system. However, county departments of social services are responsible for providing certain services and medical care to SSI recipients.

The other major public assistance program required by federal law is the Food Stamp Program.

The county social services program can be divided into three principal parts: (1) public assistance and food stamps; (2) medical care by payments to vendors of services or care; (3) services. The following is a very brief summary of the major programs in those areas:

AFDC

This federally supported categorical public assistance program provides payments to needy children deprived of parental support or care by death, desertion, or physical incapacity of one of the parents. Eligible children must be living with specified relatives or in a licensed foster home or child-caring institution. The amount of the payment is determined by need and the size of the family. Recent state legislation authorizes a flat grant approach that will be called the Consolidated Standard of Needs. There are limitations on the eligibility of children related to age, school attendance, and whether they are needed in the home. Recent federal legislation provides incentives for AFDC recipients to work, including exemption of earned income in determining family resources.

SSI and State-County General Assistance

Supplemental Security Income is payments to needy aged, blind, or disabled persons as provided by the Social Security law. This program is administered through the Social Security system by the federal government, not by county departments of social services. However, counties are responsible for services and medical care for SSI recipients. To meet this responsibility, state legislation provides for State-County General Assistance funds that may supplement SSI payments, particularly for needy persons who need residential care in domiciliary facilities or personal care to remain in their own home.

Food Stamps

Federal and state law require that each county implement the Food Stamp Program. In general, eligible families are entitled to purchase through county departments, local banks, or other approved vendors food stamps that enable the family to acquire food purchasing power greater than the cost of the stamps. Not all things available at a grocery store can be purchased with food stamps—only food.

County General Assistance

The county general assistance program should be distinguished from the State-County General Assistance program. A county may elect to have a county general assistance program to provide temporary financial assistance to needy persons or to applicants for AFDC while their applications are being processed. The level of funding and the policies for administration of county general assistance are entirely within the discretion of the board of county commissioners and the county social services board.

Medicaid

Medicaid provides medical care for needy persons through the county departments of social services. To be eligible, a family must receive AFDC or SSI or be medically indigent under specified circumstances. Medicaid provides certain services to eligible persons through vendor payments to the provider of the medical care or services administered through the Department of Human Resources.

Services

Federal and state law gives the Social Services Commission of the Department of Human Resources and county departments of social serv-

ices broad responsibilities for various services to children, families, and other eligible adults. These services might be summarized as follows:
(1) Protective services to children or elderly adults who may be neglected or abused;
(2) Child-placement services, including licensing of foster homes and supervision of children placed in licensed foster homes;
(3) Coordination of interstate placement of children;
(4) Consultation with and licensing of child-care institutions;
(5) Adoptions;
(6) Services to unmarried parents;
(7) Day care;
(8) Family planning;
(9) Psychological services;
(10) Homemaker services;
(11) Work incentive program (WIN).

FINANCING SOCIAL SERVICES

Federal Funds

The federal share of the cost of financing public assistance and service programs is determined according to formulas established in federal law. These formulas vary somewhat among the various programs. In general the federal share of the cost of public assistance is approximately 70 per cent; federal funds pay about 50 per cent of administrative costs. The balance of the cost is divided between the state and the county. If the county is eligible for equalizing funds (see below), receipt of the equalizing funds would decrease the percentage amount of the county's share.

State Funds

Social service programs are financed from three sources—state, local, and federal funds. But the critical element in this tripartite arrangement is the size of the appropriation made by the General Assembly from state tax funds, because it is this amount that determines how large the county appropriation must be on a percentage matching basis. Federal funds are provided on the basis of matching formulas contained in federal and state laws according to how much the counties spend. Thus it is essentially the size of the state appropriation that determines the dimension of the state's total social services program.

Counties do not have equal financial abilities to pay their share of the cost of social services programs. Thus, state law directs the Secretary of Human Resources to reserve a portion of the state appropriation for social services as an "equalizing fund." These state funds are distributed to the counties according to need under a formula approved by the Social Services Commission. Other state funds (known as "aid to county administration") are similarly distributed according to need to help counties pay their share of the cost of county administration.

County Funds

Recent state legislation (to be effective on a trial basis during the 1974-75 fiscal year) provides a budgeting procedure for the social services program in county government, including administration, that places a limit on county responsibility for social service financing. The county director of social services must compile annual budget estimates on forms provided by the Department of Human Resources and submit them to the county board of social services by March 15 of each year. After these figures are reviewed by the county board of social services and modified, the board must transmit these estimates to the county commissioners by April 1 of each year. The commissioners are to review, modify, approve, and transmit the estimates to the Department of Human Resources by April 15.

The Director of the Division of Social Services in the Department of Human Resources, as agent of the Department of Human Resources, must review the estimated budget submitted by each county and notify the county commissioners in each county by June 1 of each year of approval or disapproval. If the Director approves the estimate, the county's obligation may not exceed approved budget estimates. If the costs of public assistance or administration run higher than expected, the necessary funds are to be provided by the state from the State Public Assistance Contingency Fund, rather than by the county.

If the Director of the Division of Social Services disapproves the county estimates, he must recommend an appropriate county budget. To receive any funds from the State Contingency Fund, should the need arise, a county must accept this recommendation. If a board of county commissioners disputes the director's budget recommendations, the Secretary of the Department of Human Resources must make a determination of the dispute; his decision is binding on the county.

— *Mason P. Thomas, Jr.*

18 / Public Library Services

Establishment and Operation / 358
Statutory Authority / 358
Library Board of Trustees / 358
Library Employees / 359
Area Served by the Library / 359
Financing the Public Library / 361
Local Financial Support / 361
State and Federal Grants-In-Aid / 361
The State Library / 366
Interstate Library Compact / 367
Bibliography / 367

18 / PUBLIC LIBRARY SERVICES

The public library is an educational institution that exists to provide people of all ages and interests with the means of continuing education. Its function is to select, assemble, organize, and make easily and freely available to all of the people in its service area the printed and audiovisual materials that will facilitate informal self-education and enrich formal education, help people keep pace with progress in all fields of knowledge and discharge political and social obligations, and encourage recreation and constructive use of leisure time.

ESTABLISHMENT AND OPERATION

Statutory Authority

The public library—whether municipal, county, or multi-county (regional)—historically has been primarily the responsibility of local government. The state may grant authority to a local unit to establish library services by general law or special law. (Under general act, the state merely provides that any county or municipality may act; under special act, the law authorizes a local government to create the service.) Although most public libraries in North Carolina have been established and are supported by local governmental units under the general law, the provisions of special laws often are different from the provisions of statewide laws; therefore, the local governing body should know the authority under which its library was created and be familiar with this law. The law also authorizes a county or municipality to appropriate funds to support a library that provides free services to all.

Library Board of Trustees

In 1973, the General Assembly revised and amended the General Statutes relating to counties, including the enabling law for public libraries. The new Chapter 153A, Article 14, gives local governing bodies greater latitude in organizing public library services and in deciding whether to have a library board of trustees.

This chapter is adapted from earlier versions by Olga Palotai and Robert E. Phay.

Appointments to a library board are made at the discretion of the local governing body, which is authorized to determine the number of trustees (not to exceed twelve), their terms of office, removal of a trustee from office, and any compensation that the trustees might receive. Powers that may be delegated to a library board by a governing body are set out in G.S. 153A-266.

Library Employees

To serve as the chief administrator of any public library system in North Carolina, a person must have a professional librarian certificate issued by the Public Librarian Certification Commission. All employees of a public library are "for all purposes" bona fide employees of the county (or city) that supports the library and thereby are entitled to coverage by county workman's compensation insurance and are eligible for membership in the county retirement system and other fringe benefits.

Although employees of regional libraries are not mentioned specifically, the statutes (G.S. 160A-463) provide that employees of joint agencies of local governments shall enjoy the same rights and privileges to which employees of single units of the participating governments are entitled.

Area Served by the Library

The very earliest public libraries in North Carolina were municipal libraries, serving the immediate community. Local initiative and interest were instrumental in their organization and support. By the mid-twenties, the county library had been recognized as a more efficient unit of library services for North Carolina. Primarily for this reason, more libraries that provide county-wide service have been established than have libraries limited to municipal service. The fact that state aid is given only to those libraries that render service to the entire county also accounts for the preponderance of this kind of library.

Today, however, library leaders believe that only a much larger geographical unit, possibly more than a single county, can provide the organizational structure and financial base necessary to assure quality library service.

The American Library Association has set forth national standards of good library service, stressing the importance of cooperation and joint action among libraries as the best means of reaching and maintaining adequate library service. It points out that only libraries bound together formally or informally in groups called systems, sharing their services and materials, can meet the full needs of twentieth-century clientele. The trend toward broader-based library systems makes sense, not only because the per capita service cost is less if the library serves a large area but also because the quality of library service and resources can be improved through cooperation.

The Development Committee of the Public Libraries Section of the North Carolina Library Association, recognizing that good library service is economically impractical for library systems serving fewer than 50,000 people, recommends that

> Public libraries should investigate possibilities of improving service through cooperation or affiliation with other libraries in a system. This system should combine existing and potential library resources in a pattern appropriate to the area.

Toward this end, the law enables two or more units of local government to operate public libraries jointly.

Two or more units of local government are empowered to acquire jointly or construct public buildings, and they may acquire jointly the necessary land for such buildings or use land that already belongs to one of the participating governments.

Although a system of local libraries under local governmental control has been established in North Carolina, the individual libraries are beginning to function together in regional systems. Such systems make possible larger book collections and more varied services to all residents of a region and permit wiser use of tax resources. They are defined as "public authorities" and are subject to the Local Government Budget and Fiscal Control Act.

To date forty-seven counties in North Carolina have formed fifteen regional library systems. In addition to these formal organizations, other cooperative efforts are being made to enable libraries to meet increasing demands for a variety of services and materials. The Cape Fear Council of Governments published a "Regional Library Feasibility Study" in 1972 and "A Plan for Library Facilities in Brunswick, Columbus, New Hanover and Pender Counties" in June 1973. The Piedmont Triad Council of Governments (State Planning Region "G") completed a study in November 1973 that recommended for its area a number of ways to "improve user services while reducing the cost of library operations." Although the Piedmont Triad Council cuts across the boundaries of three regional libraries and includes ten library systems in all, the participating librarians are devising plans for reciprocal borrowing throughout Region G library systems, the sharing of audiovisual resources, in-service training for library staffs in Region G, and possibly the joint hiring of specialized library personnel.

In sum, the demand for quality library services and more varied library resources is evident, but the goals can be reached only through statewide cooperation and coordination.

FINANCING THE PUBLIC LIBRARY

Local Financial Support

As we have seen, library service to the general public has been considered chiefly a function of local government and, accordingly, public library financial support has come predominantly from the locality served.

As the result of a ruling some years ago by the State Supreme Court that libraries in North Carolina were not a "necessary expense" within the meaning of the North Carolina Constitution, certain constitutional and statutory limitations applied to the financing of library operations. These limitations meant that a tax to support libraries could not be levied by counties and cities unless it had been approved by the voters of the governmental unit. Libraries that had not been authorized by local referendum to receive support from ad valorem property taxes derived their local support from nontax funds including, among others, profits from ABC stores and excess income from revenue-producing enterprises such as public utilities.

Revised Article V of the State Constitution, which became effective July 1, 1973, eliminated the "necessary expense limitation" clause, thereby making libraries eligible for appropriations from ad valorem revenues. By statute, public libraries and a number of other local government functions fall into a classification for which property tax levies are subject to a rate limitation of $1.50 per $100 of appraised property valuation. (The General Statutes provide that the tax rate limitation can be increased, however, by conducting a local referendum on raising the limitation or by conducting a local referendum to levy a special tax for libraries.)

State and Federal Grants-in-Aid

Federal Aid. Although library service to the general public is a function of local government, the trend through the years has been increased aid from higher levels of government. Thus, seeing national benefit, Congress in 1956 passed the Library Services Act, Public Law 84-597, authorizing the appropriation of $7.5 million annually for five successive years to help states develop and extend public library service in rural areas.

In 1960, Congress extended the act for another five years. North Carolina qualified for its full allocation during the first year of the program (1957), and its share grew from the initial grant of $40,000 to $236,132 for 1963. In 1964, the Congress passed the Library Services and Construction Act, (LSCA) Public Law 88-269, which replaced the 1956 measure. The new law broadened and increased federal assistance for public library service. It authorized $25 million for the fiscal year ending June 30, 1964, for assistance to the states for improved and extended public library services and specified that urban areas could share in those funds on the same basis as rural areas. Congress was authorized to determine the amounts to be allocated for these improvements for the following two fiscal years. In addition, $20 million was authorized for construction of local public library buildings for the fiscal year ending June 30, 1964. Construction amounts for the following two years were determined by Congress. (The appropriations in both areas were less than authorized amounts.) The 1964 act made possible for the first time federal allocations to each state to help local public libraries build better facilities. The state library agency of each state was given full authority to plan for the use of these funds for public libraries.

The North Carolina state plan for using construction funds, already approved by the federal government, set forth criteria and procedures prescribing how the construction funds were to be managed. The general aim and purpose of the state plan was to help county and municipal governments obtain adequate physical facilities. The percentage of the total cost of each project to be allocated from federal grants varied in size according to the wealth of the county in which the facility was to be located. The per capita personal income, as estimated by the North Carolina Division of Tax Research, was used to determine the amount of federal participation. Counties with lower per capita income were eligible to receive a larger percentage of the construction cost from federal funds than wealthier counties. The percentage varied from one fiscal year to the next, depending upon the amount of money available.

Local funds were required to match the federal construction-aid funds and were to be available when such funds were applied for. Private contributions could be counted as matching funds when turned over to the local government for this purpose.

In 1966, the Library Services and Construction Act was amended. Specific appropriations were authorized for public library services for a five-year period in graduated amounts from $35 million for fiscal year 1964 to $75 million for fiscal year 1971. Public library construction funds were authorized in like manner for the five-year period, ranging upward from $40 million for fiscal year 1964 to $80 million for fiscal year 1971. For both construction and services annual appropriations were below the authorized amounts; however, construction funds for eleven libraries in the Appalachian area were supplemented by funds from the Appalachian Regional Development Act [40 App. U.S.C. § 214 (1971)]. More than fifty libraries received funds for new construction or additions to existing library buildings.

The 1966 act added two titles—"Interlibrary Cooperation" (Title III)

PUBLIC LIBRARY SERVICES   363

and "Specialized State Library Services" (Title IV)—that provide for state institutional library services and services to the physically handicapped. That act expired on June 30, 1971, but was extended for another five years by the Library Services and Construction amendments of 1971. The new law stressed services for the disadvantaged, the strengthening of national and regional information centers, and more help to administrative agencies of state libraries. It also authorized an increased federal share of support for public services and construction from 33 per cent to 50 per cent and changed the federal share for interlibrary cooperation from 50 per cent to 100 per cent.

Under the new amendments, services to the handicapped that were in Title IV of the 1966 act were moved to Title I as public services. Specific appropriations were authorized for the five-year period, beginning with $112 million for fiscal year 1972 and reaching $137.1 million for fiscal year 1976. Title II appropriations for library construction were authorized in amounts ranging upward from $80 million for fiscal year 1972 to $97 million for fiscal year 1976. As in the earlier act, $30,000 remained the basic construction allotment for each state; however, construction funds appropriated for the year ending June 30, 1973, were not released until January 1974. North Carolina's share of federal aid for Title I increased from $844,066 for fiscal year 1968 to $1,468,035 for fiscal year 1973; however, only $495,849 was made available to North Carolina until impounded funds were released in January 1974. Table 18-1 shows LSCA allotments to North Carolina for the period from 1965 to 1973.

State Aid. State government financial aid to county and regional public libraries usually takes the form of cash grants and/or services. In North Carolina the state aid fund to public libraries became available in 1941. The first appropriation of $100,000 per annum for "payment to counties" was increased during each successive session of the General Assembly until 1957, when the appropriation was set at $425,000. It remained at this figure until the General Assembly of 1965 increased it to $636,250 for 1965-66 and $686,250 for 1966-67.

In 1967, the General Assembly created by joint resolution the Commission to Study Library Support in the State of North Carolina. This commission recommended that the state gradually assume equal responsibility, with local government, for public library support. It recommended that this goal be accomplished over a period of several years with annual increases in state grants to public libraries amounting to the equivalent of approximately 20 cents per capita.

The Commission's recommendation was followed by the State Library in its request for an initial $3 million additional appropriation—$1 million for the first year and $2 million for the second year. The 1969 General Assembly, however, appropriated only half of the requested increase.

Table 18-I
LSCA Allotments to North Carolina

Year ending in	Title I P.L. Services	Title II Construction C	Title III Interlibrary Cooperation	Title IV A	Title IV B
1973	($ 679,178	((Impounded)	($ 55,036	Incl. in I	
Orig. added from impoundment	788,857)	$339,605)	117,585)		
TOTAL	1,468,035		172,621		
1972	1,087,577	204,019	52,830	Incl. in I	
1971	712,539	169,369	44,033	$39,509	$25,351
1970	405,643	-	44,033	39,509	25,351
1969	844,066	203,886	44,033	-	-
1968	844,066	613,132	43,407	-	23,750
1967	844,066	975,886	7,075	7,075	4,735
1966*	597,962	771,653	-	-	-
1965*	601,100	329,828	-	-	-

*North Carolina received additonal funds these years, reallotted from shares of states that could not match for their allotments.
Source: Records on file in the Division of the State Library, State Department of Cultural Resources, Raleigh, N. C.

In 1971 the State Aid to Public Libraries budget request again was for a $3 million increase—$1 million for the first year, and $2 million for the second. The General Assembly granted only $200,000 for each year, breaking the pattern of gradual increase as well as reducing the amount requested.

By 1973 the State Library was a division of the Department of Cultural Resources, which requested a $6 million increase in the appropriations—$2 million for the first year and $4 million for the second—in the hope of accelerating the movement slowed down the previous biennium. The General Assembly, moving toward annual sessions, acted on the first year only and appropriated a $1 million increase. The Department's request to the second session of the General Assembly in 1974 was for $1.7 million. Table 18-II, based on figures obtained from the Division of the State Library, shows the major sources of public library revenue for the fiscal year 1972-73.

Table 18-II
Sources of Library Income in North Carolina, 1972-73

	Percentage	Per Capita
City or Town	24%	$ .58
County	46	1.08
State Aid	17	.39
Federal Aid	4	.10
Other	9	.22
	100%	$2.37

In October 1972, the Congress enacted the State and Local Fiscal Assistance Act, Public Law 92-512, which authorizes general revenue-sharing money to be used by state and local governments for specific purposes over a five-year period. Libraries are one of the eight governmental functions authorized to receive these revenue-sharing funds for "ordinary and necessary capital expenditures authorized by law" and for "ordinary and necessary maintenance and operating expenses." The Fiscal Assistance Act prohibits the use of these funds as matching funds on any federal grant, however.

It is too soon to estimate the impact that general revenue-sharing will have on the public library program in North Carolina. Careful planning by library boards, library administrators, and local governing bodies is called for to insure that a fair share of these funds is allocated for improved library services to the people of each county and municipality.

State funds, designed to stimulate the improvement and expansion of public library services, are allocated among qualifying counties following the rules and regulations formulated by the State Library Division of the Department of Cultural Resources in accordance with G.S. 125-7 and G.S. 143A-195.

At present, a basic grant of $4,000 is available to each county, plus an additional grant based on the "effort index" score of the various counties. The effort index is determined by dividing the total personal income of a county or region into its library operational expenditures from local funds for the previous year. In addition to the basic and effort grants, personnel grants ($9,000 each in 1973-74) are made to county and regional libraries for certified professional personnel with the provision that at least two subprofessional employees support each professional position. Other requirements for qualifying for a personnel grant are that the positions being funded must be filled and that salaries for professional positions must be compatible with those recommended by the State Library Division. Under these provisions, libraries are eligible for one personnel grant for each 100,000 population, or fraction thereof, served. As many as four grants can be made to regional libraries that serve two or three counties and up to five grants to the larger regional libraries. The first grant must go toward the regional director's salary.

Regional grants are made to multi-county library systems that operate as a single administrative unit, the amount of the grant being correlated with population of the region and the per capita local support for library service. Thus, regions with fewer than 50,000 people may qualify for an allotment of $4,000 per county if the regional library income from local government averages at least 75 cents per capita. Regional grants per county may be increased as the per capita local government participation increases, to a maximum of $8,000 per county when the per capita library income is $1.75.

Certain limitations are placed on the uses that may be made of effort and regional grants. These are explained in the State Library Division's *Rules and Regulations for the Allocation of State Aid to Public Libraries, 1973-74*. This annual publication also specifies procedures for applying for state aid. To continue qualifying for funds, the county or regional library must not reduce its appropriation from local government sources below that of the previous year. State aid is designed to supplement local funds rather than to replace them.

THE STATE LIBRARY

The reorganization of state government enacted by the General Assembly in 1971 brought the State Library and other cultural agencies of state government under the wing of a new Department of Art, Culture and History; the Executive Organization Act of 1973 renamed the newly created agency the Department of Cultural Resources and placed the Division of the State Library under its administration.

Besides administering the state and federal financial aid programs, the Division of the State Library provides advisory and consultative services to all public libraries and to communities that may propose to establish libraries. It provides a back-up information service to all public, college, and technical institute libraries and to industries that have special libraries through a free Inward Wide Telephone Service. It also serves directly, by mail, all blind citizens of North Carolina (and those whose physical handicaps make the use of ordinary books impossible) with Talking Books (recordings), Braille, and cassette tapes, and it coordinates public library activities on a statewide basis.

The State Library, in promoting better public libraries throughout North Carolina, has helped to develop and formulate a set of standards for the state that are designed to help public libraries in North Carolina ultimately attain national standards. Increased financial support from local government is essential to realization of this goal. The cost of achieving minimum national standards was estimated by the American Library Association in 1971 to be $8.23 per capita for a library system serving approximately 200,000 people. The present expenditure in North Carolina averages $2.32 per capita. The direction is clear; the gap is obvious. Although obtaining sufficient funds for quality library service may pose problems, it is imperative to find the means to build this basic educational resource through which our people can realize the lifelong education process so essential in our rapidly changing world.

INTERSTATE LIBRARY COMPACT

The 1967 General Assembly enacted the Interstate Library Compact as Chapter 125, Article 2, of the General Statutes. The compact authorizes state library agencies of those states party to the compact to engage in joint and cooperative library programs or services. It also authorizes the creation of interstate library districts by agreement between local library agencies in two or more party states.

BIBLIOGRAPHY

American Library Association, Public Library Association. *Interim Standards for Small Public Libraries; Guidelines Toward Achieving the Goals of Public Library Service.* Chicago: 1962.

American Library Association. *Minimum Standards for Public Library Systems — 1966.* Chicago: 1967.

American Library Association, Public Libraries Division, Coordinating Committee on Revision of Public Library Standards. *Public Library Service; A Guide to Evaluation with Minimum Standards.* Chicago: 1956.

Supplements: *Cost of Public Library Service in 1959, 1960; Cost of Public Library Service in 1963; 1964.*

Downs, Robert P., ed. *Resources of North Carolina Libraries; a Report to the Governor's Commission on Library Resources.* Raleigh: The Commission, 1965.

International City Managers' Association. *Local Public Library Administration.* Chicago: 1964.

North Carolina. Legislative Commission to Study Library Support in the State of North Carolina. *Report of the Commission*, with appendix. Raleigh: The Commission, August 1968.

North Carolina Library Association, Public Libraries Section, Development Committee. *Standards for North Carolina Public Library Service in North Carolina.* Raleigh: North Carolina State Library, 1970.

North Carolina Library Association, *North Carolina Library Trustee's Pocket Handbook*. Raleigh: North Carolina State Library, 1960.

North Carolina Library Association, Personnel Manual Committee. *North Carolina Public Library Personnel Manual.* Chapel Hill: Institute of Government, 1959.

North Carolina Library Association. *Suggested Policies for Public Libraries.* Raleigh: North Carolina State Library, 1960.

Phay, Robert E. *The Public Library; A Guidebook for North Carolina Library Trustees.* Chapel Hill: Institute of Government, 1972.

Piedmont Triad Council of Governments. *Regional Library Services Study.* Greensboro, N.C.: November 1973.

Young, Virginia G. *The Library Trustee.* New York: R. R. Bowker, Co., 1964.

— *Elaine von Oesen*
Rebecca S. Ballentine

19 / Recreation

Introduction / 370
Growth of Public Recreation / 370
County Recreation in North Carolina / 371
Scope of County Recreation Programs / 371
Legal Aspects / 372
General Powers / 372
Financing Public Recreation / 372
Organization / 373
Recreation Commission or Department / 373
Professional Staff / 373
Joint Programs Involving Several Units / 374
Advisory Committee / 374
Recreation Planning / 374
Sources of Assistance / 375

19 / RECREATION

INTRODUCTION

Growth of Public Recreation

Public recreation as a local government function in the United States is of fairly recent origin, having grown out of the park and playground movement that began in such large cities as Boston and Chicago around the period 1890-1900. In the past, recreation has generally been regarded as a municipal function, and its growth in North Carolina and throughout the nation has been such that even the smaller cities and towns now provide some measure of financial support for recreation. In 1973-74, the average per capita outlay for operating costs by North Carolina municipalities that have recreation programs was about $15, for a total statewide outlay of $26,000,000. These cities and towns also spent $8,000,000 in 1973-74 for recreational facilities. In the same fiscal year, counties with recreation programs spent $1,600,000 to operate the programs and $912,000 for recreational facilities.

The acceptance of public recreation as a county function in the state has been slow, however, and the reasons seem fairly obvious. It would appear, for example, that children who live in rural areas have less time for recreation activities. Many of them spend more time traveling to and from school than city children do, and they may well spend more time on chores at home. Also, farm families are said to be generally less inclined to spend cash (including taxes) for goods and services than city families, and comparing two families with the same "real" income, the farm family tends to provide a higher proportion of its own food, clothing, and other items— including its own fun and recreation. On the face of it, there would appear to be less need in rural areas for publicly provided parks and open space or for organized recreation programs.

On the other hand, there is considerable evidence that traditional attitudes toward county parks and recreation are changing. For example, the National Association of Counties has reported that in 1950, counties in the United States operated 933 county parks totaling 200,000 acres with the help of approximately 5,000 recreation leaders. Ten years later, however, the number of county parks had almost tripled, park acreage had more than doubled, and the number of volunteer recreation leaders had increased more than eightfold.

County Recreation in North Carolina

In recent years, the growth of county recreation in North Carolina, still for the most part a rural state, has followed the national trend. According to a 1960 Institute of Government survey, thirteen counties were then providing financial support for recreation activities. By early 1974, the number of counties with recreation programs had risen to twenty-seven. By 1974, more than half of the 100 counties are providing some financial support for public recreation programs. There is every reason to believe that as the state becomes more urban, the number of counties that offer recreation programs and the scope of their services will continue to increase. This trend will probably be fortified by the general tendency of rural and suburban residents to demand higher and higher levels of governmental services of all kinds.

It can be predicted, in fact, that public recreation in some areas will eventually come to be regarded as a responsibility of the county rather than of the municipality. Large parks and major recreation facilities to serve urban populations will of necessity have to be located outside cities as urban land becomes more scarce; even today, many cities are put to major expense to provide recreation programs and services to county residents who live outside municipal boundaries. In this respect, public recreation may well be heading in the direction of welfare and similar programs, which now are generally accepted as functions of county government.

Scope of County Recreation Programs

The range of recreation services and activities in the several dozen North Carolina counties already active in this area is wide, and no two programs are exactly alike. However, most county programs fall within several broad categories. Some counties own and maintain a scattering of county parks and playgrounds in rural areas, and a few share the responsibility for these facilities with one or more towns in the county. Other counties operate summer recreation programs in small towns or unincorporated communities throughout the county. These programs typically focus on Little League baseball and similar activities. A third category of county activity includes grants of county funds (usually matching funds) to towns or communities in the county for summer programs and facilities. A fourth category of arrangements includes those county programs that, although financed by the county, are administered by the recreation department or commission of a municipality in the county. A fifth and final category of county activity, even though it stops short of the immediate provision of recreation services, is cooperative planning with municipalities in the county for park land acquisition. Greensboro and Guilford County, for instance, have actively cooperated for some time in developing plans for a metropolitan park system that will eventually benefit urban, suburban, and rural residents of the county.

In all, however, there is no uniform pattern of county involvement in recreation, in either the type of activity or the level of service. Generally, appropriations by counties for recreation are modest, and the program in each county tends to be based more on local needs and resources than on any consensus about what is appropriate.

LEGAL ASPECTS

General Powers

The North Carolina recreation enabling act is contained in G.S. Ch. 160A, Art. 18, and applies to both cities and counties. By its terms, the governing body of any county, city, or town is authorized to engage in a wide variety of recreation activities. G.S. 160A-353 specifically authorizes local governments to:

(1) Establish and conduct a system of supervised recreation;
(2) Set apart land or buildings for use as parks or playgrounds, recreational centers or facilities;
(3) Acquire lands or buildings by gift, purchase, lease, or loan or by condemnation;
(4) Accept any gift, grant, or bequest of money or other personal property or any donation for recreational use;
(5) Provide parks, playgrounds, recreation centers, and recreation facilities;
(6) Appropriate funds for public recreation programs.

The statute also provides a broad definition of what constitutes "recreation," for purposes of the enabling act:

> Recreation means activities that are diversionary in character, and aid in promoting entertainment, pleasure, relaxation, instruction, and other physical, mental, and cultural development and leisure time experiences. [G.S. 160A-352.]

Financing Public Recreation

Before the 1973 revision of Article V of the North Carolina Constitution, recreation was not a "necessary expense" and could not be financed by property tax revenues without a vote of the people. Under the revised Constitution and the enabling legislation enacted pursuant thereto in 1973, public recreation is among the purposes for which counties and cities may levy property taxes without a vote, subject to an over-all property tax rate limitation of $1.50. In addition, counties may allocate to public recreation programs any other county revenue whose use is not restricted by law. There is now no legal impediment to adequate county funding of a public recreation program.

ORGANIZATION

Recreation Commission or Department

The Recreation Enabling Law gives the county commissioners several alternatives in organizing to undertake a county recreation program.

First, they might operate the program as any other activity of the county (either exercising direct control themselves or establishing a county recreation department for that purpose) or they might establish an official county recreation commission. During the early years of a county recreation program, or when the program is exceedingly modest and the county commissioners wish to keep in close contact with it, they may be able to operate the program themselves. This arrangement might also be appropriate in cases in which all recreation services and facilities are provided by contract with a city in the county, or by agreement with another county, under G.S. 160A-355.

Or the commissioners might establish a county recreation department with a paid, professional staff, which would handle all operating details of the program subject to general policies established by the county commissioners.

However, if they feel that a separate group is needed to plan, operate, and establish program policies, or if the program is sufficiently large or diverse that they no longer wish to remain in direct control over the operating details of the program, then the county commissioners may find it desirable to create a county recreation commission. This may be done by passing an ordinance or resolution establishing the commission and vesting it with authority to operate the program. Normally the general powers and duties of the commission are spelled out in the ordinance that establishes it.

Professional Staff

Regardless of the form of organization chosen, good leadership for the program will be essential. The major requirement in this respect is for a recreation director to organize the program, train and supervise a staff, select appropriate program activities, and so on. Recreation supervisors may also be needed, depending on program requirements. Some assistance may be had in this regard through the use of volunteers, but experience indicates that volunteers should be used to *enrich* the program and not be considered as an adequate substitute for paid leadership.

Joint Programs Involving Several Units

A county that does not wish to hire and maintain its own staffs may find it advantageous to arrange for professional services or the use of certain recreation facilities through contractual agreements with a town or city in the same (or another) county, or with another county. Such arrangements are authorized by G.S. 160A-356.

These arrangements might be for a temporary summer program or for a year-round program of activities. As mentioned earlier, several cities and counties have found this approach to be an economical and fair way to provide recreation services for county residents who live in the fringe or suburban areas of larger cities and towns.

This relatively simple contractual approach will generally prove satisfactory in situations in which one or two units of government are in effect "buying" the use of recreation facilities or professional staff services from an existing program, and in which a second full-time staff is not feasible or a second policy-making body is not needed.

However, if a large number of local governments are involved, as might be the case when several counties (including perhaps the smaller towns within each county) band together to provide regional recreation services, or facilities, a more appropriate form of organization may be an independent, jointly financed recreation commission with its own staff. This approach is possible under either the general wording of G.S. 160A-355 or the general legislation authorizing interlocal cooperation found in G.S. Ch. 160A, Art. 20.

Advisory Committee

Finally, it is usually desirable to have a representative advisory committee to backstop the recreation commission and the professional staff. The advisory committee (of which no specific mention is to be found in the statutes) can be used to recruit volunteers, to advise the recreation commission and staff in matters related to planning and operation, to serve as a promotional group during the early years of the program, and in many other useful ways. If such a group is appointed, as recreation specialists advise, it not only should be geographically representative of the county, but also should include members chosen from the major civic, business, and religious organizations in the county.

RECREATION PLANNING

Recreation services and facilities, like any other governmental activity, must be carefully planned in advance if they are to operate efficiently and economically and provide an appropriate level of service. Thus, county recreation facilities, whether they consist of many buildings and sites or merely one summer athletic park, must be acquired and built with the requirements of their users in mind. Not only must park and recreation sites be properly located, but also they should be acquired before land values have risen to the point that the use of land for recreation purposes is no longer feasible. Sites and buildings should be neither too large nor too small for their intended long-term use. Major recreation facilities often require protection from possibly adverse uses of nearby property through the adoption and enforcement of a county zoning ordinance, and in many cases county subdivision regulations may be helpful in acquiring public park and recreation areas as large tracts are subdivided for residential purposes. Advance planning may also make possible the joint use of some sites for both school and recreation purposes. For these reasons, it is extremely important that the county's planning and recreation programs be closely coordinated.

SOURCES OF ASSISTANCE

The primary source of assistance for counties contemplating the establishment of a public recreation program is the Department of Natural and Economic Resources in Raleigh. Upon request, the department's staff specializing in recreation will provide a wide range of advisory services, including organization, staffing, budgeting, programming, and information about the various types of aid available to counties. There is no fee for such services. Counties are strongly urged to take advantage of the information and experience that the department has available.

— *Robert E. Stipe*

20 / Planning for Physical and Economic Development

Introduction / 378
The Need for Planning / 379
Organization and Planning / 380
Planning Board / 381
Staff Assistance / 382
Officials Concerned with Carrying Out Plans / 383
Studies and Plans / 383
Studies / 383
Plans / 385
Devices for Guiding Development / 386
Jurisdiction / 387
Types of Regulations / 388
Economic Development Measures / 388

20 / PLANNING FOR PHYSICAL AND ECONOMIC DEVELOPMENT

INTRODUCTION

Planning, regulation of physical development, and promotion of economic development are perhaps the newest, and least understood, of all county functions. Although North Carolina counties were given general authority in 1945 to create planning boards, not until 1959 (when they received power to effectuate plans through regulation of private development) was any widespread use made of this authority.[1] Even today, not all counties in the state carry on full-fledged planning programs. It is nevertheless apparent that as time goes by there will be increasing attention to this function everywhere.

"Planning" in its broadest sense means any form of rational anticipation of and preparation for future action, and everyone is accustomed to planning his own activities in some degree. Here we are referring to planning in a narrower sense, however. As used here, the term may be loosely defined as a formal and organized effort by the county government:

(1) To gather facts concerning the county's people, economy, and physical problems and resources;
(2) To identify present and probable future needs;
(3) To develop some consensus as to objectives to be sought in the county's physical and economic development;
(4) To prepare plans and programs for attaining such objectives; and

---

1. Planning legislation for particular counties may vary from the statewide pattern described herein. Great care should be taken, therefore, to determine whether the county in which one is interested is either exempt from provisions of a general statute or subject to a special local act. Exemptions normally appear in the General Statutes of North Carolina, either as codified sections or (in the case of minor deviations) as annotations to particular provisions. The county attorney should be consulted for information about any applicable special acts.

(5) To use a variety of legal and administrative devices in a coordinated way so as to carry out these plans and programs.

Because planning, with its end results, impinges so directly upon the lives of all people of the county, it can be one of the most difficult of all county functions to perform successfully. In a democracy, planning does *not* connote a small group of "supermen" telling everyone else how to conduct his life. Instead, it calls for the closest possible collaboration between governmental officials and the public at large in arriving at an *informed consensus* as to the county's needs, the objectives to be sought, and the means for attaining these objectives. A successful planning program is possible only where it has the broadest possible public understanding and support, and this can be achieved only through continuing efforts of responsible leaders both within and outside the government.

THE NEED FOR PLANNING

The nature of a planning program will differ from county to county, because problems differ from county to county. Some counties, confronted with explosive population growth, will be seeking ways to provide governmental services for new development and to guide it into a desirable pattern. Other counties, losing population and tax valuations, will be more concerned with measures to strengthen the economy. The following are typical county problems dealt with through planning.

The widespread desire of many city dwellers for "a place in the country," along with dispersion of industry into the countryside and the freedom of transportation given by the automobile, has led to a sprawling pattern of development that frequently disintegrates into "rural slums" in the absence of regulation. Rapid and uncoordinated building in areas that lack safe water supplies or adequate sewage disposal facilities; roads that appear to have been laid out by a drunken bulldozer operator and that the Department of Transportation refuses to accept because of their inadequate rights of way, unsafe layout, and substandard construction; jerry-built houses that do not meet the minimum standards of any building code; intrusion of noxious businesses into residential areas; failure to provide sites for schools, recreational areas, or other public facilities—all of these add up to gigantic headaches for rural residents and eventually for governmental authorities (not to mention the unhappy taxpayer who will be called upon to finance corrective measures). Where there are inadequate planning and regulation to avert such man-made problems, inevitably there will arise the necessity for costly "rural renewal" programs similar to the "urban renewal" programs now required in most large cities.

As cities and towns have started adopting more stringent development controls for their own protection, rural areas have become "dumping grounds" for all sorts of operations considered undesirable as neighbors: garbage dumps, junkyards, concentrations of billboards, unusually smelly and ugly manufacturing operations, etc. Because many of these operations are important from an economic standpoint, the problem for the county is not one of prohibiting them but rather of insuring that they are located where their noxious qualities will have the least damaging effects on other types of development. This too requires planning and regulation.

Equally pressing problems may infect the county's economy. Already some counties seem to have entered a vicious cycle in which their trained young people are leaving because of a lack of jobs and new industries are unwilling to come in because of a lack of young trained workers. Without continuing study of population, social, and economic trends, county leaders may not even realize that such a cycle has begun until it is well along—at which time corrective measures will have become far more difficult.

Planning is also important in the county government's own operations. When and where should such county facilities as the courthouse, schools, health centers, fire stations, etc., be located? How much space should they contain? How large should their sites be? How may sites for future county facilities be acquired and protected until they are needed? Should the county undertake construction of water and sewerage systems in rural areas? If so, where should they be located and for what capacities should they be designed? Answers to such questions are impossible without projections of the future population to be served, a visualization of the future pattern of development within the county, and regulations designed to bring this pattern into reality.

Finally, the Coastal Area Management Act of 1974 requires coastal area counties to adopt land-use plans to guide development in environmentally sensitive areas.

ORGANIZATION FOR PLANNING

Most experienced planners would agree that four elements are necessary in a successful organization for planning. The first of these is the governing board (for the county, the board of county commissioners), with adequate powers to establish the program, to finance and construct the public facilities that are called for by the plan, and to regulate private development. Second, there must be an agency to make the required studies and prepare the plans. This agency normally includes both a board of laymen (which is usually called the "planning board") and professional staff assistants. Third, there must be officials charged with administering the regulations and constructing the public facilities called for by the plan. And fourth, there is the public at large, whose understanding and support are essential.

Planning Board

The General Statutes give the county commissioners considerable latitude in determining how they will create a planning agency.

First, under G.S. 153A-321, the county may establish a *county planning board*. Such a board would be responsible only to the commissioners of the county creating it. The statute leaves the board's membership (so long as there are at least three members), organization, powers, and duties to the discretion of the commissioners.

Second, under G.S. Ch. 160A, Art. 20, a county and any other county or city or town may, by agreement, establish a *joint planning* board. The membership, powers, duties, and provisions for financial and other support of this type of board are normally spelled out in the agreement creating it.

Third, under G.S. Ch. 153A, Art. 19. a county may establish, by agreement with any number of counties and cities, a *regional planning commission*. The statute spells out in considerable detail the basic powers and duties of such a commission but leaves details as to membership and support to be fixed by the agreement that creates it.

Fourth, under G.S. 153A-398 a county may establish, by agreement with any number of counties and cities, a *regional planning and economic development commission*. Such a commission would combine the functions of both a regional planning commission and an economic development commission, established under G.S. Ch. 158, Art. 2.

Fifth, under G.S. Ch. 160A, Art. 20, Part 2, a county may establish, by agreement with any number of counties and cities, a *regional council of government*. Such a council could be closely similar to a regional planning commission in its operations.

Finally, the county may wish to secure special legislation, tailored to its specific situation, for the creation of a planning agency. The acts that authorize the City-County Planning Board of Winston-Salem and Forsyth County (Sess. Laws 1947, Ch. 677, as amended by Sess. Laws 1953, Ch. 777), the Carteret County Planning Commission (Sess. Laws 1959, Ch. 1033), and the Hickory Regional Planning Commission (Sess. Laws 1963, Ch. 477) are examples of this approach. It should be noted that a county may have its own planning board and *also* have representation on a regional planning commission.

Although the statutes cited above differ in the degree to which they spell out the powers and duties of planning boards or commissions, all such boards are responsible for making studies and plans. Some have statutory responsibility for advising on the location of new public facilities, while others do this under provisions of the ordinance that created them. The county zoning enabling act (G.S. Ch. 153A, Art. 18, Part 3) requires that a county (or joint) planning agency prepare a recommended zoning ordinance for the county initially and also make recommendations later with respect to proposed amendments. The county subdivision-regulation enabling act (G.S. Ch. 153A, Art. 18, Part 2) provides that the planning agency may be given either advisory or final authority in the approval of subdivision plats. The urban redevelopment law (G.S. Ch. 160A, Art. 22) requires findings by the planning agency as to the nature of areas proposed for renewal and review of the redevelopment commission's plan by that agency.

Basically, the planning board may be regarded as an *advisory* body, with very little power to make decisions directly affecting others. Its advice is both incorporated in and based upon plans for the county; and to the extent that these plans are sound and thoughtfully prepared, the commissioners should give considerable weight to them.

Staff Assistance

As we have noted, the planning board itself may have statutory responsibility for making studies and plans. In practice, because it is normally composed of unpaid citizens, a planning board may have neither the time to do the "legwork" involved in data collection nor the expert knowledge needed to analyze data and make plans. For this reason, it is generally considered advisable to supply the board with assistance. The statutes provide several ways to do this.

G.S. 153A-322 authorizes the commissioners to make appropriations to the planning agency, and this has been interpreted to permit the hiring of a full-time professional staff for the board. It also permits the hiring of professional planners on a consulting basis, either in lieu of a resident staff or to supplement the efforts of such a staff.

Next, the county may contract with any city, county, regional council, or planning agency for services furnished by the unit's staff (G.S. 153A-322). Regional planning commissions may, if they wish, furnish staff assistance to local planning boards in their area even without such a contract [G.S. 153A-395(7)].

Probably the most common arrangement for securing staff services, however, is through the Division of Community Assistance of the Department of Natural and Economic Resources (G.S. 143-319, G.S. 143A-128). This state agency maintains a number of regional offices around the state, each with a staff of planners available to work under contract in counties and municipalities in its area. Regional planning agencies and county planning boards are eligible for federal grants that cover a major part of the cost of such services [Section 701 of the federal Housing Act of 1954 as amended; 40 U.S.C. § 461 (1970)].

Officials Concerned with Carrying Out Plans

Because plans must be comprehensive in order to be most effective, virtually every official in the county may have a part in carrying out plans. In addition to the board of county commissioners and the planning board or commission, certain officials and agencies may have particularly important roles in this process. Among the agencies concerned with providing major public facilities pursuant to the plan objectives are the state Department of Transportation, the county board of education, the county recreation commission, and possibly a public housing authority (G.S. 157-33, -34) or an urban redevelopment commission (G.S. Ch. 160A, Art. 22). Among those concerned with regulating private development are the county inspection department (including one or more inspectors such as a building inspector, an electrical inspector, a plumbing inspector, a housing inspector, a zoning inspector, a heating and air conditioning inspector, and a fire prevention inspector) (G.S. Ch. 153A, Art. 18, Part 4), a zoning board of adjustment (G.S. 153A-345), an appearance commission (G.S. 160A, Art. 19, Part 7), and a historic district commission (G.S. 160A-395, -396). The agency most concerned with developing and carrying out economic development programs is the economic development commission (G.S. Ch. 158, Art. 2), which may have its own staff.

STUDIES AND PLANS

An essential element of the planning process is the making of studies—gathering facts that bear upon particular aspects of the county's development and analyzing those facts to identify shortcomings and opportunities. This is necessary groundwork in making plans and policies, which in their turn become a basis for providing public facilities in a coordinated way and for regulating private use of land.

Studies

The range of studies that might be made as part of a county planning program is hard to describe precisely. Such studies are intended not as academic exercises but rather as steps toward specific goals. For this reason they vary according to the nature of a particular county's problems, resources, and objectives. However, it is possible to indicate generally the types of information that a county planner may need to gather.

First, he is interested in the *land* of the county. He needs to have accurate maps indicating its contours, streams, highlands, and swamps. He needs to know where the best agricultural land is located, and where the poor land is located. He needs to know where rock outcroppings will make urban development difficult. He needs to know where the soil is capable of receiving effluent from septic tanks and where it is not, where the soil can support the weight of large buildings and where it cannot, where it is well drained and where it is not. He needs to know the bounds of natural watersheds, within which sewage collection systems will be most feasible. And he needs to know something of the pattern of land ownership and what land might be available for sale or development.

Next, he would like to know about the *natural resources* of the county. He needs information about any mineral deposits. He needs to know about the ground-water supply—how deep one must drill to find water in various areas and the characteristics of that water. He needs to know about surface waters—lakes, streams, their flow, flood levels, the extent of pollution, etc.

He wants to know about *man-made improvements* on the land. He should map the transportation facilities that exist—railroads, waterways, highways. He should map the use that is now made of the land—for agricultural, forestry, industrial, business, residential, governmental, or other purposes. He should know the patterns of development as they have evolved, where recent development has concentrated, and the rate of that development.

He should inventory *public facilities,* including their present conditions, capacity, and capability for expansion. He needs to know about power supplies, water supplies, sewerage systems, and telephone systems. He needs to know about schools, colleges, libraries, parks, museums, and theaters. He needs to know about the condition and adequacy of the courtrooms, the registry of deeds, the tax supervisor's office, and other county offices.

He should know something about the range of *public services*—law enforcement, fire protection, home demonstration, agricultural services, welfare, education, health, trash and garbage collection and disposal, and so forth.

He will certainly study the *people* of the county. He is interested in tracing the past population growth, measuring the present size of the population, and estimating its future growth, for this tells him how many school rooms, how much water storage capacity, how much land for residential purposes, etc., will be needed as the county develops. He is interested in the past, present, and probable future characteristics of that population—in terms of sex, age, race, education, and other qualities—for this gives him further clues about what public needs must be anticipated and provided for. He is interested in the past, present, and probable future distribution of that population over the land, as a further aid in estimating the needs of particular areas. He is interested in the size and characteristics of the work force, for this may be a crucial factor in the area's economic development.

PLANNING 385

He must study the *economy* of the area to determine its strengths and weaknesses and opportunities for expansion. He must know how the people make their living, how much unemployment exists, whether it is seasonal, how diversified the economy is. He must identify the resources on which the people of the county can capitalize, the drawbacks that must be eliminated, what kind of economic base the citizens prefer if they have a choice, how the local economy fits into the regional and national economy.

And he must study the *social problems* of the county, as its government assumes more and more responsibility for problems of employment, housing, education, race relations, mental health, the very young, and the very old.

In sum, while he is not interested in fact-gathering as an end in itself, he is interested in bringing together all available information concerning the past, present, and future development of the county so that soundly based plans can be prepared and decisions can be based on facts rather than hunches.

Some of this information has already been gathered by others and needs only to be located. The United States Census, power companies and other public utilities, various departments of the state and federal government—all have collected a vast amount of information. Some of it has been published, some is still "raw" data. Having discovered it, the planner must put it into a form that will be most useful—maps, charts, tables, etc.—so that the planning board or county commissioners can readily grasp the essentials of the decisions that they must make.

Other data may require extensive investigation—riding about in a car and marking observed information on a map, inspecting properties on foot, interviewing citizens, etc. Here the data-collection process outweighs the problems of presentation, but both the data and the presentation are necessary.

Finally, the planner must analyze the information he has gathered and determine what it all means. This is the most difficult process of all, and this is where the experience and ability of a professional planner become most valuable to the county.

Plans

The range of possible plans is geared to the range of the county's problems and objectives. In most counties a general *plan for physical development* will be prepared at some point in the planning process. This plan will identify the general pattern of development that is thought best for the county—where urban development should be encouraged and where it should be discouraged; which areas should be developed predominantly for residential purposes, which for industrial, which for commercial, which for agricultural; where public facilities—streets and highways, parks, schools, health centers, fire stations, water systems, sewerage systems, etc.—should be located to serve this development; which lands should, if possible, be kept as "open space"; where reservoir sites should be preserved or acquired; and so forth. (This plan may be called a "land-use plan" in counties subject to the Coastal Area Management Act.)

Detailed plans may be made for providing particular types of public facilities—an open-space plan, a park and recreation plan, a major highway plan, a water and sewer plan, a school plan.

Keyed to these plans may be an *economic development plan* or program, spelling out what type of development is to be sought, what public facilities are to be provided to encourage such development, what types of private activities are to be encouraged as an aid to this development, etc.

And there may be various types of plans and programs to meet current or emerging social problems, involving both the provision of particular facilities (such as a community center, a technical training institution, or housing for the aged) and new or expanded health, welfare, or other services.

Throughout the plan-making phase, the responsible officials must insure that they do not set impossible goals. They are charged with identifying needs and devising *feasible* ways to meet those needs; at each step they should consider how the county can accomplish what they have proposed. They must always keep in mind the county's capability (financial and otherwise) of achieving particular ends. While they should be imaginative, they should not be featherbrained. In short, the best planning is highly pragmatic.

DEVICES FOR GUIDING DEVELOPMENT

Once plans have been prepared for a county, a number of devices are available to guide development as it takes place, so that the ultimate pattern will be in accord with the plan.

Often the mere adoption and publication of a plan has profound effects on development, if the plan is a good one that makes sense to property owners in the county. Frequently an owner will be inspired to undertake development that he had not previously considered or to give up an ill-considered project that would obviously not fit in with the over-all plan for his area.

County plans adopted under the provisions of the Coastal Area Management Act will become the primary criteria for issuing or denying development permits in areas of environmental concern.

Third, the county may influence the pattern and density of development by its own actions in choosing sites for new schools, acquiring and maintaining parks and recreation areas, or providing water and sewerage service to some areas while denying such services to areas that are unsuitable for development.

Fourth, the county may keep development out of some unsuitable areas through the purchase of land or interests therein. Purchase may be outright for park or recreation purposes (G.S. Ch. 160A, Art. 18). Or for the preservation of open spaces, it may be possible to purchase only the owner's right to convert the land to urban types of development, while allowing him to continue to farm it (G.S. Ch. 160A, Art. 19, Part 4). In either event, federal grants may be available to defray a part of the cost [75 STAT. 183-185 (1961), 42 U.S.C. Ch. 8C (1970)].

Fifth, a wide range of regulatory powers is available to the county for controlling development, as outlined below.

Jurisdiction

Under the provisions of the county (G.S. Ch. 153A, Art. 18) and city (G.S. Ch. 160A, Art. 19, especially G.S. 160A-360) enabling acts for planning and regulating development, the county's jurisdiction is basically every part of the county that lies outside any city's jurisdiction.

All cities may adopt ordinances spelling out the boundaries of their extraterritorial jurisdiction, which may extend up to one mile beyond the city limits. Cities with populations over 10,000 may extend such boundaries up to two miles beyond their limits and cities over 25,000 population may extend these boundaries up to three miles, if the county commissioners first give their approval in the form of a resolution.

If a city has not adopted a boundary ordinance, the county may exercise its powers right up to the city limits.

Whether or not a city has adopted a boundary ordinance, it may by resolution authorize the county to exercise any specified regulatory powers in any specified areas within its extraterritorial jurisdiction or even within its city limits.

Once a county has begun to zone, regulate subdivisions, and enforce the State Building Code within an area, no city may thereafter extend its extraterritorial jurisdiction into that area without the county's permission.

Although normally a county must exercise its regulatory powers throughout its jurisdiction if it wishes to exercise those powers at all, the statutes allow it to zone *portions* of the county, provided that any portion zoned contains at least 640 acres and ten separate tracts of land in separate ownership. If it has elected to zone only portions of the county, it may also regulate subdivisions only in those portions zoned.

Types of Regulations

The process of converting raw land to building lots is controlled through *subdivision regulations,* which the county may adopt under G.S. Ch. 153A, Art. 18, Part 2. These normally govern the design of streets, lot layouts, provision for water supply and sewage disposal, and similar matters. The *zoning ordinance,* adopted under G.S. Ch. 153A, Art. 18, Part 3, divides the county into districts and within each district specifies the use that may be made of property and the placement and size of any buildings. However, all bona fide agricultural or farming operations are excluded from such regulation.

Special types of zoning are *historic district zoning* for the preservation of the special attributes of historic areas (G.S. Ch. 160A, Art. 19, Part 3A) and *airport zoning* for the protection of airports against structures that will endanger aircraft because of their height (G.S. Ch. 63, Art. 4).

A third major regulatory tool is the *building code,* which governs the materials and manner of construction of new buildings. At present, the construction of every building in the state, other than farm buildings, is subject to the State Building Code enacted by the Building Code Council (G.S. Ch. 143, Art. 9). The commissioners may adopt modified building regulations, if their modifications are approved by the Building Code Council [G.S. 143-138(e)]. In any event, by creating an inspection department (G.S. Ch. 153A, Art. 18, Part 4), the county may take primary responsibility for enforcing the Code, subject to the State Commissioner of Insurance (G.S. 143-139).

Closely related legal tools are the *fire prevention code,* which the county may adopt with the approval of the State Building Code Council (G.S. 153A-235), and the *minimum housing standards ordinance* (or housing code) (G.S. Ch. 160A, Art. 19, Part 6); both deal with substandard conditions.

More recently the county has also been given responsibilities in the area of environmental protection (see Chapter 22 of this book). These include such matters as floodway regulation, requirements of environmental impact statements, sedimentation control, septic tank regulation, and new regional land-use management systems.

ECONOMIC DEVELOPMENT MEASURES

Although the state and federal governments have been concerned with problems of economic development almost from the beginning of our history, most local governments have been content until comparatively recently to leave such problems to private agencies—the Chamber of Commerce, industrial development corporations, individual realtors, and

PLANNING 389

businessmen generally. A perceptible shift in attitude has now taken place, however, and many local governments have begun to take the lead in economic development efforts.

Any municipality, county, or group of cities and counties may create an *economic development commission,* furnish it with a full-time staff, and finance various development efforts (G.S. Ch. 158, Art. 2). Under the statutes, this commission shall:

(1) Receive from any municipal, county, joint, or regional planning board or commission with jurisdiction within its area an economic development program for part or all of the area;
(2) Formulate projects for carrying out such economic development program, through attraction of new industries, encouragement for existing industries, encouragement of agricultural development, encouragement of new business and industrial ventures by local as well as foreign capital, and other activities of a similar nature;
(3) Conduct industrial surveys as needed, advertise in periodicals or other communications media, furnish advice and assistance to business and industrial prospects which may locate in its area, furnish advice and assistance to existing businesses and industries, furnish advice and assistance to persons seeking to establish new businesses and industries, and engage in related activities;
(4) Encourage the formation of private business development corporations or associations which may carry out such projects as securing and preparing sites for industrial development, constructing industrial buildings, or rendering financial or managerial assistance to businesses and industries; furnish advice and assistance to such corporations or associations;
(5) Carry on such other activities as may be necessary in the proper exercise of the functions described herein. [G.S. 158-13.]

These activities may be financed from surplus funds of the county or from the proceeds of taxes levied for such purposes pursuant to statutory authority contained in Article 1 or Article 3 of G.S. Ch. 158 or in a special act applying to a particular governmental unit.

It will be noted that the North Carolina statutes extend no authority for undertaking certain industrial development measures that are used in some other states. The reason is that such measures would probably be held to violate the State Constitution.

For example, granting tax exemptions or preferential tax treatment to new industries would probably violate Article I, section 32, and Article V, section 2, of our Constitution. Similarly, governmental construction of an industrial building to be turned over to a new industry free of charge or at a very low rental would probably be held to violate Article I, section 32; also, such construction would probably not be a "public purpose" for which public funds could be spent [N.C. CONST. art. V, § 2 and § 4(3)]. An attempt by the 1967 General Assembly to provide for this type of assistance (G.S. Ch. 123A) was promptly ruled unconstitutional by the State Supreme Court in *Mitchell v. Financing Authority* [273 N.C. 137 (1968)]. A second attempt, in modified form, by the 1971 General Assembly [G.S. Ch. 159A] was similarly invalidated in *Stanley, Edwards, Henderson v. Dept. Conservation and Development* [284 N.C. 15 (1973)].

On the other hand, there is no reason why a *private* association or development corporation could not prepare industrial sites or buildings for sale, lease, or gift to a new industry, as suggested by subsection (4) of the statutory listing of the economic development commission's duties.

A great many federal, state, and private agencies are actively engaged in assisting economic development programs, of course, and one major contribution that a county economic development commission can make is to bring the possibility of such aid to the attention of interested local groups.

Other measures that a county may take to further economic development include:

(1) Planning board surveys and plans, designed to identify resources for attracting particular industries and to prepare for handling any problems that stem from industrial growth;

(2) Industrial zoning, designed to identify potential industrial sites and protect them against types of development that would lessen their attractiveness to industry;

(3) Provision of adequate governmental facilities (particularly water and sewage systems) to serve industrial sites thus identified and protected (the county may also encourage the Department of Transportation to provide adequate access roads to such sites); and

(4) Provision of fire and police protection, garbage collection, and other services desired by new industries.

Finally, the things that make an area attractive to its ordinary citizens are likely to be equally attractive to industrial prospects. An aggressive program of planning for a "first-class" living environment almost certainly will yield many unexpected benefits of this kind.

— *Philip P. Green, Jr.*

21 / Interlocal Cooperation and City-County Consolidation

Interlocal Cooperation / 392
Types of Cooperation / 393
Authority for Cooperation / 394
Provisions of Interlocal Agreements / 394
City-County Consolidation / 395

21 / INTERLOCAL COOPERATION AND CITY-COUNTY CONSOLIDATION

INTERLOCAL COOPERATION

Cooperation among local governments has increased greatly in recent years. As urbanization has spilled beyond city limits, counties have had to begin providing urban services. They have often found that an efficient way of providing these services is by cooperation with one or more cities within the county. In this way, a county, as it begins a new activity, may benefit from a city's experience in that activity. Also, counties have continued and expanded cooperation among themselves in providing services more traditional to county government.

Cooperation offers several advantages. First, it may be the most efficient and least expensive way of providing a new service. As a county begins inspection services, a contract with an on-going city inspection department can provide experienced services immediately, with no administrative overhead. To take another example, a county by itself may not need on a full-time basis or be able to afford specialized services such as more sophisticated types of police activities. However, if a county and one or more cities in the county joined, or a county and an adjacent county joined, such a service might be financially feasible and fully used. Second, through cooperation governments may achieve economies of scale, lowering the per-unit cost of a service and perhaps providing it at a higher level. A good example is a district health department. Third, cooperation permits more effective response to problems that refuse to respect governmental boundaries—for example, air pollution that drifts across governmental boundaries. Fourth, by cooperating, two units may coordinate functions that each is carrying on independently. Water and sewer services just beyond city limits are an example of this coordination; counties must often work with the city to establish policies on extensions, supplies, costs, and the like. Fifth, cooperation permits local governments to adjust inequitable situations. Often, for example, cities provide recreation programs used by people from throughout the county, and so many counties contribute to these programs. Finally, cooperation is flexible. It usually can begin by simple action of governing boards. A unit may engage in several cooperative ventures, each differing from the others in scope, administrative structure, and financial support. A cooperative relationship established for one service may provide a model for another, but it in no way establishes a mold.

Types of Cooperation

Cooperation between local governments may assume a variety of forms. The most frequent categories are:

Contributions. Occasionally one government will provide a program that benefits the property or citizens of another government, but without financial support from the beneficiaries. In that case, the government that benefits might contribute funds to the government that provides. County support of a city recreation program would be such a contribution.

Mutual Aid Contracts. This category involves two or more governments that agree to come to each other's aid (if possible) in emergencies, whether police, fire, or natural disaster.

Transfer of Functions. Sometimes a county and city, each authorized to perform a particular function, will agree that the county should assume total responsibility. This process has frequently occurred with libraries, hospitals, and most recently, solid waste disposal.

Service Contracts. This category includes all agreements in which one government contracts with another to provide a service, either an administrative service to the receiving government itself or a service provided directly to the citizens of that government. A county might contract to collect the taxes of a city, or to provide data-processing for the city; or a city might contract to inspect buildings throughout the county.

Joint Agreements. The line between "joint agreements" and "service contracts" is often a thin one, but in theory the former involves two or more units exercising jointly a power that each could exercise individually. A city and a county might employ a joint manager, or two counties a joint social services director. City-county planning boards would fit under this category, as would councils of governments and other regional councils.

New Units of Government. Infrequently, two or more local governments will cooperatively create a new political subdivision, intended to provide a service to citizens of each of the creating governments. This form of cooperation is not often found in North Carolina, but examples would include some airport authorities, water and sewer authorities, metropolitan water or sewerage districts, and regional housing authorities.

Authority for Cooperation

The General Assembly, through a series of statutes, has provided ample authority for cooperation by counties. Table 21-1 sets out the principal statutes authorizing counties to cooperate with other local governments.

Provisions of Interlocal Agreements

Some types of cooperative arrangements are quite simple. When one government contributes to an on-going program of another, the contributing government typically does not concern itself with the administration of the program; it simply includes an appropriation in its budget ordinance. The amount of the appropriation may have been negotiated, but the negotiations probably would not have extended to other subjects. The same disinterest in administration would probably attach to a transfer of function; once the transfer is made, the function becomes the sole responsibility of one of the governments.

Other arrangements, however, become more complex, and negotiations may be difficult. Questions arise concerning financing, operations, administration, property, and many other matters. This chapter cannot suggest correct solutions—needs, administrative structures, traditions and services involved all differ—or even all the questions. But it can point out the most common decisions that two negotiating governments might face. Perhaps the list could then suggest other questions more peculiar to the particular situation:

Administrative Structure
 Should the units jointly supervise the function, or should one simply contract for the other to provide it for both?

Finances
 Are user charges to be used?
  Should the agreement establish the schedule of charges?
  Should the agreement establish the basis of charges?
  How should charges be modified?
  Should charges be the province of the operating government alone?
 On what basis are costs to be divided?
  What should be included as costs attributable to the activity?
  What is the timing and manner of payment between governments?
 What budgeting procedures should be established?
 Are special assessments to be used? On what basis?
 In capital projects, how are expenditure decisions to be made?

Operations
 What is the territorial scope of activity?
 What performance levels are expected?
  Can these be modified? How?

In capital projects, what specifications are required?
On facilities, what limitations or priorities on use are necessary?
Personnel
  How are personnel selected?
  Whose employees are they?
  Should there be special provisions in regard to position classification, pay plan, fringe benefits?
Property
  How are decisions to buy real or major personal property to be made?
  How are sites selected?
  How are specifications established?
  How will acquisition be made?
  Who will own property?
  How will property be disposed of?
Miscellaneous
  What reports are required?
  What records must be kept?
  What rights of inspection should be allowed?
  How will potential tort liabilities be paid?
Joint Agencies
  How will this be structured?
    Size, terms, who appoints
    Meetings
    Powers and duties
    Budgeting provisions
    Reports and records
Duration
Termination and Renewal Provisions

— David M. Lawrence

CITY-COUNTY CONSOLIDATION

City-county consolidation is the merger of a county government with one or more city governments. As a general rule, the c_ty government is abolished and the county government is legally transformed into one that has all the powers and functions previously held by both the county and city governments.

In North Carolina, interest in city-county consolidation has a long history, beginning with a 1927 plan to consolidate Mecklenburg County

Table 21-I
Statutes Authorizing Counties to Cooperate with Other Local Governments

Function	G.S. Citation
General powers of cooperation	
Administrative and governmental powers	160A-460 et seq.
Property transactions	160A-274
Buildings	153A-164
Councils of governments	160A-470 et seq.
Consolidation study commissions	153A-401 et seq.
Elections	
Registration	163-288
Conduct	163-285
Voting machines	163-161
Planning and regulation of development	
Transfer of territorial jurisdiction	160A-360
Planning contracts	153A-322
Historic district commissions	160A-396
Historic properties commissions	160A-399.2
Appearance commissions	160A-451
Inspection services	153A-353
Housing	157-35, -39.5
Regional planning commissions	153A-391 et seq.
Regional economic development commission	158-8 et seq.
Environmental matters	
Air pollution control	143-215.112
Shoreline protection	104B-6
Public safety	
Law enforcement	
Training	153A-211
Auxiliary police	160A-283
Emergency assistance	160A-288
Local confinement facilities	153A-219
Fire protection	160A-293
Civil disorders	14-288.12, -288.14
Civil defense	166-9 et seq.
Ambulance services	153A-250
Health services	
Public health	130-14
Mental health	122-35.19, 122-35.5
Alcoholism programs	122-35.16
Hospitals	131-126.20 -126.27. -28.2
Social services	
Social services directors	108-17
Human relations programs	160A-492
Manpower programs	160A-492
Community action programs	160A-492

Function	G.S. Citation
Education	
Merger of school administrative units	115-74.1, -74.2
Community colleges	115A-37
Library services	153A-270
Recreation	160A-355
Public enterprises	
Airports	63-56
	153A-278
Water services	153A-278
Sewer services	153A-278
Solid waste services	153A-278
	160A-192(b)
Off-street parking	153A-278
Utility emergencies	160A-318
Bus and mass transit	153A-278

and the City of Charlotte that was never submitted to the voters. Since that time there have been two more unsuccessful attempts to consolidate Charlotte and Mecklenburg, two unsuccessful efforts in Wilmington and New Hanover County, and three failures in Durham and Durham County. In each of these instances, special enabling legislation was needed from the General Assembly to undertake a consolidation study and submit the issue to the voters.

Special legislation for each consolidation study and proposal is no longer necessary since the enactment in 1973 of Article 20 of G.S. Chapter 153A, which authorizes counties and cities to create charter or governmental study commissions.

— *Warren J. Wicker*

22 / Environmental Affairs

Air Pollution / 400
Occupational Safety and Health / 402
Water Pollution / 402
Septic Tanks / 403
Sedimentation Control / 404
Pesticides / 405
Floodway and Floodplain Management / 405
Environmental Impact Statements / 406
Soil Conservation, Small Watershed, and Drainage Programs / 407
Soil Conservation Programs / 407
Small Watersheds / 407
Drainage Districts / 409
County Involvement in Soil Conservation and Drainage Programs / 409
County Involvement in Small Watershed Work / 409
Opportunities for County Participation / 409
Duties of County Officials / 410
References / 411
The Environment and Land Use / 411
Coastal Area Management / 411
Other Land-Use Programs / 412

22 / ENVIRONMENTAL AFFAIRS

The last edition of this book contained a chapter concerning soil conservation, watershed and drainage programs. Since the last edition, four legislative sessions have dramatically expanded the subject of environmental law, as Table 22-1 shows. Although some of this expansion affects only state government functions, local government is increasingly involved. Reflecting the increasing involvement of local government, the scope of this chapter has been enlarged to cover environmental protection and resource management programs generally.

AIR POLLUTION

Under existing state and federal legislation, the federal government sets general standards for air quality, while the state government, under close supervision from the federal government (the Environmental Protection Agency [EPA]), develops the administrative machinery for achieving these goals and standards. North Carolina's state implementation plan was one of the first to be approved by EPA. The North Carolina program is operated by the State Environmental Management Commission (EMC), formerly the Board of Water and Air Resources.

Local governments (counties, cities, regional groupings of cities and counties) in North Carolina can operate local air pollution control programs, but only if the local unit can demonstrate to the satisfaction of the EMC its ability to run an effective program. The powers of local programs and the procedure for obtaining state approval are spelled out in G.S. 143-215.112. Any county that is interested in conducting or participating in an air pollution control program should review this statute carefully, since it sets out the alternatives and requirements for local programs in some detail.

Local programs that have full state approval at this time are those in Forsyth, Gaston, and Mecklenburg counties; Western North Carolina Regional (Buncombe and Haywood counties); and the "Unifour" area (Alexander, Burke, Caldwell, and Catawba counties). Partial approval has been given to local programs in Cleveland, Cumberland, Durham,

Guilford, and Rowan counties. Programs given partial approval cover such functions as open burning and dark smoke control, as well as monitoring in most cases.

Several recent developments stress the connection between land-use and air pollution controls. These developments include EPA requirements that state implementation plans include land-use and transportation controls to supplement air quality controls; that states consider the need for air quality maintenance controls in metropolitan areas; and that state programs control so-called "complex sources" of air pollution. (A typical "complex source" would be a large shopping center, with a high level of air contamination from motor vehicles.) Also related is the so-called "nondegradation" requirement that pure air that is already cleaner than national standards not be allowed to deteriorate to the level of the national standards.

On some of these matters county planning staffs may be able to play an important part in ensuring that a reasonable balance is maintained between the need for air pollution control and the need for opportunities for development. It may be in the best interest of the county for its county planning staff to keep a close watch on developments in this area where air pollution control and land-use planning are so closely related.

No units of government (federal, state, or local) are exempt from complying with air pollution regulations merely because of their status as government agencies.

Table 22-1
North Carolina Environmental Legislation: 1967-1974

Appalachian and Carolina Trails Acts	Occupational Safety and Health Act
Bikeway laws	Oil pollution control
Clean Water Bond Act ($150 million)	Pesticide control
Coastal Area Management Act	Rights of withdrawal in stored water
Coastal Wetlands Act	Salt water fishing program
Constitutional amendment: Environmental Bill of Rights	Scenic river (framework act and New River designation)
Constitutional amendment (proposed) on industrial development pollution-abatement revenue bonds	Sedimentation control
	Septic tank waste control
	Small water and sewer system regulation (State Utilities Commission)
Environmental Policy Act	
Estuarine protection legislation (dredge and fill permits, coastal management study)	Small watershed and drainage laws revisions
	Southeastern Environmental Compact
Farmland taxes	Surface mining control
Floodway regulation	State Land Policy Act
Land Conservancy Act	Tightened water and air pollution controls (penalties, reporting, etc.)
Local and regional water supply and waste disposal	

OCCUPATIONAL SAFETY AND HEALTH

Congress has passed an Occupational Safety and Health Act (OSHA) that imposes standards on employers for the protection of employees' health and safety. Like most federal environmental and health protection laws, OSHA contemplates a coordinated federal-state program, with standards set nationally and administered largely by the states.

Although this chapter does not attempt to cover health legislation generally, OSHA is noted briefly here for two reasons. First, it provides, in one sense, the in-plant equivalent of the protections established by clean air laws for the air environment. Thus an in-plant air quality problem is likely to be covered by OSHA rather than by clean air laws. Second, there is some overlapping and duplication between OSHA and environmental protection laws. For example, for the protection of farm workers the administrators of OSHA have imposed restrictions on application of pesticides. These restrictions are in addition to (and in some ways may even conflict with) the provisions of pesticide control legislation (see "Pesticides," below).

North Carolina has adopted the state legislation required to put the state government in a position to administer this program: the Occupational Safety and Health Law of North Carolina (G.S. Ch. 95, Art. 16). It is administered by the State Department of Labor.

Private employers were subject to the requirements of OSHA and related state laws from the beginning. Governmental employers (state and local government) were required to comply with standards set under these laws beginning July 1, 1974.

WATER POLLUTION

The basic system of water pollution control is similar in general outline to the one that operates in the air pollution field. The federal government provides leadership in setting goals and standards, while the state government is largely responsible for providing the machinery to achieve them. Local government's role, however, is smaller in regard to water pollution than in regard to air pollution.

Federal legislation sets long-term national water quality goals. The standards that will be required to meet these goals will become increasingly stringent during the next decade as the nation works toward a goal of achieving recreational water quality for all its waters by 1983. The federal government (EPA) has been working to help the states bring their water pollution control laws and programs into compliance with federal standards. North Carolina's water pollution legislation has now been brought into substantial compliance with federal minimum requirements. The EMC is in the process of substantially enlarging its staff to meet minimum EPA recommendations.

There is a large-scale program of federal subsidies to help local government build sewage treatment plants. The present federal formula provides federal subsidies of up to 75 per cent of the cost. In North Carolina this is supplemented by state aid under the Clean Water Bond Act of 1971. (The state also assists the construction of local water supply systems under this act.) Counties are beginning to develop or participate in county-wide or multi-county waste treatment and collection systems.

The very important responsibilities placed on local governments (primarily cities) by the water pollution laws to collect and treat their sewage properly should be noted. Counties that have assumed treatment responsibility are presumably in the same position. Failure to meet the responsibility may result in the assessment of heavy penalties on local governments and local officials.

Unlike the situation in regard to air pollution, there is currently (1974) no statutory authority for delegating the state's *regulatory* responsibilities concerning water pollution control to local governments. In some respects, however, county health department or county environmental protection departments participate in the water pollution abatement effort, mainly in regard to wastes from septic tanks, which are discussed in the next heading.

A significant recent addition to water pollution control programs is the so-called "208 plans" (named after the statute that gave rise to them, Section 208 of the Federal Water Pollution Control Act). 208 plans are comprehensive regional sewage and waste management plans, developed after a long process of study and hearings. Their purpose is to coordinate state and local waste management efforts within a region (such as standard metropolitan statistical area). Under these programs, water pollution controls would be correlated with land-use plans and controls. In those regions that develop 208 plans, including several already under way in North Carolina, the 208 plan may well turn out to be the most important aspect of a county's involvement in water pollution control.

SEPTIC TANKS

Local sanitarians employed by county health departments have traditionally been responsible for inspecting and supervising installation of septic tanks. In recent years, as septic tanks have been used for larger projects and in more densely built-up areas, septic tank wastes have become an increasing concern for the EMC (with its general mandate for water pollution control) as well as for the health authorities. As a result, it is sometimes difficult to separate the respective jurisdictions and responsibilities of the water and health authorities concerning this subject. The 1973 General Assembly addressed itself to this problem and passed legislation that drew a jurisdictional line based on capacity of treatment units. Under this legislation, septic tanks and similar treatment facilities with a capacity smaller than 3,000 gallons will continue to be the responsibility of state and local health authorities; larger units will be the responsibility of the EMC. (A cautionary note: further revision of these laws is under study at this writing, late in 1974.)

Another 1973 law (the Ground Absorption Sewage Disposal System Act of 1973) sought to upgrade the county health department's procedures for inspecting septic tanks by incorporating the practices and standards of some of the stronger county health departments. This act requires that an improvements permit be secured from the local health department before construction of a dwelling is begun or a mobile home is moved onto a site (other than in mobile home parks, which were thought to be already adequately regulated). Field inspection and tests are required before this permit can be issued.

Even then, the dwelling may not be occupied until the department determines that its sewage disposal system (septic tank or otherwise) has been properly installed. When the installation is approved, the department is to issue a certificate of completion. To reinforce these provisions, the act provides that no other permit may be issued for construction on a conventional dwelling until an improvements permit has been issued; and no permit for electrical or other construction work on a mobile home or for location on a particular site may be issued until a certificate of completion has been issued.

SEDIMENTATION CONTROL

Sedimentation pollution control is a specialized aspect of water pollution control. It involves preventing the silting of streams that would result from uncontrolled runoff from construction projects, logging activities, farming, etc. Sedimentation pollution control programs are relative newcomers to the political scene. In most states (including North Carolina), they have not yet been incorporated into the general water pollution control agency.

Under the Sedimentation Pollution Control Law of 1973, the General Assembly created a Sedimentation Control Commission within the Department of Natural and Economic Resources and gave it the authority to develop and supervise a cooperative state-local program to control the pollution of streams by sediment and silt. A principal function of this commission will be to review local ordinances and programs for compliance with state standards and criteria. Any county (or city) that wishes to adopt a sediment control ordinance should contact the Sedimentation Control Commission, which will help the county develop a satisfactory ordinance and program.

The new law also lays down three statutory standards that apply statewide. First, it forbids "land-disturbing activities" in close proximity to a lake or natural watercourse without a buffer zone sufficient to confine visible siltation within the 25 per cent of the zone nearest the land-disturbing activity. Second, it forbids the grading of slopes to an angle greater than can be retained by vegetative cover or other erosion-control methods. And, third, it requires that planting or other ground cover be provided on graded land within thirty days after grading is complete and on any portion of a tract greater than one acre on which active construction is not taking place.

The Sedimentation Control Law covers only residential, commercial, and industrial construction activities; it does not apply to timbering or agricultural activities. It applies to local and state governmental land-disturbing activities as well as to private or commercial work. Thus, county projects must comply with the law.

PESTICIDES

Federal laws and programs set general standards for pesticides control, which must be met by state laws and programs, if a state is to retain state control over its permit system for the use of pesticides. North Carolina enacted in 1971 a comprehensive pesticides law that clearly meets minimum federal standards in most respects. Principal elements of the North Carolina program are regulation of the sale and use of "restricted-use pesticides," licensing of pesticides dealers who sell restricted-use pesticides, licensing of commercial pesticides applicators and consultants, and registration of pesticides. The North Carolina Pesticide Board is the policy-making agency for the state program, and the Commissioner of Agriculture has the administrative responsibility. EPA is responsible for the federal program.

Local governments have no responsibilities for regulating the use or sale of pesticides. However, they are subject to the licensing requirements and regulations of the Pesticide Board. Local and state government agencies that use or apply pesticides, as well as commercial operators, must obtain licenses.

FLOODWAY AND FLOODPLAIN MANAGEMENT

Counties and cities in North Carolina, under their general zoning powers, have long had the legal authority to adopt floodplain zoning ordinances. In this fashion, special zones or districts can be established to regulate land use in floodplain areas, or floodplain managment provisions can be added to existing zones.

State legislation passed in 1971 specifies in detail the procedure for adoption and administration of controls over the use of floodways. Essentially, this statute prohibits construction in a floodway that has been officially delineated without a permit from the appropriate city or county government except for certain uses that may be made as a matter of right (such as farming, parking areas, recreational areas, streets, utility and railroad facilities, dams, docks, ramps, temporary facilities such as circuses, etc.) This puts cities and counties in the position of having to adopt ordinances providing for floodway permits in order to permit any construction within the floodway other than the exempted uses. A 1973 amendment empowers the EMC to trigger the process of adopting a floodway permit system by delineating the floodway where local governments have not done so. Except for this authority, state government in North Carolina is generally limited to the role of providing technical assistance to local governments with respect to floodplain and floodway managment.

Any floodway or floodplain ordinance that is adopted by a county or city should take into consideration the Federal Flood Insurance Program, administered by the Federal Insurance Administration (a branch of the Department of Housing and Urban Development). Under this new program, after March 1, 1974, federal mortgage guarantees and other housing assistance programs are not available to communities with flood hazards unless the communities have adopted approved floodway or floodplain controls. Information on this subject can be obtained from EMC or from HUD.

The "floodway" of a stream is essentially the channel and banks that carry normal stream flow and moderate flooding (defined by statute in North Carolina as the "100-year flood"). The "floodplain" refers to the broader area that receives and carries large floods that overflow the banks of a stream and spread out extensively into surrounding areas.

ENVIRONMENTAL IMPACT STATEMENTS

The North Carolina Environmental Policy Act of 1971 (effective through August 31, 1977) requires that environmental impact statements be filed by state agencies in connection with all "actions involving expenditure of public moneys for projects and programs significantly affecting the quality of the environment." (A similar requirement applies to federal projects and programs under federal law.) A provision in the North Carolina statute, G.S. 113A-108, authorizes counties and cities to require environmental impact statements in connection with "major development projects" (those larger than two acres) of private developers and special-purpose governments. This would cover such projects as shopping centers, subdivisions, and industrial or commercial developments.

Environmental impact analysis provides an opportunity for a thorough (and sometimes very lengthy) ventilation of the possible environmental consequences of important developments. A county that wants to take advantage of this opportunity can either adopt a separate environmental impact ordinance or insert similar provisions in its county zoning ordinance or subdivision control ordinance, under G. S. 113A-108. Whether one approach or the other is preferable will depend upon the county's objectives.

SOIL CONSERVATION, SMALL WATERSHED, AND DRAINAGE PROGRAMS

Soil Conservation Programs

North Carolina, like most of the states, has adopted an enabling statute, G.S. Ch. 139, Art. 1, to serve as a framework for its soil conservation program. Under this statute, soil and water conservation districts (originally "soil conservation districts") may be formed by interested farmers through a petition procedure supervised by the State Soil and Water Conservation Committee. Once formed, the districts coordinated by the State Committee and assisted by the U.S. Soil Conservation Service (SCS) carry on programs of soil erosion control and land treatment within their jurisdiction—which may be a single county or several counties. (Currently there are eighty-nine single-county districts, and three multi-county districts covering the remaining counties. The multi-county districts are all located in the coastal area). These districts have no taxing powers and are financed by voluntary contributions supplemented by state appropriations. Although the districts nominally are vested with certain regulatory powers concerning farm land use, their objectives have been secured largely by cooperative, voluntary action by participating farmers.

Small Watersheds

The so-called "small watershed" program is an extension of the soil conservation movement into related water conservation activities. Historically, the small watershed program originated in P.L. 83-566 of 1954, a federal aid statute that authorized the Soil Conservation Service (SCS) to aid local sponsors of small projects in controlling flood damage and sedimentation, improving drainage, and conserving water through storage.

In addition to this SCS-assisted small watershed program, a comparable activity, known as the "tributary areas development" program, is sponsored by the TVA in the Tennessee Valley section of western North Carolina. Localized flood control and navigation improvement projects are also sponsored by the U.S. Army Corps of Engineers with county or municipal cooperation, and sometimes assisted by state cost-sharing.

A typical Piedmont or Mountain small watershed project in North Carolina may involve one or more small impoundments that provide for flood storage, a sedimentation pool, and downstream channel clearance. It may also include limited storage for water supply and recreational use, as well as areas for conservation of fish and wildlife habitat. Eastern Carolina projects usually emphasize drainage improvements rather than flood prevention.

The federal government aids these projects under P.L. 83-566 by paying all costs of construction for flood prevention, paying part of the construction costs for water conservation features (including drainage and irrigation), contributing to costs for recreational features and fish and wildlife enhancement, providing planning services, and making loans to help finance the local share of the costs. Local sponsors must initiate and maintain the projects, obtain easements, and secure agreements with landowners to carry out needed soil conservation measures. In North Carolina the state government has appropriated an average of about $200,000 annually in recent years to help plan, organize, and coordinate small watershed work, plus another $160,000 or more annually for soil and water conservation programs.

Local sponsorship of small watershed projects in North Carolina may take various forms. Thus, the principal local sponsor can be a watershed improvement district, a drainage district, or a county, working in cooperation with the appropriate soil and water conservation districts. A decade of experience has indicated that county-sponsored programs have met with most favor in the Piedmont and Mountain sections, and either county or drainage district programs in the East. Local revenue sources under our general enabling statutes are benefit assessments for drainage districts and watershed improvement districts and ad valorem property taxes for county-sponsored projects. Under the County Finance Act (G.S. 159-48), counties may also borrow funds for small watershed projects. Counties and municipalities may borrow to finance present or future water supplies in conjunction with watershed projects under G.S. 139-37.1.

Special acts vary these powers in some respects. For example, fifteen counties have secured special acts permitting the levy of a property tax for watershed purposes without the need for a referendum. (A countywide vote is required by general law, under G.S. 139-39. Five counties have established county programs by county-wide vote.)

Drainage Districts

While drainage districts may serve as sponsors of federally aided small watershed projects, programs of farm drainage and land reclamation in North Carolina, especially in the Coastal Plains, have long antedated P.L. 83-566.

Under G.S. Ch. 156, subch. 3, drainage districts may be organized with the approval of the clerk of superior court following an engineering survey by a board of viewers. The procedures to be followed by the clerk of superior court—beginning with the filing of a landowner petition to create a district, and concluding with his adjudication on the final report of the board of viewers—are spelled out in G.S. 156-54 through -78. As previously mentioned, drainage districts are empowered to levy benefit assessments, and they may condemn necessary rights of way and drainage outlets. G.S. Ch. 156 (subch. 1, 2, and 4), it may be added, also spells out procedures for drainage undertakings by individual landowners and corporations and to a very limited extent by certain counties.

County Involvement in Soil Conservation and Drainage Programs

Counties are not involved in the creation, operation, or supervision of soil and water conservation districts. However, G.S. 153A-440 authorizes counties to cooperate with and support soil and water conservation work and to appropriate for this purpose revenues not limited as to use by law. Acting under this authority, a number of counties have assisted the districts in such ways as furnishing office space and helping to pay secretarial salaries.

No county participation is required in the organization or operation of drainage districts except in the collection of district assessments, which is by law made a responsibility of the county tax collector. The procedures to be followed in the levy and collection of these assessments are set forth in detail by G.S. 156-94 et seq.

County Involvement in Small Watershed Work

Opportunities for County Participation. A county may directly undertake a small watershed program pursuant to G.S. Ch. 139, Art. 3, with financing by county-wide taxes. The program may be conducted by the board of county commissioners itself or through a watershed improvement commission created by the board. Or, the board of county commissioners may designate its soil and water conservation district to conduct the program. To finance this activity, the board of commissioners with the approval of the voters may levy a special tax of not more than 25 cents per $100. As noted earlier, some counties have eliminated the voter-approval requirement by means of special legislation authorizing special tax levies without a vote, ranging from 1 cent to 25 cents per $100 valuation.

As an alternative to direct operation, under G.S. 139-37 a county may participate in the small watershed program of a watershed improvement district by contributing funds, services, or materials. Such contributions may be made for works or projects that will provide drainage or flood protection benefits to property within the county or provide public water supply benefits to the county.

It should be pointed out that the creation of any additional watershed improvement districts has been prohibited since 1971 and only a few of these districts were created before 1971. Thus, this is a relatively minor organizational alternative.

In addition to direct operation and financial assistance, counties may also act as co-sponsors with other landowners by having county-owned property included in either a drainage district or watershed improvement district, subject to assessments. Procedural complications and enforcement problems, however, make this the least attractive avenue for county participation.

Duties of County Officials. Certain functions are imposed by law upon various county officials in the organization and operation of both county watershed programs and watershed improvement districts.

In the case of a county program, under the general law the board of county commissioners has the power to initiate the program by calling a special election upon the levy of a watershed improvement tax. (Under the special acts that dispense with a vote, the county commissioners have been empowered to initiate the work directly without a county-wide election.) Once a program has been established, the county commissioners determine the tax rate within specified limits. The commissioners also operate the program or may delegate its operation to a watershed improvement commission or soil and water conservation district. Finally, the county commissioners have certain functions regarding the exercise of condemnation powers for watershed purposes, subject to review by the State Soil and Water Conservation Committee.

The county board of elections is responsible by law for conducting elections of watershed improvement district trustees in conjunction with the general elections. Because the boundaries of most watershed improvement districts do not coincide with precincts, and because of the possibility of multi-county districts, the conduct of trustee elections is likely to be a difficult task that requires careful planning.

Collection of watershed improvement district assessments (like drainage assessments) is a statutory responsibility of the county tax collector. The procedures are substantially similar to the usual tax collection procedures. Before collection, the tax collector's only contact with district assessments is to receive a copy of the assessment roll filed with him by the district. The board of county commissioners is also assigned some minor functions in the collection of district assessments.

References

The Institute of Government, in cooperation with the State Soil and Water Conservation Committee and the State Conservationist, has prepared a set of guides concerning the organization of small watershed programs. Among these are guides dealing with county commissioner responsibilities, election procedures, and opportunities for county participation in small watershed programs. Copies are available from the Institute without charge.

Soon after enactment of the original small watershed enabling legislation, several articles were published on this legislation during 1959 and 1960 in the Institute of Government's magazine *Popular Government*. A report of the Legislative Research Commission in 1971 on small watershed and drainage laws contains a brief history of small watershed and drainage legislation.

THE ENVIRONMENT AND LAND USE

Coastal Area Management

The 1974 General Assembly enacted a Coastal Area Management Act. The basic objective of this act is to establish a comprehensive plan for the protection, preservation, orderly development, and management of the coastal area of North Carolina. Twenty counties are covered by the act: Beaufort, Bertie, Brunswick, Camden, Carteret, Chowan, Craven, Currituck, Dare, Gates, Hertford, Hyde, New Hanover, Onslow, Pamlico, Pasquotank, Pender, Perquimans, Tyrrell, and Washington.

The three main features of the act are designed to insure that the following will have been accomplished by 1977:

(1) That each of the 20 coastal area counties will be covered by a land-use plan, hopefully prepared by local government, and in basic harmony with the plans adopted for the other 19 coastal area counties.
(2) That all critical areas that need to be considered for protection and possible preservation in each county will have been designated so-called areas of environmental concern.

(3) That any proposed development, change, or other use of land within any of the designated areas of environmental concern will be subject to review by means of development permits under the terms of this act. Generally, local government will handle permits for minor developments (in most cases those under 20 acres) and the Coastal Resources Commission will handle permits for major developments.

The thrust of this act is to establish a cooperative state-local program of coastal land management. It will be local government's responsibility to establish local land-use plans and issue permits for minor development in areas of environmental concern. It will be state government's responsibility to adopt guidelines and standards for local land-use plans; to establish areas of environmental concern; to issue permits for major developments in areas of environmental concern; and to assume the responsibilities of local government if and when a local government body does not exercise its initiatives. Enforcement will be a concurrent state-local responsibility.

The basic state agencies involved in the process provided by this act are a newly created Coastal Resources Commission and Coastal Resources Advisory Council, as well as the Secretary of Natural and Economic Resources and the Secretary of Administration.

The basic local agencies involved in the processes provided by this act are the counties, cities, and multi-county planning districts in the 20 coastal area counties.

Funding for the coastal program during its first fiscal year will include $200,000 in direct state appropriations and $300,000 in matching federal grants. Additional funds are expected from other sources. Altogether, it is hoped that more than $500,000 will be available in planning grants to local government.

It should be obvious that counties can have a strategic role to play in the coastal area management program. Each coastal area county nominates four persons to the Coastal Resources Commission and designates one member of the Advisory Council. If they wish, the coastal area counties can be the dominant partner in the planning process and can play an important part in enforcement. The act offers these counties an extraordinary opportunity to upgrade and strengthen their land-use planning and management capability with state assistance.

Other Land-Use Programs

A Mountain Area Management Bill that was proposed in 1974 would have applied the principles of the Coastal Act to 24 western counties. Although this legislation was not enacted in 1974, it has been reintroduced in 1975, applicable this time to 26 counties.

The third bill in the 1974 land-use legislation package, the State Land Policy Act, was enacted along with the Coastal Act. The act calls for development of a land classification system for all land in North Carolina, to be used as the basis for evaluating land capability and suitability for major use classifications. Not less than four or more than eight classifications are to be established. A substantial opportunity for local input is guaranteed by a provision that the recommended classifications must be revised in light of consensus proposals of local planning agencies.

The act also directs that state land policies be articulated to govern the use of publicly owned lands and to provide guidance for such processes as advanced land acquisition, location of new towns, and review of projects of regional impact. All of these functions will be the responsibility of a State Land Policy Council, which will consist of cabinet officers, legislative leaders, and local government spokesmen.

The Land Policy Council will be setting policy for the entire state, with special emphasis on the counties not covered by the Coastal Act. Counties can participate directly in the work of the Land Policy Council through their representation on the Council. County planning agencies also have the opportunity to review the proposed land classifications, as previously noted.

— *Milton S. Heath, Jr.*

23 / Public Enterprises

Introduction / 416
Water and Sewerage Services / 417
Introduction / 417
Financing Water and Sewerage Services / 418
  Local Taxes / 418
  User Rates and Charges / 418
  Payments from Property / 419
    A special assessment / 419
    Subdivision requirements / 419
    Payment in advance / 419
    Acreage charges / 420
    Special connection charges / 420
  Special Services Charges / 420
  State and Federal Grants / 420
Patterns of County Financing and Provision of Services / 422
City-County Financing Agreements / 426
Solid Waste Collection and Disposal / 427
Introduction / 427
Regulation / 427
  County Boards of Health / 427
  County Commissioners—Health / 428
  County Commissioners—Business / 428
Provision of Services / 429
  Authority / 429
  General / 429
  Collection / 430
  Disposal / 430

23 / PUBLIC ENTERPRISES

INTRODUCTION

County governments in North Carolina are authorized to operate six public enterprises (G.S. Ch. 153A, Art. 15)—(1) water supply and distribution systems, (2) sewage collection and disposal systems, (3) solid waste collection and disposal systems, (4) airports, (5) off-street parking facilities, (6) bus lines and mass transit systems.

Except for airports, which were first authorized for county governments in 1929, all are fairly recent authorizations. Counties were first authorized to provide water and sewerage services in 1955 and solid waste disposal in 1961. Off-street parking facilities and bus lines and mass transit systems were added to the list of enterprises authorized for counties in 1974. (By special acts, a few counties were authorized to provide some of these enterprises earlier than the dates given for counties generally.)

While in some cases the original enterprise authorizations were limited as to areas that could be served or the source of financing, counties now have quite broad authority and flexibility in providing service and in financing.

Counties may own and operate all the enterprises both inside and outside their boundaries and condemn land needed in connection with their operation. Both general obligation and revenue bonds may be issued for these purposes. Counties may levy property taxes for all the enterprises and may do so without a vote of the people except for bus lines and mass transit systems. Rates, fees, and charges may be imposed for all of these enterprises, and a county may join with other counties or cities to undertake joint operation of any of them.

Of the six public enterprises, only the three chief activities—water, sewerage, and solid waste—will be discussed in this chapter. While airports were the first of the enterprises authorized for counties, they are still only a minor function and involve fewer than half of the counties.

No county is yet (1974) involved in operating bus lines or mass transit systems, and only a few—mostly in connection with new county office buildings and courthouses—provide off-street parking facilities.

The statutes provide a few additional powers and impose a few limitations on county actions with respect to particular enterprises. These will be noted below in the discussions of individual enterprises. But in general, counties have broad discretion in undertaking, organizing, and financing these public activities.

WATER AND SEWERAGE SERVICES

Introduction

North Carolina's growing urban population and the emphasis on attracting new industries, especially during the 1950s and 1960s, have produced increased needs for water and sewerage services outside municipal boundaries. For the most part, these requirements have been met by the joint efforts of cities and towns, developers, and industries. But county governments have increasingly become involved in providing these services.

The early county efforts were almost all in response to industrial needs, but since the late 1960s the needs of residential and commercial development have received increased attention from county governments. Almost every county in the state has completed one or more county-wide surveys of water and sewerage needs and developed preliminary projections as to where future facilities may be provided. Federal funds that became available for planning purposes in the mid-sixties (especially those through the Farmers Home Administration) and the planning prerequisites to other federal grants (particularly those through the Economic Development Administration and those authorized by the Housing and Urban Development Act of 1965) encouraged area-wide and metropolitan planning by both cities and counties. More recently, the regulations of the Environmental Protection Agency, the increase in federal grants for water pollution control, and the approval by the state's voters of $300 million in Clean Water Bonds in 1972 have not only increased county interest in meeting the needs but also provided part of the financing.

While an exact count is not available, surveys suggest that 75 or more of the state's 100 counties have joined in the financing of one or more water or sewer extensions or other facilities in the past 15 years. Reports from the North Carolina Local Government Commission show that 15 counties have issued bonds for water and sewerage purposes in the first four years of the 1970s and that their total authorized bond issues in the same period come to $29,700,000.

Financing Water and Sewerage Services

County governments in North Carolina have five principal sources of funds that may be used to finance water and sewerage services. These are set out in Table 23-I, together with the general principle of revenue-raising that the use of each represents.

All water and sewerage services provided by county and city governments in North Carolina are financed by some combination of the sources listed in the table. In fact, the classification is one that would include almost all revenues of a county. Various nontax revenues of a county (ABC funds, interest, etc.) are not listed separately. There are no legal bars to the use of these nontax funds, but to the extent that they are used, a county uses local tax receipts for other purposes that the nontax funds might otherwise have financed. Thus, in this discussion, nontax funds are considered the equivalent of local taxes.

Local Taxes. The property tax and the local sales tax are the two chief local tax measures. Proceeds of both may be used to finance water and sewerage services. Both are classified in economic terms as "ability to pay" taxes since the amount each taxpayer contributes is based on the value of his property or on how much he spends, both assumed to reflect ability to pay. For neither tax is the taxpayer's obligation related to use of the utility systems and his direct benefit from them. Almost all counties have used local tax funds (or the equivalent nontax proceeds) to finance water and sewerage services.

User Rates and Charges. These are the monthly or quarterly charges made to customers of the utilities based on their consumption of water or use of the sewerage system. In most systems the amount of the charge reflects the amount of use and thus is related to the benefit the customer receives directly. All utility systems employ user rates, but only rarely

Table 23-I
Sources of Funds for Financing Water and Sewerage Services and Revenue-Raising Principle of Each

Source of Funds	Principle
A. Local taxes	Ability to pay
B. Service rates and charges	Benefit
C. Payments from property	Benefit
1. Special assessments	
2. Subdivision requirements	
3. Payments in advance	
4. Acreage charges	
5. Special connection charges	
D. Special service charges (tap fees, hydrant rentals, etc.)	Benefit
E. State and federal grants	Ability to pay

PUBLIC ENTERPRISES 419

are the rates set at a level that will cover all utility costs. Furthermore, while proceeds from rates are considered in the financing of all systems, in most city-county arrangements in this state the proceeds flow through the city government and are not available directly to the county government for appropriation. (Where a county operates the system or a county and a city share the proceeds, the proceeds do become available for direct county appropriation.) The key consideration is the disposition of the proceeds. If agreement on disposition is reached in a joint enterprise involving two or more units, which unit the proceeds flow through is not of much importance.

Payments from Property. The presence of water and sewer lines provides special benefits to the property the lines serve. Increasingly, cities and counties in North Carolina are adopting financing policies that require the owners of abutting property to bear part or all of the cost of installing the water and sewer lines to serve their property. The five devices listed in Table 23-1 under the heading Payments from Property are the techniques for securing payment that are most frequently used. (Terminology is not standard. Some of the devices listed in the table may have other names in some places.)

A *special assessment* is a charge against property for part or all of the cost of making an improvement. It is in the nature of a tax, and once a special assessment is lodged against a lot or tract, that property is available to satisfy the payment of the special assessment in the same manner as if a property tax had been levied. The major advantage in its use is that the property stands behind the charge. Also, the charge is not related to *use* of the utility; in theory, the presence of the line has added value to the property because the line is *available* for use, so that the special assessment is seen as fair even if the owner does not connect. All counties have authority to impose special assessments for utility extensions, but few have done so. Guilford may be the only one.

Subdivision requirements. When these regulations are used by a county or city, the developer is required to install utilities to the unit's specifications and dedicate them to the unit when they are complete. The financing is thus normally a private matter and the funds to install the facilities do not flow through the unit's treasury. The cost of these installations is then, it is assumed, passed on to those who buy property in the subdivision. As with special assessments, that cost becomes a part of the cost of the developed lot or tract. This technique is widely used by cities. From the unit's administrative standpoint, it is the simplest method of all.

Payment in advance. Where a unit plans to make an extension but does not want to use special assessments and the property to be served is already in diverse ownership, property owners may be required to pay in advance so that the unit will have funds available to make the extension. Usually, the charge is on the basis of frontage and at a level that would correspond with what would be imposed if special assessments were used. This method is quite useful where extensions are short and the owners of the property to be served are able to make payments in advance.

Acreage charges. Acreage charges have been developed by units that have concluded that the full cost of extending utilities should be met by the properties to be served. In most cases, these charges are designed to cover each lot's or tract's proportionate share of the cost of providing major trunk lines in the water and sewer systems as opposed to smaller distribution and collection lines to which direct connection is made from each premise. For example, in many residential areas a 6-inch water line is installed to provide direct service to abutting property. But between such a 6-inch line and the water treatment plant there may be a network of major distribution lines of 12, 16, or 24 inches in size or even larger. These bigger lines are necessary to bring adequate water to large areas. It is thus said that each lot or tract adds to the capacity demand of these larger mains and each parcel should therefore be charged for its share. Charges of about $300 an acre are typical. Normally, acreage charges are collected at the time application for services is made. Perhaps 30 or more cities and counties in the state now use acreage charges or some close equivalent.

Special connection charges. Under a variety of names, special connection charges are used to recover extension costs from the property being served. In most cases, they are a substitute for one of the four devices described above or a combination of two or more. For example, a unit that does not impose special assessments might use a special charge at the time of connection to collect the same amount and on the same basis. Or a single special connection charge might be used that would combine the equivalent of the special assessment and the acreage charge.

Special Services Charges. The operation of a utility system involves a number of services that are provided directly for the benefit of a particular customer—making a tap and setting a meter, turning services on and off, installing private fire hydrants or sprinkler connections, installing temporary services, and the like. Usually special charges are made for these services, often at a level to cover the actual cost.

State and Federal Grants. In recent years significant amounts of support for water and sewerage facilities have been available through state and federal grants. Given the state and federal tax systems, this means that the funds are largely raised from state and national taxpayers through the general sales tax and the individual and corporate income taxes, all of which are levied on the ability-to-pay principle. To the extent that these are used, local utility systems are being supported on a statewide and nationwide basis by taxpayers some of whom are not served directly by any community utility system. This approach to financing utilities is quite similar to the approach used in financing education, parks and recreation, and many other general governmental functions.

As the foregoing discussion suggests, counties and cities in North Carolina use a variety of combinations of revenue sources to finance water and sewerage systems. Differing views as to need and equity as well as different conditions and community traditions lead to different financing arrangements. A community actively seeking new industrial growth may be less inclined to impose high extension costs on users than one with a no-growth bent. A community that has a tradition of financing all extensions from taxes and user charges may find it difficult to change to the use of special assessments. There has been, however, a slight trend toward making the water and sewerage utilities self-supporting insofar as local financing is concerned. (Almost all units will accept state and federal grants.) Units with self-supporting utility systems have tended to adopt financing policies that related elements of system cost with particular revenue sources as shown in Table 23-II.

Most of the water and sewerage systems operated by the state's larger cities are self-supporting (except for state and federal grants), including all operation and maintenance, extensions, and debt service on utility bonds. Not all, however, use the arrangements noted above. For example, those that do not use acreage charges tend to combine the costs of major lines with the cost of supply and treatment works (usually financed initially with bond proceeds) and these costs are then ultimately met through user rates and charges.

Table 23-II
Typical Pattern of Financing for Self-supporting System

Element of Cost	Sources of Funds
A. Supply and treatment works	Rates (plus grants when available)
B. Operation and maintenance	Rates
C. Major lines	Acreage charges (plus grants when available)
D. Minor lines	Special assessments, subdivision requirements, payments in advance, and special connection charges
E. Special services	Special service charges

The general financing plan outlined above may be illustrated to show its meaning for an individual customer of the system. A homeowner with a half-acre lot to which service is being extended by special assessment would typically face charges of the following order for water. (The levels of charges are typical and are given for purpose of illustration. They will obviously vary from system to system.)

Initial Charges   *Amount*
Special assessment for line in front of property
    ($3 per foot for 100 feet) $300
Service connection and meter (actual cost) 150
Acreage charge (for share of major distribution
    lines serving the area—$300 per acre) 150
                                             Total $600

Monthly Charges
Monthly user charge for water consumed; this charge
    includes costs of water supply and treatment, maintenance and repair of system, and administration $7

The flexibility granted to counties enables them to arrange the financing (cities have equal flexibility) in whatever manner appears most reasonable and equitable.

Patterns of County Financing and Provision of Services

Four patterns of county financing and action have developed as county governments have joined with cities to extend water and sewerage services.

First, in many cases the county has simply borne part of the cost of the extension outside the city, and the city has owned the lines and been completely responsible for their operation. For example, Wake County, acting under a special act and using ABC revenues, appropriated over $100,000 in 1954 to extend water and sewer lines to a new industry locating outside Raleigh. The lines were built to Raleigh's specifications, were deeded to the city when completed, and are operated and maintained by the city. Since that time Wake has financed a number of other extensions with the same arrangement. Robeson, Vance, Warren, Haywood, Lee, Cherokee, Buncombe, and several other counties have all made expenditures for water or sewer lines in a similar manner.

The second approach is essentially the same as the first except that ownership of the lines remains with the county. In these cases all or part of the cost of the extension was borne by the county, and the lines were then leased to the city, at a nominal sum, for operation and maintenance.

Catawba, Cleveland, and Lincoln counties, among others, have used this method. Cleveland County issued about $400,000 in general obligation bonds to finance one such project that provided lines to serve a new major industry in the county.

The third pattern that has developed calls for reimbursement of the county for its initial outlays. Under this plan, by agreement between the county and the city, the county is reimbursed, in whole or in part, from fees and charges or from the sale of water. The city is uniformly responsible for operation and maintenance, but there is a specific agreement as to the collection of rates and charges and the payment of part (or all) of these to the county. For example, Rockingham County has financed extensions outside the City of Reidsville with the provision that half of the water revenues from the line (rates outside the city are double those inside) will be paid to the county until it is completely reimbursed. Davidson County has constructed lines outside the City of Lexington and will receive all tap fees on the lines for ten years, or until it is fully reimbursed, whichever is first. Ownership of the lines will pass to the city after payments to the county cease. Guilford County has entered into a formal agreement with the City of Greensboro under which the county expects to finance a number of water and sewer extensions in the years ahead. The agreement provides for the collection of an acreage charge that is remitted to the county (on county-financed lines) and for the county to share in the revenue from water customers. The plan also provides for the city to purchase the county's interest in all county-financed lines upon annexation. Ownership and full responsibility for operation and maintenance are with the city from the beginning. Durham, Edgecombe, Rowan, and Wayne counties have all made similar expenditures with provision for reimbursement.

In the same class but slightly different in emphasis are the agreements between Wake County and Raleigh and similar agreements that Wake has with most of the other cities in the county. These agreements look to the steady extension of utility services throughout the county where needs exist. They give the county the initial responsibility for arranging financing within its funding limits. Special connection charges (in lieu of special assessments) and acreage charges are used to recover county outlays. Ownership and operation of the systems will be the responsibility of the city whose lines are being extended. If the county does not have funds available for a particular extension, or if the extension does not meet the standards for county participation, the applicant for service may finance his own extension. Cities are also free to make extensions from their own funds.

Agreements directed to the same ends but with different features are used in Buncombe and Cumberland counties among others.

The fourth pattern involves direct county provision of services. Several counties—Anson, Durham, Forsyth, and Mecklenburg among others—

have made substantial outlays for county water and sewerage systems in addition to, or in lieu of, joint financing with a city.

Anson County received a combination revenue bond loan and grant of $4,000,000 in 1966 from the Economic Development Administration. The county's voters then approved a $750,000 general obligation bond issue to add to the EDA funds and enable the county to implement preliminary plans for a county-operated, county-wide water supply and distribution system. The system is designed to serve all the municipalities within the county and the areas between them. Some of the municipalities purchase water "wholesale" from the county; in others, the county serves customers directly. Anson was the first county in the state with such a system in operation.

Durham County was the first in the state to build a sewage collection system. The Durham system serves the Research Triangle Park area and was financed from a revenue bond issue. The county has contracted with the City of Durham to operate and maintain the system.

In early 1968 Forsyth County voters approved a general obligation bond issue of $5,000,000 for the development of county water systems. The Forsyth systems are operated and maintained by the county. The systems near Winston-Salem and located in territory likely to be annexed within a few years were built to the same specifications employed by the city, and the city's water supply system was used as a source of water. The county expects to use wells as a source of water for outlying systems that may be built.

Mecklenburg County agreed in 1967 to finance a large water line in the southern portion of the county to meet the needs of industrial growth. Later, Mecklenburg voters approved a $9,500,000 water bond issue to finance a much larger water distribution system and a $2,000,000 bond issue to finance sewer extensions outside municipal boundaries. Initially, the Mecklenburg systems were operated directly by the county, but in early 1973 the governments of Mecklenburg County and the City of Charlotte created a joint department that is responsible for all water and sewerage services provided through the two governments.

The demand for county action in providing utilities arises largely because of the rapid growth of suburban areas. For orderly and healthful development in these areas, water and sewerage services need to be present *before* extensive development takes place. Cities are frequently reluctant and unable (legally and/or financially) to extend services to these areas, and individuals, small developers, and industries are also often unable to do so. The county, as a general unit of government with jurisdiction over the full area, comes naturally into the picture. To date, in North Carolina, county participation has been essentially financial, except for Buncombe County (where for many years the county government has served as the management agency for a number of local water districts); the activity by Anson, Durham, Forsyth, and Mecklenburg counties noted above; and the beginning development of county systems such as those in Harnett, Montgomery, and Richmond counties. The general procedure has been for the city to expand its systems because this has usually been more economical than constructing new systems with separate supply and treatment works. The county has helped with financing, and there is a trend for joint agreements to provide for some form of reimbursement as described above.

This approach—stressing municipal ownership and operation of facilities and county participation in financing—is in accord with the principles underlying North Carolina's municipal annexation procedures and the division of governmental powers and functions among the state, the counties, and the municipalities. These principles call for the extension of municipal boundaries and the full range of municipal types of services (water and sewerage services, higher levels of police protection, fire protection, streets, sanitation, etc.) to areas that become urban in character. But needs for water and sewerage services often arise before an area has become fully urban. In these cases, if the needs are to be met by local government, the county becomes the logical unit to help provide these services, at least on a transitional basis.

Since 1964 the Farmers Home Administration has been authorized to make grants to public bodies and loans to both public bodies and private, nonprofit corporations to finance water and waste-disposal systems for small towns, communities, and rural areas. A number of nonprofit corporations have been formed in North Carolina since that time to supply water to rural communities, using loans from FHA to finance the initial installation of the necessary facilities. In some cases the associations secure water from a neighboring city or town; in other cases wells are used as a source of supply. County governments in North Carolina have authority to serve as the unit for building and operating such small community water systems and are eligible to secure loans from FHA in the same manner as the nonprofit associations. But no county government has undertaken to serve as the managing unit for community systems, even though self-supporting and differing rates might be used for each separate system. As the need for interconnections between small community systems increases, it appears probable that some county governments will become the operating and managing units for community and rural water supplies.

While some counties will become active in providing community water systems and others (such as Anson and Forsyth) may find it desirable to become a major supplier of water and sewerage services, the experience of recent years suggests that most counties will probably serve only a financial and transitional role in providing these services for many years. In this area, as in most other aspects of county government, the traditional North Carolina approach of working out specific details on a county-by-county basis will undoubtedly continue, and a variety of arrangements will be found over the state.

City-County Financing Agreements

Because situations differ, the arrangments made between counties and cities in joint financing of water and sewerage services will necessarily vary from county to county, and perhaps within a single county from one time to another. While there is no standard agreement that can be recommended, certain factors should be kept in mind and, when necessary, included in all such agreements. Special conditions in some circumstances may, of course, call for consideration of other factors not listed here.

1. Responsibility for financing the cost of the construction of the facilities should be set forth. The financing of facilities may be borne by one unit or shared by all units; or certain portions of an improvement may be financed by one unit and other portions by the remaining units.

2. Ownership of all facilities and rights in all easements should be established.

3. If initial ownership is by the county and the county does not anticipate entering into water and sewerage operations directly, transfer of ownership should be provided for.

4. The agreement should specify any change in ownership that would take place upon annexation by the city of areas in which the facilities are located, or anticipate any problems that might arise if ownership did not rest with the city after the annexation.

5. The procedure and circumstances under which further extension of any facility may take place should be covered. Any unit might be empowered to extend on its own, or joint approval might be required.

6. The unit responsible for prescribing the specifications for all facilities should be established. Specifications should cover the size and quality of all materials used and the location of all facilities.

7. The level of rates, fees, and other charges to customers should be agreed upon. This would include the level of water rates, sewer charges, tap fees, acreage charges, fire protection charges, and other miscellaneous charges. Either stipulated rates or rates scaled to those inside the city might be used.

8. Changes, if any, in levels of rates or other fees and charges upon annexation of the facilities by the city should be anticipated, with regard to both the initial financing and the financing of future extensions.

9. The source and amount of all reimbursements to the county or city, if any, should be set forth—including the term during which reimbursement is to be made.

10. Responsibility for operation, maintenance, and control of the facilities—including the control of taps and the collection of all rates and charges—should be established.

SOLID WASTE COLLECTION AND DISPOSAL

Introduction

Solid waste collection and disposal is today a problem wherever people live, whether in rural or urban areas. Many of the goods we consume come in containers that are difficult to dispose of. This problem affects farmers and suburbanites as well as city dwellers, and the littered roadsides, beaches, and mountain paths—as well as unsightly dumps along many highways—all attest to its extent The fact that dumping trash along highway rights of way, or on another's property, is a criminal act (G.S. 14-134.1 and -399) has been of little value in solving the problem, because enforcement is exceedingly difficult. Moreover, the real need is for positive action to provide adequate and satisfactory collection and disposal.

Cities for many years have offered collection and disposal services, and in recent years counties have started providing them also. North Carolina counties have been slower to do this than counties in many other states, but most now provide services of some type.

County involvement takes two forms: regulation of practices of private persons, and provision of services. County regulatory activity may be undertaken by the county boards of health or, in some cases, by the boards of county commissioners. Only the commissioners are authorized to provide services.

Regulation

County Boards of Health. The authority of county boards of health to regulate the collection and disposal of solid waste is based on the broad rule-making powers set forth in G.S. 130-17, which gives local boards of health authority to make such rules and regulations ". . . as are necessary to protect and advance the public health."

Regulations adopted by the boards of health may cover all aspects of collection and disposal that affect the public health. Such regulations typically cover four major areas:

(1) The type of containers in which waste is placed;

(2) Sanitation standards for equipment used in the collection of garbage and other refuse;
(3) Standards and methods for disposal; and
(4) Requirements relating to the licensing of collectors.

In most of the counties that regulate collection and disposal, a permit is required before a private individual may provide collection service. Such a permit is issued only after the board of health has found that the equipment to be used is adequate and that provision for the sanitary disposal of wastes collected has been made. Regulations covering containers in which waste is placed while awaiting collection apply to individual homeowners, businesses, and others responsible for the accumulation of refuse. Collection permits may be revoked for violation of regulations. G.S. 130-203 makes violation of local health regulations a misdemeanor and provides for a fine of not more than $50 or imprisonment not to exceed 30 days.

Among the counties that have regulations adopted by the local board of health are: Cleveland, Craven, Cumberland, Davidson, Durham, Forsyth, Gaston, Guilford, Henderson, Mecklenburg, Mitchell, New Hanover, Polk, Rutherford, Wilson, and Yancey. Copies of a recommended model set of regulations are available from the Solid Waste and Vector Control Branch, Division of Health Services, Department of Human Resources.

Statewide regulations relating to the collection and disposal of solid wastes were adopted by the State Board of Health in March of 1971. These generally parallel the provisions found in the local regulations then extant. Since that time very few additional counties have adopted local regulations.

County Commissioners—Health. G.S. 153A-132.1 and -136 grant authority to the boards of commissioners in all counties to make rules and regulations with respect to the collection and disposal of solid wastes. This authority essentially parallels that normally exercised by the county boards of health. It is, however, limited to the areas of the county outside municipal boundaries, while the authority of boards of health is county-wide. Only a few boards of commissioners have taken action under these statutes.

County Commissioners—Business. All counties in the state have authority to regulate the "business" aspects of solid waste collection and disposal under the provisions of G.S. 153A-136. This statute grants authority to the commissioners to regulate the collection and disposal of solid wastes by persons, firms, and corporations, both private and public. County regulatory authority may be exercised only outside city boundaries unless the city governing board by resolution permits the regulatory ordinance to be effective inside the city as well (G.S. 153A-122).

PUBLIC ENTERPRISES 429

In adopting ordinances under the authority of this statute, the board of commissioners may:
(1) Issue licenses for the commercial collection and disposal of solid wastes and charge a fee for the licenses;
(2) Prohibit commercial collection and disposal by unlicensed persons;
(3) Grant licensed persons exclusive rights to collect commercially in designated areas; and
(4) Regulate the fees charged for collection and disposal services by licensed or franchised persons.

Action under this statute has usually been taken to assure adequate service to all areas of a county. Often a small private collector with inadequate equipment starts a service, perhaps with a lower fee than is offered by an existing collector, and soon has financial trouble. The result is frequently a business loss for the operator and periods without collection for the homeowner. In some cases, the county commissioners have established uniform rates for the different levels of service (once- or twice-a-week collection, from front or back yards). More often, however, both rates and exclusive collection rights for certain collectors in designated areas have been established in an attempt to assure collectors enough business to justify their investment in adequate equipment.

Among the counties that have adopted regulations of this type are Alamance, Alexander, Anson, Buncombe, Burke, Catawba, Cleveland, Columbus, Guilford, Iredell, Lincoln, Mitchell, Stanly, and Yancey.

Provision of Services

Authority. All counties are authorized to provide solid waste collection and disposal services outside municipal boundaries. Within these areas counties are specifically authorized to:
(1) Establish and operate collection services;
(2) Establish and operate disposal facilities;
(3) Jointly, with cities and towns, establish and operate collection services and disposal facilities; and
(4) Charge fees for collection services and the use of disposal facilities.

If a county undertakes to provide collection services, the statute requires that fees be charged that are adequate to meet the costs of collection (G.S. 153A-292). And if a county levies county-wide taxes on property to support any of the cost of the disposal facilities, it may not charge disposal fees for the use of the facilities by municipalities within the county. These provisions are designed to prevent inequities in county taxing and services with respect to solid wastes.

General. Activity and services by North Carolina county governments in regard to solid wastes expanded greatly between 1968 and

1974. During this period a county-wide study of solid waste problems and possible solutions was made in each of the 100 counties. During this period also the State Division of Health Services was making a great effort to improve collection methods and develop approved methods of disposal throughout the state. The combination of state and local action produced remarkable progress.

In 1968 there were 479 disposal sites in the state that were operated by cities, towns, counties, and private persons. None of these would have met today's standards, and only 23 were at that time classed as "sanitary landfills." By mid-1974 the number of disposal sites had been reduced to 151. Of these, 10 were operated by industries, 38 by cities, and 103 by counties. Fewer than a dozen of these failed to meet current standards. Expressed another way, state-approved landfills were in operation in 96 of the state's counties. Only four counties—all small—were without at least one approved disposal facility.

Collection. Few counties provide house-to-house collection services. In 1974 three counties are known to provide direct collection services. Dare County, under a contract with a private collector, provides collection services for most of Roanoke Island. Camden and Jones counties provide a "mail box" collection service. The mail box system operates on a fee basis through the purchase of plastic bags by the homeowner. These bags are filled with refuse and placed beside the mail box for collection once each week.

Disposal. Two types of disposal service may be offered by county governments—container-transport systems and landfills.

In 1974 almost two-thirds of the state's counties operate a container-transport ("green box") system: truck-tended solid waste boxes are located all along the highways in areas of the county that are too sparsely populated to permit door-to-door collection of solid wastes by either the county or private collectors. Citizens individually take their refuse to the boxes for deposit. Specially designed packer trucks collect the wastes from the boxes on a regular schedule for transport to the landfill. Most of these systems are owned and operated by the county, but a few counties provide the service through contracts with private firms. Alexander, Ashe, Burke, Chatham, and Orange are among the counties that provide container-transport services.

In mid 1974 over two-thirds of the counties provide solid waste disposal facilities. At least four counties—Guilford, Forsyth, Orange, and Wilson—had joint city-county financing of facilities that were available to all cities and private haulers in the county. In all four, financing was from a combination of general revenues and special fees.

At least three other counties—Pasquotank, Person, and Stanly—make payments to a city to operate a county-owned landfill that is available to all persons and governmental units within the county. The cities in these instances may provide additional support above the county-wide level provided by the county.

Finally, at least 61 counties operate and finance landfills that are available to all users within the county. Of these landfills, those in 53 counties were financed from general county revenues (e.g., Anson, Brunswick, Haywood, Union, Rowan, Stokes and Yadkin), and eight (e.g., Randolph) were financed from a fee schedule.

The recent tremendous increase in solid waste collection and disposal activities by counties indicates that by 1980 solid waste disposal will be almost an exclusive county government function statewide. (In a few places, regional arrangements—involving several counties— may be developed; in fact, some joint county activity is already going on.) Solid waste collection appears likely to continue as a city function for areas within cities. Outside cities, the present patterns suggest that reliance on franchised private collectors will continue for the more densely populated areas and that "mail box" collections and "green boxes" will bring collection and disposal services to sparsely populated areas.

— *Warren J. Wicker*

24 / Fire Protection

Introduction / 434
Alternative Approaches / 435
County Fire Departments / 435
Contracts with Municipalities / 435
Tax-Supported Rural Fire Districts / 436
County Service Districts / 437
Associations That Contract for Fire Protection / 438
Volunteer Fire Departments / 438
Selection of Approach / 439
County Fire Marshals / 440
Fire Prevention Codes / 441
Further Assistance / 441

24 / FIRE PROTECTION

INTRODUCTION

Rural fire protection as a function of county government in North Carolina dates almost entirely from the period following World War II. Historically, fire protection was a most important function of early cities and towns, whose compact development with largely wooden buildings presented a constant danger of a community-wide conflagration. But in rural areas, characterized by widely separated farm buildings, fire protection was regarded as a matter of concern to the individual property owner rather than to the community. Only in recent times, when rural areas became subject to an urban type of development and when rural citizens began demanding the same kinds of governmental services as those enjoyed by urban dwellers, have county governments been called upon to furnish fire protection.

Counties first became concerned with fire problems around 1900, when the sheriff was authorized to investigate the possibility of arson when fires occurred outside municipal corporate limits. The concept of county firefighting service emerged only in 1939, when counties were authorized to contract with municipal fire departments to provide service beyond town limits; and not until 1945 were counties empowered to establish and maintain departments of their own, Another approach was made possible by a statute enacted in 1951 that authorized the creation of rural fire protection districts supported by special taxes levied within the district, if district residents voted for such an arrangement. The 1973 General Assembly, in an effort to make municipal types of services more available to county residents, enacted the County Service District Act, which permits the establishment of districts for fire protection, as well as for certain other designated purposes, without a popular vote.

A number of counties have secured special acts that authorize the payment of specified amounts to municipal fire departments or rural volunteer departments to furnish fire protection. Also, groups of county residents have formed associations for the purpose of contracting for fire protection with various public and private agencies without the benefit of special implementing legislation. In recent years acts authorizing the appointment of county fire marshals have been passed and county fire prevention codes have been enacted, which has further strengthened county fire protection efforts.

ALTERNATIVE APPROACHES

County fire protection may be provided by several methods or by a combination of methods:

(a) By creating a county fire department;
(b) By contracting with one or more municipalities or volunteer fire departments to furnish fire protection in rural areas;
(c) By creating one or more rural fire protection districts;
(d) By creating a county service district or districts to furnish fire protection; or
(e) By associations formed by groups of citizens to contract for fire protection services.

County Fire Departments

Article 11 of G.S. Chapter 153A provides: "A county may establish, organize, equip, support, and maintain a fire department; may prescribe the duties of the fire department; may provide assistance to incorporated volunteer fire departments; may contract for fire fighting or prevention services with one or more counties, cities, or other units of local government or with an agency of the state government; and may for these purposes appropriate funds not otherwise limited as to use by law."

Most counties have not established fire departments as such. Past practice has been to enter into agreements with volunteer departments to furnish fire protection in designated rural areas for a fixed fee ("financial assistance"). These volunteer departments for all intents and purposes then function as a county department. The area protected by an individual volunteer department is usually referred to as a fire district. Quite often a county government, in fixing fire district boundaries, asks for help from the North Carolina Fire Insurance Rating Bureau in Raleigh. Such a cooperative effort can mean that these districts receive an improved rating for fire insurance purposes. An improved rating, of course, means savings for property owners by virtue of reduced fire insurance premiums.

Contracts with Municipalities

Article 3 of G.S. Chapter 69 authorizes a county to contract for rural fire protection services with any municipality (even one not located within the county) if the governing boards of both city and county have, by resolution, accepted the terms of Article 3. A county is expressly authorized to pay an annual fee to compensate a city for providing the equipment and carrying the insurance necessary to enable it to answer calls in rural areas. The statute sets forth a basis for arriving at the amount to be paid for fire protection services, but the statutory formula is not binding on the contracting parties, who may agree on a different schedule of fees. Counties and municipalities are authorized to make appropriations necessary to carry out their contractual relationship and to fund fire protection activities by levying property taxes as well as by allocating other revenues whose use is not restricted by law.

Regardless of the terms of a fire protection contract, statutory provisions require that a municipality not be left unprotected by having all of its personnel or equipment sent more than two miles beyond the corporate limits.

A fireman who answers a call outside the city by which he is employed or who is in volunteer service has the same authority, rights, privileges, and immunities that he has while responding to a call within his home municipality. A municipality that dispatches its fire department to an emergency outside the city is deemed to be exercising a governmental function and thus has all the privileges and immunities attendant upon the exercise of that function within its corporate limits.

Tax-Supported Rural Fire Districts

County-wide fire protection is the exception, and the inhabitants of most rural areas must rely on the services of a volunteer department or a tax-supported fire protection district. The first step in establishing a tax district is to present the county commissioners with a petition signed by at least 15 per cent of the resident freeholders of an area outside the corporate limits of a city or town. (To be a freeholder one must own an estate in land or other realty.) The area to be included in the district must be described in the petition and the proposed district must be given a name.

The question of levying a special tax for the purpose of providing fire protection is submitted to the qualified voters of the proposed district. Those who own realty in the district but do not reside therein are not "qualified voters" and may not vote in the election. This special tax is collected on all taxable property in the district, real and personal, but may not exceed 15 cents per $100 valuation. [By special acts Wake County has authorized a levy of 50 cents per $100 (Ch. 169, 1955 Session Laws), and Granville County a levy of 3 cents per $100 (Ch. 790, 1957 Session Laws).] A method is also provided whereby an existing district that has previously authorized a tax of 10 cents per $100 valuation may vote on whether to increase the tax to 15 cents a $100. The fact that a tax of 15 cents per $100 is authorized evidently does not require that the full amount be levied, and many districts that have authorized the 15-cent levy are actually taxed at a lower rate.

In the past the election was called and conducted by the county commissioners, but a recently enacted statute now requires that the election be conducted by the county board of elections. The form of the ballot is prescribed by statute. If a majority of those casting ballots vote "in favor of tax for fire protection in _____ Fire Protection District," the county commissioners then select the means of providing such protection. The statutes provide several alternative methods of furnishing fire protection:

(1) By contracting with an incorporated city or town;
(2) By contracting with an incorporated nonprofit volunteer or community fire department;
(3) By contracting with the State Department of Conservation and Development;
(4) By using the county's fire department if it has one;
(5) By establishing a fire department within the district;
(6) By using a combination of the above.

The taxes collected for fire protection purposes go into a special fund administered by the board of county commissioners or by a three-member "fire protection district commission" appointed by the county commissioners. Fire protection district commissioners must be qualified voters who reside in the district; they serve for two-year terms and are subject to the county commissioners' supervision.

The statutes also authorize an election to determine whether an existing fire district should be abolished. This election is also called upon petition of 15 per cent of the resident freeholders within the district. Fire district boundaries may be increased or decreased; this may be accomplished by petition, so that another election is not necessary. When all or any part of a district is annexed by a municipality that furnishes fire protection, the annexed territory ceases to be a fire district (or part of a fire district), and fire district taxes may no longer be collected in the annexed area.

County Service Districts

The County Service District Act of 1973 empowered boards of county commissioners to create special districts to furnish several urban services, including fire protection.

The county commissioners must hold a public hearing, after giving statutory notice, before they adopt a resolution to create a new district; in order to justify establishing a district, the board must find that:

(1) There is a demonstrable need for one or more of the authorized services;
(2) The proposed services cannot practically be provided on a county-wide basis;
(3) The proposed services can be provided to the district without unreasonable or burdensome tax levies; and
(4) There is a demonstrable demand for the proposed services by those who live in the district.

No territory lying within a municipality or a sanitary district may be included within a service district without the approval of the governing body of the city or sanitary district. It should be noted that, contrary to the requirement for a rural fire protection district, no election need be held to establish a county service district. The resolution of the county commissioners that defines and in effect creates the district becomes effective at the beginning of the fiscal year following its adoption.

The county service district shares one important characteristic with the rural fire protection district: those who own property within the district usually are required to pay additional taxes to support the services provided within the district. Counties are expressly authorized to levy property taxes, within a service district, in addition to those levied throughout the county, to finance services within the district at a higher level than other county residents receive. A county may, however, allocate to a district any other revenues whose use is not restricted by law.

Associations That Contract for Fire Protection

Occasionally individuals or associations of individuals who live outside a municipality will contract with a city or a volunteer fire department so that for a fixed fee they receive the protection of a municipal or other accredited department. This type of contract is expressly authorized by G.S. Chapter 160A. Areas so protected may be approved by the Fire Insurance Rating Bureau, and property owners thereby secure a reduced fire insurance rate.

VOLUNTEER FIRE DEPARTMENTS

Whatever approach is used to furnish rural fire protection, probably one or more volunteer fire departments will be created or contracted with. For example, no county in this state has a fully paid fire department, and counties usually contract with volunteer departments to furnish protection to rural residents. Likewise, when a tax-supported fire district is established, fire protection services are usually provided by a volunteer department.

Volunteer fire departments may be incorporated pursuant to the Non-Profit Corporation Act, as contained in G.S. Chapter 55A. The corporation is legally created when one or more incorporators sign the Articles of Incorporation, have this document notorized, and then file the articles in the office of the North Carolina Secretary of State in Raleigh.

Requirements in this state for creating a nonprofit corporation are not complex. Any person or persons who are eighteen years of age or older may act as the incorporators. The law does not even require that the incorporators be residents of North Carolina. The initial board of directors is named in the Articles of Incorporation, and at the organizational meeting the directors adopt by-laws and elect officers. Corporate officers consist of a president, at least one vice-president, a secretary, and a treasurer, plus any other officers deemed necessary. Unless the corporation charter or by-laws provide otherwise, all officers are elected or appointed annually by the board of directors.

SELECTION OF APPROACH

Each of the alternatives outlined above for furnishing county fire protection has some advantage as well as disadvantages. A paid professional county-wide department, for example, would provide municipal-quality fire protection to county residents, but this alternative would also be prohibitively expensive for most counties. The customary practice of counties' contracting with volunteer departments to furnish protection in rural areas is relatively inexpensive, since no salaries need be paid; but this system leaves the county government without any real control over the fire protection services.

Contracting with a city for fire protection to be furnished by a municipal department has the advantage of relieving the county of the responsibility for organizing, training, administering, and maintaining a department. Also, many city departments are staffed by highly trained personnel and have excellent equipment. But not all cities will agree to furnish protection to outlying rural areas; and in any event a city department's first duty and highest priority is to protect life and property within the city's corporate limits. The North Carolina Fire Insurance Rating Bureau requires that certain equipment and personnel remain within the city at all times and thus the full resources of a city department are never available to county residents.

Establishment of a tax-supported rural fire protection district is attractive because it can be accomplished without increasing the tax burden on county residents who do not own property within the district. If this alternative is chosen, the cost of the fire protection is placed entirely on those who will receive the service. This approach has the disadvantage of requiring a successful district-wide election as a prerequisite to the creation of the district. If an election is not feasible, the county commissioners may be asked to establish a county service district to furnish fire protection.

The final alternative, encouraging groups of rural residents to contract with a city or volunteer department for fire protection, creates few if any problems for the county government. Unfortunately, most county residents lack the initiative and expertise to organize and contract for such an arrangement.

COUNTY FIRE MARSHALS

Counties are authorized by statute to appoint a fire marshal and to employ whatever assistants may be required. The county is not required to appoint a fire marshal and may instead assign the fire marshal's duties to another qualified county officer or employee. The following duties for a fire marshal have been suggested by the Fire and Rescue Service Division of the State Department of Insurance:

(1) To keep the county manager and the board of county commissioners informed of the progress and development of rural fire departments.
(2) To keep the county manager and the board of county commissioners informed of any matters pertaining to the present and future expansion of rural fire departments.
(3) To act as liaison between fire departments and the county manager or board of county commissioners.
(4) To help organize and develop new fire departments.
(5) To be the county manager's and commissioners' adviser concerning requirements of the North Carolina Fire Insurance Rating Bureau.
(6) To help develop a comprehensive training program for all rural fire departments.
(7) To advise fire departments on equipment purchases and problems.
(8) To advise fire departments on the availability of civil defense surplus equipment.
(9) To make periodic inspections of all departments to see that they conform to the minimum standards of the North Carolina Fire Insurance Rating Bureau.
(10) To make fire prevention inspections of schools, as required by G.S. Ch. 115, and of day-care facilities as authorized by G.S. 110-91(5).
(11) To make fire prevention inspections of places of public gathering.
(12) To investigate (along with other officials) fires of a suspicious nature so as to determine their cause.
(13) To help fire departments develop a fire prevention program in their respective districts.
(14) To help school authorities develop a fire prevention program for each school.
(15) To coordinate all fire departments within the county in a mutual aid program.
(16) To coordinate the activities of all fire departments in a "call system or calling system" so that each department will be assured of prompt notification of all fire calls.
(17) To administer the county fire prevention code and other safety ordinances.

FIRE PREVENTION CODES

A county may by ordinance adopt a fire prevention code that will be effective in all areas of the county not covered by a municipal fire prevention code. Any published technical code promulgated by a public agency may be adopted by reference in the ordinance. (If so, then an official copy of the technical code so adopted must be available for public inspection in the office of the clerk to the county commissioners.) Also, the State Building Code Council must approve the code before it is adopted. Contents of county fire prevention codes are not specified by state law. County commissions have full authority to determine the contents of the codes subject to approval by the State Building Code Council. However, it is anticipated that a code similar to the one recommended by the American Insurance Association (the successor to the National Board of Fire Underwriters) will be adopted in whole or in part by most counties.

County fire prevention codes are enforced by fire prevention inspectors. These inspectors' duties are determined by the board of county commissioners but must also be approved by the State Building Code Council. Appointing inspectors does not necessarily mean that additional personnel must be hired, since the law specifically provides that other county officers or employees may perform the duties assigned to inspectors.

FURTHER ASSISTANCE

This chapter is a brief summary of North Carolina's county fire protection laws. The subject is treated in depth in the Institute's publication *Fire Protection Law*. This book also contains forms for creating fire protection districts, a sample contract between a unit of local government and a homeowners' association for fire protection, and a sample corporate charter for a volunteer fire department. Agencies other than the Institute of Government that might be helpful in resolving problems related to fire protection include the North Carolina League of Municipalities, the North Carolina Association of County Commissioners, the State Department of Insurance, and the North Carolina Fire Insurance Rating Bureau.

— *Ben F. Loeb, Jr.*

164